FLORA of THE YELLOWSTONE

by WHITNEY TILT

A guide to the wildflowers, shrubs & trees, ferns, and grass-like plants of the Greater Yellowstone Region of Idaho, Montana, and Wyoming

ISBN 978-1-4951-6004-2

Book Design by Whitney Tilt | Graphic Design by Ixtla Vaughan

Published by the Gallatin Valley Land Trust
Bozeman, Montana

Printed in the USA

THREE FORKS
BOZEMAN
YELLOWSTONE R.
LIVINGSTON
MADISON R.
GALLATIN
ENNIS
GRAVELLYS
RED LODGE
GRANITE PEAK 12799'
MONTANA
GARDNER
ELECTRIC PEAK 10969'
CLARKS FK.
BLACK BUTTE 10544'
YELLOWSTONE
SHOSHONE R.
RED ROCK LAKES
PARK
W. YELLOWSTONE
HENRY'S LAKE
CODY
CENTENNIALS
SO. FORK
IDAHO
ASHTON
2 OCEAN PASS
WYOMING
HENRY'S FK.
GRAND TETON 13770'
TOGWOTTEE PASS 9544'
S. FK. SNAKE R.
DRIGGS
ELK REFUGE
DUBOIS
IDAHO FALLS
JACKSON
CONTINENTAL DIVIDE
WIND R.
WIND RIVER RANGE
ALPINE
SALT RIVER

TABLE OF CONTENTS

Subalpine environment, Beehive Basin. Photo by W. Tilt

INTRODUCTION

My initiation as a plant watcher in the Northern Rockies began while "moving pipe" in the Teton Valley of Idaho in the 1970s. Anyone who has experienced the joys of moving 40-foot-long irrigation pipe twice daily across acres of fields knows that it provides plenty of time for your mind to wander. Directing my gaze downward from the ramparts of the Grand Tetons, wildflowers scattered across the field gave punctuation to the green expanse of grass. Over the years rambling across the Greater Yellowstone Region, my interest only continued to grow.

Returning to the region in 2001, I began enjoying the vast network of public lands. Whether walking the dog, hiking, riding, cross-country skiing, these lands and the trails that connect them stitch people together with the landscape. Finding our way outside into these wildlands is essential to restoring our vital link to nature as well as a reminder for us that we are the land's stewards, and that we cannot take these lands, and our access to them, for granted.

In 2011, I authored *Flora of Montana's Gallatin Region, Greater Yellowstone's Northwest Corner.* The book arose out of the simple need for a book that focused on the characteristic plants of the Greater Yellowstone Region. Most of my friends who were self-styled "plant nerds" carried four to seven books to cover the basic flora, never mind the botanical equivalent of "LBJs" ('little brown jobs' for birders) that required a land lens and dichotomous key. *Flora of Montana's Gallatin Region* was published in partnership with the Gallatin Valley Land Trust who received all revenue from the sale of the book, along with the Big Sky Community Corporation and several other non-profit educational organizations. The book's publication also lead me into the world of mobile apps, and a partnership with Katie Gibson to form High Country Apps. To date, the collaboration has produced numerous apps for plants across the Pacific Northwest and Rocky Mountains and beyond, including the "Flora of Yellowstone" (www.highcountryapps.com).

This book builds on these foundations and is the product of an ongoing journey of discovery, land snorkeling across the Greater Yellowstone Region.

THE GUIDE

Flora of the Yellowstone presents more than 400 wildflowers, trees and shrubs, ferns, and grass-like plants found in the region. These species meet a combination of three criteria: They are 1) "readily encountered," meaning they are relatively common and observable, 2) easily identifiable with some attention to detail but no special botanical training, and 3) representative of the much larger plant community found in the region. They include plants that flower once every 60 years, plants that are a favorite food of grizzly bears, and others that are deadly poisonous. Some of these plants are found only in the Northern Rocky Mountains while others are found growing across the United States and beyond. Taken together, their forms, colors, and habits are diverse and compelling.

The majority of species captured here are native plants. However, as an increasingly large number of non-native plants are becoming naturalized, and "exotic aliens" – those introduced plants considered "harmful" for one or more reasons – are often a conspicuous part of our flora, the most commonly encountered non-native species are presented here as well.

Designed for ease of use, this guide intentionally spares the user from the full force of botanical minutia by not attempting to identify every ADC (the dreaded "Another Damned Composite") or species of penstemon you might encounter.

Species in this field guide are organized by type (herb, shrub-tree, fern, and grass-like). Within each plant type, species are presented in order of: Scientific Family, Genus, and Species – with a few exceptions where closely-related plants have been placed together for ease of reference, e.g. *Centaurea* (knapweed) placed next to *Cirsium* (thistles), and the cinquefoils (*Drymocallis* with *Potentilla*).

SPECIES DESCRIPTIONS

Common Name: Many plants have a single distinctive common name, while others have numerous common names, many of which may apply to more than one species. While not always accurate, common names are often wonderfully descriptive and more easily remembered by many of us than scientific names.

Scientific Name: In botany, the scientific name is distinctive. Botanists don't always agree, however, so in some instances more than one scientific name has been applied to the plant – such synonyms are provided as appropriate. The names can be equally descriptive, such as "hirsutus" to describe a hairy plant or "vulgaris" meaning common, as in lowly (applied to many invasive species).

Family: Plant families unite disparate species under a set of common characteristics, such as flower structure (see page 20 for plant family descriptions).

In response to improved phylogenic research, scientists are reclassifying species into entirely different families. Nowadays there is a need for "Family Synonyms" as some of us turn to the Scrophulariaceae to locate a favorite penstemon only to find it's been reclassified to the Plantaginaceae.

Description: The plant's physical characteristics are described. Many plant species exhibit a wide variety of flowers and leaf styles, and their size and general appearance is heavily influenced by habitat, weather, and the plant's maturity. A graphic symbol depicts whether a plant is:

native (N) or **non-native/introduced** (I)

Tidbits: A potpourri of additional information is given here, including further comments on the plant's appearance, human and wildlife uses, name origins, and other interesting details, such as which plants are favorites of grizzly bears.

Habitat: The ecotype and vegetative zone where the plant is commonly found is an important component of plant identification. Many plants occur across several habitats while others have tighter niches.

Flowering Time: Plants bloom and go to seed throughout the growing season. Flowering time is provided in full months as applied to the plant's range throughout the Northern Rocky Mountains. Flowering times are highly variable in response to elevations, topography, and annual climate.

THE REGION AND ITS FLORA

The Greater Yellowstone Region sits astride the spine of the Rocky Mountains, marking the transition east to west from the Great Plains to the Great Basin and Snake River Plain. For the purposes of this field guide, the region is defined as the lands bounded to the north by the Bridger and Crazy Mountains in Montana; to the south by the Salt River and Wind River Ranges in Wyoming; to the east by the Absaroka Range in Montana and Wyoming; and to the west by the Tobacco Root and Gravelly Ranges in Montana and the Big Hole Mountains of Idaho (see map at front of book). The guide's floral concentration includes Yellowstone and Grand Teton National Parks and the surrounding national forests. It will serve its user well throughout much of the Northern Rocky Mountain Region.

The region is a land sculpted by mountains, rivers, and titanic volcanic forces – most prominently the Yellowstone Caldera and the region's geothermal wonders. The region's rivers bend to this geology, flowing to both the Atlantic and Pacific oceans. The Yellowstone and Missouri rivers travel some 2,300 miles to mix with the saline waters of the Gulf of Mexico. The Henry's Fork and Snake River drain to the Columbia and then to the Pacific Ocean. And at the southern extent of the region, the Green River flows south to the Colorado River, the Sea of Cortez, and the Pacific Ocean. Collectively, this convergence of landscapes results in a medley of soils and climates that, in turn, create a diversity of plants and animals.

In a region etched by mountains and rivers, topography has a profound effect on habitats. At the lower elevations there are floodplains with their associated wetlands, willow thickets, and meadows. Above the effects of seasonal flood waters are dryer grasslands and sagebrush benches. Along an ongoing skirmish line, shrub-steppe interacts with parklands of aspen and conifers. Moving up in elevation, the conifers win out – lodgepole pine, Douglas-fir, Engelmann spruce, subalpine fir, and whitebark pine flank the mountains as they rise to more than 9,000 feet. Throughout this ecological narrative, the interplay of geology, soils and exposure all make their subtle influences known.

The climate is dominated by long, cold winters and short, relatively dry summers with continual variations of temperature and moisture. The vagaries of weather and climate are typically extreme in mountain regions, and the impacts of global climate change make such variations even more erratic in recent decades. Obviously, plants and animals living in this climate must adapt to these harsh and variable conditions, migrate, or bow to extinction. Yet, even given these challenges, the Greater Yellowstone Region is home to more than 2,000 species of vascular plants.

OF LATITUDE AND ELEVATION

Anyone who has spent time in the Northern Rockies understands firsthand that weather is a highly variable thing – one moment it's sunny and warm, next it is windy with snow in the air. At high elevations, temperatures fluctuate quickly as heat is gained rapidly through radiation and lost just as quickly through the thinner atmosphere. Temperatures in the mountains are generally cool relative to surrounding plains and get cooler as one ascends in elevation. As a rule of thumb, temperatures cool 1-2° F for every 300 feet of elevation gained. Mountain areas may also be cooled by colder, denser air flowing downslope from snowfields and glaciers above. Plants and animals at higher elevations are also exposed to greater amounts of ultraviolet radiation as the thinning atmosphere absorbs less and less solar radiation.

Latitude, elevation, and aspect all play a role in determining climate, which in turn plays a major role in determining the flora of a specific area. Ascending 300 feet in elevation is analogous to traveling north more than 150 miles. The alpine zones encountered in the Absaroka-Beartooth Wilderness, at approximately 9,000-10,000 feet, are akin to the tundra found at sea level in the far north. As used in this field guide, four basic vegetative zones are defined for the Greater Yellowstone Region.

VEGATATIVE ZONES

Alpine	Prairie Grasslands, river valleys, and scrublands. **Elevation: 3,000-5,500'**
Subalpine	Defined as the treed or forested areas with lodgepole pine, Douglas-fir, other conifers, and aspen commonly found. **Elevation: 4,500-8,000'**
Montane	Transition zone whose lower reaches are characterized by subalpine fir upwards through krummholz (bent, crooked, twisted trees) to timberline. **Elevation: 6,500-9,000'**
Plains, Valleys, Foothills	Extends upward from timberline to end of vegetation on exposed rock and permanent snow and ice fields. **Elevation: 9,000'+**

PLANT WATCHING TIPS

Blooming times for wildflowers are as variable as the weather in the Greater Yellowstone Region. Foothill flowers appear as early as mid-March. As days pass, blooming wildflowers spread upward across the montane and subalpine until the alpine areas reach their maximum bloom in late-July and August. Meanwhile the summer heat has dried the foothill flowers to a rustling brown. By mid-October most flowers are gone to seed, though their fruits and stalks often remain.

When you go off in search of wildflowers, near and far, bring some basics. For me this includes: raingear and an extra layer of warmth, hat, sunglasses, lip balm and sunblock, water, and a snack. Altitude sickness is a reality for some people, so drink plenty of water and take your time. Lightning injures and kills a number of people in the Rockies every year. Watch the skies and leave yourself plenty of time to move to safety before a storm shows you who's boss (hint: it is, you're not).

It is a tribute to the beauty of plants that we want to know their names and learn about their characteristics. The best way to achieve this knowledge is to have a discerning eye, a good field guide or two (or a mobile app from High Country Apps), and an unhurried pace. Think of it as "land snorkeling."

A Caution on edibility. Many of the plants in this guide are edible. An astonishing number of plants in this guide are also highly toxic. To make matters worse, many edible plants have one or more look-alikes that are inedible at best or poisonous at worst. Information on edibility in this guide is provided as a matter of general interest – it makes no allowances for misidentification, allergies, or other factors. Do not eat any plant you do not know to be edible. In addition, many wild plants are quickly extirpated from areas as a result of indiscriminate harvesting.

Camas (*Camassia quamash*) and White Mulesears (*Wyethia helianthoides*) fill a meadow in Harriman State Park. Photo by W. Tilt.

WALK THE WALK

The Greater Yellowstone Region is endowed with hundreds of miles of trails on public and private lands. These trails provide a wealth of opportunity, including afternoon jogs along the foothills, day hikes to remote waterfalls, and backcountry overnights crossing entire mountain ranges. Rewards for the trail user come in many forms, from an exercised dog to standing atop Electric Peak. Regardless of access, the region's trails and other access should be viewed as a privilege – a privilege which needs to be continually earned and not be taken for granted. In enjoying the outdoors, remember P-L-S:

Practice courtesy to the land, its owners and other users. Trails are shared by hikers, bikers, motorized users, horseback riders, and hunters alike. They are also used by wildlife. All share the same right of access and enjoy it as much as you do. On private lands, continued access depends on the landowner's generosity. Needless to say, extend this courtesy to the plant life by refraining from such acts as picking the wildflowers or breaking off living branches for dog toys or campfires.

Leave the land better. Find room in your pack for that odd piece of trash, and practice your aim by kicking those "horse apples" off the trail. Dog owners, keep evidence of your dog's passage off the trails as well. Leave wildlife and wildflowers in their place and whenever possible, and stay on the trail. It doesn't take long for furtive trails to become permanent.

Support organizations that work for the outdoors. The Gallatin Valley Land Trust, Yellowstone Association, Yellowstone Park Foundation, and many other nonprofit organizations are working to conserve and educate. The region's national parks, national forests, and other public lands are units of state and federal agencies supported by increasingly insufficient tax dollars. Their success depends on community support. We are the direct beneficiaries of their efforts every day. Support them with your time, talents, and treasury.

SOURCES AND RESOURCES

A number of resources were essential for this field guide:

Flora of Montana, W.E. Booth & J.C. Wright, Montana State University (1966)
Manual of Montana Vascular Plants, Peter Lesica, Brit Press (2012)
Montana Plant Life (CD-ROM), Plant-Life.org (2007)
Plants of the Rocky Mountains, Linda Kershaw et al, Lone Pine (1998)
Vascular Plants of the Greater Yellowstone Area, Erwin F. Evert (2010)
Weeds of the West, Tom Wilson et al, Western Society of Weed Science (1992)
Wildflowers of Montana, Donald Schiemann, Montana Press (2005)
Dictionary of Plant Names, Allen J. Comber, Timber Press (1994)
Latin for Gardeners, Lorraine Harrison, University of Chicago Press (2012)

In addition, *Trees to Know in Oregon* (Edward Jensen et al, 1994, Oregon State University) and a number of other field guides and websites provided important information on individual species. Terry Willard's *Edible and Medicinal Plants of the Rocky Mountains and Neighboring Territories* and *Montana Plant Life* provided much of the ethno-botanical information.

The Burke Museum of Natural History (www.washington.edu/burkemuseum), Lady Bird Johnson Wildflower Center (www.wildflower.org/plants), Southwest Colorado Wildflowers Ferns & Trees (www.swcoloradowildflowers.com), and USDA Natural Resources Conservation Service Plants Database (http://plants.usda.gov) were essential on-line resources for this publication. For the grasses, *Grasses of Montana*, Matt Lavin and Cathy Seibert, Montana State University (2009); Fire Effects Information System (www.fs.fed.us/database/feis); and Range Grasses of Utah, Utah State University (http://extension.usu.edu/rangeplants) were the primary references.

The plant illustrations utilized throughout this guide were provided by USDA Natural Resources Conservation Service Plants Database (http://plants.usda.gov), Flora of North America (www.eFloras.org), and Karl Urban, Umatilla National Forest (www.nps.gov/plants/color/northwest).

DEDICATION AND ACKNOWLEDGEMENTS

This guide is the result of a cadre of talented professionals and a good deal of cooperation. I do not count myself among that cadre. In making the field guide as useful and accurate as possible, I owe my sincere thanks to many people for their botanical expertise, thoughtful insights, sharing of favorite pictures, and countless rounds of editing. For the field guide's strengths, I thank my contributors. I alone assume the responsibility for acts of omission and misidentification. I welcome all comments and corrections.

The field guide is an expansion of the *Flora of Montana's Gallatin Region*, published in 2011. In turn, the project grows out of research I undertook along with Marianne Salas to produce a "Flora of Silver Tip Ranch and Surrounds" for our friend Gerry Ohrstrom and the other owners of Silver Tip Ranch in 2009.

To Matt Lavin, professor of botany at Montana State University, I extend my appreciation for his encyclopedic grasp of the region's flora, painstaking review of draft species accounts, and his patience. Similarly I owe a debt of gratitude to Gerry Carr, David Giblin, Steve Hegji, Shannon Kimbal, Ben Ledger, and Al Schneider for their botanical expertise, and willingness to share it. *Flora of the Montana's Gallatin* benefitted greatly from Big Sky naturalists Katie Alvin, Leslie Stoltz, Denise Wade, and Jessica Wiese, and Gallatin National Forest biologists Jodie Canfield, Reggie Clark, Rachel Feigly, Susan Lamont, and Sally Senger. Their input continues to be reflected here.

To Rip McIntosh and Marianne Salas, I owe my thanks for years of sharing an enjoyment of wild things that translates into many wonderful pictures and much heedful advice throughout both books.

What would a field guide be without photographs? Along with Tim, Rip, and Marianne, my deep appreciation to Gerald D. Carr (Oregon Flora Image Project, www.botany.hawaii.edu/faculty/carr/ofp/ofp_index.htm), Steve Hegji (*Wasatch Wildflowers*), Carolyn Hopper, Hank Jorgensen (http://snowbirdpix.com), Ben Legler (Burke Museum, http://biology.burke.washington.edu), and Al Schneider (www.swcoloradowildflowers.com) for their generous sharing of outstanding photographs.

As to the artistic presentation of this field guide, I acknowledge a talented bunch. The painting which graces the book's cover, Sticky Geraniums, is courtesy of artist

Clyde Aspevig. Clyde and artist wife, Carol Guzman, have coined the term "land snorkeling" for taking the time to look closer at the nature around us. It is an honor to have their talent and enthusiasm as part of this project. The map found on the inside cover is testament to the artistic talents of Daphne Gillam, who graciously donated her time to capture the field guide's scope in water colors. You don't realize how many moving parts there are until you attempt to align them coherently in one place. For that I also am very much in debt to Megan Regnerus and Jae Evans for their technical editing prowess, and Ixtla Vaughan and Kimberly Geer for their design skills and infinite patience in the layout process.

Lastly, to my wife, Sarah Davies Tilt, who along with canines Blaze, Chace, and Charlie, accompanied me on countless hikes and patiently tolerated my continual photographing, note-taking, and side trips – never mind the countless hours at my desk pulling this field guide together.

As with *Flora of Montana's Gallatin Region*, it was my goal to deliver *Flora of the Yellowstone* to the Gallatin Valley Land Trust and other partners at no cost to their already tight budgets. To realize this wonderful idea, I was fortunate to be able to turn to Gerry Ohrstrom and the Yellowstone Club Community Foundation who provided the core funding for this project. All proceeds from the sale of *Flora of Montana's Gallatin Region* went to support the good work of the Gallatin Valley Land Trust, Big Sky Community Corporation, and other non-profit organizations. *Flora of the Yellowstone* continues that tradition, so 100 percent of the revenue from the sale of this field guide will have a direct impact on the people and wildlands that comprise the Greater Yellowstone Region through the work of Gallatin Valley Land Trust, the Yellowstone Park Foundation, and others.

Get out in the outdoors and enjoy. Feel free to infect others with your enthusiasm and love of the land.

— Whitney Tilt, Bozeman, Montana, 2015

Author tries his luck fishing in Yellowstone National Park. Good news is the wildflowers and plant life are always biting. Photo by Frank Sulloway.

Page 200 Page 130 Page 176 Page 175 Page 190

Page 111 Page 327 Page 112 Page 289 Page 274-275

Page 337 Page 247 Page 128 Page 253 Page 346

Page 160 Page 193 Page 345 Page 181 Page 262

Page 132 Page 238-239 Page 125 Page 102 Page 225

Page 95 Page 81 Page 67 Page 68 Page 96

Page 127 Page 186 Page 268 Page 30 Page 119

WHITE/CREAM

Page 113 Page 122 Page 44 Page 43 Page 48
Page 47 Page 189 Page 174 Page 324 Page 318
Page 49 Page 286 Page 244 Page 183 Page 29
Page 104 Page 276 Page 341 Page 339 Page 252
Page 154 Page 152 Page 348 Page 342 Page 277
Page 278 Page 33 Page 294 Page 336 Page 304
Page 307 Page 287 Page 34 Page 347 Page 45

Page 83 Page 242 Page 32 Page 35 Page 41
Page 31 Page 326 Page 39 Page 140 Page 145
Page 143 Page 141 Page 142 Page 216 Page 219
Page 323 Page 133 Page 157 Page 257 Page 207
Page 208 Page 205 Page 280 Page 279 Page 180
Page 310 Page 311 Page 264 Page 263 Page 240
Page 270 Page 269 Page 265 Page 375 Page 274

Page 186	Page 267	Page 123	Page 108	Page 167
Page 52	Page 52	Page 53	Page 55	Page 74
Page 75	Page 76	Page 77	Page 78	Page 54
Page 58	Page 73	Page 73	Page 72	Page 101
Page 89	Page 86	Page 87	Page 90	Page 312
Page 84	Page 83	Page 100	Page 65	Page 66
Page 98	Page 93	Page 131	Page 295	Page 57

Page 296	Page 297	Page 121	Page 116	Page 120
Page 114	Page 282	Page 282	Page 92	Page 91
Page 88	Page 298	Page 322	Page 97	Page 36
Page 37	Page 40	Page 39	Page 118	Page 343
Page 221	Page 150	Page 146	Page 321	Page 115
Page 153	Page 214	Page 215	Page 215	Page 211
Page 293	Page 299	Page 227	Page 228	Page 313

Page 355 Page 354 Page 307 Page 254 Page 213

Page 178 Page 196 Page 223 Page 290 Page 206

Page 136 Page 46 Page 79 Page 188 Page 103

Page 325 Page 130 Page 316 Page 187 Page 344

Page 197 Page 198 Page 161 Page 317 Page 105

Page 253 Page 194 Page 195 Page 126 Page 61

Page 63 Page 59 Page 62 Page 60 Page 51

Page 154 | Page 42 | Page 315 | Page 305 | Page 305
Page 134 | Page 314 | Page 317 | Page 320 | Page 185
Page 271 | Page 271 | Page 64 | Page 248 | Page 212
Page 201 | Page 199 | Page 243 | Page 210 | Page 209
Page 237 | Page 246 | Page 224 | Page 151 | Page 218
Page 144 | Page 30 | Page 129 | Page 217 | Page 249
Page 250 | Page 50 | Page 170 | Page 135 | Page 202

Page 306 Page 266 Page 169 Page 240 Page 184
Page 283 Page 226 Page 234 Page 235 Page 80
Page 99 Page 99 Page 69 Page 70 Page 73
Page 94 Page 106 Page 107 Page 124 Page 236
Page 124 Page 191 Page 110 Page 109 Page 256
Page 258 Page 261 Page 165 Page 162 Page 171
Page 164 Page 166 Page 172 Page 163 Page 173

Page 149 Page 149 Page 225 Page 147 Page 148

Page 155 Page 232 Page 231 Page 241 Page 82

Page 138 Page 137 Page 177 Page 229 Page 260

Page 159 Page 158 Page 230 Page 251 Page 259

Page 284 Page 288 Page 168 Page 204 Page 203

Page 179 Page 182 Page 283 Page 222 Page 156

Page 56 Page 245 Page 266 Page 281 Page 285

Page 192 | Page 356 | Page 301/302 | Page 363 | Page 363

Page 220 | Page 85 | Page 256 | Page 261 | Page 349-351

Page 338 | Page 305 | Page 307 | Page 294 | Page 322

Page 347 | Page 151 | Page 341 | Page 315 | Page 320

Page 182 | Page 181 | Page 314 | Page 323 | Page 344

Page 303 | Page 284 | Page 252 | Page 43 | Page 313

Page 312 | Page 293 | Page 304 | Page 346 | Page 345

Page 339 Page 302 Page 326 Page 337 Page 324

Page 325 Page 342 Page 319 Page 299 Page 310

Page 311 Page 113 Page 310 Page 311 Page 306

Page 356 Page 291 Page 292 Page 122 Page 353-355

Page 352 Page 343 Page 147 Page 145 Page 328

Page 321 Page 269 Page 300/301 Page 331 Page 332/334

Page 330 Page 335 Page 333 Page 333 Page 329

Aceraceae
(Maple)

Tree with deciduous, opposite leaves that are usually simple and palmately lobed but may be pinnately compound. Flowers regular, sometimes perfect, in clusters. Sepals 4-6, petals 4-6 or lacking. Stamens 4-12 (usually 8), pistil 1. Fruit a samara.

Agavaceae
(Agave)

Leaves usually long and pointed, tipped with spines, margins with spines or fibers, and arranged as a rosette around a stout flower stem. Flowers numerous, often large, showy, fleshy; usually perfect. Corolla parts in threes. Stamens 6, pistil 1. Fruit 3-chambered fleshy or more often dried, firm, almost woody with numerous seeds.

Amaryllidaceae
(Amaryllis)

Perennial herbs, plants from bulbs; leaves simple, linear, parallel-veined, mostly basal, alternate; flowers in clusters, often showy; tepals (sepals and petals that look identical) 6, free or fused; stamens 6; ovary inferior; fruit a capsule.

Anacardiaceae
(Sumac)

Vines or shrubs, some plants toxic, may produce contact dermatitis; leaves compound, deciduous, alternate; sepals 5, fused below; petals 5, free; fruit a drupe.

Apiaceae
(Parsley/Carrot)

Annual, biennial, perennial herbs, stems often hollow, ribbed, some species highly toxic when consumed, some species producing contact dermatitis; leaves basal and along stems, compound, often fragrant, alternate. Flowers in umbrella-like clusters (umbels); sepals 5 (sometimes absent), free; petals 5, free; stamens 5; ovary inferior. Fruit a schizocarp.

Apocynaceae
(Dogbane)

Perennial herbs, plants with milky sap; leaves opposite or whorled, entire; flowers 1 or in clusters of many axillary or terminal blossoms; sepals 5, fused below, 5 lobes often reflexed; petals 5, fused in bell shape, lobes 5; stamens 5; ovaries 2, superior; fruit a follicle.

Asparagaceae
(Asparagus)

Perennial herbs, plants from bulbs or rhizomes; leaves simple, parallel-veined, basal or alternate; flowers in clusters or solitary; tepals (sepals and petals that look identical) 6, free or fused; stamens 6; ovary superior; fruit a capsule or berry.

Asteraceae
(Sunflower/Aster/Daisy/Composite)

Annual, biennial, perennial herbs, shrubs. Leaves simple or compound, alternate, opposite, or whorled. Flowers, few to many clustered into heads (e.g., daisy) enclosed by cluster of bracts (involucre), often green but sometimes spiny. Three flower types: 1) ray flowers, bilaterally symmetrical with a long, flat, strap-like portion and often surrounding disk flowers; 2) disk flowers, radially symmetrical, in center of flower-heads, usually surrounded by ray flowers; 3) flowers bilaterally symmetrical, similar in appearance to ray flowers but never accompanied by ray or disk flowers. Fruit an achene.

Balsaminaceae
(Touch-me-not)

Annual herbs. Stems with watery sap. Leaves simple, alternate. Flowers bilaterally symmetrical, single or in clusters; sepals 3 with 2 small and green and the other large, colored and forming a spur; petals 5, fused into unequal lobes; stamens 5; ovary superior; fruit a capsule, explodes when ripe, seeds many.

Berberidaceae
(Barberry)

Perennial herbs, shrubs, plants spreading to erect from rhizomes. Leaves simple or pinnately compound. Sepals and petals 6 or 9 in whorls of 3. Fruit a berry, usually purple-black.

Betulaceae
(Birch)

Shrubs and trees with alternate and simple serrated leaves. Male inflorescence a catkin; female inflorescence in clusters, spikes, or, typically, catkins. Stamens 2 to many, styles 2. Fruit is a 1-seeded nut. Dried catkins persist.

Boraginaceae
(Borage/Forget-Me-Not)

Annual, biennial, perennial herbs, plants with hispid hairs. Leaves usually simple, entire. Flowers in clusters or 1-sided coil, uncoiling in seed; sepals and petals 5, fused below, five-lobed, petals forming tube; stamens 5, alternating with petals; ovary superior, splitting in fruit to produce 4 nutlets.

Brassicaceae
(Mustard)

Annual, perennial herbs, subshrubs. Leaves are alternate. Sepals 4, free; petals 4, free, forming a cross shape; stamens usually 6 with 4 higher than other 2; ovary superior; seedpods either long and thin or somewhat globe-shaped, divided in center by a papery division with seeds on either side.

Cactaceae
(Cactus)

Perennial herbs with highly modified stems that are thick, fleshy, round to flat, and green for photosynthesizing; leaves highly modified into spines; flowers solitary; sepals 5 to many, free; petals many, free; stamens many; ovary superior or inferior; fruit a berry.

Campanuaceae
(Bellflower)

Annual, perennial herbs, often with white, milky sap; leaves simple, alternate; flowers radially or bilaterally symmetrical, in clusters, spikes, or solitary; sepals 5, free or fused below; petals 5, fused for part or all of length; stamens 5; ovary inferior, style 1 with 2-5 branches; fruit a capsule with many seeds.

Caprifoliaceae
(Honeysuckle)

Shrubs or woody vines; leaves simple or compound, opposite; flowers radially or bilaterally symmetrical, in clusters or single; sepals 5, fused below; petals 5, fused below; stamens 5, alternating with petals; ovary inferior, style 1; fruit a berry. See also Linnaeaceae.

Caryophyllaceae
(Pink)

Annual, biennial, perennial herbs; leaves opposite, often simple; area where leaf attaches to stem often swollen; flowers solitary to many; sepals 4-5, free or fused, sometimes inflated when fused; petals 4-5, usually notched or divided, free; stamens usually 5 or 10; fruit a capsule, usually with many seeds.

Celastraceae
(Staff Tree)

Perennial herbs, shrubs; leaves simple, along the stem or basal, evergreen or deciduous, opposite; flowers in clusters or solitary, axillary or terminal; sepals 4-5, fused below; petals 4-5, free; stamens 4-5, fused with sepals and petals to form hypanthium; ovary superior; fruit a capsule or berry.

Cleomaceae
(Cleome)

Annual herbs with alternate, petiolate, palmate leaves. Flowers regular, perfect, in racemes, 4 sepals, 4 petals. Stamens 6 to many, 1 pistil. Fruit a 1-celled, many seeded, linear capsule. Commonly malodorous.

Convolvulaceae
(Morning Glory)

Annual, perennial herbs, usually twining or trailing, some members non-green parasitic plants; Leaves are alternate when present, simple; flowers single or in clusters, often twisting in bud; sepals 5, free; petals 5, tubular or bell-shaped; stamens 5; ovary superior, styles 1-2; fruit typically a capsule.

Cornaceae (Dogwood)	Perennial herbs, shrubs, trees; leaves simple, usually with arched, parallel veins, opposite or whorled; flowers tiny, in dense cluster atop showy, white bracts; sepals 4, fused below; petals 4-5 (or absent), free; stamens 4-5, alternating with petals; ovary inferior; fruit a drupe (single-seeded berry).
Crassulaceae (Stonecrop)	Annual, perennial herbs, plants fleshy; leaves simple, basal and along stems, alternate or opposite; flowers in clusters, usually with bracts; sepals 3-5, free; petals 3-5, free or fused; stamens same number as sepals; ovary superior; fruit a capsule with many seeds.
Cupressaceae (Cypress)	Ancient family. Shrubs or trees commonly resinous and aromatic. Leaves are evergreen, overlapping scale-like, or needle-like. Male cones are small, female cones with 1 to several seeds are much larger and dry or fleshy at maturity.
Cyperaceae (Sedge)	Perennial herbs; leaves grass-like, V-shaped at base, basal; flowers in spikes that are either all male, all female, or a mix of male and female; sepals and petals lacking; stamens 3; ovary superior and surrounded by a sac (perigynium), styles 2-3; fruit an achene. Stems are usually 3-sided and solid.
Dennstaedtiaceae (Bracken Fern) ***Dryopteridaceae*** (Wood Fern)	Ferns in general are non-flowering plants with scaly or hairy, creeping rhizomes; in bud, leaves are coiled i 358n a fiddlehead form; leaves have petioles, are simple or mostly compound, and are often hairy or scaly. Fertile and sterile leaves may have same shape. Shape, position, and structure of spore cases separates species into genera and families.
Elaeagnaceae (Oleaster)	Shrub or trees, commonly thorny, with simple leaves coated with very showy scales or hairs (observable with a hand lens). Flowers perfect or imperfect, regular, small but clustered in large numbers. Perianth four-lobed. 4-8 stamens, 1 pistil. Fruit is hard dry seed enclosed in often edible fleshy growth.
Equisetaceae (Horsetail)	One of the most ancient land plants. Perennial, stems annual or perennial, typically hollow, jointed, ribbed. Leaves small and scale-like. Spores numerous.
Ericaceae (Heath/Heather)	Perennial herbs, shrubs, trees; leaves simple, evergreen or deciduous; flowers in cluster or solitary, usually with bracts; sepals 5, free; petals 4-5, free or fused; stamens 8-10; ovary inferior or superior; fruit a capsule, berry, or drupe (single-seeded berry). The Pyrolaceae (Wintergreen Family) is sometimes presented as a separate family.
Euphorbiaceae (Spurge)	Annual, perennial herbs, plants with milky sap; leaves usually simple, alternate or opposite; flowers in clusters, axillary or terminal, monoecious (separate male and female flowers on same plant) or dioecious (male and female flowers on separate plants), petal-like bracts present; sepals 3-5, free or fused below; petals absent; stamens 1 to many; ovary superior, often hanging to one side; fruit a capsule.

Fabaceae
(Pea/Bean/Legume)

Herbs to trees; leaves nearly always compound, alternate; flowers "pea-like," usually in clusters; sepals 5, fused below; petals 5 with different shapes: 1 at top that is bent backwards (banner), 2 on the side (wings), and 2 down low with crescent shape (keel); ovary superior; fruit pod a legume, often inflated, with a row of seeds attached along one edge.

Gentianaceae
(Gentian)

Annual, perennial herbs; leaves simple, opposite or whorled; flowers often large, in clusters or solitary; sepals 5, fused below; petals 5, fused below, forming narrowed tube with spreading lobes, sinuses between petal lobes often with pleat-like appendages; stamens 4-5, fused to tube, alternating with petal lobes; ovary superior on a stalk; fruit a capsule.

Geraniaceae
(Geranium)

Annual, perennial herbs; leaves palmately lobed or divided, simple or compound; flowers in loose cluster; sepals 5, free; petals 5, free; stamens 5 or 10; ovary superior, stigmas 5; fruit a mericarp (ripened ovary splitting into 5 individual seeds), seed clings to elongated style and coils, driving seed into soil.

Grossulariaceae
(Currant/Gooseberry)

Shrubs, plants with or without spines; leaves simple, palmately 3- to five-lobed, alternate; flowers usually in hanging clusters; sepals 5, showy, fused below and spreading above; petals 5, shorter and less showy than sepals, alternating with them; stamens 5, fusing with sepals and petals to form hypanthium; ovary inferior, style 1; fruit a berry with many seeds.

Hydrangeaceae
(Hydrangea/Mock Orange)

Shrubs or vines; leaves simple, entire or toothed, opposite; flowers in clusters or solitary; sepals 4-6, free or fused below; petals 4-6, free; stamens twice as many or more than petals; fruit a capsule with many small seeds.

Hydrophyllaceae
(Waterleaf)

Perennial, biennial, or annual often hairy herbs or shrubs. Leaves simple or deeply divided into 5-7 parts. Flowers perfect, regular with parts in fives, usually coiled like a scorpion's tail. Fruit a long capsule.

Hypericaceae
(St. John's Wort)

Annual, perennial herbs, shrubs; leaves simple, opposite or whorled, often with black dots or clear glands; flowers in clusters or solitary; sepals 5, fused below; petals 5, free; stamens many, free or fused into clusters; ovary superior, style with 3 branches; fruit a capsule. Some treat as a subfamily of the Clusiaceae.

Iridaceae
(Iris)

Perennial herbs, plants often from rhizomes; leaves simple, linear, parallel-veined, equitant (fan-like arrangement) at base; sepals 3, free; petals 3, free; ovary inferior; fruit a capsule.

Juncaceae
(Rush)

Generally slow-growing, rhizomatous, herbaceous plants that resemble grasses superficially. Leaves are evergreen, alternate, in a basal aggregation on an erect stem; leaves are tristichous (3 rows of leaves up the stem, each row of leaves arising one-third of the way around the stem from the previous leaf). Flowers in loose cymes, small and insignificant. Monocot with all of flower parts in multiples of three. Fruit is usually a nonfleshy, 3-sectioned dehiscent capsule containing many seeds.

Lamiaceae
(Mint)

Annual or perennial herbs, subshrubs, stems four-sided (square), plants often but not always with mint smell; leaves entire to deeply lobed, opposite; flowers bilaterally symmetrical, usually clustered around stem in whorls or at top of stem; sepals 5, in part fused; petals 5, fused, typically two-lipped, upper lip entire or lobed, flat to hood-shaped, lower lip 3-lobed; stamens 4; ovary superior; fruit a nutlet.

Liliaceae
(Lily)

Perennial herbs, plants from bulbs or rhizomes; leaves simple, parallel-veined, basal or along stem, alternate, opposite, or whorled; tepals (sepals and petals that look identical) 6; stamens 3 or 6; ovary superior, style 1; fruit a berry or capsule. See also Amaryllidaceae, Asparagaceae, and Melanthiaceae.

Linaceae
(Flax)

Annual, perennial herbs; leaves often linear, alternate, opposite, or whorled; sepals 4-5, free; petals 4-5, free; stamens 4-5, alternating with petals, fused at base and surrounding ovary; ovary superior, styles 2-5; fruit a dehiscent capsule, usually 10-seeded.

Linnaeaceae
(Twin Flower)

Trailing shrubs; leaves simple, opposite; sepals 5, fused below; petals 5, fused below; stamens 4, attached to fused section of petals, alternating with petal lobes; ovary inferior, style 1; fruit a capsule.

Loasaceae
(Blazing Star)

Annual, perennial herbs, plants with rough or stinging hairs; leaves simple, alternate, pinnately lobed; sepals 5, free, persistent in seed; petals 5, free; stamens many; ovary inferior; fruit a capsule with many seeds.

Malvaceae
(Mallow)

Annual, biennial, perennial herbs, leaves and stems often with sticky sap; leaves lobed, palmately veined, somewhat maple-like, alternate; sepals 5, fused below; petals 5, mostly free; stamens 5 to many, fused at base forming column around ovary; ovary superior, stigmas 5-10, generally extending above stamens; fruit a capsule or mericarp (mature ovary splitting into many individual seeds).

Melanthiaceae
(False Hellebore)

Perennial herbs, plants from bulbs or rhizomes; leaves simple, alternate, basal, or whorled; flowers in spikes or solitary; tepals (sepals and petals that look identical) 6, free or fused; stamens 6; ovary superior to partly inferior, styles 3; fruit a capsule.

Montiaceae
(Miner's Lettuce)

Annual, perennial herbs, usually fleshy, lacking hairs; leaves simple, alternate or opposite; sepals usually 2, free; petals 1-20, free; stamens 1 to many; ovary superior, often with 3 styles, possibly up to 8; fruit a capsule.

Nymphaeaceae
(Waterlily)

Perennial herbs, plants aquatic; leaves floating or submersed, arising on long petioles from underwater rhizomes, alternate; flowers solitary, large and showy; sepals 4-12, free, petal-like; petals many (sometimes absent), some stamen-like; stamens many; ovary superior, 1 to many; fruit a fleshy capsule.

Oleaceae
(Olive)

Trees or shrubs with opposite and simple or pinnately compound leaves; flowers are unisexual or bisexual, generally small in size, and most commonly four-lobed; and the fruit is variable.

Onagraceae
(Evening Primrose)

Annual, perennial herbs; leaves basal or along stem, simple, alternate, opposite, or whorled; flowers in spikes, clusters, or solitary, often open at dusk or dawn, fading to darker color with age; sepals 4, free; petals 4, free; stamens 4 or 8, fused to sepals and petals to form hypanthium; ovary inferior; fruit usually a capsule.

Orchidaceae
(Orchid)

Perennial herbs; leaves with parallel veins, simple; flowers bilaterally symmetrical; sepals 3, free; petals 3, free, lowermost usually highly modified and quite different in appearance; stamen 1, fused with stigma; ovary inferior; fruit a capsule with many seeds.

Orobanchaceae
(Broomrape)

Annual, perennial herbs, some plants leafless, non-green and parasitic, other plants green and semi-parasitic; flowers bilaterally symmetrical, in spike, clusters, or solitary; sepals 5, fused below or not; petals 5, fused below, two-lipped; stamens 4; ovary superior; fruit a capsule with many small seeds.

Paeoniaceae
(Peony)

Perennial herbs or shrubby plants. Leaves are alternate and divided into three lobes. Flowers radially symmetrical, bisexual, and large, with 5 sepals, 5 petals (sometimes 10), and an indefinitely large number of stamens. The female parts are superior and consist of 2-5 large fleshy pistils containing many ovules, which develop into large seeds.

Papaveraceae
(Poppy)

Annual, perennial herbs, plants often with milky sap; sepals 2 or 3, free, falling as flower bud opens; petals 4-6, free, dropping all at once; stamens many; ovary superior; fruit a capsule.

Phrymaceae
(Lopseed)

Annual, perennial herbs; leaves simple, opposite; flowers usually bilaterally symmetrical, in clusters or solitary, axillary or terminal; sepals 5, fused below; petals 5, fused below, often two-lipped; stamens 4, in two pairs; ovary superior; fruit a capsule.

Pinaceae
(Pine)

Ancient family of evergreen trees with scaly bark. Leaves of two kinds: thin and scale-like at the base of short branches and long, green needle-like borne singly or in clusters of 2-5 on spur branches. Male pollen-producing cones are narrow, elongated; female cones similarly shaped but much larger and woody, maturing in 1 or 2 seasons and not falling apart at maturity.

Plantaginaceae
(Plantain)

Annual, biennial, perennial herbs, some plants aquatic; leaves simple, alternate, opposite, or whorled; flowers bilaterally or radially symmetrical, in clusters with 1 to many flowers; sepals 4-5, fused below; petals 4-5, fused below, sometimes two-lipped; stamens 2 or 4; ovary superior; fruit a capsule.

Poaceae
(Grass)

Annual, perennial plants with hollow, jointed stems (culms) and narrow, parallel-veined alternate leaves, attached to the stem by a sheath. Flowers in spikelets aggregated in open, compound panicles, racemes or cylindrical spikes. Each flower with 2 scale-like bracts (lemma and palet) which enclose the pistil and stamens. Each spikelet subtended by a pair of scales (glumes).

Polemoniaceae
(Phlox)

Annual, perennial herbs, subshrubs; leaves simple or compound, alternate or opposite, arranged along stem and/or in basal rosette; flowers in clusters, heads, or solitary; sepals 5, fused below, often with translucent tissue between veins; petals 5, fused below, bell-shaped or a short tube with 5 flattened lobes and open throat at top; stamens 5; ovary superior, style 1 with 3 stigmatic lobes; fruit a capsule with 1 to many seeds.

Polygonaceae
(Buckwheat)

Annual, perennial herbs, subshrubs; leaves simple, alternate or whorled, attachment to stem enclosed within papery sheath (ocrea); flowers in clusters, axillary or terminal; tepals (sepals and petals that look identical) 2-6, free or fused below, usually in 2 whorls; stamens 3, 6-9; ovary superior; fruit an achene.

Primulaceae
(Primrose)

Annual, perennial herbs, hairless or with glands; leaves simple, often basal; flowers often on long, leafless stem (scape); sepals 4-5, fused below, often persisting; petals 4-5, fused below, often spreading or reflexed; stamens 4-5, opposite the petals; ovary superior, style 1, stigma head-like; fruit a capsule with few to many small seeds.

Pteridaceae
(Maidenhair Fern)

Largest fern family comprising some 50 genera and over 950 species. Ferns in general are non-flowering plants with scaly or hairy, creeping rhizomes; in bud, leaves are coiled in a fiddlehead form; leaves have petioles, are simple or mostly compound, and are often hairy or scaly. Fertile and sterile leaves may have same shape. Shape, position, and structure of spore cases separates species into genera and families.

Ranunculaceae
(Buttercup)

Annual, perennial herbs, vines; leaves simple or compound, usually alternate, sometimes opposite; flowers radially or bilaterally symmetrical; sepals 5 to many, green, withering early or petal-like when petals absent; petals 5 to many, sometimes absent; stamens 10 to many; ovary superior, 1 to many, not fused; fruit a berry, follicle, or achene (single seed).

Rhamnaceae
(Buckthorn)

Shrub or tree; leaves simple, often clustered on short shoots, usually alternate; flowers in small to large clusters at top of stems or solitary in axils; sepals 4-5, free; petals 4-5 (sometimes lacking), free; stamens 4-5, fusing with sepals and petals to form hypanthium around or attached to ovary; ovary superior, style 1, undivided or with 2-3 branches; fruit a capsule or drupe (single-seeded berry).

Rosaceae
(Rose)

Herbs, vines, shrubs, trees; leaves simple, pinnately or palmately compound, with appendages (stipules) at base, alternate; flowers in clusters or solitary; sepals 5, free; petals 5, free; stamens 5 to many; ovaries 1 to many, inferior or superior; fruit a berry, achene (single seed), or follicle.

Rubiaceae
(Madder/Bedstraw)

Annual, perennial herbs, stems four-sided; leaves opposite or whorled; flowers solitary or in clusters; sepals 4-5 or absent, fused below; petals 4, fused below, free lobes forming a cross; stamens 4-5; ovary inferior; fruit a nutlet or capsule.

Salicaceae
(Willow)

Dwarf shrubs to large trees. Leaves are alternate, simple, entire. Flowers not perfect in catkins. Male flowers of 1 to many stamens, female of a single pistil. Fruit is a capsule with numerous small seeds, each bearing a tuft of white, silky hairs.

Sarcobataceae
(Greasewood)

Perennial, deciduous shrubs with spiny branches and succulent leaves. The flowers are unisexual, with the male and female flowers on the same plant.

Saxifragaceae
(Saxifrage)

Annual or perennial herbs, plant glabrous or hairy, usually glandular when hairy; leaves linear to round, entire to maple-like lobing; flowers solitary or in clusters; sepals 5, fused below; petals 5, sometimes spotted, fused below; stamens 10, fusing with sepals and petals to form a hypanthium; ovary inferior to superior; fruit a capsule.

Scrophulariaceae
(Figwort/Snapdragon)

Annual, biennial, or perennial herbs, stems round or square; leaves simple, alternate or opposite; flowers radially to bilaterally symmetrical, usually in spikes; sepals 4-5, fused below; petals 4-5, fused below; stamens usually 4 in two pairs, sometimes sterile staminode present; ovary superior; fruit a capsule with many seeds. See also Phrymaceae and Plantaginaceae.

Solanaceae
(Nightshade/Potato)

Annual or perennial herbs; leaves simple, entire or deeply lobed, alternate; sepals 5, fused below; petals 5, fused below, tube often trumpet-shaped or flattened; stamens 5; ovary superior, style 1 and undivided; fruit a berry or capsule.

Typhaceae
(Cattail)

Perennial herbs, plants aquatic or in wetlands, stems round and stiff; leaves simple, flat, parallel veins; flowers in cylindrical spikes or spherical heads, male and female flowers separate (monoecious), male flowers above females; sepals and petals lacking; stamens 1 to several; ovary superior; fruit a follicle.

Urticaceae
(Nettle)

Annual, perennial herbs, some plants with stinging hairs; leaves simple, toothed, alternate or opposite; flowers single to clustered, axillary, male and female flowers on same plant (monoecious) or on different plants (dioecious); sepals 4-5, free; petals absent; stamens 4-5, opposite the sepals; ovary superior; fruit an achene.

Valerianaceae
(Valerian)

Annual, perennial herbs, plants often with strong, unpleasant odor; leaves simple or pinnately lobed or compound, opposite; flowers in dense clusters, bilaterally symmetrical; sepals fused, lobes 0 or 5-15; petals 5, fused below, often two-lipped with spur or swollen base; stamens 1-3; ovary inferior; fruit an achene.

Violaceae
(Violet)

Annual, perennial herbs; leaves basal or along stem, sometimes both; flowers bilaterally symmetrical, usually solitary; sepals 5, free; petals 5, free, larger petal at bottom with spur or pouch at base; stamens 5; ovary superior; fruit a capsule, seeds often with fleshy appendage.

INTRODUCTION TO SPECIES ACCOUNTS

FORBS/HERBS
Pages 29-290

Forbs are non-grasslike herbaceous plants that inlcude what we commonly recognize as wildflowers. Herbs are plants that do not have persistent above-ground stems, dying back to the ground at the end of the growing season; they lack woody, above-ground stems.

Forbs may be **annual**, living only one season; **biennial**, living 2 years, typically flowering and producing fruit in the second year; or **perennial**, growing for 3 years or more, typically producing flowers and fruit each year, after their first year. The vast majority of wildflowers depicted in these following pages are perennials.

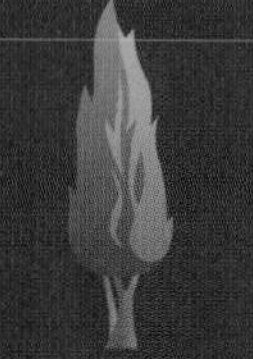

SHRUBS/TREES
Pages 291-356

Shrubs and trees are woody plants, as compared with forbs that have non-woody above-ground stems. The woody stems are defining, not the plant's size. Consequently Pink Mountain Heather (*Phyllodoce empetriformis*), though seldom more than 10" tall, is considered a shrub, not a forb.

Shrubs are typically multi-stemmed and less than 30' when mature. Trees are single-stemmed woody plants that are generally self-supporting and taller than 30' in stature when mature. Small trees may be considered shrubs.

A simple key to confiers found in the region is found on page 385.

FERNS
Pages 357-359

Ferns are vascular plants with stems and leaves common to other "higher" plants but neither flowers or seeds. Ferns have been part of the earth's flora for 300 million years. In fact, the Carboniferous Period is known as the Age of Ferns. Six species of fern most common to this region are featured. To learn more about ferns, visit the American Fern Society online.

Fern Allies are a diverse group of seedless vascular plants that are not true ferns, but like ferns, they reproduce by spores. Horsetails (Equisetaceae) are one of the most ancient land plants still in existence. All living horsetails are in the genus *Equisetum*. Two species are featured in this guide.

GRASS-LIKE
Pages 360-385

Graminoids include the true grasses (*Poaceae*), Rushes (*Juncaceae*), and Sedges (*Cyperaceae*). Appreciation of graminoids is too often left to the agrostologist. To help remedy this, this guide presents a sampling of 51 species found in the region.

True grasses (*Poaceae*) are herbaceous monocots with round hollow stems, 2-ranked leaves that arise on opposite sides of the stem, and flowers modified into glumes, lemmas, and paleas. There are more than 260 grass species found in Montana alone. Of these, some 20 percent are non-native.

Sedges (*Cyperaceae*) typically have 3-sided solid stems, 3-ranked evergreen leaves that arise from 3 different sides of the stem, and scale-like flowers.

Rushes (*Juncaceae*) have round solid stems, evergreen leaves arising from plant bases forming tufts, and flowers that comprise 3 sepals and 3 petals. To help distinguish sedges from rushes, I remember the adage from high school botany, "Sedges have edges, rushes are round."

SOAPWEED YUCCA
(SPANISH BAYONET)

FIELD DESCRIPTION:

Evergreen perennial herb, 1-5′ tall, bearing conspicuous cream-to-greenish-white blossoms rising on a tall stalk above stiff, narrow (~0.5″ wide), sharp-pointed leaves. Arranged in raceme, flowers are 2-4″ long with 6 broad, thick tepals surrounding 6 stamens and a green style. Leaves are numerous, thick, dagger-like, covered with a fine powder, in an upright overlapping swirl. Fruits in woody capsules with numerous black seeds.

SUBALPINE
MONTANE
FOOTHILLS

Flowering: June - August

Habitat: Moist soils in meadows and along stream banks, foothills to subalpine

TIDBITS

Soapweed Yucca provides both food and cover to a range of wildlife. Its flowers and fruits are edible, its leaves used in basket making, and a soap was traditionally made from the plant's roots. Yuccas are pollinated by their very own moth, the Yucca or Pronuba moth, which is the only known pollinator of the various species of yuccas. The moth drills a hole into the maturing seed capsule and deposits its eggs (look for it on the seed capsule). Yucca is a Carib name for Cassava and was applied, for some unknown reason, to this genus by Linnaeus. Cassava and yucca are not related. *Glauca* from the Greek for gray-green in reference to the leaves.

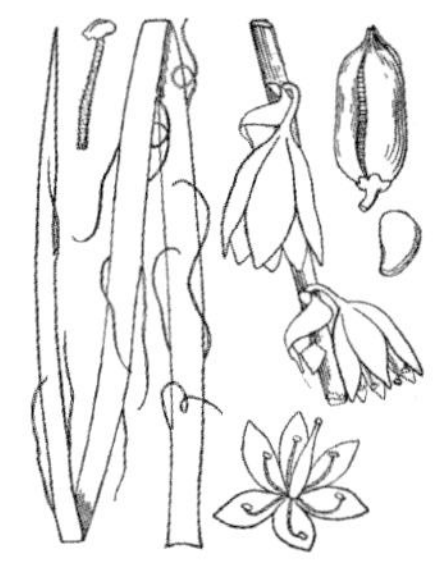

Photos: Bozeman, MT, July (W. Tilt); Illustration: USDA-NRCS Plants Database

WILD ONION

Allium sp. • Amaryllidaceae (Amaryllis Family)

FIELD DESCRIPTION:

Short-Styled Onion *(Allium brevistylum)* is a perennial herb with an onion or garlic-like odor, 10-20" tall. Erect cluster of pink-to-rose-purple flowers and papery bracts on stalks join at base like staves of an umbrella. Short, flat, grass-like leaves arise from base of stem. Stem flattens near top and flowering umbel does not bend or nod.

Nodding Onion *(Allium cernuum)* is a perennial herb with onion smell, 6-20" tall, growing from egg-shaped bulb. Leaves basal consisting of 3-7 flat, grass-like blades. Smooth round flower stem curves downward near its tip supporting an umbel of white-pinkish flowers. Bell-shaped flowers have 6 rounded petals and 6 yellow-tipped stamens that extend beyond the petals.

Flowering: June - August

Habitat: Open to moist soils, montane to subalpine

TIDBITS

Bulbs and leaves are edible raw or cooked. Flowers can also be eaten raw and used as garnish in salad. Bear, elk and other animals also eat wild onions. The more than 500 species of onion in the world are distinguished by the same 3-parted flower structure: 3 sepals, 3 petals, 3 fused carpels and 6 stamens. Recently reclassified from the *Liliaceae* to the *Amaryllidaceae*.

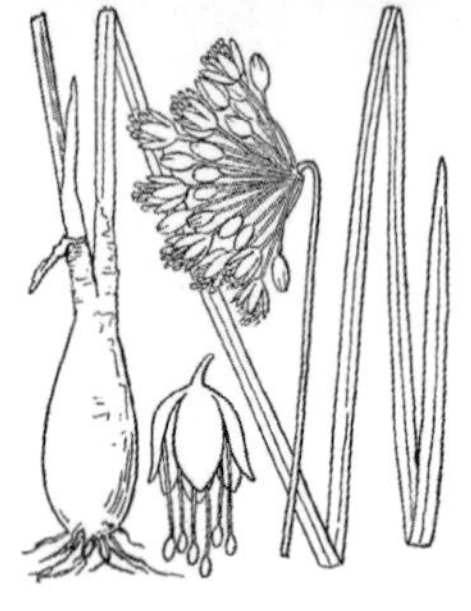

Thumbnail & reference photos (*A. breistylum*): Slough Creek, MT, June (W. Tilt); Inset and illustration (*A. cernuum*): Gallatin Range, June (W. Tilt); Illustration USDA-NRCS Planta Database

WHITE ANGELICA
(SHARPTOOTH ANGELICA)

FIELD DESCRIPTION:

Perennial herb with smooth, erect stems 1-5′ tall. Leaves are arranged in an alternate pattern along the stem. Each leaf is divided into segments, which are further divided into smaller leaflets (twice pinnate). Leaflets are oval in outline, 1-4″ long and sharply toothed along the margins. Tiny white flowers form a 2-tiered, flat-topped flower cluster resembling an umbrella (compound umbel). Each flower matures into a compound fruit (schizocarp) that splits into 2 single-seeded fruits (mericarps). The schizocarp is oval in outline and flattened in cross section. Each mericarp has a thin, wavy wing running along its outer edge.

MONTANE

Flowering: July - August

Habitat: Moist forests and meadows, in aspen groves and along streams, montane

TIDBITS

Frequently found in northern and western portion of the Yellowstone region in wet soils, 5,300-8,300′ in elevation. The stems, roots, and crushed fruit have a distinct anise-like smell. White angelica is an important food for grizzly and black bears throughout the summer. The genus name *Angelica* derives from supposed medicinal properties disclosed by an angel; the species name *arguta* means sharp-toothed for the shape of the leaves.

Photos: Ferry Co. WA, July (Gerald D. Carr); Illustration: USDA-NRCS Plants Database

WATER HEMLOCK
(SPOTTED WATER HEMLOCK)

Cicuta maculata • Apiaceae (Parsley Family)

TIDBITS

All parts of this tall, stout wetland plant are poisonous. While the notorious "hemlock" that killed Socrates in ancient Greece was Poison Hemlock (*Conium maculatum*), Water Hemlock is considered equally lethal. The leaflets can be distinguished from similar, non-toxic species in the Parsley Family by having veins that fork at their tips, with one branch ending at the tip of the leaflet and the other in the V-shaped sinus between adjacent leaflet lobes. Cut stems and roots may exude a yellow, oily, highly toxic liquid that smells like parsnips. *Cicuta* is the ancient Latin name for this plant. *Maculata* means "spotted."

FIELD DESCRIPTION:

Robust perennial herb, 1.5-6′ tall, with thick hollow, partitioned stems supporting flat-topped, umbrella-like flower clusters (compound umbels) of small, five-petaled, white-to-greenish flowers. Leaves are pinnately compound, alternate with lance-shaped leaflets with saw-toothed margins. Narrow, serrated leaves have veins that fork at their tips, with 1 branch ending at the tip of the leaflet and the other in the V-shaped sinus between adjacent leaflet lobes. Stems thickened and chambered at base. Sap often oily, yellow, and foul smelling. Fruits are flattened, egg-shaped achenes in drying umbels.

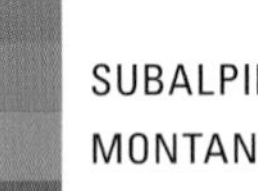

Flowering: June - September

Habitat: Moist soils along streams and sloughs, montane to subalpine

Photos: SW Colorado, June (Al Schneider); Illustration: USDA-NRCS Plants Database

Conium maculatum • Apiaceae (Parsley Family)

POISON HEMLOCK

FIELD DESCRIPTION:

Robust perennial herb, 1-8′ tall, with thick, hairless, purple-spotted hollow stems. Leaves large, alternate, petioled, feathery, and pinnately divided (fern-like, ternate-pinnate), individual leaflet segments small. Flower-heads in numerous open, flat-topped, umbrella-like clusters (compound umbels) of small, five-petaled, white-to-greenish flowers. Fruits are flattened, egg-shaped achenes with wavy ribs in drying umbels.

Flowering: June - August

Habitat: Moist soils, disturbed areas, along roads, ditches, and fields, plains to montane

TIDBITS

A native of Eurasia, all parts of this plant are extremely poisonous. Poison Hemlock is notorious for the execution of Socrates in ancient Greece. Even small amounts can be deadly. Plant looks superficially similar to other members of the Parsley Family, such as Wild Carrot (*Daucus carota*). Purple spotted stems are a good field mark, but avoid all parsley-like species unless you are an expert in distinguishing the various species. *Conium,* from the Greek konas (to whirl), in reference to vertigo, one of the symptoms of ingesting the plant; and *maculata* means "spotted."

Photos: Benton Co., OR, June (Gerald D. Carr); Illustration: USDA-NRCS Plants Database

COW PARSNIP

Heracleum maximum • Apiaceae (Parsley Family)
(Synonym: *Heracleum lanatum*)

FIELD DESCRIPTION:

Large perennial herb, 3-7′ tall, that towers over surrounding vegetation. Tall, hollow, very hairy stems support large (up to 12″ in diameter), flat-topped umbels of white flowers, with smaller umbels arising from leaf axils. Individual flowers comprised of 5 deeply lobed petals. Flower smell is strong, sweet, and a bit overpowering. Large maple-like leaves, 12-16″ across, are palmately lobed into 3 leaflets, alternate with inflated stems that are winged at their base. Fruits are flattened, ribbed disks with 2 broad wings.

Flowering: June - July

Habitat: Moist soils in wet meadows and along streams, montane to subalpine

Photos: Slough Creek, July (W. Tilt); Illustration: USDA-NRCS Plants Database

TIDBITS

The stalks and roots of Cow Parsnip are often peeled and roasted as a vegetable. The plant is rich in minerals and favored by grazing animals, hence the common name. The very young leaves of the plant are eaten in salads or cooked. In herbal medicine, this plant has long been used to treat epilepsy and a number of other ailments. Mature plants often have an unpleasant smell. Cow Parsnip may be confused with Water Hemlock, which is extremely poisonous. The genus was named for Hercules for the plant was thought to have potent powers, and its large size is also herculean.

Ligusticum filicinum • Apiaceae (Parsley Family)

FERNLEAF LOVAGE
(FERNLEAF LICORICEROOT)

FIELD DESCRIPTION:

Tall, leafy, perennial herb, 2-4′ tall. Small, white, five-petaled flowers arranged in delicate, flat-topped compound umbels, typically found on both the central and side stalks. Leaves basal and alternate, divided into fine, fern-like segments. Bracts are generally absent beneath umbels. Basal leaves are large while stem leaves fewer and reduced in size. Fruits are oblong with narrowly winged ribs.

SUBALPINE
MONTANE

Flowering: July - August

Habitat: Open, wooded slopes, montane to subalpine

Photos: Targhee Ski Resort, ID, August (W. Tilt)

TIDBITS

Fearnleaf Lovage is a delicate-looking plant with showy white flowers and finely cut leaves. The plant is common to the Tetons and other scattered areas at altitude. The Parsley Family is characterized by umbrella-shaped flower-heads and mostly parsley-like leaves. Many of the family's members are edible, like carrots and dill, but some are very poisonous, like Water Hemlock. The genus name, *Ligusticum*, is named after the Italian city of Liguria, and *filicinum* from the Latin "filum" (thread) in reference to the finely-cut, fern-like leaves.

COUS BISCUITROOT (COUS)

Lomatium cous • Apiaceae (Parsley Family)

FIELD DESCRIPTION:

Perennial herb, 4-10" tall, with yellow, five-petaled flowers arranged in dense, compound umbels. Conspicuous oblanceolate bracts present beneath flower-heads. Flower stalks are usually leafless. Basal leaves are parsley-like, shiny, dark-green, and 3-5 times pinnately dissected. Fruits are oblong with ridges upright on flower-head. Root is starchy tuber, varying in shape from long and slender to beet-like.

TIDBITS

Showy yellow flowers and parsley-like leaves mark this small-statured plant found along rocky trails. The root of cous is edible, as are all the biscuitroots, hence the common name. The journals of Lewis and Clark in 1805 noted Native Americans trading beads in exchange for cous on the Columbia River. The roots were pounded, roasted, and shaped into cakes. The cakes lasted for years and were light enough to carry during seasonal migrations and for trading. When boiled in water, the cakes created a thick soup. *Lomatium* from the Greek *loma* meaning "fringe" or "border," referring to the winged seed, and *cous* from the Chinookan language.

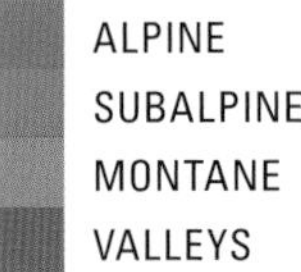

Flowering: April - July

Habitat: Dry rocky soils on open slopes, meadows and sagebrush steppes, valleys to alpine zones

Photos: Bridger Mountains, MT, May (Matt Lavin); Seedhead: Gallatin Mountains, MT, June (W. Tilt)

Lomatium dissectum • Apiaceae (Parsley Family)

FERNLEAF BISCUITROOT

FIELD DESCRIPTION:

Perennial herb, 1-4' tall, with fern-like leaves and flowers arranged in dense, compound umbels. Individual, small, usually yellow (but sometimes red/purple) flowers are at tips of long stalks in flat-topped clusters that open widely on long rays as the flowers mature. Narrow green involucre bracts present beneath each cluster. Flower stalks hollow and purple at base. Leaves arise from base on very long petioles with a few alternate leaves on stem. Leaves pinnately divided 3-5 times into slender, lacy, rough-textured segments. Fruits are flattened and elliptical with corky wings. Plant grows from a large woody taproot.

MONTANE
FOOTHILLS

Flowering: May - June

Habitat: Dry hillsides and meadows, foothills to montane

TIDBITS

Fernleaf Biscuitroot is a member of the Parsley Family, which includes mainly aromatic herbs with hollow stems and fern-like leaves. Large starchy roots of biscuitroots are edible, and were traditionally used in a number of ways including as flour to make meal cakes which were taken on long journeys. The Blackfoot Indians ground biscuitroot into flour and baked into loaves with a hole in the center so it could be lashed and packed for travel. *Loma* is Greek for "border" and refers to the small wings of the fruit. *Dissectum* from the Latin for "cut into many deep lobes."

Photos: Bozeman, MT, June-July (W. Tilt); Going to seed: Bozeman, MT (Matt Lavin)

BIGSEED BISCUITROOT
(WHITE BISCUITROOT, DESERT PARSLEY)

Lomatium macrocarpum • Apiaceae (Parsley Family)

TIDBITS

One of the "wild parsleys," Bigseed Biscuitroot grows from a large starchy taproot that is edible. The root is typically peeled before being eaten raw or cooked. Like all the biscuitroots, the root can be dried and ground into flour and used for a variety of purposes. Flowers are generally white in the Yellowstone region but may also be purplish or yellow. The Parsley Family includes many edible species, including carrot, parsnip, and dill, but also the deadly Poison and Water hemlocks. Both the plant's scientific and common names reference the plant's large seeds.

FIELD DESCRIPTION:

Spreading to erect perennial herb, 4-10" tall, with grayish-white-to-purplish-white flowers arranged in dense rounded clusters (umbels). Conspicuous narrow green bracts present under umbels. Numerous stems arising from taproot bear purplish peduncles topped with flower clusters. Leaves resemble those of the carrot with a grayish-green appearance caused by fine hairs. Basal leaves are gray-green, pubescent, triangle and pinnately divided 1-3 times into small lance-shaped segments. Fruits are brown, hairless, and distinctly winged along the margins.

VALLEYS-FOOTHILLS

Flowering: May - July

Habitat: Open, dry, rocky soils of sagebrush flats and hillsides, valleys to foothills

Thumbnail photo: Bozeman, MT, June (W. Tilt); Reference photo: Bozeman, MT, May (Matt Lavin); Seedhead: Bozeman, MT, July (Matt Lavin)

NINELEAF BISCUITROOT

FIELD DESCRIPTION:

Erect perennial herb, 8-30" tall, with tiny, yellow flowers in compact, flat-topped clusters (umbels) that are twice-divided. Involucre bracts are linear and acute. Leaves are mainly basal (on long petioles), divided 2-3 times into long linear grass-like segments. Plant has a parsley-like fragrance.

MONTANE
FOOTHILLS

Flowering: May - July

Habitat: Dry to moist open sites, foothills to montane

Photos: Bozeman, MT, June (Matt Lavin)

TIDBITS

The peanut-sized roots of Nineleaf Biscuitroot are edible either raw or cooked. Many animals, including ground squirrels and other rodents, feed on them. Biscuitroot was a staple of many Native American tribes. The species name, *triternatum*, refers to three times ternate, i.e., leaves are split 3-times, then again 3 times, and then again (although this species does sometimes split into 3s only twice). Lewis & Clark collected this species and several other biscuitroots that were previously undescribed by science as they aren't found east of the Mississippi River.

WESTERN SWEET CICELY

Osmorhiza occidentalis • Apiaceae (Parsley Family)

FIELD DESCRIPTION:

Perennial herb from 2-4′ tall, strongly aromatic. Leaves pinnate. Petioles of lower leaves 2-12″ long, the upper ones reduced. Lower leaf blades to 10″ long, upper ones markedly smaller. Peduncles 2-8″ long, Flower-heads are 3-5 umbels, yellow-to-greenish flowers on elongated rays (stems). Petals green-white to green-yellow. Fruits black with stiff hairs, up to 1″ long.

Flowering: June - August

Habitat: Woodlands, moist or dry soils, meadows, shrublands, montane to subalpine

TIDBITS

Western Sweet Cicely is one of 4-5 species of *Osmorhiza* found in the Yellowstone region, typically characterized by dainty flower-heads, compound leaves, and fragrant roots. The seed pods of sweet cicely are distinctive, both to species identification and as they are easily dislodged to be carried away on pants, socks, and dogs. Blunt Sweet Cicely (*O. depauperata*) and Aniseroot (*O. longistylis*) are two other species likely encountered in the region. Stems, leaves, seeds, and roots of Western Sweet Cicely have a pleasant anise flavor and the genus name, *Osmorhiza*, is from the Greek for "smelly root."

Thumbnail photos: Top: Yakima, WA, June (Walter Siegmund, Wikimedia Commons); Bottom: SW Colorado, June & August (Al Schneider); Reference photo:Yakima, WA, June (Walter Siegmund, Wikimedia Commons)

Perideridia gairdneri • Apiaceae (Parsley Family)

GAIRDNER'S YAMPAH

FIELD DESCRIPTION:

Erect, slender perennial herb, 15-40" tall, with a caraway-like fragrance. Basal leaves pinnately divided 1-2 times into long, narrow segments; stem Leaves are alternate along the stem, once (rarely twice) pinnate into long narrow segments. Flat-topped clusters (umbels) of tiny white flowers with uneven, spreading stalks, 1 to several in number. Fruit is a fleshy round bulb.

MONTANA
FOOTHILLS

Flowering: July - August

Habitat: Dry to moist slopes, foothills to montane

Photos: Driggs, ID, June (W. Tilt); Illustration: USDA-NRCS Plants Database

TIDBITS

Gairdner's Yampah was an important food for many Native American tribes. Roots of the plant have a sweet nutty flavor and were traditionally roasted or boiled. The tuberous roots of yampah are also known to be important foods of both grizzly bears and burrowing rodents. *Perideridia* from the Greek for "with a leather coat," referring to the leathery skin of the tuberous edible roots of this plant. Caution: Never eat a carrot-like plant unless you are sure of its identity. Many similar looking plants are poisonous.

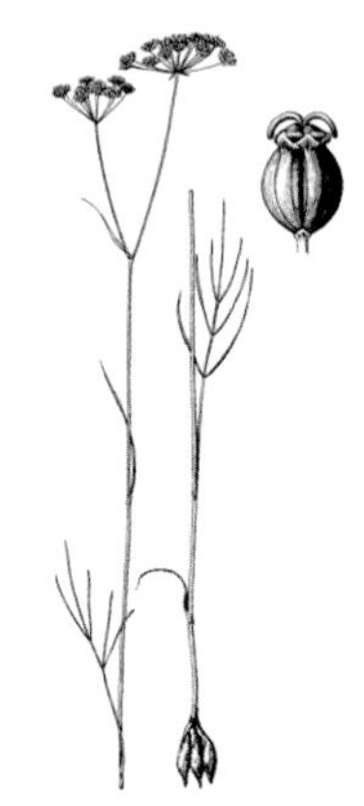

SPREADING DOGBANE

Apocynum androsaemifolium • Apocynaceae (Dogbane Family)

FIELD DESCRIPTION:

Bushy perennial herb, 8-20" tall, with opposite, drooping leaves. Leaves are ovate-oblong, smooth on short stalks, and usually hairy on underside. Small white-pink clusters of flowers arise from axils of terminal leaves. Flowers are bell-shaped with 5 fused petals often with red stripes on the inside. Stems have milky sap. Fruits are long, reddish, slender, cylindrical pods in pairs. Mature pods contain numerous seeds with tufts of silky hairs.

SUBALPINE
MONTANE
FOOTHILLS

Flowering: June - September

Habitat: Dry, well-drained soils on open hillsides and forests, foothills to subalpine

TIDBITS

Dogbane is most noticeable in the late summer and fall when its leaves turn a bright yellow along roadways and trails. *Apocynum* is Greek for "away dog," i.e., "dogbane," and animals avoid eating it. Plant has a wide variety of traditional medicine uses, from the treatment of kidney complaints to treating pinworms. Stem fibers can be used to make thread and cord. This species is also commonly called Indian Hemp, a name shared with *Apocynum cannabinum* and other plant species as well. *Androsaemifolium* is Latin for "man's blood-colored flower," perhaps a reference to the plant's reddish stems.

Photos: Bozeman, July (W. Tilt); Illustration: USDA-NRCS Plants Database

FALSE SOLOMON'S SEAL
(FALSE LILY OF THE VALLEY)

FIELD DESCRIPTION:

Leafy perennial herb, 2-3′ tall, with numerous tiny white flowers, with 3 petals and 3 sepals, in a dense panicle atop an erect or slightly bent stem. Alternate, long, broad leaves with pointed tips either clasp the stem or are held on short stalks. Later in the season, a head of light green-brown berries on reddish stems replaces the panicle of white flowers.

SUBALPINE
MONTANE

Flowering: May - July

Habitat: Most soils in woods and stream banks, montane to subalpine

TIDBITS

A common, widespread plant that goes by numerous common names, including False Spikenard and Solomon's Plume. Its taller stature, wider leaves, and numerous tiny white flowers in a dense panicle distinguish it from Starry Lily-of-the-Valley (*Maianthemum stellatum*). The 2 species are commonly found in the same habitats. Both are commonly cultivated in gardens. *Maianthemum* means "May Flower," and *racemosum* describes the inflorescence. Recently reclassified from the Liliaceae to the Asparagaceae.

Photos: Bozeman, MT (W. Tilt);
Illustration: USDA-NRCS Plants Database

STAR-FLOWERED FALSE SOLOMON'S SEAL

Maianthemum stellatum • Asparagaceae (Asparagus)
(Synonym: *Smilacina stellata*)

FIELD DESCRIPTION:

Perennial herb, 8-24" tall, with arching form. Five to 10 white star-like flowers, comprised of 3 petals and 3 sepals (6 tepals) are arranged in an unbranched inflorescence atop an unbranched leafy stem. Leaves are alternate, lance-shaped, and stalkless with prominent parallel veins. Fruits are greenish-yellow initially, and darkening to reddish-blue-black as they fully mature.

TIDBITS

Six-petaled star flowers arranged in a raceme, narrow leaves, and dense colonies of plants help distinguish Star-Flowered False Solomon's Seal from False Solomon's Seal. Berries striped when they first emerge before maturing into red-brown then blue-black berries. *Stellatum* from the Latin for "star" – an apt description of the plant's flowers. Recently reclassified from the Liliaceae to the Asparagaceae.

Flowering: May - June

Habitat: Moist soils in woods and stream banks, montane to subalpine

Thumbnail photo: SW Colorado, May (AL Schneider); Reference photo: Slough Creek, June (W. Tilt); Illustration: USDA-NRCS Plants Database

Achillea millefolium • Asteraceae (Sunflower Family)

YARROW

FIELD DESCRIPTION:

Perennial herb, 8-40" tall, with white flowers (sometimes pinkish) with yellow disks. Tiny flowers collectively create flat-topped flower-head clusters. Leaves are highly aromatic, alternate, fern-like, pinnately divided 2-3 times into fine segments. Single or clumped stems, branched near top and covered with soft, woolly hairs arise from rhizomes below the ground.

MONTANE
VALLEYS

Flowering: May - September

Habitat: Plains, hills and slopes, from valleys to montane

Thumbnail photo: Bozeman, MT, July (Matt Lavin); Reference photo: Gallatin Range, MT, July (W. Tilt); Illustration: USDA-NRCS Plants Database

TIDBITS

Achillea references one or more of the myths surrounding Achilles, his invincibility, and the battle of Troy. Legend tells us that Achilles was dunked into a bath of Yarrow tea at birth protecting his body from harm, save the heels by which he was held. Another piece of lore has Achilles using an ointment made from Yarrow to treat the wounds of his fellow soldiers. The leaves of Yarrow are said to be effective in stopping bleeding and the plant has been used for thousands of years as a medicinal plant for treating everything from mosquito bites to colds and flu.

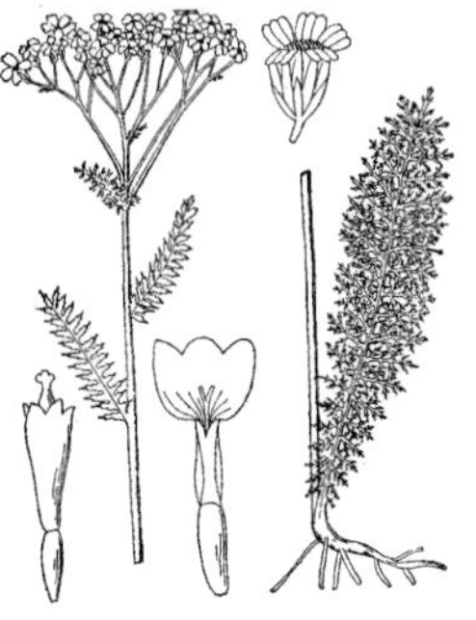

ORANGE AGOSERIS (ORANGE MOUNTAIN DANDELION)

Agoseris aurantiaca • Asteraceae (Sunflower Family)

FIELD DESCRIPTION:

Perennial herb, 4-24" tall, with solitary leafless stems and milky sap. Each stem topped by orange (rarely yellow) flower consisting of only ray flowers, which often turn pink-purplish with age. Outer tips of rays squared with 5 small teeth. Narrow, lance-shaped leaves in basal rosette. Leaves are long-stalked with smooth-edged margins or with scattered teeth or small lobes. Fruits are smooth achenes with long, slender beaks and pappus of clustered white hairs.

TIDBITS

The only orange-flowered *Agoseris*, the flower resembles the common dandelion in general form, and is often referred to as "mountain dandelion." Widespread and common in western North America, Orange Agoseris also resembles Orange Hawkweed (*Hieracium aurantiacum*), an invasive exotic, distinguished by its multiple flower-heads per stem. *Agoseris* from the Greek for "goat chicory," and *aurantiaca* from the Latin for "orange."

MONTANE
FOOTHILLS

Flowering: June - August

Habitat: Open meadows and woodlands, foothills to montane

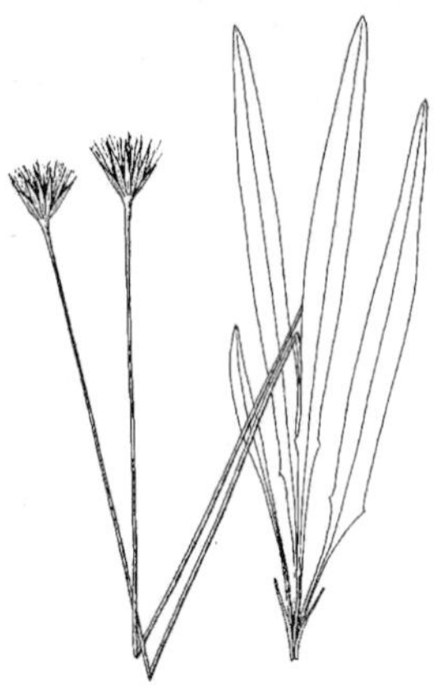

Thumbnail photo: Beehive Basin, MT, July (Rip McIntosh); Reference photo: Glacier NP, MT, July (W. Tilt); Illustration: USDA-NRCS Plants Database

Anaphalis margaritacea • Asteraceae (Sunflower Family)

PEARLY EVERLASTING

FIELD DESCRIPTION:

Perennial herb, 8-36" tall, with white, woolly, leafy stems topped by roundish dense clusters of flower-heads with pearly-white bracts. Flowers comprise white papery involucral bracts surrounding yellowish (turning brown) disk flowers. Leaves are alternate along the length of the stem, linear- to lance-shaped, with dense, hairy undersides and a conspicuous mid-vein.

MONTANE

Flowering: July - September

Habitat: Forest openings and meadows, montane

TIDBITS

The pale green leaves of Pearly Everlasting often provide an eye-catching contrast with the surrounding vegetation. Its flowers dry well and are a favorite in floral arrangements. Pearly Everlasting may be confused with pussytoes, but Pearly Everlasting has lance-shaped leaves distributed alternately along the stem and lacks basal leaves. *Margaritacea* from the Latin for "pearl."

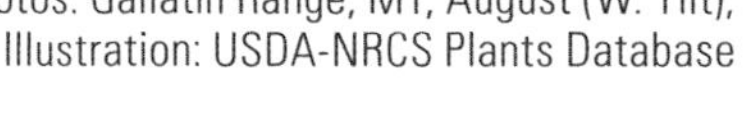

Photos: Gallatin Range, MT, August (W. Tilt); Illustration: USDA-NRCS Plants Database

SMALL-LEAF PUSSYTOES

Antennaria parvifolia • Asteraceae (Sunflower Family)

FIELD DESCRIPTION:

Perennial herb, 1-6" tall, mat forming from stolons. Leaves are simple, alternate, mostly basal, and hairy on both sides; basal leaves are generally spatulate shaped while stem leaves more linear. Inflorescence is relatively large, closely packed cyme with 2 to 6 heads of flowers. Corollas made up of disk flowers. Papery phyllaries are white with pink tips. Fruits are glabrous, angled achenes.

SUBALPINE
MONTANE
FOOTHILLS

Flowering: June - September

Habitat: Dry sunny hillsides, wooded slopes, forest openings, foothills to subalpine

TIDBITS

Frequently found in open areas and forest edges, Small-Leaf Pussytoes are low (1-6" tall), mat-forming plants with fuzzy white flower-heads. Of little interest to grazing wildlife and livestock, the plant responds favorably to grazing pressure. The common name "pussytoes" refers to the tightly packed flower-head's resemblance to the bottom of a cat's paw. The genus *Antennaria* refers to antennae-like floral parts and *parvifolia* means "small leaves." Pussytoes can be difficult to identify to the exact species as the species readily hybridizes and also often forms seed asexually, without pollination. This results in a good deal of taxonomic confusion.

Photos: Bitterroot Valley, MT, July (W. Tilt); Illustration: USDA-NRCS Plants Database

RACEME PUSSYTOES
(WOODS PUSSYTOES)

FIELD DESCRIPTION:

Perennial herb, 5-20" tall, with erect stems and leafy stolons. Basal leaves elliptical to oval with petioles; basal leaves green and nearly hairless above and white, woolly underneath. Stem leaves reduced in size, alternate, and lance-shaped. Flower-heads round, comprising disc flowers (no ray flowers), in open elongate clusters (racemes) atop green stalks. Flower-heads generally white in color but variable from white to greenish-brown. Fruits are achenes with pappus of long white bristles.

SUBALPINE
MONTANE

Flowering: May - July

Habitat: Moist, cool soils, commonly in open wooded areas, often on disturbed sites, montane to subalpine

Photos: Gallatin Range, MT, July (W. Tilt); Plant detail: Ferry Co., WA, July (Gerald D. Carr)

TIDBITS

While most pussytoes prefer open areas, Raceme Pussytoes tolerates shade and is found in open forested areas, particularly north facing slopes. The plant spreads vegetatively from above ground stolons. Genus name *Antennaria* from the Latin "antenna" in reference to the appearance of the pappus. *Racemosa* refers taking the form of a raceme. Plants have little known food value for wildlife.

ROSY PUSSYTOES
(LITTLELEAF PUSSYTOES)

Antennaria rosea • Asteraceae (Sunflower Family)
(Synonym: *Antennaria mircophylla*)

FIELD DESCRIPTION:

Mat-forming, stoloniferous perennial herb, 2-12" tall. Erect stems are topped with 3-20 flower-heads arranged in small tight clusters. Flower bracts range in color from white to rosy pink. Basal leaves are small, spoon-shaped, and woolly on both sides. Leaves along stem few and narrowly lance-shaped. Male and female flowers occur on separate plants.

TIDBITS

Antennaria species are distinctive with flower clusters resembling fluffy cat toes. There is a good deal of debate among taxonomists as to the classification of individual species. Rosy Pussytoes, however, are often distinctive, producing flowering heads surrounded by pink bracts. Fruits of some pussytoes have long, white, hair-like bristles. Pussytoes can be distinguished from Pearly Everlasting by the presence of basal leaves. The genus *Antennaria* refers to antennae-like floral parts.

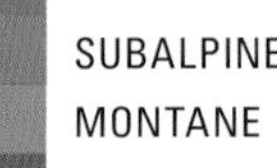

Flowering: May - July

Habitat: Dry open meadows and open woods, montane to subalpine

Photos: Yellowstone NP, August (W. Tilt & Rip McIntosh); Illustration: USDA-NRCS Plants Database

COMMON BURDOCK

Arctium minus • Asteraceae (Sunflower Family)

FIELD DESCRIPTION:

Large-leaved perennial herb, 3-8′ tall, with round, pinkish-purple, bur-like flower-heads borne in leaf axils or at end of branches. Flower-heads comprise only disk flowers amid overlapping bracts with narrow inward-pointing hooks. Leaves are alternate, egg- to heart-shaped, and broadest at the leaf base. First-year plant is a rosette of large, cordate, thick-hairy leaves. Second year growth is an erect, many-branched stem. Flower-heads mature into prickly brownish burs.

VALLEYS-FOOTHILLS

Flowering: July - October

Habitat: Roadsides and disturbed soils, valleys to foothills

Photos: Bozeman, MT, August (W. Tilt); Illustration: USDA-NRCS Plants Database

TIDBITS

A native of Europe, now established across the U.S. States, burdock is considered a noxious weed in many locales. Its large leaves are conspicuous and its fruits well-known to dog owners since the burs become deeply ensnared in an animal's coat. Burdock is considered one of the foremost detoxifying herbs in herbal medicine and a poultice of its leaves can be used to soothe sunburn and skin irritations from poison ivy and the like. The Great Burdock (*A. lappa*) has larger, stalked flower-heads. The Common Cocklebur (*Xanthium strumarium*) is another large bur-producing plant, though its burs are fused to a nut-like seed case.

HEARTLEAF ARNICA

Arnica cordifolia • Asteraceae (Sunflower Family)

FIELD DESCRIPTION:

Perennial herb, 5-24" tall, with solitary stems supporting 2-4 pairs of opposite, often heart-shaped leaves. Lowermost leaves are largest and long-stalked, becoming smaller and usually sessile higher on the stem. Leaves typically have coarsely toothed margins. Flower-head (almost always single, sometimes 2 or 3) with 9-15 rays with shallow teeth on their ends and numerous disk flowers in central button. Involucral bracts are glandular, somewhat rounded to pointed, with long, spreading hairs.

TIDBITS

All western species of *Arnica* have paired leaves on the stems. Mountain Arnica (*A. latiifolia*) is similar to Heartleaf Arnica but also has a number of differences. As compared with *A. cordifolia*, the petioles of lower stem leaves are shorter than leaf blades; phyllaries lack tuft of hairs at tips; and leaves are not cordate. Heartleaf Arnica is commonly used as an external liniment to treat sprains and other pain. Since the plant is toxic and can cause blistering in the intestinal tract, it should not be taken internally or applied to broken skin. *Arnica* means "lamb's skin," in reference to its downy-soft leaves. *Cordifolia* means "heart-leaf."

SUBALPINE
MONTANE

Flowering: May - July

Habitat: Dry open meadows and open woods, montane to subalpine

Photos: Gallatin Range, MT, July (W. Tilt); Illustration: USDA-NRCS Plants Database

LONGLEAF ARNICA
(SPEARLEAF ARNICA)

FIELD DESCRIPTION:

Perennial herb, 12-28" tall, usually forming clumps of stems sprouting from creeping rhizomes. The foliage is short-hairy and glandular. Lance-shaped leaves grow opposite each other, with 5 to 7 pairs usually produced per flowering stem. Leaves have entire margins, are 2-6" long and lack petioles (stalks). Several yellow flower-heads, each 1-2" in diameter, are grouped at the top of the stem. Flower-heads consist of a central cluster of disk flowers surrounded by 8 to 13 ray flowers. Fruits are tiny achenes tipped with a tuft of yellow to brown, barbed bristles.

SUBALPINE

Flowering: July - August

Habitat: Wet, stony soil of slopes and meadows, subalpine

TIDBITS

Also known as Seep-spring Arnica, Longleaf Arnica is found high in the mountains in wet meadows and around seeps. Its smooth-edged leaves and tendency to grow in clumps is characteristic. Homeopathic preparations of arnica are widely marketed, commonly to treat sprains and other pain. However, arnicas typically contain the toxin helenalin which can be poisonous and contact with the plant can also cause skin irritation. The genus name *Arnica* from the Greek arnakis for "lamb's skin," in reference to the texture of the leaves.

Thumbnail photo: Harney Co., OR, August (Gerald D. Carr); Reference photo: Northern Utah, July (Steve Hegji); Illustration: USDA-NRCS Plants Database

RYDBERG'S ARNICA

Arnica rydbergii • Asteraceae (Sunflower Family)

FIELD DESCRIPTION:

Low-growing perennial herb with glandular, hairy foliage. Flowering stems usually bear a solitary flower-head. Occasionally 2-3 flower-heads are produced per plant. Flowering stems are often separate from clusters of basal leaves. Leaves are elliptic to lance-shaped in outline, about 2" long and may be toothless or slightly toothed along the margins; 3-4 leaf pairs arranged opposite each other along erect stems; only the basal leaves have petioles. Flowers are produced in densely clustered, broadly conical flower-heads at the top of stems. A central button of dark yellow disk flowers is surrounded by 7-10 yellow ray flowers, each about 0.75 long. Fruits are densely short-hairy achenes.

ALPINE
SUBALPINE

Flowering: July - August

Habitat: Stony, shallow soil of meadows and slopes, subalpine to alpine

TIDBITS

Found isolated or in scattered patches, this bright yellow arnica prefers subalpine and alpine rocky areas. Its pairs of widely spaced stem leaves can be slightly serrated. Basal leaves are clustered and usually have petioles. The plant is commonly used as an external liniment to treat sprains and other pain. Since the plant is toxic and can cause blistering in the intestinal tract, it should not be taken internally or applied to broken skin. The species name was given in 1899 by Edward Greene to honor Per Axel Rydberg, who wrote *Flora of the Rocky Mountains and Adjacent Plains* in 1917.

Thumbnail & inset photos: SW Colorado, July (Al Schneider); Reference photo: City of Rocks National Preserve, ID (Walter Keck, Wikipedia)

TWIN ARNICA

FIELD DESCRIPTION:

Slender perennial herb with narrowly lance-shaped leaves, 1.5-5" long. Leaves grow in a basal cluster and in pairs opposite each other along the stem. The leaf bases are sometimes slightly hairy. Solitary (sometimes 2-3) yellow flower-heads are produced at the top of stems. Each flower-head is composed of a tightly clustered, central button of disk flowers surrounded by radiating, petal-like ray flowers. The fruit is an achene a few millimeters long with a white pappus.

Flowering: June - July

Habitat: Dry, open soils, grasslands, foothills to montane

Photos: Bozeman, MT, June (Matt Lavin)

TIDBITS

Also known as Bunch Arnica or Grassland Arnica, Twin Arnica tolerates dry conditions and is found in open sagebrush, grasslands and other dry open areas in the region. While the plant commonly sports a pair of conspicuous yellow flat-topped flowers, it commonly has 3 flower-heads. Species is similar in appearance to *Arnica rydbergii* which is half as tall and grows mostly high in mountains. Many arnicas contain the toxin helenalin which can be poisonous if large amounts of the plant are eaten, and contact can also cause skin irritation. The specific name *sororia* means "sisterly."

FIELD SAGEWORT
(TALL WORMWOOD)

Artemisia campestris • Asteraceae (Sunflower Family)
(Synonyms: *Artemisia caudata, Artemisia borealis*)

FIELD DESCRIPTION:

Biennial or short-lived perennial herb, 4-30" tall, highly variable in form and habit. One-to-many reddish stems arise from a woody base. Basal leaves in rosette, pinnately divided 2-3 times. Leaflets seldom more than 1" wide, glabrous to silky-hairy. Basal leaves may or may not persist. Stem leaves similar to basal leaves but alternate, smaller, and less divided. Flowers are inconspicuous, arranged in spike or panicle-like inflorescences with 6-40 disk flowers. Involucral bracts are smooth. Fruits are hairless achenes without a pappus. Plant is somewhat aromatic.

SUBALPINE
MONTANE

Flowering: July - September

Habitat: Open sites with loose soils, often in sandy soils, montane to subalpine

TIDBITS

A plant of many names, including Boreal Wormwood and Prairie Sagewort, numerous subspecies, and multiple synonyms, Field Sagewort is found throughout North America. The reddish stems, glabrous involucral bracts, and basal dissected leaves clustered into a distinct rosette are conspicuous traits for this species. Tarragon (*A. dracunculus*) is a similar species in appearance but lacks the basal rosette of leaves and the lower leaves generally fall off. The genus is named in honor of the Greek goddess Artemis. *Campestris* means "of the fields."

Photos: Bozeman, MT, September (Matt Lavin)

Artemisia ludoviciana • Asteraceae (Sunflower Family)

WHITE SAGEBRUSH
(LOUISIANA WORMWOOD)

FIELD DESCRIPTION:

Aromatic perennial herb/semi-shrub, 6-36" tall. White woolly-hairy stems, usually numerous in large patches. Silvery-sage green leaves are alternate, long, and narrow. Leaves present mainly along stem, margins are entire, lobed, or pinnately incised, may have toothed notches. Inflorescence is a narrow, open-to-dense panicle, 2-12" long. Numerous flower-heads consist of downy silver-white flower buds that mature into small yellowish disk flowers, branched and nodding. Seeds are small brown achenes.

MONTANE
FOOTHILLS

Flowering: June - July

Habitat: Dry, open prairie and sagebrush, foothills to montane

Thumbnail photo: Multnomah Co,, OR, September (Gerald D. Carr); Reference photo: Bozeman, MT, September (W. Tilt); Illustration: USDA-NRCS Plants Database

TIDBITS

White Sagebrush is a common plant scattered amongst the larger sagebrush in largely undisturbed plant communities, where it provides important forage for pronghorn and other wildlife. White Sagebrush is similar in overall appearance to small specimens of Silver Sagebrush (*A. cana*), but Silver Sagebrush is a shrub and has woody stems. White Sagebrush also exhibits a variety of leaf widths and shapes while the leaves of Silver Sagebrush are fairly uniform. Native Americans utilize a number of the sagebrushes for incense and ceremonial purposes. Ludoviciana means "of or relating to Louisiana," as in the Louisiana Territory.

ARROWLEAF BALSAMROOT

Balsamorhiza sagittata • Asteraceae (Sunflower Family)

FIELD DESCRIPTION:

Large-leaved perennial herb, 8-36" tall, with yellow-rayed, yellow-disked flowers at end of stems. Long, arrow-shaped, silvery-green leaves, often up to 4" wide and 6-9" long, with long stalks. Leaves mainly basal, leaf margins are entire. Young leaves have felt-like woolly hairs that give the plant a velvety-gray appearance.

MONTANE
FOOTHILLS

Flowering: May - June

Habitat: Open hills and sage flats from foothills to montane

TIDBITS

This large, conspicuous plant with showy yellow flowers fills the sagebrush hillsides with splashes of yellow in the spring and early summer. As the summer comes on, leaves turn brown and persist through the fall, rattling in the wind. The plant may be confused with various mulesears (*Wyethia sp*). species, but the leaves of balsamroot are about 4" inches wide, 6-9" long, and arrowhead-shaped while mulesears leaves are 2-4" wide, up to 16" long, and shaped like the ears of a mule. Balsamroot also tends to bloom several weeks earlier than Mulesears. Traditionally the seeds, young shoots, and roots of balsamroot were eaten by Native Americans. *Balsamorhiza* refers to the balsam-like taste and smell of the root (*rhiza* in Greek), and *sagittata* is from the Latin for "arrow," as in Sagittarius, the legendary archer.

Photos: Slough Creek, MT, June (W. Tilt)

Carduus nutans • Asteraceae (Sunflower Family)

NODDING THISTLE
(MUSK THISTLE)

FIELD DESCRIPTION:

Erect biennial, 1-6′ tall. Basal rosette up to 3′ in diameter. Stems leafy with spines and winged appearance. Leaves are alternate, lance-shaped, and deeply lobed; dark green, edges serrated with lobes tipped with white spines. Flowers, mostly solitary, often nodding, deep rose-to-purple disk florets, with triangular, spine-tipped bracts often bent back (recurved) at base. Seeds are hairless achenes with pappus of barbed hair-like bristles.

MONTANE
VALLEYS

Flowering: June - September

Habitat: Rangeland, pastures, roadsides and other disturbed areas, valleys to montane

Photos: Smith River, MT, July (W. Tilt); Illustration: USDA-NRCS Plants Database

TIDBITS

Introduced from Eurasia in the early 1800s, Nodding Thistle is now widely established in various regions of the world and North America. It is definitely not a plant you want to unexpectedly brush up against as it is well armored with sharp spines. The plant is considered a noxious weed in many states. Nodding Thistle is distinguished from *Cirsium* species by its simple and slightly barbed (rather than feathery) pappus hairs. Linnaeus named this genus and species in 1753. *Carduus* from the Latin for "thistle" and *nutans* is Latin for "nodding."

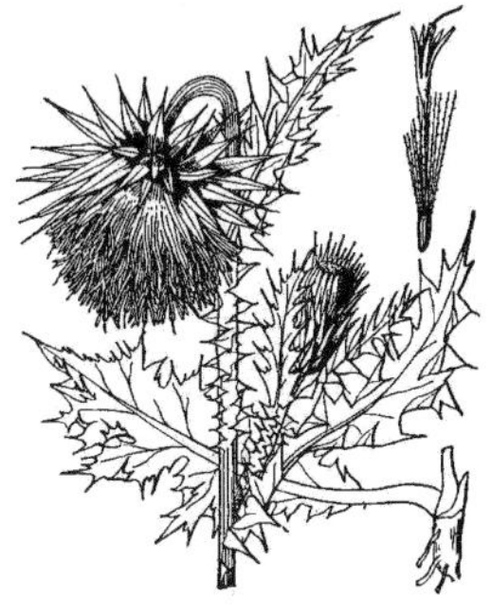

SPOTTED KNAPWEED

Centaurea stoebe • Asteraceae (Sunflower Family)
(Synonyms: *Centaurea biebersteinii, Centaurea maculosa*)

FIELD DESCRIPTION:

Erect, branching biennial to short-lived perennial herb, 1-4′ tall. Single pink-purple flower on terminal branches, with disk florets only. Bracts below florets have dark tips that appear spotted. Stem leaves are alternate with sandpaper-like surface. Leaves are pinnately cut into narrow lobes, somewhat short-hairy, commonly with translucent dots. One-to-many branches grow out of a basal rosette of deeply lobed, grayish-green leaves radiating from a common center. Fruits are achenes with pappus of white, hair-like bristles.

VALLEYS-FOOTHILLS

Flowering: June - September

Habitat: Dry sandy or gravelly disturbed soils, valleys and foothills

Photos: Bridger Range, MT, July (Matt Lavin); Illustration: USDA-NRCS Plants Database

TIDBITS

A native of eastern Europe, Spotted Knapweed is now spread across much of the West. It is a prolific seed producer allowing it to quickly establish itself on disturbed ground. The genus is named for the centaur, the Greek mythological half-man, half-horse, famous for his knowledge of medicinal plants. Russian Knapweed (*C. repens*) is a bushier plant; flower bracts have rounded, papery tips, and lack black spots, spines, or sharp tips. Diffuse Knapweed (*C. diffusa*) has greatly divided, feathery leaves covered with small hairs; numerous whitish flowers growing singly or in clusters at end of stems; bracts are yellow-green, triangular, with spine tips.

CANADA THISTLE

FIELD DESCRIPTION:

Erect, branching perennial herb, 2-5' tall, that forms colonies from its root system. Leaves are alternate, oblanceolote to elliptical, sharply toothed to deeply lobed, with spiny tips. Leaves short-petiolate, commonly white-woolly on undersides, and lowest are usually deciduous. Cylindrical pink-purple flower-heads arise from terminal branches. Flowers are numerous on open, spineless stalks. Flower-heads are comprised of disk flowers. Unlike other thistles, the male and female flowers appear on separate plants. Fruits are ribbed achenes, are borne on numerous, feathery white-brownish pappus hairs.

MONTANE
VALLEYS

Flowering: June - August

Habitat: Fields, pasture, and along roadsides, valleys to montane

Photos: Bozeman, MT, July (Matt Lavin & W. Tilt); Illustration: USDA-NRCS Plants Database

TIDBITS

An invasive plant introduced to North America from Eurasia (not Canada), commonly found in large patches, having spread by deep rhizomes. The plant is favorite food of the Painted Lady Butterfly caterpillar. The Bull Thistle (*C. vulgare*) and Nodding Thistle (*Carduus nutans*) are 2 other introduced thistles. As compared to Canada Thistle, they have spiny-winged stems, pinnately cut leaves with bristly hairs, and larger, showier flower-heads. *Cirsium* from the Greek for "dilated vein," from the bygone belief that a thistle distillate opens clogged veins.

ELK THISTLE
(EVERTS' THISTLE)

Cirsium scariosum • Asteraceae (Sunflower Family)

FIELD DESCRIPTION:

Leafy, thick perennial, 8-40" tall with 1-8 creamy white-to-pink-to-purple disk flowers forming a large flower-head. Fleshy stem with large grayish-green leaves that clasp the stem at their base. Leaves have spine-tipped lobes on their margins and smooth upper surfaces. Stems and leaves are covered with long white hairs that extend into the flower-heads.

MONTANE
FOOTHILLS

Flowering: June - July

Habitat: Dry open grasslands and meadows, foothills to montane

TIDBITS

Elk Thistle is a native thistle that can stand 6' tall or lie plastered to the ground. Its stemless flowers, tucked into the leaf axils, and very light green herbage are distinctive. Elk Thistle was first collected for science by Thomas Nuttall in Idaho in the 1830s. The plant's other common name recognizes Truman Everts, a member of the Washburn Expedition that explored Yellowstone National Park in 1870. Separated from his party, Everts subsisted on thistle roots for nearly a month until rescued, near death.

Photos: Slough Creek, MT, June (W. Tilt); Going to seed: Big Sky, MT, August (Rip McIntosh)

Cirsium vulgare • Asteraceae (Sunflower Family)
(Synonym: *Cirsium lanceolatum*)

BULL THISTLE
(SPEAR THISTLE)

FIELD DESCRIPTION:

Stout and branched biennial, 1-5′ tall. Stems are slightly to densely hairy with spiny wings extending down from base of leaves. Leaves pinnately cut, bristly haired on upper surface and white-woolly on lower surface. Leaves dark green on both upper and lower surface. Flowers comprised of rose-purple disk florets, numerous on plants, with bracts that are spine-tipped. Seeds small and curved with white fluffy plume.

MONTANE
VALLEYS

Flowering: July - September

Habitat: Rangeland, pastures, roadsides and other disturbed areas, valleys to montane

Photos: Bozeman, MT, August (Matt Lavin & W. Tilt); Illustration: USDA-NRCS Plants Database

TIDBITS

Introduced from Eurasia and now widely established throughout the region, Bull Thistle is considered a noxious weed in many states. It is distinguished by large rose-purple flower-heads, spiny-winged stems, and leaf hairs that make leaves feel rough to touch. Its spine-tipped involucral bracts also tend to arch outward more so than in other species of *Cirsium*. The roots, stems, and young flower buds of *Cirsium* species are nutritious and can be eaten raw. As thistles are widespread and easy to identify, they have been useful as emergency foods (see Elk Thistle for story of Truman Everts).

DUSTY MAIDEN

Chaenactis douglasii • Asteraceae (Sunflower Family)

FIELD DESCRIPTION:

Biennial or perennial herb, typically 10-20" tall. Stems single with gray woolly or cobwebby hairs. Leaves are alternate, fernlike, pinnately divided 1-3 times into narrow segments, reduced in size as they ascend stem. Leaflet segments are narrow, thick, and curled. White, at times pinkish, flower-heads in flat-topped clusters comprised of numerous disk flowers in glandular cups with anthers thrust out. Involucral bracts glandular and often hairy. Fruits hairy club-shaped achenes.

TIDBITS

The leaves of Dusty Maiden resemble those of a carrot with a covering of cobwebby hairs, hence the dusty appearance. Var. *douglasii* has a simple caudex and leafy leaves found in valleys to montane, while var. *alpina* is mat-forming with a branched caudex growing in alpine areas. Some Native American tribes used this plant as a dressing for burns, wounds, and sores. *Douglasii* honors David Douglas (of Douglas-fir fame), a 19th century Scottish botanist and explorer. *Chaenactis* from the Greek for "open rays" in apparent reference to the protruding styles.

FOOTHILLS

Flowering: April - June

Habitat: Dry sandy and rocky soils, foothills

Photos: Bozeman, MT, July (Matt Lavin); Illustration: USDA-NRCS Plants Database

TAPERTIP HAWKBEARD

FIELD DESCRIPTION:

Perennial herb, up to 3' tall, with upright stems, branching at the top. Leaves are slightly to moderately hairy, the lower ones up to 15" long, pinnately lobed, the lobes and terminal portion of the leaf tapering to a long point. Leaves higher on the stem are much smaller and have few lobes. The 20-75 flower-heads are narrow, 1/2" high and 1/4" wide, and cylindrical in shape, especially before they open. The flowers are yellow, with corollas less than 1" across, each flower-head containing only 5-10 ray flowers, and no disk flowers.

SUBALPINE
MONTANE
FOOTHILLS

Flowering: May - July

Habitat: Sagebrush, mountain brush, and open fores, foothills to subalpine

TIDBITS

Also known as Long-leaved or Mountain Hawksbeard, the branching top, long, deeply cut, gray-green leaves, and small flower-heads distinguish the plant from other hawksbeard species. Hawksbeards (not to be confused with genus *Hieracium*, or the hawkweeds) are characterized by flower-heads comprised of only ray flowers, and stems and leaves with milky sap. Hawksbeards are very palatable to domestic sheep and can be overgrazed where sheep are present. *Crepis* from the Greek *krepis* for "slipper" or "boot," in possible reference to shape of the fruit. *Acuminata* meaning "tapering to a long point."

Photos: Harney Co., OR, May (Gerald D. Carr); Leaf detail: Northern Utah, June (Steve Hegil)

WESTERN HAWKSBEARD
(LARGEFLOWER HAWKSBEARD)

Crepis occidentalis • Asteraceae (Sunflower Family)

FIELD DESCRIPTION:

Perennial herb, 4-15" tall with gray, felt-like hair on stems and a woody taproot. Plants often grows in dense, upright clusters with candelabra-like branching. Basal leaves deeply lobed, often with backward-toothed margins, up to 12" in length. Stem leaves are few, alternate, and greatly reduced in size. Flower-heads yellow comprising 10-40 ray flowers and no disk flowers, similar in appearance to those of a Dandelion. Flower-heads are cupped, arising out of a vase-like calyx. Phyllaries are narrow, pointed, and often covered with short, black-tipped hairs. Fruits are achenes with pappus of whitish hair-like bristles.

TIDBITS

Hawksbeards are commonly characterized by flower-heads that only have ray flowers and stems and leaves with milky sap. The hawkbeards, dandelions, and agoseris species can be confusing to identify. They all have generally similar flower-head appearance with distinctions found in leaf shape, seed appearance, and other characteristics. In dry locations or dry years, Western Hawksbeard may only grow 5" tall, while in more favorable conditions it can reach 12-15". Crepis meaning "sandal" (of possible reference to its seed) and occidentalis from the Latin for "western."

VALLEYS-FOOTHILLS

Flowering: May - July

Habitat: Open dry soils, valleys to foothills

Photos: Harney Co., OR, May (Gerald D. Carr); Illustration: USDA-NRCS Plants Database

Erigeron compositus • Asteraceae (Sunflower Family)

CUTLEAF DAISY
(FERNLEAF FLEABANE)

FIELD DESCRIPTION:

Perennial herb, 1-10" tall, with low cushion form and glandular-hairy herbage. Leaves mainly basal, fan-shaped, mostly cut 2-3 times into narrow segments. Stem leaves few and reduced in size upward on the plant, simple or ternate. Flower-heads solitary, rays 20-60, ranging in color from white to pink to bluish-purple with center of yellow disk flowers. Involucre bracts spreading, glandular, hairy, commonly purple at the tips, and in 1 row. Fruits are two-nerved, hairy achenes with white hair-like pappus.

Flowering: July - September

Habitat: Dry areas, rocky slopes, meadows, tundra, montane to alpine

Photos: Butte Co., ID, May (Matt Lavin); Illustration: Karl Urban, Umatilla National Forest, OR

TIDBITS

Deeply cut basal leaves help distinguish this species from other *Erigeron*. Rayless forms of Cutleaf Daisy are also common. Frederick Pursh named this species in 1814 from a specimen collected by Meriwether Lewis in 1806. *Erigeron* is the largest genus of the Asteraceae in the region. Generally speaking *Erigeron* species have showy flower-heads consisting of yellow disk flowers and narrow ray flowers that mostly arise singly on each stem. Involucral bracts are narrow and mostly equal in length. By some accounts, the name "fleabane" arises because the seeds are "so like fleas!"

BUFF FLEABANE

Erigeron ochroleucus • Asteraceae (Sunflower Family)

FIELD DESCRIPTION:

Perennial herb from taproot and thick caudex, up to 10 inches. Stems erect, often decumbent. Stems, bracts, and leaves hairy. Leaves, mostly basal, linear-oblanceolate, 2-7 mm long, margins entire; stem leaves reduced near the top; surfaces pubescent with short, stiff appressed hairs. Flower-heads usually solitary at stem ends, ray florets white or sometimes blue, 8-12 mm long. Hairs on involucral bracts often have red-purple cross walls. Fruits are achenes.

TIDBITS

Buff Fleabane is a common wildflower in the sagebrush community of the Yellowstone region. The plant is found at all elevations with the dwarf, high-elevation plants often with blue rays. This fleabane is variable across its range with white-to-purplish flowered forms, as well as forms with conspicuously spreading or appressed stem hairs. Typical of *Erigeron* species, Buff Fleabane has a showy flower-head, consisting of yellow disk flowers and narrow ray flowers arising singly on each stem and narrow involucral bracts mostly equal in length.

Flowering: June - August

Habitat: Open dry soils, grasslands and sagebrush steppe, valleys to alpine

Photos: Phillips Co., MT, July (Matt Lavin)

SUBALPINE FLEABANE

Erigeron peregrinus • Asteraceae (Sunflower Family)
(Synonym: *Erigeron glacialis*)

FIELD DESCRIPTION:

Herbaceous perennial growing from short, fibrous rhizomes. Stems grow up to 27" tall and bear solitary, showy, purple and yellow flower-heads. The leaves are highly variable, ranging from elongated to spoon-shaped in outline. Basal leaves are largest (up to 8"), gradually becoming smaller toward the top of the stem. Flower-heads are about 1" wide with purple ray flowers along the perimeter and yellow disk flowers clustered in the center of each head. The leaf-like involucral bracts surrounding each flower-head are dotted with tiny hairs and glands and feel slightly sticky.

Flowering: May - July

Habitat: Sagebrush, mountain brush, and open forest, foothills to subalpine

Photos: North Cascades NP, WA, September (Ben Legler); Illustration: USDA-NRCS Plants Database

TIDBITS

Subalpine Fleabane is a showy component of montane and high-elevation meadows in summer bloom. Along with paintbrush and arnica, it adds its color to moist meadows and stream sides. Subalpine Fleabane is sometimes mistaken for other alpine asters that also commonly occur in these habitats. The involucral bracts of Subalpine Fleabane are sticky-feeling due to the presence of tiny glandular hairs. Most *Erigeron* species have very narrow ray flowers, typically about 1 millimeter; those of Subalpine Fleabane are about 2 millimeters.

SHAGGY FLEABANE

Erigeron pumilus • Asteraceae (Sunflower Family)

FIELD DESCRIPTION:

Perennial herb, up to 20" tall, light green foliage, covered with short white hairs, from a thick, woody base. Narrow basal leaves up to 3" long and 1/4" wide, slightly wider near the tip; stem leaves similar but reduced in size. Flower-heads single to many per stem, about 1/2" wide and 1/4" tall. The bracts on the outside of the flower-head are all about the same length and taper to a long point. Each flower-head contains 50-100 ray flowers, 1/2" or more in length, white, pink, or lavender. The pappus is double, the inner of coarse bristles, the outer of bristles or scales. The fruit is a two-nerved achene.

SUBALPINE
MONTANE
FOOTHILLS

Flowering: May - August

Habitat: Dry, sandy, gravelly soils, foothills to subalpine

TIDBITS

Shaggy Fleabane is a frequently encountered "daisy" throughout the region's sagebrush-grasslands and Limber Pine woodlands from 3,600' to 7,600' elevation, preferring sandy, gravelly soils. The plant is characterized by numerous blossoms, giving it a bouquet appearance. *Pumilus* means "dwarf," which reflects the short stature of this plant. Compare with *Townsendia*, which is shorter stemmed and has larger flower heads, and also with other asters that have leafy stems and more than one flower head per stem.

Photos: Boise, ID, June (Matt Lavin); Illustration: USDA-NRCS Plants Database

Erigeron speciosus • Asteraceae (Sunflower Family)

ASPEN DAISY
(SHOWY FLEABANE)

FIELD DESCRIPTION:

Perennial herb with a leafy stem, 7-30" tall, branching near the top into leafless stalks; each stalk with a single flower-head at the end. Flower consists of many narrow pink, lavender, or white rays surrounding button of yellow disk flowers. Flower-heads are 1.5-2" wide, with involucre bract,s all about the same length lined up side by side, not overlapping. Leaves long, lanceolate, smooth, commonly with 3 obvious veins. Leaf bases joined to the stem about halfway around and, therefore, are slightly clasping.

SUBALPINE
MONTANE
FOOTHILLS

Flowering: June - September

Habitat: Meadows and forest openings, foothills to sub-alpine

Photos: Madison Range, MT, July (Rip McIntosh & W. Tilt)

TIDBITS

Erigeron from the Greek eri ("early") and *geron* ("old man" as in geriatric) suggesting "gets old early" in reference to the fact that many fleabanes bloom in the spring and often go to seed when other flowers are just getting started. Alternatively, *erio* from the Greek for "woolly," with *Erigeron* meaning "woolly old man" in reference to the grizzly appearing fruiting heads. *Speciosus* from the Latin for "showy" or "beautiful." Early European settlers in North America stuffed mattresses with fleabane and hung clusters of plants in their cabins to drive out fleas, hence fleabane. The custom persisted for generations, though the plant appears to have no insect-repelling properties. Other accounts, however, state the name "fleabane" arises because the seeds appeared "so like fleas!"

BLANKETFLOWER

Gaillardia aristata • Asteraceae (Sunflower Family)

FIELD DESCRIPTION:

Perennial herb, 8-24" tall, with yellow ray flowers. Flowers are 2-3" across with 3 lobes on the tip of each ray petal; disk flowers form a red-brown cluster in the center. Reddish color often extends up into rays. One or several stems arise from a slender taproot. Leaves are alternate on the stem and can be entire, divided, or variously toothed. The leaves, stems and receptacles are covered with coarse, long hairs. Fruits are hairy achenes with stiff white bristles.

MONTANE
FOOTHILLS

Flowering: June - September

Habitat: Dry meadows and other open places, foothills to montane

TIDBITS

The three-lobed ray flower of Blanketflower helps distinguish this varied-colored wildflower. Many popular cultivars of this plant can be found in home gardens. Blanketflower has been used to treat a wide number of ailments, including hair loss, nasal congestion, sunstroke, and even saddle sores. *Gaillardia* after Gaillard de Charentonneau, a French amateur botanist. *Aristata,* means "bristled" in reference to the stiff awns on the fruit. Meriwether Lewis collected the first specimens of this plant for science in Montana, 1806.

Photos: Bozeman, MT, June (W. Tilt); Illustration: USDA-NRCS Plants Database

Grindelia squarrosa • Asteraceae (Sunflower Family)

CURLY-CUP GUMWEED

FIELD DESCRIPTION:

Highly aromatic, sticky biennial or short-lived perennial, often shrubby herb, 8-23" tall. Numerous yellow flower-heads consisting of 25-40 rays with disk flowers in the center. Each flower-head has overlapping rows of very obvious backward-curling green bracts. Leaves are oblong, hairless, toothed, and often dotted with resinous glands.

Flowering: July - September

Habitat: Dry, open slopes in valleys and foothills

VALLEYS-FOOTHILLS

Photos: Bozeman, MT, August (Matt Lavin);
Illustration: USDA-NRCS Plants Database

TIDBITS

The name "gumweed" is apt, as the upper portions of the plant are quite sticky from the glandular hairs that abound on the plant. Another common name for this plant is "rosin weed." The plant has numerous traditional applications, including treating poison ivy blisters and bronchial asthma. *Grindelia* after David Grindel, a German botanist in the 18th century, and *squarrosa* from the Latin for "rough." Meriwether Lewis collected this plant for science on the banks of the Missouri River, probably in 1806.

ONE-FLOWER SUNFLOWER

Helianthella uniflora • Asteraceae (Sunflower Family)

FIELD DESCRIPTION:

Erect perennial, 1-2' tall, with leafy and hairy stems. Leaves oblong-lanceolate, entire and 3-veined. Upper leaves commonly alternate while lower leaves are opposite on stem. Single bright yellow flower-head atop stem comprises 12-14 ray flowers surrounding disk of generally same shade of yellow. Involucral bracts are narrow, pointed to blunt, and loosely clasping.

TIDBITS

A denizen of undisturbed sagebrush flats and mountain meadows, One-Flower Sunflower accents the gray green of sagebrush with their bright yellow blooms. Distinguishing *Helianthella* species from the true sunflowers (*Helianthus*) is often a challenge. Look for 4 traits: 1) ray and disk flowers are equally yellow in *Helianthella*, whereas in *Helianthus* the disk flowers are often darker yellow compared to the ray flowers; 2) involucral bracts of *Helianthella* tend to be much narrower and more loosely clasping compared to those of *Helianthus*; 3) *Helianthus* generally has toothed leaves and larger flower-heads; and 4) *Helianthus* prefers trailside and roadside habitats.

MONTANE
FOOTHILLS

Flowering: May - August

Habitat: Open sagebrush flats and hillsides, foothills to montane

Photos: Bozeman, MT, June/July (Matt Lavin)

Helianthus annuus • Asteraceae (Sunflower Family)

FIELD DESCRIPTION:

Erect annual, mostly 3-6′ tall and 4′ wide with rough-hairy stems and leaves. Large flower-head comprised of bright yellow rays around a reddish-brown disk. Involucral bracts usually hairy on margins, ovate-oblong and narrowing to pointed tip. Flower-heads are generally solitary on stems. Leaves large, alternate on upper stem, and opposite on lower portion, egg- to heart-shaped with margins that are smooth to irregularly toothed.

VALLEYS-FOOTHILLS

Flowering: July - September

Habitat: Open areas, especially along roadways and disturbed areas, valleys and foothills

TIDBITS

Common along the region's byways, especially in August, this species has been cultivated since pre-Columbian times for its edible seeds which can be eaten raw or roasted. Traditionally sunflower seeds were used in a variety of ways for food and medicines, including ground into flour and baked into cakes suitable for travel. *Helianthus* from the Greek for "sun flower." Sunflowers are generally coarse plants with simple, bristly leaves. As a result of many cultivars, the showy flowers of *Helianthus* come in shades of yellow, orange, red, cream, purple, and bronze.

Photos: Gallatin Range, MT, August (W. Tilt); Illustration: USDA-NRCS Plants Database

PRAIRIE SUNFLOWER

Helianthus petiolaris • Asteraceae (Sunflower Family)

FIELD DESCRIPTION:

Annual, usually 3' tall, from taproot. Stems erect and commonly branched. Overall plant hairy. Leaves are alternate, with petiole; blades entire to serrate. Flower-heads solitary or few, about 3" across. Disks are purplish-brown and corolla lobes dark red to purplish. Involucre bracts lanceolate and ciliate. Fruits are a hairy achene.

TIDBITS

As its common name suggests, the Prairie Sunflower is native to the dry prairie grasslands of the western United States. The species is very similar to the Annual Sunflower (*Helianthus annuus*) and its seeds can be just as tasty. Prairie Sunflower is a shorter plant with elongated, rather than heart-shaped leaves. Its leaves tend to be smaller and more narrowly lanceolate as compared with those of the Annual Sunflower. The two species grow in very similar habitats and do hybridize. *Petiolaris* from the Latin for "having a petiole."

Flowering: May - September

Habitat: Forested, disturbed, roadsides, foothills

Thumbnail photo: Big Horn, WY, June (Matt Lavin); Reference photo: Colfax Co., NM, August (Ben Legler); Illustration: USDA-NRCS Plants Database

GOLDENEYE
(SHOWY GOLDENEYE)

Heliomeris multiflora • Asteraceae (Sunflower Family)
(Synonym: *Viguiera multiflora*)

FIELD DESCRIPTION:

Erect, perennial herb, 2-4′ tall, with slender stems and numerous yellow composite flowers. Disk flowers domelike, golden-yellow, surrounded by 10-14 yellow ray flowers. Involucral bracts linear and overlapping. Dark olive drab leaves mostly opposite (may be alternate near top), lance-shaped, rough, and toothed. Lower leaves short-stalked becoming stalkless above. Stems fine-hairy and highly branched. Fruits are hairless, flattened, four-sided achenes with no pappus.

SUBALPINE
MONTANE
VALLEYS

Flowering: July - September

Habitat: Dry, often disturbed, soils, valleys to subalpine

Photos: Madison Range, MT, July (Rip McIntosh); Illustration: USDA-NRCS Plants Database

TIDBITS

A domelike center disk that looks like a golden eye gives this plant its common name. Goldeneye is highly branched, bushy with numerous flowerheads that fill montane meadows with blooms that last for many weeks. Central disk flowers start green and change to golden-yellow as the summer progresses. *Helios* from the Greek for "sun" and *meris* for "part of." William Gambel collected the first specimen of this plant for science, probably in the 1840s.

GOLDEN ASTER
(HAIRY GOLDEN ASTER)

Heterotheca villosa • Asteraceae (Sunflower Family)
(Synonym: *Chrysopsis villosa*)

FIELD DESCRIPTION:

Spreading, clump-forming perennial herb, to 20" tall and wide, with grey-green to blue-green, silky-hairy foliage, and yellow composite flowers. Flower-heads in short, open, flat-topped clusters comprised of a yellow disk surrounded by 10-25 yellow ray flowers. Involucral bracts lance-shaped in overlapping rows. Leaves are alternate, lance-shaped to oblong with entire margins. Fruits are flattened, hairy, with long, hair-like pappus.

MONTANE
FOOTHILLS

Flowering: June - August

Habitat: Open, well-drained soils in grasslands and woodlands, often on disturbed sites, foothills to montane

TIDBITS

Golden Aster's soft, woolly foliage sets it apart from most other yellow-flowered, daisy-like plants that occupy similar habitats. It is a highly variable plant with many local forms. Golden Aster is a long-blooming species with an aromatic sage-like smell. The genus name, *Chrysopsis*, for "golden," while the species name, *villosa*, means "soft-hairy" in reference to the gray hairs on leaves and stems.

Photos: Bozeman, MT, July (Matt Lavin); Illustration: USDA-NRCS Plants Database

Hieracium aurantiacum • Asteraceae (Sunflower Family)

ORANGE HAWKWEED

FIELD DESCRIPTION:

Introduced perennial herb, 10-20" tall. Clusters of reddish orange flower-heads are comprised of ray flowers that are notched at tip. Involucre densely hairy with glandular hairs. Leaves, mostly basal, oblong to spoon-shaped, petiolate, and entire. Leaves and stems covered with stiff hairs, generally leafless (1-2 small leaves may be alternately arranged on stem), and stem exudes a milky sap. Fruit is dark achene with white pappus.

MONTANE
FOOTHILLS

Flowering: June - September

Habitat: Open fields and woods, especially on disturbed soil, foothills to montane

Photos: Upper Boulder River, MT, July (W. Tilt); Illustration: USDA-NRCS Plants Database

TIDBITS

Orange Hawkweed, also known as "Devil's Paintbrush," is an invasive species capable of rapid spread (plant can be both rhizomatous and stoloniferous) and the plant tolerates poor soils. Orange Hawkweed thrives in disturbed areas, such as roadsides, gravel pits, and pastures. It can also invade meadows and forested areas and is well-adapted to life at higher elevations. The plant is capable of forming dense mats that crowd out other vegetation. As the plant flowers, white-fuzzy stolons extend outward, generating new plants. It is distinguished from Orange Agoseris (*Agoseris aurantiaca*) by its multiple flower-heads per stem.

BLUE LETTUCE

Lactuca pulchella • Asteraceae (Sunflower Family)
(Synonym: *Lactuca oblongifolia, Lactuca tatarica*)

FIELD DESCRIPTION:

Perennial herb, 15-36" tall, with erect stems and milky sap. Leaves are alternate, narrowly lance-shaped with entire margins. Underside of leaves often has a waxy coating. Lower leaves often lobed. Showy flower-heads with numerous blue-purple flowers comprised of 20-50 ray florets. Fruits are ribbed achenes with stout beak and pappus of white bristle hairs. Overall foliage is pale bluish-green.

MONTANE
VALLEYS

Flowering: June - September

Habitat: Moist open soil, disturbed sites, valleys to montane

TIDBITS

Blue Lettuce is considered a non-native by some botanists, while others accept it as native and distinct from its European cousins. The plant does, however, have weedy, invasive tendencies. The milky sap from Blue Lettuce contains lactucarium which has been used for pain relief and other symptoms. Lactucarium has narcotic effects and ingestion can cause drowsiness and restlessness and, in extreme cases, can cause death through cardiac paralysis.

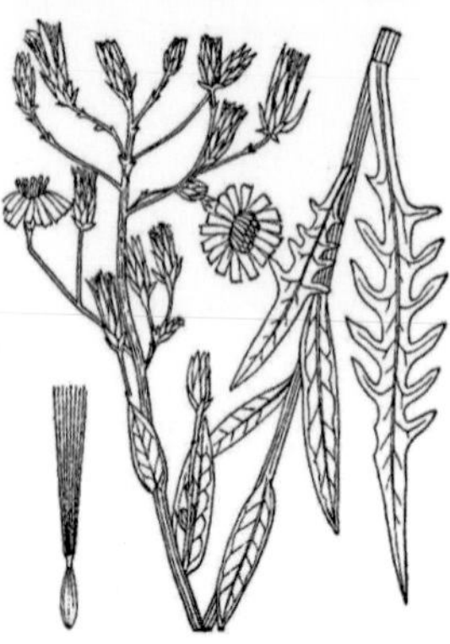

Photos: Boulder River, MT, July (W. Tilt); Illustration: USDA-NRCS Plants Database

Leucanthemum vulgare • Asteraceae (Sunflower Family)
(Synonym: *Chrysanthemum leucanthemum*)

OXEYE DAISY

FIELD DESCRIPTION:

Perennial herb, 10-20" tall. Clusters of reddish orange flower-heads are comprised of ray flowers that are notched at tip. Involucre densely hairy with glandular hairs. Leaves, mostly basal, oblong to spoon-shaped, petiolate, and entire. Leaves and stems covered with stiff hairs, generally leafless (1-2 small leaves may be alternately arranged on stem), and stem exudes a milky sap. Fruit is dark achene with white pappus.

Flowering: June - September

Habitat: Disturbed soils in fields, pastures, and roadsides, valleys to montane

Photos: Gallatin Range, MT, July (W. Tilt); Illustration: USDA-NRCS Plants Database

TIDBITS

The Oxeye Daisy was intentionally introduced from Europe as a garden plant. The plant has taken to its adopted country, spreading widely and the plant is considered an invasive species in many states. The seeds of Oxeye Daisy are often included in so-called "wildflower" seed packs, helping spread this invasive species even wider. Flowers are long-lived, large, and attractive. The plant is used in a wide range of medical applications including the treatment of whooping cough. *Leucanthemum* from the Greek for "white flower," and *vulgare* from the Latin for "common."

GAYFEATHER (DOTTED BLAZINGSTAR)

Liatris punctata • Asteraceae (Sunflower Family)

FIELD DESCRIPTION:

Perennial herb, 9-36" tall, with cluster of unbranched stems topped with spike of showy purple flowers. Flower-heads are comprised of 4-6 disk flowers with overlapping bracts surrounding 5 tiny petals. Leaves are alternate, stiff, glabrous, and entire. Small dots are apparent on leaves' lower surface. Flower-heads mature into a mass of white, feathery bristles.

TIDBITS

Gayfeather is one of the last flowers of the season to bloom at lower elevations. The plant is an important source of nectar for many species of butterflies and other wildlife species browse it. The roots of Gayfeather have traditionally been used to help treat a range of kidney, bladder, and other ailments. Deep-rooted and long-lived (35 or more years), Gayfeather is drought-tolerant and a common addition to gardens. The origin of *Liatris* is obscured by time while *punctata* is from the Latin for "with spots" in reference to the dots found on its leaves.

VALLEYS-FOOTHILLS

Flowering: July - September

Habitat: Dry open plains and sage flats, valleys and foothills

Photos: Bozeman, MT, August (W. Tilt); Going to seed: Bozeman, MT, October (W. Tilt)

PRAIRIE CONEFLOWER (MEXICAN HAT)

FIELD DESCRIPTION:

Erect perennial, 1-3' tall. Upper portion of stem is leafless, holding a single flower-head. Flower-heads comprise 3-7 yellow ray flowers, typically bent downward, surrounding a raised cylindrical disk. Leaves are alternate, hairy, and pinnately cut into 5-9 linear segments with smooth margins.

VALLEYS-FOOTHILLS

Flowering: June - August

Habitat: Dry plains, valleys and foothills

Photos: Big Timber, MT, July (W. Tilt);
Illustration: USDA-NRCS Plants Database

TIDBITS

A tall finger-like column with a bottom fringe of yellow petals identifies the Prairie Coneflower at a distance. The yellow petals may also have rich red-brown tones as well. The flowers attract a range of pollinators. Traditionally a tea was made from the leaves and flower-heads, while the Cheyenne Indians reportedly boiled the leaves and stems to make a solution to draw poison out of rattlesnake bites. The plant's appearance has lead to a rich variety of descriptive common names including Mexican Hat, Thimble Flower, and Long-Headed Coneflower.

CUTLEAF CONEFLOWER

Rudbeckia laciniata • Asteraceae (Sunflower Family)

FIELD DESCRIPTION:

Erect perennial herb, growing up to 6′ tall. Large flower-heads with a yellow-green-to-brown disk surrounded by 6-16 dropping, yellow ray flowers. Involucral bracts green, spreading, ovate in 1 row. Tall single-to-slightly-branched stems have alternate, long, broad leaves, deeply palmate to pinnately cut into toothed segments. Center disks elongate and become brownish, as seeds ripen.

MONTANE
FOOTHILLS

Flowering: July - September

Habitat: Moist soils, foothills to montane

TIDBITS

Cutleaf Coneflower is one of several sunflower species sometimes called "Black-Eyed Susan." Often found in shaded wet soils, the plant's flower-head has an unkempt appearance. The Black-Eyed Susan commonly found in gardens, *Rudbeckia hirta*, escapes cultivation and is somewhat similar in appearance, but it has lance-shaped leaves and its petals do not noticeably droop. Linnaeus named the genus in honor of one of his teachers, Olaus Rudbeckius, and his father. *Laciniata* from the Latin for "torn or rent," in likely reference to the plant's deeply cut leaves.

Photos: Gallatin Range, MT, August (W. Tilt); Illustration: USDA-NRCS Plants Database

Rudbeckia occidentalis • Asteraceae (Sunflower Family)

WESTERN CONEFLOWER

FIELD DESCRIPTION:

Erect perennial herb, 1-5′ tall, with large leaves and dark-brown-to-black, cone-shaped "flowers." Tall, mostly unbranched stems have alternate, broadly ovate-to-elliptical leaves, up to 9" long and 6" wide; leaf rough hairy; leaf margins entire to serrate. Leafless stalks bear one or more flower-heads about 1" high comprising numerous tiny disc flowers, yellow at tip but overall dark purple-brown in appearance; no ray flowers present.

MONTANE
FOOTHILLS

Flowering: June - August

Habitat: Moist soils in meadows and forest openings, foothills to montane

TIDBITS

Unmistakable and distinctive, the Western Coneflower is the "flower without the petals." It has no ray flowers, just an array of purplish phyllaries around a purple-brown dome of disk florets. The cones become twice as tall and darker when in seed. Coneflowers are a favorite object for kids to pick and throw. Hint: do not pick from the saddle of a horse then throw at nearby rider unless you want a bucking bronco show. Another apt name is Western Chocolate Cone, which certainly bees and other pollinators think the flower to be. Linnaeus named the genus in honor of one of his teachers, Olaus Rudbeckius, and his father.

Photos: Big Timber, MT, July (W. Tilt)

WOOLLY GROUNDSEL (GRAY RAGWORT)

Senecio canus • Asteraceae (Sunflower Family)
(Synonym: *Packera cana*)

FIELD DESCRIPTION:

Silvery-gray, woolly perennial herb, 5-12" tall, with heavy fibrous roots. Leaves and stems densely covered with felt-like matted hairs. Leaves mainly basal, linear to lance shaped, margins are usually entire but occassionaly lobed, on long petioles. Stem Leaves are alternate, few, smaller, narrow, toothed, or lobed. Flower-heads in branched flat-topped clusters (corymbs) at the top of the stem. Yellow ray flowers, 8 to 13, around a yellow button of disk flowers. Fruits are hairless, ribbed achenes.

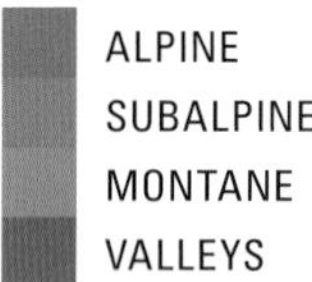

Flowering: May - August

Habitat: Dry open sites, valleys to alpine

TIDBITS

Also known as Gray Ragwort, the plant is common throughout the Yellowstone region from valley floors to alpine ridges. Groundsel is derived from the Anglo-Saxon for "ground-swallowing," an assumed reference to the plant's ability to spread rapidly across the land. As a genus, *Senecio* is a large genus of well over 1,000 species worldwide. The name stems from the Latin *senex* for "an old man" and canus for "gray," in reference to the woolly or "hoary" appearance of many of the species.

Photos: Blaine Co., ID, June (Matt Lavin); Illustration: USDA-NRCS Plants Database

Senecio crassulus • Asteraceae (Sunflower Family)

THICKLEAF GROUNDSEL (THICK-LEAF RAGWORT)

FIELD DESCRIPTION:

Perennial herb, 6-18" tall, with erect stems and glabrous herbage. Leaves thick, succulent, lanceolate to elliptic, somewhat hairy, with toothed margins. Lower leaves broadly petiolate; stem leaves gradually reduced upward, becoming sessile and clasping. Flower-heads solitary or 2-12 in clusters, ray flowers 8-13, yellow, surrounding center of disk flowers. Involucres to 1/2" high and almost twice as wide, with 8-21 bracts, green to brown, black tips with tufted hairs. Fruits are glabrous achenes.

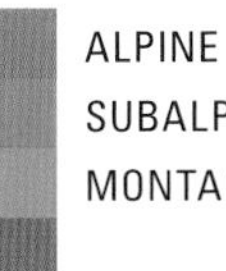

ALPINE
SUBALPINE
MONTANE

Flowering: June - September

Habitat: Grassy, sandy, gravel areas, woodland openings, meadows, montane to alpine

Thumbnail and inset photos: SW Colorado, July (Al Schneider); Reference photo: High Uinta, UT, July (© Andrey Zharkikh)

TIDBITS

Thickleaf Groundsel is a common plant of upper elevation meadows. Its common name, Meadow Butterweed, alludes to the plant's attractiveness to butterflies and other pollinators. Flower-heads are large and showy with yellow-on-yellow ray and disc flowers. The involucres bulge, hence the species name *crassulus*, from *crass*, Latin for "thick." *Senecio* arises from the Latin *senex* for "an old man," in reference to the plant's pappus hairs. Ragwort is an expressive term for plants in early English herbal tradition, having supposed aphrodisiac virtues. Later the name became associated with the groundsels.

WESTERN GROUNDSEL
(LAMBSTONGUE RAGWORT)

Senecio integerrimus • Asteraceae (Sunflower Family)

FIELD DESCRIPTION:

Stout, erect perennial herb, 8-27" tall, with numerous yellow flower-heads in a terminal cluster. Flower-heads have narrow yellow rays and purple-black tipped bracts. The central head is often larger with thicker stalk. Basal Leaves are alternate, spoon-shaped and stalked. Leaves somewhat fleshy, stiff-hairy, entire to irregularly toothed, and twice as long as wide. Stem leaves few, linear-lance-shaped, growing smaller upwards on the stalk. Stems are erect, single. Entire plant commonly cobwebby-hairy when young, becoming hairless as it matures.

MONTANE
FOOTHILLS

Flowering: May - July

Habitat: Moderately dry to rather moist open areas and open woods, foothills to montane

TIDBITS

Senecio is a large genus with several dozen species occurring in the Rocky Mountain region. The bracts of Western Groundsel are often tipped in black. Arrow-leaved Groundsel (*S. triangularis*) is similar in appearance to Western Groundsel but distinguished by large triangular leaves and a preference for higher elevations and moister soils. Folklore tells of witches turning groundsel into horses when no broomsticks were handy. *Integerrimus* from the Latin for "entire," perhaps referring to the smooth-edged leaves.

Thumbnail photo: Benton Co., OR, ID, June (Gerald D. Carr); Reference photo: Bingham, ID, June (Matt Lavin); Illustration: USDA-NRCS Plants Database

Senecio streptanthifolius • Asteraceae (Sunflower Family)
(Synonym: *Packera streptanthifolia*)

ROCKY MOUNTAIN GROUNDSEL
(ROCKY MTN BUTTERWEED)

FIELD DESCRIPTION:

Perennial herb, 6-24" tall with glabrous stems arising from short, woody base or rhizome. Leaves basal and alternate on stem, simple, somewhat succulent, entire to coarsely toothed. Basal leaves ovate to rounded on petioles; upper stem leaves reduced in size, becoming sessile. Flower-heads broadly cylindrical in umbel-like arrays. Ray and disk flowers yellow. Fruit is achene with white bristles on top.

SUBALPINE
MONTANE

Flowering: May - August

Habitat: Moderately dry to moist open areas and woods, montane to subalpine

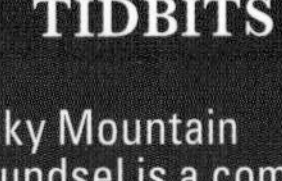

TIDBITS

Rocky Mountain Groundsel is a common yellow flower along trails in montane meadows and forest. The plant's leaf shape is highly variable and there are numerous varieties of the species. Thomas Nuttall was the first to collect it in Oregon in the 1830s, naming the plant *Senecio cymbalarioides*. Since that time the plant has gone through a number of name changes, and the species has no fewer than 7 synonyms that have been in use at some time. *Streptanthifolia* from the Greek streptos for "twisted" and *folius* for "foliage."

Photos: Gallatin Range, MT, July (W. Tilt)

ARROWLEAF GROUNDSEL
(TRIANGLELEAF RAGWORT)

Senecio triangularis • Asteraceae (Sunflower Family)

FIELD DESCRIPTION:

Perennial herb, 2-5′ tall, often growing in large clumps in damp to wet areas. Leafy to apex of plant, glabrous or sparingly hairy near nodes. Leaves glabrous, 2-8″ long, about one-quarter as wide, alternate, triangular, and sharply toothed on margin. Several yellow flower-heads in a flattened cluster, each with 6-12 yellow ray flowers (about 0.5″ long), surrounding yellow disk flowers.

MONTANE

Flowering: June - September

Habitat: Stream banks and moist soils, montane

TIDBITS

Arrowleaf Groundsel is distinguished from other *Senecio* species by its large triangular leaves. It occurs at higher elevations and in moister soils than Western Groundsel (*S. integerrimus*). Tall Ragwort (*Senecio serra*) is another similar appearing groundsel that occupies similar habitats, but the leaves of *S. serra* are not triangular. Groundsels have a rich folklore including fairies using the plants to travel from place to place, and witches turning groundsel into horses when a broom stick wasn't handy.

Photos: Bear Canyon, MT, July (W. Tilt); Illustration: USDA-NRCS Plants Database

CANADA GOLDENROD

Solidago canadensis • Asteraceae (Sunflower Family)

FIELD DESCRIPTION:

Hairy unbranched perennial herb, 10-60" tall, with showy yellow flower-heads in pyramids, cones, or cylinders, often arching and borne on just one side of the flower stem. Flower-heads contain 9-17 yellow ray flowers with yellow disks. Leaves are alternate, narrow, sparsely hairy. Margins entire or less commonly serrate. Leaves long and narrow, enlarged at either end or in middle, up to 4" long, gradually reduced in size as they ascend the stem. Young leaves are three-nerved (midrib and 2 parallel lateral veins are prominent). Flowers replaced with showy cluster of seeds tipped with tuft of white hairs (pappus).

MONTANE
VALLEYS

Flowering: July - October

Habitat: Moist soils in open area, valleys to montane

TIDBITS

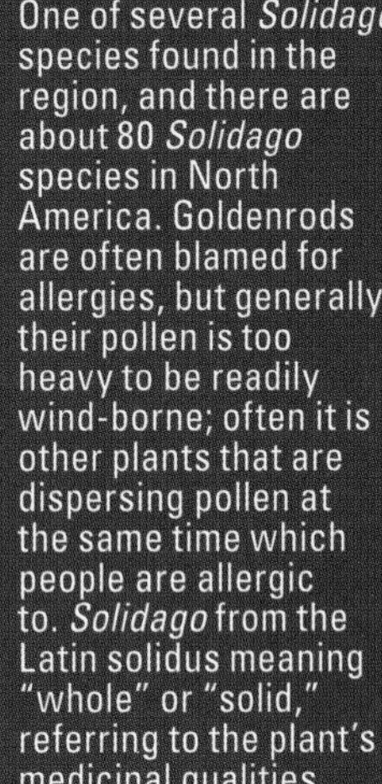

One of several *Solidago* species found in the region, and there are about 80 *Solidago* species in North America. Goldenrods are often blamed for allergies, but generally their pollen is too heavy to be readily wind-borne; often it is other plants that are dispersing pollen at the same time which people are allergic to. *Solidago* from the Latin solidus meaning "whole" or "solid," referring to the plant's medicinal qualities.

Thumbnail & seedhead: Gallatin Range, MT, July & October (W. Tilt); Reference photo: Teton Co, WY, September (Matt Lavin); Illustration: USDA-NRCS Plants Database

MOUNTAIN GOLDENROD

Solidago multiradiata • Asteraceae (Sunflower Family)

FIELD DESCRIPTION:

Perennial herb, 8-18" tall, with branched caudex. Numerous basal leaves and stems commonly form a dense clump. Crinkly hairs on upper stem and petiole bases; lower stem leaves and basal leaves to 6" long and as much as an inch wide, varying in shape and tapering to a conspicuously ciliate petiole. Inflorescence tight or loose, usually the former. Bracts are green on the tip and have a prominent mid-vein. Ray flowers, about 13 in number, yellow, short (about 0.2" long). Fruit an achene.

TIDBITS

Mountain Goldenrod is a common plant in alpine and subalpine meadows. The large number of ray flowers (usually 13) helps to distinguish the species from other goldenrod species. *Solidago* species have a wide range of traditional uses from herbal tea and diuretic to antiseptic lotion and yellow dye. *Solidago* from the Latin solidus meaning "whole" or "solid," in apparent reference to the plant's medicinal qualities.

ALPINE
SUBALPINE
MONTANE
FOOTHILLS

Flowering: June - September

Habitat: Forests, meadows, foothills to alpine

Photos: Teton Co., WY, September (Matt Lavin); Illustration: USDA-NRCS Plants Database

Sonchus arvensis • Asteraceae (Sunflower Family)

SOWTHISTLE

FIELD DESCRIPTION:

Perennial herb, to 3' tall, with horizontal, spreading rootstocks. Stems less leafy upward on stem. Lower leaves pinnate, lobes spiny, upper leaves pinnate or unlobed, glabrous. Flower-heads in clusters. Ray flowers only. Involucres to 0.2" high, glandular. Fruit an achene, 0.2" long with longitudinal ribs and a tuft of hair at the tip.

MONTANE

Flowering: June - September

Habitat: Disturbed soils, fields, roadsides, montane

TIDBITS

Also known as Field Milk-Thistle, Sowthistle spreads quickly from horizontal roots and provides abundant forage for many small mammals. Each plant has numerous flower-heads with just a few open at any given time. Stems are hollow and have a bitter milky sap. Sowthistle is utilized by a range of wildlife and its young leaves have been eaten raw or cooked since ancient times in southern Europe. *Sonchus* from the ancient Greek name for the plant, and *arvensis* means "of the fields."

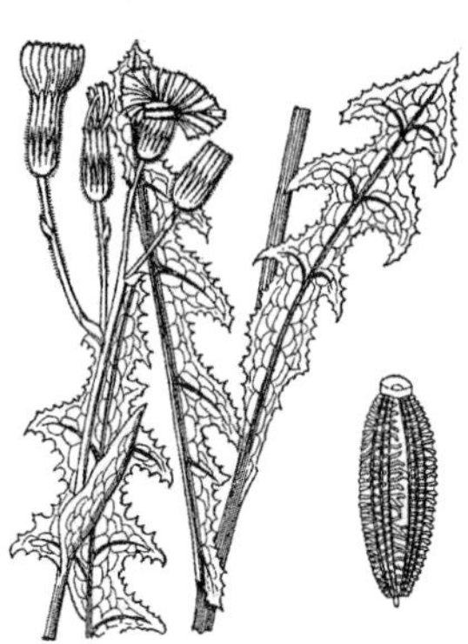

Photos: Gallatin Range, MT, July (W. Tilt); Illustration: USDA-NRCS Plants Database

LONGLEAF ASTER
(WESTERN ASTER)

Symphyotrichum ascendens • Asteraceae (Sunflower)

FIELD DESCRIPTION:

Perennial herb, 5-40" tall, that spreads by rhizomes. Basal leaves long and narrow, entire and smooth. Stem leaves shorter and somewhat thicker. Flower-heads comprised of 15-40 lavender-pink ray flowers surrounding a yellow disk. Involucral bracts are green and outwardly curved in several offset, overlapping rows.

TIDBITS

Longleaf Aster is common in moderately disturbed sites and rarely found in open, dry, intact habitats. Dependent on soils, Longleaf Aster can absorb selenium, which may cause it to be poisonous. The genus Aster is now generally restricted to Old World species with most New World species reclassified into other genera, including *Symphyotrichum*. All continue to be treated under the tribe Astereae. Aster from the Greek for "star." *Ascends* from the Latin for "rising upward."

MONTANE
FOOTHILLS

Flowering: June - September

Habitat: Wet to dry open areas, foothills to montane

Photos: Bozeman, MT, September (Matt Lavin); Illustration: USDA-NRCS Plants Database

Symphyotrichum ericoides • Asteraceae (Sunflower)
(Synonyms: *Aster ericoides, Aster pansus*)

WHITE HEATH ASTER
(MANY-FLOWERED ASTER)

FIELD DESCRIPTION:

Bushy perennial, 10-40" high, with numerous white composite flowers arising from ends of multiple stems. Numerous small white ray flowers with center of yellow disk flowers. Leaves are alternate, numerous, narrow, and linear, resembling the leaves of heather. Leaf often tipped with small spine and texture rough with stiff hairs. Fruit are achenes with tufts of white bristles. Stems from thickened base and an extensive root system of rhizomes and stolons.

VALLEYS-FOOTHILLS

Flowering: July - September

Habitat: Open, dry or wet soils, in meadows and along streams, plains to foothills

Photos: Madison River Valley, MT, August (Rip McIntosh); Illustration: USDA-NRCS Plants Database

TIDBITS

Distinguishable from other white-flowered asters by its general bushy appearance; dense arrays of small white flower-heads; short narrow leaves; and the blunt point of the involucre bracts as compared to other asters that have sharply pointed bracts. The plant's showy flowers make it popular in gardens where one of its varieties is named "snow flurry." The plant tolerates alkaline conditions and is often found in disturbed areas. *Ericoides* translates to "similar to Heath" (as in *Ericaceae*).

WHITE PRAIRIE ASTER
(CLUSTER ASTER)

Symphyotrichum falcatum • Asteraceae (Sunflower)
(Synonym: Aster falcatus)

FIELD DESCRIPTION:

Perennial herb, 12-24" tall, congested with short, hairy leaves and numerous flower-heads. Individual flower-heads are comprised of 20-35 narrow, white rays around small, light-yellow center disk. Involucre bracts are green, overlapping, and bent backward. Coarse spreading hairs are present on leaves and stems. Plant spreads by rhizomes, often forming dense stands of evenly scattered stems.

TIDBITS

White Prairie Aster is a common late-summer and fall wildflower. It has an unkempt appearance and an overall fuzzy look due to many short, stiff hairs. The genus *Symphyotrichum* displaced the more euphonious *Aster* for this species, as well as the majority of other former *Aster* species. The name is a particular tongue-twister, derived from the Greek *symphyos for* "coming together" and *trich* for "hair." *Falcatum* from the Latin for "shaped like a sickle" is assumed to be a reference to the backward-bending bracts.

Flowering: August - September

Habitat: Dry open sites, in foothills to montane

Thumbnail photo: Bozeman, MT, August (Matt Lavin); Reference photo: Bozeman, MT, August (W. Tilt); Illustration: USDA-NRCS Plants Database

Tanacetum vulgare • Asteraceae (Sunflower Family)

COMMON TANSY

FIELD DESCRIPTION:

Aromatic perennial herb, 16" to 6' tall. Numerous yellow, button-like disk flowers, formed into flat-topped branching clusters at end of stems. Leaves are alternate, fern-like, with pinnately divided leaves. Leaf axis is winged. Small pitted glands on leaves produce a strong odor. Stems are often purplish-red. Browned flowers persist into fall and early winter. Seeds are yellowish-brown and capped with a toothed crown.

MONTANE
VALLEYS

Flowering: July - October

Habitat: Moist disturbed soils in fields, roadsides and stream sides, valleys to montane

TIDBITS

An introduced garden plant from Europe that escaped cultivation, Common Tansy earned its *vulgare* (common or ordinary) label for its weedy nature as the plant is capable of overtaking large tracts of moist, disturbed soils. A number of traditional medicinal and household uses led to widespread introductions of Common Tansy throughout Europe and North America. For example, corpses were wrapped with Common Tansy as an embalming substitute and buried with the deceased to help repel vermin. The plant may be toxic in large doses or with long-term consumption.

Photos: Bozeman, MT, August (Matt Lavin); Illustration: USDA-NRCS Plants Database

COMMON DANDELION

Taraxacum officinale • Asteraceae (Sunflower Family)

FIELD DESCRIPTION:

Perennial plants, 2-20" tall, from a deep root. Leaves from 2-15" long and up to 4" wide, pinnatifid to pinnately lobed. Stems hairy to almost smooth and often hairy right below the flower-head. Outer bracts of the involucre narrow, lance-shaped, and strongly curved back. All ray flowers, yellow. Fruit an achene.

TIDBITS

Dandelions are among the longest blooming and most adaptable plants in the region. They seed easily from the wind-dispersed seeds carried on the fluff of pappus hairs. Dandelion leaves and flowers have been eaten for centuries, but they are also Enemy #1 to millions of home owners seeking a weed-free lawn. In the mountains, the dandelion follows trails into the backcountry, carried by humans, horses, and other travelers. The common name is a condensation of the French "dent de lion" (lion's tooth), referring to the teeth on the leaves.

SUBALPINE
MONTANE
FOOTHILLS

Flowering: April - October

Habitat: Lawns, vacant lots, meadows, foothills to subalpine

Thumbnail photo: Bozeman, MT, July (Matt Lavin); Reference photo: Bozeman, MT, July (W. Tilt); Illustration: USDA-NRCS Plants Database

PARRY'S TOWNSENDIA

Townsendia parryi • Asteraceae (Sunflower Family)

FIELD DESCRIPTION:

Showy annual, biennial, or short-lived perennial herb, 6-12" tall, with stout, leafless stems rising from a cluster of basal leaves. Large flower-heads, 1.5 to 3.5" in diameter, comprise lavender or purple-blue rays around a button of yellow disk flowers. Involucral bracts lance-shaped, sharp-pointed, in multiple rows, with a distinct fringe on their margin. Basal leaves spatulate, tapering toward base. Stem leaves few and reduced in size upwards.

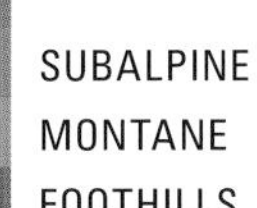

SUBALPINE
MONTANE
FOOTHILLS

Flowering: May - August

Habitat: Open, generally dry soils, foothills to subalpine

TIDBITS

Also known as Parry's Townsend Daisy, the flower of Parry's Townsendia often appears oversized for its supporting plant. Found on stony ground, at all elevations in the Yellowstone region, this showy flower is named for Charles C. Parry, the first botanist in the U.S. Department of Agriculture in first half of 19th century who contributed significantly to the nation's botanical knowledge. Hooker's Townsendia (*T. hookeri*) is a similar species with white ray flowers and short stems.

Photos: Bozeman, MT, August (W. Tilt)

YELLOW SALSIFY (GOATSBEARD)

Tragopogon dubius • Asteraceae (Sunflower Family)

FIELD DESCRIPTION:

Biennial herb, 1-3' tall. Yellow flower-head with ray florets, surrounded by 10-14 green involucral bracts (conspicuously longer than ray petals). Stem is triangular in cross-section, hollow, with milky sap. Leaves are alternate, long, linear, tapering from base toward tip. Seed head is conspicuous globe of white feathery bristles.

TIDBITS

Introduced from Europe, salsify has spread across much of North America. Salisify means "plant that follows the sun." The flowers open at sunup, follow the sun, and close tightly around noon on cloudy days, earning them the name "Jack-go- to-bed-at-noon." The plant can become weedy in rangelands and roadsides. Four other species of salsify are reported in the region. *Tragopogon* from the Greek for "goat beard," in reference to the plant's large feathery seed heads.

Flowering: June - August

Habitat: Trail sides and other open, relatively dry places, commonly disturbed areas, valleys to montane

Thumbnail & seedhead photos: Bozeman, MT, June (Whitney Tilt); Reference photo: Bingham Co., ID, June (Matt Lavin)

Wyethia amplexicaulis • Asteraceae (Sunflower Family)

YELLOW MULESEARS

FIELD DESCRIPTION:

Perennial herb, 10-36" tall, with upright stems. Basal leaves, 4-16" long, upright and shiny, stem leaves much smaller, rounded, and clasping the stem. Flower-heads large, 1.5" high and up to 2" wide, with the corolla up to 6" across, having 6-16 bright yellow rays and numerous yellow disk florets. The achenes are three- or four-angled with the pappus a crown of scales.

MONTANE
FOOTHILLS

Flowering: May - July

Habitat: Meadows and parklands, foothills to montane

TIDBITS

Yellow Mulesears often grow in open, montane areas where the plant forms large colonies. Large leaves give this species its name "mule's ears." Black bears and deer will forage on Yellow Mulesears in the early spring, though domestic livestock tend to avoid it. *Amplexicaulis* means "clasping stem," referring to the growth habit of the leaves on the stem. *Wyethia* recognizes Nathaniel Wyeth, a Massachusetts businessman who led two overland expeditions to Oregon in 1832 and 1834. The botanist Thomas Nutall accompanied the second expedition, during which Nutall named this plant for Wyeth.

Photos: Island Park, ID, July (Matt Lavin): Note the White Mulesears (*W. helianthoides)* in background

WHITE MULESEARS
(WHITE-RAYED WYETHIA)

Wyethia helianthoides • Asteraceae (Sunflower Family)

FIELD DESCRIPTION:

Perennial herb, 7-36" tall, with white flowers and large, dark-green, shiny leaves. Flowers are typically solitary on each stem, about 4" in diameter, consisting of white ray flowers surrounding a center of yellow disk flowers. Leaves large (up to 2' in length), elliptical, entire with short petioles, arising from root crown. Leaves noticeably covered with silky hairs. Stem leaves smaller, alternate and stalkless.

MONTANE

Flowering: May - June

Habitat: Moist meadows, montane

TIDBITS

Large leaves give this herb its name, "mule's ears." The species was identified in Idaho in 1833 by the noted explorer Nathaniel Wyeth. *Helianthoides* means sunflower-like. White Mulesears are often mixed in with yellow-flowered members of the genus, such as Yellow Mulesears (*W. amplexicaulis*). These 2 species often hybridize, producing pale yellow flowers. Mulesears can be confused with the balsamroots (*Balsamorhiza*), but the two can be distinguished by the presence of stem leaves in *Wyethia* and exclusively basal leaves in *Balsamorhiza*.

Thumbnail photo: Mesa Falls ID, June (W. Tilt); Other photos: Box Canyon, ID, July (Matt Lavin)

Impatiens ecalcarata • Balsaminaceae (Touch-me-not)

SPURLESS TOUCH-ME-NOT

FIELD DESCRIPTION:

Succulent perennial herb, 16-40" tall. Leaves simple, alternate, lanceolate with toothed margins and smooth surface. Yellow-orange, snapdragon-like flowers, mostly in twos, from leaf axils, unspotted, pouched with lateral pair of sepals fused. Stems hairless and freely branched. Fruit are 5-celled capsules that explosively disperse seeds when mature.

MONTANE

VALLEYS

Flowering: August - September

Habitat: Moist areas, along streams and ditches, valleys to montane

Photos: Bozeman, MT, September (Matt Lavin)

TIDBITS

Spurless Touch-Me-Not is 1 of 2 native impatiens found in the region in wet, organic soils. Pale Yellow Jewelweed (*I. aurella*) is a similar-looking plant with a recurved spur and a 1-2 mm long capsule, as opposed to *I. ecalcarata* with a non-spurred sepal and longer capsule. *Impatiens*, as in "impatient," referring to the explosive release of seeds when the ripe capsule is touched. This is also the origin of the name "Touch-Me-Not." The stem juices of jewelweeds have traditionally been used in treatment of nettle stings and poison ivy rash.

MINER'S CANDLE
(BUTTE CANDLE)

Cryptantha celosioides • Boraginaceae (Borage Family)

FIELD DESCRIPTION:

Biennial or short-lived perennial, 5-20" tall, with single unbranched stem, decorated with clusters of small, five-petaled white flowers. Flowers in small clusters around upper portion of the stem, tubal with 5 lobes and yellowish throat. Stems and leaves hairy. Basal leaves are commonly spatulate. Stem leaves smaller and wider at upper end. Fruits are 4 ovate nutlets.

TIDBITS

Miner's Candle is named for its showy spike of white, five-petaled flowers, sometimes called White Forget-Me-Not in reference to its flower with a prominent eye and yellowish center. The plant's common name alludes to the plant's candle-like appearance and early mining efforts in the American West when the preferred lighting method was a simple candle stuck to miners' caps or mine shaft walls with a wad of clay. There are several members of *Cryptantha* potentially found in the region with *Cryptantha celosioides* the most commonly encountered.

MONTANE
FOOTHILLS

Flowering: May - June

Habitat: Dry soils, foothills to montane

Reference photo: Paradise Valley, MT, June (W. Tilt);
Reference photo: Klickitat Co., WA, April (Gerald D. Carr);
Illustration: USDA-NRCS Plants Database

Cynoglossum officinale • Boraginaceae (Borage Family)

HOUNDSTONGUE

FIELD DESCRIPTION:

Single-stemmed biennial herb, 1-4' tall, with numerous lance-shaped, soft-hairy leaves. Clusters of red-purple flowers have 5 petals fused in a funnel shape. Terminal branches unfurl like scorpion tails to reveal racemes of flowers. Plant forms a rosette in its first year of growth and a flowering stem in the second year. Rosette is circle of large (up to 12") hairy leaves that are rough to the touch and lack teeth or lobes. Fruits a flattened nutlet with short, barbed prickles.

MONTANE

VALLEYS-FOOTHILLS

Flowering: May - July

Habitat: Dry, sandy disturbed soils, valleys to montane

Thumbnail photo: Bozeman, MT, June (Matt Lavin); Reference photo: Bear Canyon, MT, June (W. Tilt); Illustration: USDA-NRCS Plants Database

TIDBITS

A native of Europe, Houndstongue is considered a noxious weed in many areas. The plant's common name arises from two attributes: its leaf vein pattern and the roughness of its rosette leaves. The most likely reference to your dog, however, is the burs embedded in the fur. The plant can cause human skin reactions and contains alkaloids which are toxic to animals and humans. *Cynoglossum* from the Greek for "dog's tongue" and *officinale* ("sold in shops") for a plant considered a medicinal herb sold in an apothecary shop.

FORGET-ME-NOT
(ALPINE & MOUNTAIN)

Eritrichium sp./Myosostis sp. • Boraginaceae (Borage)

FIELD DESCRIPTION:

Alpine Forget-Me-Not *(Eritrichium nanum)* is a dwarf cushion-like perennial, 1-4" tall, soft-hairy overall. Leaves are alternate, oblong to ovate, densely clustered, long-hairy, tips often tufted. Flowers in tight, showy, terminal clusters of light blue-lavender, five-lobed flowers with yellow (some pinkish) eyes. Fruits are glabrous nutlets with flanges across the backs.

Mountain Forget-me-not *(Myosotis alpestris)* is a perennial herb, 4-10" tall. Overall plant sparsely hairy with erect, simple stems. Leaves are alternate, lance- to spoon-shaped with soft hairs. Basal leaves have petioles while higher stem leaves do not. Flowers, showy, blue (rarely white), five-lobed, with yellow (at times pinkish) eyes. Hooked hairs present on calyx. Fruits are black, shiny nutlets.

TIDBITS

The Mountain Forget-Me-Not is a circumboreal species and a favorite wherever it is found. At higher elevations, plant may be confused with Alpine Forget-Me-Not, but the latter is a cushion-plant. At lower elevations, forget-me-nots may be confused with stickseeds (*Hackelia sp.*). Both have the characteristic small pale- to dark-blue flowers and yellow or white centers. Stickseeds are generally taller plants with a "weedy" appearance and prickles on their fruits. Forget-me-nots are generally lower growing with denser flower presentations. Forget-me-nots are often worn or used as a sign of faithfulness and enduring love. Legend has it that a knight and his lady were walking along a river. Stooping to pick flowers for his love, the knight slipped and tumbled into the river. As the weight of his armor dragged him under, the knight threw the bouquet to his love and called out, "Forget me not!"

ALPINE
SUBALPINE
MONTANE

Flowering: June - August

Habitat: Meadows, moist open slopes, rocky soils, montane to alpine

Top (*Myosotis alpestris*):Bozeman, MT, June (W. Tilt); bottom (*Eritrichium nanum*): Beartooth Plateau, July (Gordon Wiltsie)

MANY-FLOWERED STICKSEED

FIELD DESCRIPTION:

Biennial or short-lived perennial herb, 12-48" tall. Basal leaves oblanceolate and petiolate, commonly smaller than stem leaves; stem leaves numerous, well developed, becoming sessile and more elliptic upward on stem; texture rough-hairy. Flowers pale blue, funnel-shaped, five-lobed, densely arranged on elongate stalks that droop as the flowers mature. Fruits are 4 teardrop nutlets armed with rows of barbed prickles.

SUBALPINE
MONTANE
FOOTHILLS

Flowering: June - August

Habitat: Moist soils in meadows and along stream banks, foothills to subalpine

Thumbnail photo: Beehive Basin, MT, July (Rip McIntosh); Reference photo: Bear Canyon, MT, June (W. Tilt)

TIDBITS

Stickseeds have barbed prickles on their fruits that snag passing fur and clothing, like that other Boraginaceae member, Houndstongue. Stickseeds appear as leggy forget-me-nots. Both stickseeds and forget-me-nots have small pale- to dark-blue flowers with 5 lobes and yellow or white centers. Stickseeds are generally a taller plant, have prickles on their nut-like fruits, and a "weedy" appearance. Forget-me-nots (*Myosotis* and *Eritrichium*) are generally lower growing with denser flower presentations, and their nutlets lack prickles.

WESTERN STONESEED (WESTERN GROMWELL)

Lithospermum ruderale • Boraginaceae (Borage Family)

FIELD DESCRIPTION:

Stiff-stemmed, bushy perennial herb, 10-20" tall, with multiple unbranched hairy stems and a woody caudex. Small, obscure, pale yellow flowers arranged in clusters tucked deeply into the axils of upper leaves. Flowers comprised of a small tube of fused petals spreading into 5 lobes. Leaves are alternate, dark green, lanceolate to linear, hairy, stalkless, becoming more numerous toward the top of the plant. Fruits are shiny, hard, egg-shaped brownish nutlets.

MONTANE
VALLEYS

Flowering: May - July

Habitat: Dry plains, hillsides, sagebrush steppes and open forests, valleys to montane

TIDBITS

Western Stoneseed is also known as "Yellow Puccoon." Puccoon is a Native American word for plants that yield a purple dye that can be extracted from its roots. Western Stoneseed has been used for centuries as a female contraceptive. Yellow Gromwell (*Lithospermum incisum*), favoring sandy soils at lower elevations, has larger, bright yellow-orange flowers with fringed petals. *Lithospermum* from the Latin for "stone seed," and refers to the plant's hard, shiny seeds that have been used as beads. *Ruderale* in reference to growing on waste ground or among rubbish, as in "ruderal."

Photos: Bozeman, MT, May (W. Tilt); Seeds: Bozeman, MT, July (W. Tilt)

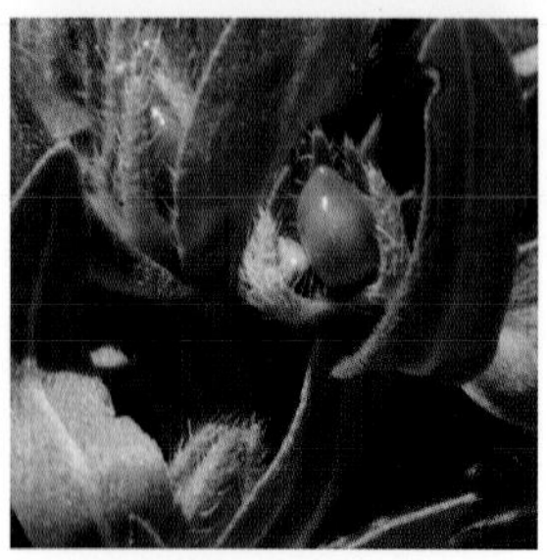

Mertensia ciliata • Boraginaceae (Borage Family)

MOUNTAIN BLUEBELLS

FIELD DESCRIPTION:

Perennial herb, 1-4′ tall, with blue, tubular, five-lobed flowers hanging in clusters from the top of stems. Blue-green leaves are alternate along stem, hairy on margins (ciliate), pointed, oval to lance-shaped. Mature flowers turn pink and the style may protrude from the flower. Plants commonly grow in large patches in moist sites.

ALPINE
SUBALPINE
MONTANE

Flowering: June - August

Habitat: Moist soils along stream banks, montane to alpine

TIDBITS

Mountain Bluebells often grow in large patches. In bloom they fill the air with an soft, appealling scent. Numerous species of *Mertensia* are found in the Rocky Mountains. The flowers are edible raw and the plant has several reported medicinal uses. Another bluebell species, Leafy Bluebells (*M. oblongifolia*), is smaller in stature with numerous lance-shaped basal leaves, and prefers drier sites. *Ciliata* from the Latin for "small hair."

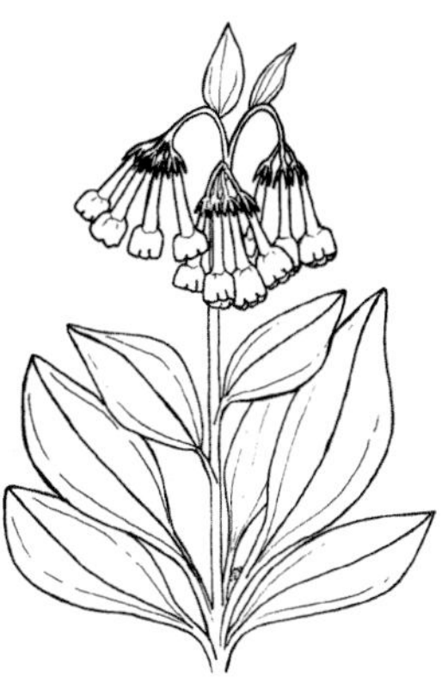

Photos: Bozeman, MT, June (W. Tilt); Illustration: USDA-NRCS Plants Database

SAGEBRUSH BLUEBELLS

Mertensia oblongifolia • Boraginaceae (Borage Family)

FIELD DESCRIPTION:

Perennial herb, 4-12" tall, with one-to-many stems from tuber-like root and often a branched caudex. Basal leaves (rare on flowering plants) with short petioles. Stem leaves sessile, to 3" long, oblong or elliptic, entire margins, and rounded at tip; slightly hairy above, smooth underneath. Flower clusters densely packed, corrolla blue, tubular, funnel-shaped, five-lobed. Tubes glabrous, 2-4 times as long as wide. Fruits comprise 4 wrinkled nutlets.

SUBALPINE
MONTANE
FOOTHILLS

Flowering: April - June

Habitat: Sagebrush and mountain brush communities; foothills to subalpine

TIDBITS

Mertensia oblongifolia is 1 of 6 bluebells found on the greater Yellowstone Region according to Erwin Evert's *Vascular Plants of the Greater Yellowstone Area.* Its short stature, large, almost hairless oblong leaves, and densely packed flower cluster make it easily distinguishable from the other bluebells. The genus *Mertensia* was named by German botanist Karl Mertens in honor of his father, Franz Mertens. The species name *oblongifolia* refers to the oblong leaves.

Thumbnail & inset photos: Bozeman, MT, May (Matt Lavin); Reference photo: Gallatin Range, MT, May (W. Tilt)

Arabis drummondii• Brassicaceae (Mustard Family)
(Synonym: *Boechera stricta*)

DRUMMOND'S ROCKCRESS
(CANADIAN ROCKCRESS)

FIELD DESCRIPTION:

Biennial or short-lived perennial, up to 3' tall, 1 or more stems, usually glabrous or some hairs at base. Basal leaves to 3" long, wider toward tips, entire, nearly glabrous. Stem leaves usually longer than internodes (distance between point of leaf attachment), numerous, to 2" long, clasping. Sepals less than 0.25" long, petals less than 0.5" long, white to pink. Seed pods from 1.5-4" long, erect and held upward.

SUBALPINE
MONTANE

Flowering: May - August

Habitat: Gravelly and rocky slopes, forest openings, meadows, along trails, montane to subalpine

Thumbnail & left reference: Beehive Basin, MT, July (R. McIntosh); Right reference photo (seedheads): Bozeman, MT (W. Tilt); Illustration: USDA-NRCS Plants Database

TIDBITS

Drummond's Rockcress is common in montane meadows, forest openings and rocky fell fields. Its slender and small stature can easily escape notice. Plants continue to elongate and flower for many weeks, typical of the mustards. Drummond's Rockcress is most conspicuous when the plant goes to seed, developing long and upright seed pods. *Drummondii* honors naturalist Thomas Drummond who first collected the seeds of this plant in the northern Rockies. *Stricta* refers to the "strict" upright posture of the stem and the seed pods.

HOARY ALYSSUM
(HOARY FALSE MADWORT)

Berteroa incana • Brassicaceae (Mustard Family)

FIELD DESCRIPTION:

Annual, biennial or short-lived perennial herb, 1-3' tall. Stem covered with short, gray hairs. Basal leaves oblanceolate, entire on slender stalks. Stem leaves similar to basal but alternate, reduced to small bracts as they ascend stem. Flowers in long clusters on upper stem but only top flowers bloom. Flowers comprise 4 white petals and 6 stamens with flattened filaments. Fruits in oblong, inflated pods covered in star-shaped hairs.

VALLEYS - FOOTHILLS

Flowering: May - August

Habitat: Disturbed soils and fields, valleys to foothills

TIDBITS

A weedy exotic from Europe now naturalized across much of the United States, Hoary Alyssum is capable of spreading rapidly by seed, inhabiting roadsides and similarly disturbed areas. The plant can be toxic, particularly to horses, causing swelling of legs, fever, and stiffness of joints. Hoary Alyssum is one of the longest-blooming flowers in the region. It is similar in appearance to Perennial Pepperweed (*Lepidium latifolium*), another noxious weed that favors moist areas.

Photos: Bozeman, MT, July (W. Tilt); Illustration: USDA-NRCS Plants Database

Capsella bursa-pastoris • Brassicaceae (Mustard Family)

SHEPHERD'S PURSE

FIELD DESCRIPTION:

Annual herb, 4-18" tall. Stem smooth or finely hairy and commonly branched. Leaves broadly lance-shaped, pinnately lobed or toothed, and stalked. Basal leaves in rosette and stem Leaves are alternate, smaller, and clasping. Small inconspicuous white flowers comprised of 4 petals, 4 green sepals, 6 stamens, and a single pistil. Flowers begin in dense, rounded clusters, then elongate into racemes as fruit develop. Fruits distinctive flattened heart-shaped pods containing numerous seeds.

SUBALPINE
MONTANE
VALLEYS

Flowering: May - July

Habitat: Disturbed soils and fields, valleys to subalpine

TIDBITS

A weedy mustard species introduced from Europe, Shepherd's Purse now occurs in almost every county of every state in the United States. A single plant can produce up to 40,000 seeds. The plant is also a host for several diseases of cultivated plants. Shepherd's Purse is an apt description of the plant's seed, which resembles a green-brown purse.

Thumbnail & seed photo: Bozeman, MT, June (Whitney Tilt); Reference photo: Bozeman, MT, May (Matt Lavin); Illustration: USDA-NRCS Plants Database

COMMON TANSYMUSTARD

Descurainia sophia • Brassicaceae (Mustard Family)

TIDBITS

Introduced from Europe, species of tansymustard are widely found across the northern Rocky Mountain region. They are a variable genus with considerable disagreement among botanists as to their nomenclature. Characteristics that help separate various *Descurainia* (and various mustards in general) are: degree to which seed pods are flattened; length and shape of pods; and position of pods to stem (i.e., horizontally, vertically).

FIELD DESCRIPTION:

Annual herb, 8-40" tall, with airy branching bearing clusters of small yellow flowers. Leaves are alternate, pinnately divided 2-3 times, cut into narrow segments. Stems grey-green with tufted hairs, pubescent with branched hairs, or nearly glabrous. Yellow flower-heads in elongating racemes consist of small, four-petaled, cross-shaped flowers. Fruits are pods with 2-3 longitudinal nerves 0.5-1.25" long.

MONTANE
VALLEYS

Flowering: May - August

Habitat: Disturbed soils, along trails, roadsides, pastures and cultivated fields, valleys to montane

Photos: Bozeman, MT, July (Matt Lavin); Illustration: USDA-NRCS Plants Database

Draba oligosperma • Brassicaceae (Mustard Family)

YELLOWSTONE DRABA

FIELD DESCRIPTION:

Low-growing perennial that forms small cushions to larger mats. Its flowering stems reach a maximum height of 8". Dense tufts of narrowly oblong leaves are produced at the plant base. Each leaf is 0.25-0.5" long and usually hairy, especially on the lower surface. A cluster of 2-to-8 yellow flowers is produced at the top of a leafless stem. Flowers are four-petaled and less than 0.25" long. Fruit are inflated, oval, hairy pods 0.25-0.5" long.

ALPINE

Flowering: July - August

Habitat: Meadows, cliffs and exposed slopes, alpine

Thumbnail photo: Wasatch Range UT, July (Steve Hegji); Reference photo: Wilsall MT, May (Matt Lavin); Illustration: Flora of North America (www.efloras.org)

TIDBITS

There are 24 species of draba named in Erwin Evert's *Vascular Plants of the Yellowstone Area*, many of which are hard to differentiate from each other. Yellowstone Draba often flowers before the stem elongates, keeping its flowers close to the shelter of its basal leaf cluster. As temperatures warm and insects become more active, the stem elongates making the flowers more conspicuous to pollinators. *Draba* from the Greek for "acrid" and the specific name means "few seeded."

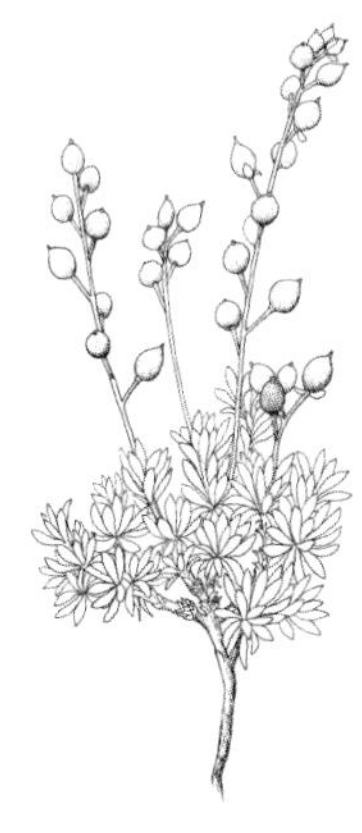

WESTERN WALLFLOWER

Erysimum capitatum • Brassicaceae (Mustard Family)
(Synonym: *Erysimum asperum*, var. *arkansanum*)

FIELD DESCRIPTION:

Single-stemmed (occasionally branched) biennial or short-lived perennial herb, 8-30" tall, with showy, typically yellow (but may be orange or lavender) flowers in dense rounded terminal cluster. Individual flowers have 4 petals and pouch-shaped outer sepals. Basal leaves are linear-elliptical with entire to sharply -toothed margins. Stem leaves are alternate and linear with overall grayish-green appearance. Seed pods are four-sided, quite thin, up to 4" long, and grow outward and upward, often parallel to stem.

TIDBITS

Also known as Sanddune Wallflower or Prairie Rocket, the species' bright spike of yellow flowers is conspicuous among the greening vegetation. It is also one of several wildflowers to have the sobriquet "prairie rocket." *Erysimum capitatum* is variable in appearance, and similar in appearance to *E. asperum*, with some botanists considering them the same species. Flowers are attractive to a number of butterfly species, making it a common garden plant. *Erysimum*, from the Greek for "help" or "save," is a reference to the centuries old belief that the plant had medicinal properties. *Capitatum*, from the Latin for "head," refers to the rounded, head-shaped flower cluster.

SUBALPINE
MONTANE
VALLEYS

Flowering: May - August

Habitat: Well-drained, dry sandy soils, valleys and foothills to subalpine

Thumbnail photo: Bozeman, MT, June (W. Tilt); Reference photo: Tobacco Root Range, June (W. Tilt); Formation of seed head: Bozeman, MT, July (W. Tilt)

Hesperis matronalis • Brassicaceae (Mustard Family)

DAME'S ROCKET

FIELD DESCRIPTION:

Erect biennial or short-lived perennial, 2-3' tall. Flowers pink-purple (occasionally white), four-petaled with 4 sepals. Flowers cluster in elongated racemes arising from axils of upper leaves. Leaves are alternate, lance-shaped, and sharply toothed. Leaves decrease in size upward on the stem. Lower leaves stalked, becoming stalkless higher on plant. Stems and leaves long-hairy. Fruits are long thin pods, narrowing between seeds.

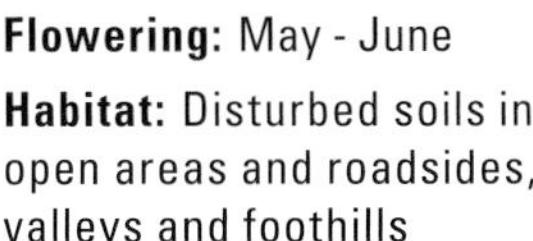

VALLEYS - FOOTHILLS

Flowering: May - June

Habitat: Disturbed soils in open areas and roadsides, valleys and foothills

TIDBITS

A showy weed introduced from Eurasia in colonial times as an ornamental. Dame's Rocket escaped cultivation, commonly through planting of wildflower seed mixes. Dame's Rocket is a prolific seed producer and can become locally invasive. The young leaves are rich in vitamin C and can be eaten raw as a cress substitute in salads. The plant is also cultivated for its seed-oil which is used in perfumes. *Hesperis* from the Greek for "nightfall," possibly because this plant is known to be more sweet-scented in the evening. *Matronalis* means "of matrons."

Photos: Bozeman, MT, June (W. Tilt); Illustration: USDA-NRCS Plants Database

DYER'S WOAD

Isatis tinctoria • Brassicaceae (Mustard Family)

FIELD DESCRIPTION:

Biennial or a short-lived perennial, up to 4' in height, with deep taproot. First year form is typically a rosette with second year flowering stage. May stay in rosette form 2-3 years. Leaves are blue-green, lance-shaped, pubescent, with a cream-colored mid-vein that extends the whole length of the leaf. Rosette leaves up to 7" long, crenulate (small-rounded teeth on margin), broadest near tip and taper to a petiole. Stem leaves are alternate, margins mostly entire, sessile (no petiole) and clasp the stem. Flowers are bright yellow, 4 petals, 4 sepals and 6 stamens (2 shorter than other 4) borne in showy racemes at the ends of the branches. Fruits are oblong, flattened seed pods containing a single brownish-yellow cylindrical seed. Pods hang down from stem and turn from green to blue-black as they dry. Plants are monocarpic, dying after they produce seed.

TIDBITS

Dyer's Woad produces a blue substance used for centuries as a form of dye for pottery, textiles, and body paint. The Romans battled Northern European tribes dyed head to toe with war paint made from the plant. Dyer's Woad is a native of Eurasia but was intentionally introduced to North America during the 1700s for use as a dye before indigo began to be imported from the West Indies. In traditional medicine, Dyer's Woad has been used as an astringent and the root is used to treat mumps, throat ailments, hepatitis, headache, and fever. Dyer's Woad escaped cultivation and spread across the western United States as a contaminant in alfalfa seed. Dyer's Woad is listed as a noxious weed in the region as a result of its rapid growth rate and prolific seed production.

VALLEYS

Flowering: May - August

Habitat: Dry rocky soils on hillsides, rangeland, uncultivated fields, roadsides, and waste areas

Photos: Wasatch Front UT, May (Matt Lavin)

Lepidium sp. • Brassicaceae (Mustard Family)
(Synonym: *Cardaria sp.*)

WHITETOP COMPLEX
(HOARY CRESS)

FIELD DESCRIPTION:

Deep-rooted perennial herb, 8-24" tall, with numerous white flowers borne in dense, elongated flat-topped clusters. Characteristic of the Mustard Family, individual flowers have 4 petals arranged in a cross. Leaves are alternate, bluish-green, lanceolate, often with finely toothed margins. Leaves are covered with soft white hairs. Plant spreads by rhizomes. Fruits are roundish, inflated, two-valved pods.

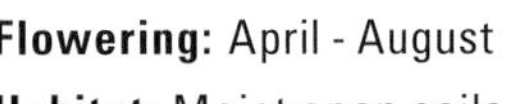

PLAINS-FOOTHILLS

Flowering: April - August

Habitat: Moist open soils including riparian areas, pastures, and roadsides, plains-foothills

Thumbnail photo: Bozeman, MT, June (W. Tilt); Reference photo: Bozeman, MT, June (Matt Lavin); Illustration (*L. draba*): USDA-NRCS Plants Database

TIDBITS

A number of *Lepidium* species were introduced from Europe in the 1800s and spread rapidly. Often classified as a noxious weed, whitetops spread from underground rhizomes, crowding out native species, and reducing crop yields. Numerous closely-related and similar-appearing species are commonly combined into the "Whitetop Complex" and include *L. draba*, *L. latifolium*, and *L. perfoliatum*. As the other common name, pepperweed and heartpod, suggest, the seed has been used as a pepper substitute and its shape is broadly round or heart-shaped.

TWINPOD

Physaria didymocarpa • Brassicaceae (Mustard Family)

FIELD DESCRIPTION:

Twinpod grows from a branched root crown, forming a tuft of grayish-green leaves covered with appressed hair. Stems are typically 1-4" inches long and prostrate. Twinpod's leaves are primarily basal, with a few stem leaves growing in an alternate pattern. Basal leaves are spoon-shaped, 0.75-2" long and often have shallow teeth along their margins. Stem leaves are much smaller and very narrow. Yellow flowers are produced in a loose, elongated cluster at the top of the stem. Each flower has 4 petals and is about 0.75" long. The fruit of this plant are inflated, two-lobed pods 0.5-1.25" tall. The pods are usually wider than tall and are produced on spreading stalks.

MONTANE
FOOTHILLS

Flowering: May - June

Habitat: Dry, sparsely vegetated soil of meadows and grasslands, foothills to montane

TIDBITS

A mustard native to the western United States, twinpods are challenging to identify to species. *Physaria didymocarpa* is the most commonly encountered in the Yellowstone region. Twinpods are similar in appearance to bladderpods (*Lesquerella sp.*), but fruits of twinpods are divided into 2 balloon-like sacs while bladderpod fruits are round orbs with slender style at tip. The juice of twinpod has been used in traditional medicine to treat sore throats and stomach ailments. *Physaria* is derived from the Greek *physa* for "bladder," and *didymocarpa* means "twin-fruited."

Photos: Gallatin Co., MT, May (Matt Lavin); Illustration: USDA-NRCS Plants Database

Sisymbrium loeselii • Brassicaceae (Mustard Family)

SMALL TUMBLEMUSTARD (HEDGE MUSTARD)

FIELD DESCRIPTION:

Leafy annual, 2-4' tall with weedy habit. Stems are erect, branched with coarse hairs, especially near the base. Leaves are alternate, hairy, stalked, and deeply divided into narrow-to-angular lobes. Leaf margin irregularly toothed, terminal lobe largest with 2-4 pairs of lateral lobes, commonly curving backward. Flower-heads are densely packed rounded clusters at end of stems that elongate as the plant matures. Flowers yellow with 4 rounded petals and 6 greenish stamens. Fruit is a long slender pod, 0.75-1.5" long, with the brown stub of the style evident at the tip.

PLAINS-FOOTHILLS

Flowering: May - August

Habitat: Open disturbed soils of roadsides, waste areas, and fields, plains to foothills

TIDBITS

Small Tumblemustard is native to Eurasia but now spread widely across North America. It is one of several "wild mustards" that readily colonize disturbed ground and can form dense stands. As the common name suggests, tumblemustards easily uproot and tumble with the wind, spreading their seeds along the way. Large Tumblemustard (*S. altissimum*) is more common in rangelands and higher elevation habitats. Tumbleweed mustards are allelopathic, producing chemicals that inhibit growth of other species near them.

Photos: Bozeman, MT, July (Matt Lavin)

PENNYCRESS
(STINKWEED)

Thlaspi arvense • Brassicaceae (Mustard Family)

FIELD DESCRIPTION:

Taprooted annual, 6-18" tall, with hairless, simple to freely branched stems. Leaves stalkless or clasping, with irregularly lobed margins and ear-shaped notches at base. Small white flowers in open clusters at tips of branches comprised of 4 petals and 4 green sepals. Fruits are flat, oval-round, winged, and notched at tip.

TIDBITS

Introduced from Europe, Pennycress is now widely distributed across the United States. It is one of the most easily recognized mustards with its large and distinctive round penny-like fruits. The species is commonly found in cropland, fallow fields, and other disturbed areas where it is considered an agricultural pest when it reduces yields of desired crops. Young leaves are edible raw or cooked and the plant has a number of recognized medicinal uses. Some references note the plant's potential toxicity to livestock. Like many mustards, the seeds are high in oil and a potential source for biodiesel.

VALLEYS-FOOTHILLS

Flowering: May - August

Habitat: On disturbed soils, valley to foothills

Photos: East End, MT, July (Matt Lavin); Illustration: USDA-NRCS Plants Database

Opuntia polyacantha • Cactaceae (Cactus Family)

PRICKLY PEAR CACTUS

FIELD DESCRIPTION:

Spiny perennial herb, 4-10" tall, forming spreading clumps. Rounded succulent pads are covered with bundles of straight 2-5" spines that may be slightly barbed. Very short, stiff, brown hairs arise from few areoles. Yellow flowers with numerous overlapping petals arise from buds on margins of pads. Pear-shaped fruits, about 1" wide, are fleshy and short-spiny.

VALLEYS-FOOTHILLS

Flowering: May - July

Habitat: Dry, sandy, gravelly soils, valleys to foothills

TIDBITS

The most common cactus of the region, the Prickly Pear Cactus is broadly distribed across western North America and found in a variety of habitats, including shrub-steppe and prairie. Its flowers may be peach-colored, yellow, or pink. Prickly pear fruits are edible, raw or cooked, and are consumed by a range of wildlife. The flesh of the plant is reported to be of particular interest to wildlife and livestock after wildfires have singed the spines off. In addition to the obvious spines, plants have minute barbed hairs that are difficult to see and remove from skin. *Opuntia* is the Greek name of a plant that grew near Opus, and *polyacantha* means "many spines."

Thumbnail photo: Yellowstone NP, June (Marianne Salas); Pink flower: SW Colorado, April (Al Schneider); Reference photo: Shields River Valley, MT, June (W. Tilt)

HARENBELL (SCOTTISH BLUEBELLS)

Campanula rotundifolia • Campanulaceae (Bellflower)

FIELD DESCRIPTION:

Slender perennial herb, 4-36" tall, with milky sap. Blue-violet bell-shaped flowers hang in clusters along the top parts of nodding, thread-like, mostly unbranched stems that grow in small to very large patches. Flowers with 5-pointed lobes that gently curve back, a 3-part stigma on a style about as long as the corolla, and 5 lavender stamens. Basal leaves on long petioles with broadly ovate to cordate blades, margins may be entire or toothed. Stem Leaves are alternate and linear. Fruits are hanging capsules.

SUBALPINE
MONTANE
VALLEYS

Flowering: June-September

Habitat: Meadows and slopes, valleys to subalpine

TIDBITS

Harebells add a dainty splash of color to the understory along trails in the region. They are found in both the Old World and the New World. In Scotland, they are known as bluebells. The common name "harebell" arises from the folk belief that witches used juice squeezed from the flower to turn themselves into hares. The plant is also known as Puck's Thimble and was traditionally linked to fairies and witches. *Campanula* is derived from the Latin for "bell." *Rotundifolio* is somewhat misleading as the plant's leaves are more cordate than round.

Thumbnail photo: Beehive Basin, MT, July (Rip McIntosh); Reference photo: Bozeman, MT, July (W. Tilt); Illustration: USDA-NRCS Plants Database

FIELD CHICKWEED

FIELD DESCRIPTION:

Perennial herb, 4-12" tall, often growing in large mats. White flowers have 5 deeply notched petals about 3 times as long as the sepals, 10 stamens, and 5 styles. Bracts below flowers are lance-shaped with thin, yellowish, membranous margin. Slender, lance-shaped leaves arranged opposite on stems with secondary leaves arising from axils of larger primary leaves. Fruit is a capsule.

ALPINE
SUBALPINE
MONTANE
FOOTHILLS

Flowering: April - August

Habitat: Dry open meadows and rocky sites, foothills to alpine

Photos: Mt. Ellis, May (W. Tilt); Illustration: USDA-NRCS Plants Database

TIDBITS

Chickweeds are common plants found along in meadows and along paths and roadsides. There are a number of similar-looking chickweeds in the region, such as non-native Mouse-ear Chickweed (*C. fontanum*). In general, the shoots of young plants are edible. Chickweeds have traditionally been used for a wide range of medicinal purposes, such as astringents to cause tissues to contract and a strong tea made from the plant is noted for soothing itchy skin. *Cerastium* from the Greek for "horned," in reference to its curved seed capsule.

MOSS CAMPION (CUSHION PINK)

Silene acaulis • Caryophyllaceae (Pink Family)

FIELD DESCRIPTION:

Perennial herb, 1-3" tall, forming cushions 2-10" in diameter. Leaves mainly basal, short, narrow linear, and bright green. Flowers are pinkish-purple, tubular with 5 spreading petals. Each petal is notched into 2 lobes. Flowers borne singly on stems and often profuse in number. Fruits are 3-chambered capsules.

ALPINE
SUBALPINE

Flowering: June - August

Habitat: Rocky soils and outcrops, subalpine to alpine

TIDBITS

When in bloom Moss Campion is hard to miss, producing brilliant high country floral displays. It is a common, and widespread plant found throughout mountainous western North America and at the higher latitudes around the Northern Hemisphere. Moss Campion is a pioneer species, establishing itself where the ground is disturbed. The notched flower petals of Moss Campion are "pinked" on their tips - thus the common family name. *Silene* is the Greek name for a related plant, and *acaulis* is Latin for "short-stemmed."

Reference photo: Wikimedia (Andrew Bossi); Thumbnail photo: SW Colorado, June (Al Schneider); Illustration: USDA-NRCS Plants Database

Silene latifolia • Caryophyllaceae (Pink Family)
(Synonym: *Lychnis alba*)

WHITE CAMPION
(WHITE COCKLE)

FIELD DESCRIPTION:

Perennial herb, 18-35" tall, with showy white flowers and prominent calyx. Flowers with 5 white, deeply notched petals. Calyx is a long, striped tube with glandular hairs. Male and female flowers on different plants (dioecious): male flower is 10-nerved, while the female flower is larger, 20-nerved, and becomes more inflated as it matures. Stem leaves opposite, oblong to lanceolate. Basal leaves spatulate. Stems are stiff-hairy and glandular on upper portions. Fruits are round, 1-celled capsules.

VALLEYS-FOOTHILLS

Flowering: June - August

Habitat: Fields, pastures, and open woods, often in disturbed areas, valleys to foothills

Photos: Gallatin Range, MT, July (W. Tilt); Illustration: USDA-NRCS Plants Database

TIDBITS

White Campion is a native of Europe that has become widely distributed across North America, favoring disturbed sites and waste areas. Like many weedy species, White Campion can cause headaches in the production of small grains and grass, as its seeds are difficult to separate from those of clover, alfalfa, and timothy. The root of White Campion has been use as a substitute for soap. The plant's inflated calyx is distinctive of the campions. Like other members of the Caryophyllaceae, the flower petals of White Campion have been "pinked," hence the common family name.

FRINGED GRASS-OF-PARNASSUS

Parnassia fimbriata • Celastriaceae (Staff-Tree Family)

FIELD DESCRIPTION:

Perennial herb, 8-14" tall, with slender, hairless, unbranched stems. A single white star-like flower with 5 petals tops the stem. Petals marked with 5-7 greenish-yellow veins, and lower edges delicately fringed. Five fertile stamens (white and anther-tipped) alternate with 5 sterile yellow stamens. Leaves are glossy, basal, heart- to kidney-shaped, on short petioles. A single heart-shaped leaf clasps the stem at its midpoint.

SUBALPINE
MONTANE

Flowering: July - September

Habitat: Wet soils in meadows and along stream banks, montane to subalpine

TIDBITS

Coming across Fringed Grass-of-Parnassus while hiking is a delight. The plant was first described in ancient Greece at Mount Parnassus, sacred to Apollo and home of the Muses. Fimbriata from the Latin for "fringed." Small-flowered Grass- of-Parnassus (*Parnassia parviflora*) differs from Fringed Grass-of-Parnassus in having smooth, not fringed, petal margins; leaf blades are obtuse rather than heart-shaped; and presence of the stem leaf below the middle.

Thumbnail photo: Glacier Natl. Park, MT, August (Gerald D. Carr); Reference photo: Linn Co. OR, August (Gerald D. Carr); Illustration: USDA-NRCS Plants Database

Peritoma serrulata • Cleomaceae (Cleome Family)
(Synonym: *Cleome serrulata*)

ROCKY MOUNTAIN BEEPLANT

FIELD DESCRIPTION:

Annual herb, 10-36" tall, freely-branching from taproots. Leaves are alternate, trifoliate, divided into 3 lanceolate leaflets, longer than petioles. Flowers are pink-purple leafy clusters (racemes) with individual flowers four-parted and cross-shaped, at ends of branches. Six conspicuous stamens protrude beyond the petals. Clusters continue to elongate during growing season. Fruits are linear cylindrical pods, tapered at both ends, green turning reddish-brown.

Flowering: May - August

Habitat: Dry, open, often disturbed soils, plains to montane

Photos: Truly, MT, August (Matt Lavin); Illustration: USDA-NRCS Plants Database

TIDBITS

Attractive pink flowers, with long stamens, attract bees and other pollinators, as its common name "beeplant" suggests. The plant is said to have kept both Native Americans and settlers from starvation with flour made from its seeds. The species was named by Frederick Pursh in 1814 from a collection made by Meriwether Lewis in August, 1804. *Serrulata* means "fine toothed." The species was formerly included in the Capparaecea (Caper Family).

BINDWEED
(FIELD MORNING-GLORY)

Convolvulus arvensis • Convolvulaceae (Morning-Glory)

FIELD DESCRIPTION:

Trailing, and climbing perennial herb, 1-4' long, with alternate, arrow-shaped leaves with sharp pointed lobes. One or 2 showy white to pink-purple flowers arise from leaf axils. Flower-head is broadly funnel-shaped with 2 small bracts on the flower stalk below the sepals. Four seeds are produced in a round capsule.

TIDBITS

At blooming time, fields and roadsides are often bedecked with myriads of Bindweed flowers. A native of Europe, Bindweed, as its name suggests, grows vine-like over the ground and vegetation, often forming dense tangles that crowd out native vegetation. Bindweed's extensive root system resists mechanical and chemical control efforts, and the plant's seeds may remain viable upwards of 30 years. These traits combine with Bindweed's trailing nature to make the plant a successful and often unwanted weed. *Convolvulus* from the Latin for "enfold" or "coil."

VALLEYS-FOOTHILLS

Flowering: May - September

Habitat: Moist disturbed areas in cultivated fields, pastures and roadsides, valleys to foothills

Photos: Bozeman, MT, June (W. Tilt & Matt Lavin); Illustration: USDA-NRCS Plants Database

Sedum lanceolatum • Crassulaceae (Stonecrop Family)

LANCELEAF STONECROP

FIELD DESCRIPTION:

Succulent perennial herb, 6-12" tall, with prominent, star-shaped yellow flowers in compact, flat-topped cluster. Flowers have 5 lanceolate and pointed petals, sometimes red-tinged. Stamens are long and obvious. Fleshy linear leaves are blunt-tipped and alternate on stems. Stems are green, yellow, or red and hairless. Basal leaves vary in color from green to reddish brown.

ALPINE
SUBALPINE
MONTANE
FOOTHILLS

Flowering: June - August

Habitat: Exposed rocky and gravelly dry soils, foothills to alpine

Photos: Paradise Valley, MT, July (W. Tilt)
Illustration: USDA-NRCS Plants Database

TIDBITS

The name "stonecrop" arises from 1 of 2 origins: 'cropping up amid stones' or the 'harvest (crop) of stones.' Regardless, stonecrops are cultivated widely in gardens and a colorful delight on hard, stony ground. Adapted to dry climates, stonecrops conserve water by closing small pores on their leaves during the day. Rich in vitamins A and C, the plant has been used to treat burns, bites, and wounds. *Sedum* from the Latin "to sit," and *lanceolatum* describes the lance-like leaf shape.

ONE-FLOWERED WINTERGREEN
(ONE-FLOWERED PYROLA)

Moneses uniflora • Ericaceae (Heath Family)
(Synonym: *Pyrola uniflora*)

FIELD DESCRIPTION:

Perennial herb, 2-6" tall on single upright stem. Leaves mostly basal, oval to round, toothed, not leathery, 1-2" long. Flowers white, single, five-petaled and waxy with 10-stamens, flower center prominent green rounded ovary, fragrant, and nodding deeply. Fruit is a 5-angled capsule.

TIDBITS

A dainty wildflower found in dry to moist spruce forests. Because the plant spreads from underground roots, it is common to find two or more plants within a few feet of each other. The deep green, serrated, round basal leaves are often more noticeable than the nodding flower-head. You will very commonly find One-Flowered Wintergreen in the company of other Ericaceae, especially One-Sided Wintergreen (*Orthilia secunda*) whose leaves are similar. *Moneses* from the Greek for "one delight," hence another common name, Single Delight.

SUBALPINE
MONTANE

Flowering: June - August

Habitat: Moist, shady coniferous forests, montane to subalpine

Thumbnail photo: Yellowstone NP, July (W. Tilt); Reference photo: Snohomish Co., WA, June (Ben Legler); Illustration: USDA-NRCS Plants Database

Orthilia secunda • Ericaceae (Heath Family)
(Synonym: *Pyrola secunda*)

ONE-SIDED WINTERGREEN
(SIDEBELLS PYROLA)

FIELD DESCRIPTION:

Perennial evergreen herb, 2-6" tall. White to pale green urn-shaped, five-petaled flowers, each with projecting style, are arranged along one side of bent stalk in a raceme. Leaves thin, elliptical to roundish, with finely toothed margins. Leaves appear basal but are alternate on lower stem. Fruits are round, five-chambered capsules with persistent styles.

SUBALPINE
MONTANE

Flowering: June - August
Habitat: Coniferous forests, montane to subalpine

Thumbnail photo: South Leigh Creek, ID, August (W. Tilt); Reference photo: Mt. Blackmore, MT, August (W. Tilt); Illustration: USDA-NRCS Plants Database

TIDBITS

The common name is apt and its one-sided flower stalks are distinctive. Leaves remain green throughout the winter, hence the "wintergreen" title. The plant also attracts attention by its habit of growing in large numbers around the base of Engelmann Spruce. One-Sided Wintergreen is circumboreal, found throughout much of the northern hemisphere. Herbalists use the plant for gynecological disorders and inflammations. *Orthilia* denotes straight or upright in reference to the style, and *secunda* is a reference to the plant's one-sided inflorescence.

PINK WINTERGREEN
(PINK PYROLA)

Pyrola asarifolia • Ericaceae (Heath Family)
(Synonym: *Pyrola rotundifolia*)

FIELD DESCRIPTION:

N

Perennial evergreen herb, 4-12" tall, with leathery, shiny leaves and nodding pink-purplish, five-petaled flowers. Flower stems are single and leafless. Flowers are cup-shaped with long curved styles, typically 10-25 in an elongated cluster, facing downward. Round to elliptical leaves, often round-toothed, are arranged in basal rosettes. Fruits are round, five-chambered capsules with persistent curved styles.

SUBALPINE
MONTANE
FOOTHILLS

Flowering: June - August

Habitat: Moist wooded sites, foothills to subalpine

TIDBITS

Pink Wintergreen often grows in colonies of large, shiny green mats of leaves. The plants may be obscured by taller vegetation in boggy meadows or they may be more conspicuous in moist open forests. *Pyrola* species have traditionally been used for a range of herbal and medicinal use, including as an astringent, diuretic and anti-spasmodic. *Pyrola* from the Latin for "pear tree" in reference to the resemblance of Pyrola's basal leaves to those of a pear. Recently reclassified from Pyrolaceae to the Ericaceae.

Photos: Boulder River, MT, July (W. Tilt); Illustration: USDA-NRCS Plants Database

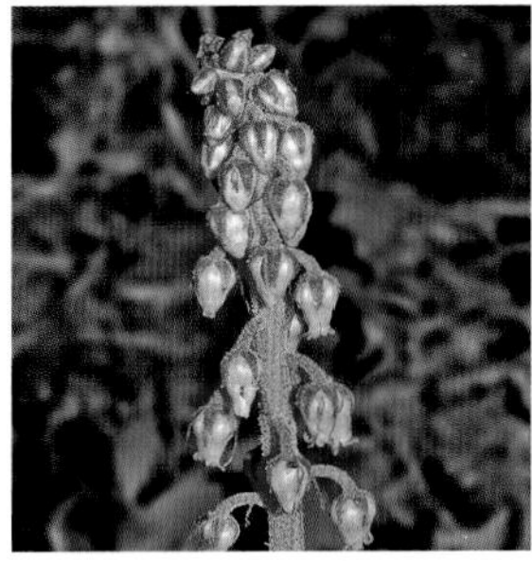

FIELD DESCRIPTION:

Upright perennial herb, 6-44" tall, with yellow, pliable stems when very young and then reddish brown, stiff, unbranched stems. Flowers pale yellow, vase-shaped, and five-petaled on curved stalks pointing down. Leaves are alternate and reduced to scales along stem. Fruits are spherical capsules.

MONTANE

Flowering: June - August

Habitat: Coniferous forests montane

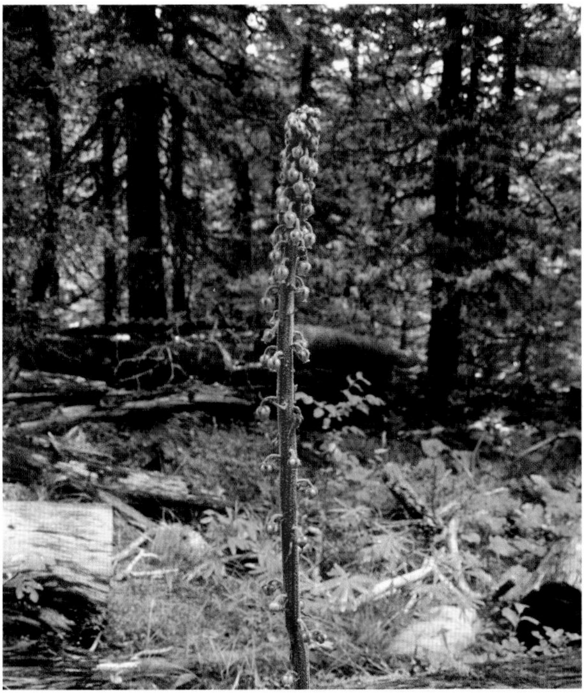

Photo: Big Hole Range, ID, June (W. Tilt); Illustration: USDA-NRCS Plants Database

TIDBITS

Conspicuously standing amid the greens and browns of the forest floor, Pinedrops are parasites, obtaining their nutrients from mycorrhizal fungi associated with neighboring tree roots. Indian Pipe (*Monotropa uniflora*) and Pinesap (*Monotropa hypopitys*) are other parasites that have white fleshy stems that become black with age. Once considered "saprophytes," living off decaying organic matter, it has now been established that they are "epi-parasites," living off fungi which in turn consume living and non-living material. *Pterospora* from the Greek for "winged seeds," and *andromedea* for "male genitals."

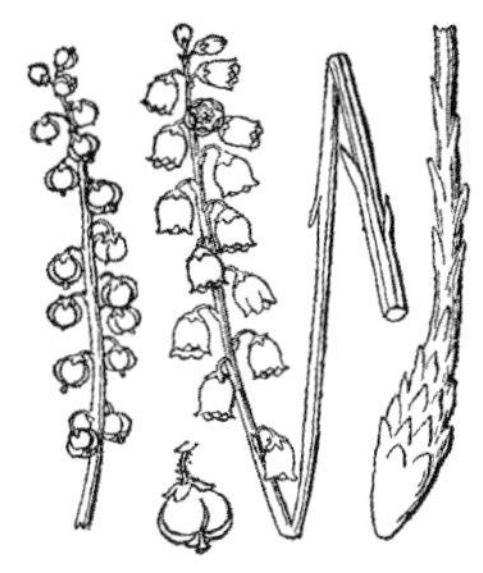

LEAFY SPURGE

Euphorbia esula • Euphorbiaceae (Spurge Family)

FIELD DESCRIPTION:

Perennial herb, 1-3' tall, with a heavy root system. Small, greenish, cuplike flowers are framed by a pair of conspicuous yellow-green, heart-shaped bracts. Flowers are arranged in an umbel. Leaves are alternate and narrow. Stem and leaves exude a milky latex sap. Seeds borne in smooth thee-lobed capsules.

TIDBITS

Native to Europe, Leafy Spurge was introduced to North America in the early 1800s and is now distributed across most of the northern United States. Leafy Spurge displaces native vegetation by aggressive use of available water and nutrients and production of plant toxins that prevent growth of other plants around it. Rootstalks penetrate deep into soil and the plant is capable of reproducing vegetatively as well as by seeds. Milky sap can cause rashes and blisters on exposed skin. Plant is toxic to many animals, though sheep are able to eat it and are often used as control agents. Leafy Spurge is considered a noxious weed throughout the Rocky Mountain region.

MONTANE
VALLEYS-FOOTHILLS

Flowering: May - June

Habitat: Disturbed soils in fields, pastures, roadsides and waterways, valleys to montane

Thumbnail photo: Butte Co., ID, August (Matt Lavin); Reference photo: Bozeman, MT, June (W. Tilt); Illustration: USDA-NRCS Plants Database

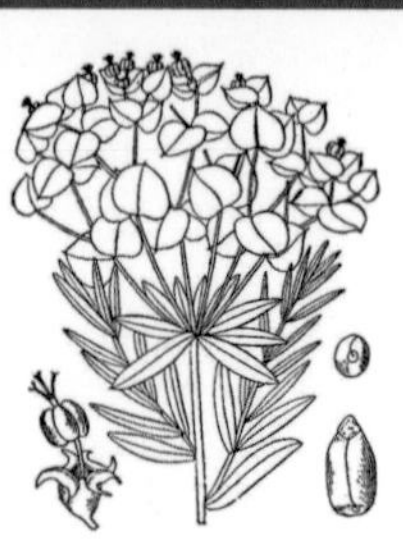

Astragalus adsurgens • Fabaceae (Pea Family)

PRAIRIE MILKVETCH
(STANDING MILKVETCH)

FIELD DESCRIPTION:

Long-lived perennial, stems to 18" tall, erect. Leaves to 5" long, leaflets 15-23, to 1" long and 0.3" wide, oblong to elliptic. Peduncles to 6" long. Racemes 16-50 flowered, flowers erect. Pedicels very short. Calyx less than 0.5" long, short-cylindrical, hairy. Flowers to slightly over 0.5" long, pink purple. Pods erect, sessile, ovoid-oblong, to 0.5" long and 0.2" thick, with 2 valves.

MONTANE
PLAINS

Flowering: May - August

Habitat: Gravelly sites, bare rock, stony soils, river banks, dry hillsides, plains to montane

TIDBITS

Prairie Milkvetch is wide-ranging through western North America as well as widely dispersed in Asia. Decumbent stems symmetrically radiating from a central point combined with a spike-like flowering or fruiting head is distinctive of this species. As true for most milkvetches, the pod is the most useful feature in identifying species. The flower may be the most conspicuous but is of little assistance in identifying *Astragalus* species. *Adsurens* from the Latin for "rising upward."

Photos: Bozeman, MT, July, (Matt Lavin); Seedpods on right

FIELD MILKVETCH

Astragalus agrestis • Fabaceae (Pea Family)

FIELD DESCRIPTION:

Perennial herb, 3-13" tall, spreading from rhizomes. Sparsely to moderately hairy. Stems erect or sprawling often in clumps. Leaves to 4" long, leaflets 13-23, narrowly elliptic to lance-shaped, hairy both sides. Peduncles to 6" long. Racemes 5-15 flowered, the flowers erect. Flowers to 1" long, pink purple, light yellow-white, or almost white.

TIDBITS

Field Milkvetch has tight clusters of ascending flowers, tightly packed clusters of erect seed pods, and habit of spreading over large areas via rhizomes. These characteristics help distinguish Field Milkvetch from other *Astragalus*, one of the largest genera in North America with more than 500 taxa. *Astragalus* from the Greek for "ankle bone," possibly a reference to Ancient Greeks using rattling bones for dice and the rattling of dry *Astragalus* seeds in the pod. A large number of milkvetch species are potentially toxic, producing nitrotoxins, alkaloids, or by accumulating selenium.

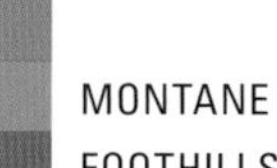

Flowering: May - September

Habitat: Meadows and openings in sagebrush and aspen forests, foothills to montane

Photos: Bozeman, MT, June (Matt Lavin); Illustration: USDA-NRCS Plants Database

FIELD DESCRIPTION:

Pubescent perennial, 1-10" tall, from rhizomes, often forming dense colonies. Stems decumbent to ascending. Leaves to 6" long, leaflets 15-26, 3-8" long, 0.1-0.4" wide. Ovate to elliptic or oblong, short appressed hairs above and below. Peduncles 1-6" long. Racemes 5-17 flowered, the flowers erect to sometimes declined, flowers to 0.5" long pinkish-purple. Pods drooping, hairy, with one or more grooves running lengthwise.

ALPINE
SUBALPINE
MONTANE

Flowering: June - September

Habitat: Meadows, wet areas, open forests, montane to alpine

TIDBITS

Alpine Milkvetch is considered one the most common and widely distributed species of *Astragalus* in North America and the world. Although the plant and its flowers are small, it is relatively easy to spot because it is often found in large colonies and there are numerous colorful flowers on each stalk. Alpine Milkvetch's attractive flowers range through shades of purple combined with white. Leaflets typically arch, have no tendrils, and are not present on the flower stalk.

Photos: Teton Co., WY, September (Matt Lavin); Illustration: USDA-NRCS Plants Database

DRUMMOND'S MILKVETCH

Astragalus drummondii • Fabaceae (Pea Family)

FIELD DESCRIPTION:

Bushy perennial herb, 16-36" tall, with woolly foliage, giving the plant a gray-green color. White-cream, drooping flowers are arranged in a dense, elongate raceme. Pinnately compound leaves are alternate, gray-green with 13-31 oblong leaflets. Leaflets entire with fine hairs on underside. Stems thick and hairy. Flowers give rise to hairless pods, 0.6 to 1.5" long, straight or curved.

MONTANE
FOOTHILLS

Flowering: June - August

Habitat: Dry slopes, foothills to lower montane

TIDBITS

Showy flowers draw one's attention to Drummond's Milkvetch, one of the many *Astragalus* found in the Rocky Mountain region. Distinguishing individual species of *Astragalus* is challenging and close examination of the pods is often necessary to determine the exact species. Alkaloids in milkvetches produce crazed behavior in livestock, and hence they are also commonly known as "locoweed." *Astragalus* from the Greek for "anklebone," in reference to the shape of seed pods or perhaps a reference to rattling bones uses for dice and the rattling of dry *Astragalus* seeds in their pods.

Photos: Bozeman, MT, June (W. Tilt); Illustration: USDA-NRCS Plants Database

Astragalus gilviflorus • Fabaceae (Pea Family)

PLAINS MILKVETCH

FIELD DESCRIPTION:

Perennial herb, 3-7" tall, with no stems forming dense low mats. Pea-shaped flowers are white-to-yellowish with purple-tipped keel. Keel shorter than wings. Leaves silvery-gray with 3 leaflets and pair of thin membranous sharp-pointed stipules at base. Pods are flat silky-hairy, leathery, stalkless, rounded to oval in cross-section.

VALLEYS-FOOTHILLS

Flowering: May - July

Habitat: Hillsides and other dry open areas, valleys and foothills

Photos: Bozeman, MT, June (W. Tilt)

TIDBITS

Plains Milkvetch forms a low cushion of white flowers interspersed amid silver-gray leaves. Astragalus is a large group of plants, and distinguishing individual species can be a challenge as there are many similar-looking species, and the seed pods are often the most distinctive identifier. A number of the milkvetches accumulate selenium to potentially toxic levels, depending on the soils where they grow. Livestock and wildlife consuming these plants in sufficient amounts are known to exhibit "crazy" behaviors that give rise to the common names "locoweed" or "crazyweed."

TIMBER MILKVETCH
(WEEDY MILKVETCH)

Astragalus miser • Fabaceae (Pea Family)

FIELD DESCRIPTION:

Trailing to erect perennial, 4-14" tall. Leaves are alternate, mostly from base, with narrow oblanceolate leaflets. Stipules present and joined around stem. White, pea-like flowers in loose clusters with a prominent purple-pink pointed keel tip that is distinctive. Fruits are stalkless, laterally compressed, hanging pods.

TIDBITS

Timber Milkvetch is a highly variable species. In spite of its common name, the species prefers open sites at upper elevations. Certain populations of this plant, as well as certain other *Astragalus* species, contain miserotoxin. While some populations are apparently innocuous, others have sufficient miserotoxin to cause sickness and death in cattle and sheep. Early signs of poisoning are the development of a placid, stupefied state, excessive frothy salivation, and increasing incoordination. There are reports of honeybees foraging on Timber Milkvetch flowers being poisoned as well.

SUBALPINE
MONTANE
FOOTHILLS

Flowering: May - July

Habitat: Moist to dry soils in meadows and ridges, foothills to subalpine

Photos: Bozeman, MT, June & September (Matt Lavin); Seedpods at left

WILD LICORICE

FIELD DESCRIPTION:

Erect, branching perennial herb, 1-3′ tall, with sticky stems. Leaves are alternate, pinnately compound, with 7-15 lance-shaped leaflets. Leaflets have sessile glands that appear as dots under magnification. Mature stems often reddish. Pea-like, yellowish-white flowers arise from the leaf axils in dense racemes. Seed pods are large, obvious, brown, bur-like, and armed with hooked bristles.

MONTANE

VALLEYS-FOOTHILLS

Flowering: June - August

Habitat: Disturbed soils along river bottoms and other moist areas, valleys to lower montane

TIDBITS

Wild Licorice readily colonizes disturbed soils and its bur-like seed pods readily attach themselves to you and your pets. The roots are edible and contain glycyrrhizin, with a taste sweeter than sugar. The root has been used both for medicinal uses and flavoring. When roasted, roots of Wild Licorice are reported to taste like sweet potato and certain Native American tribes chewed the root for its sweetness and to keep the mouth moist. The generic name *Glycyrrhiza* from the Greek for "sweet root."

Photos: Paradise Valley, July (W. Tilt); Illustration: USDA-NRCS Plants Database

NORTHERN SWEETVETCH

Hedysarum boreale • Fabaceae (Pea Family)

FIELD DESCRIPTION:

Reclining to erect perennial herb, 2-3′ tall, with leafy, gray-hairy stems. Flowers are pink-purple, arranged in elongated racemes. Keel petals longer than wing petals. Leaves are alternate, pinnately divided into 7-13 oblong leaflets. Leaves often hairy, especially on lower surface, at times glandular. Pair of brown, leathery stipules found at base of leaf. Fruits are flattened, wrinkled pods (loments) with constrictions around individual seeds.

MONTANE

Flowering: May - August

Habitat: Open, partial shaded slopes, montane

TIDBITS

Northern Sweetvetch is also known as Plains Sweetbroom, suggesting its use to sweep out dwellings, leaving a fresh smell behind. The young roots of Northern Sweetvetch can be eaten for their sweet, licorice taste, and they are enjoyed by grizzly bears and other wildlife in the spring, hence one of its other common names, Bear Root. The plant may be appropriate for range restoration given its nitrogen-fixing ability. The plant is highly variable in form, particularly in flower size and the amount of pubescence. *Hedysarum* from the Greek *hedys* for "sweet."

Thumbnail photo: Bozeman, MT, June (Matt Lavin);
Reference photo: Butte, ID, June (Matt Lavin);
Illustration: USDA-NRCS Plants Database

Hedysarum sulphurescens • Fabaceae (Pea Family)

WHITE SWEETVETCH
(YELLOW SWEETVETCH)

FIELD DESCRIPTION:

Bushy, highly branched perennial herb, 1-2' tall. The white-to-cream, pea-like flowers are arranged in long, showy racemes. Leaves are alternate, pinnately divided into 9 or more oblong dark green leaflets. Leaflets are prominently veined and sharp pointed. Stipules present and membranous. The fruit is a flattened pod, containing 2-4 seeds, with constrictions (loments) between each seed. Edges of seeds narrowly winged.

SUBALPINE
MONTANE
VALLEYS-FOOTHILLS

Flowering: June - August

Habitat: Dry to moderately moist soils in open or lightly shaded areas, valleys to subalpine

TIDBITS

White Sweetvetch is a common member of the Pea Family with distinctive pea flowers, conspicuous veins on underside of leaflets, and pods resembling a flattened string of beads. The jointed seed pod is distinctive to *Hedysarum*. Unlike the American Vetch (*Vicia americana*), White Sweetvetch does not have tendrils at the end of its leaves and has an upright form rather than sprawling. The plant is a favorite of bears, which dig up the roots early in the season. The young roots of sweetvetch can be eaten for their sweet licorice taste.

Thumbnail photo: Bozeman, MT, July (Matt Lavin); Reference photo: Slough Creek, MT, July (W. Tilt); Seedpod: Bozeman, MT, January (Matt Lavin)

BIRDSFOOT TREFOIL
(BIRDFOOT DEER-VETCH)

Lotus corniculatus • Fabaceae (Pea Family)

FIELD DESCRIPTION:

Low-growing perennial, with stems that can reach 2' long. Flowers bright yellow pea-like, red-tinged, and clustered in groups of 3-15 in umbels. Leaves are alternate, finely toothed, pinnately compound, divided into 5 leaflets. Top 3 leaflets shaped like a bird's foot and 2 leaflets at base of leaf stalk. Stems and leaves can be hairless to long-hairy. Fruits are brown-black cylindrical pods, persistent style at apex, in head-like clusters.

TIDBITS

Introduced from Europe, Birdsfoot Trefoil is widely distributed across the United States. Its bright yellow flowers arising from low green foliage is a common mid-summer sight along roadways. At first glance the plant's leaves resemble clover, but a closer inspection reveals 5 rather than 3 leaflets. In small quantities the plant is reported to stimulate respiration and improve digestion. In larger quantities Birdfoot Trefoil is poisonous, capable of causing respiratory failure and death.

VALLEYS-FOOTHILLS

Flowering: May - September

Habitat: Disturbed soils, along roads and sidewalks, valleys to foothills

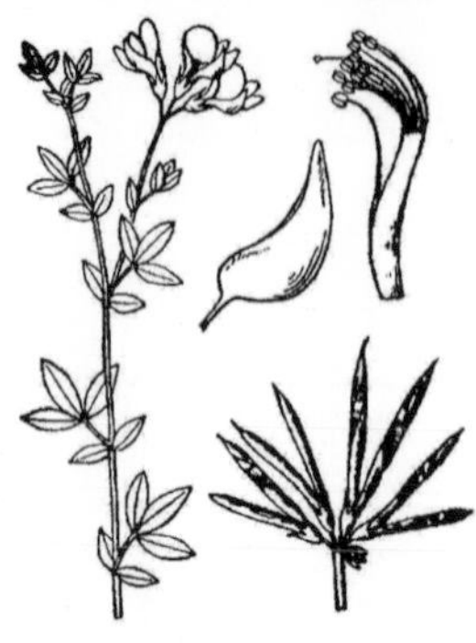

Photos: Bozeman, MT, July (W. Tilt); Illustration: USDA-NRCS Plants Database

Lupinus argenteus • Fabaceae (Pea Family)

SILVERY LUPINE

FIELD DESCRIPTION:

Perennial herb, to 36" tall, with one-to-several, occasionally branched stems, covered with hairs and topped with long, showy spikes of flowers. Flowers blue-to-purple, sometimes pink, at times white or bi-colored; whorled, in conical clusters, atop stems, clusters to over 12" long. Leaves are alternate, stalked, palmately compound, and silvery-green. Leaves, stems, seedpods, and sepals are silver-hairy. Seeds in hairy pods.

Flowering: May - July

Habitat: Dry slopes, sagebrush, meadows and woodlands, from valleys to montane

Thumbnail photos: Bozeman, MT, July (Matt Lavin); Reference photo: Slough Creek, MT, July (W. Tilt); Illustration: USDA-NRCS Plants Database

TIDBITS

An iconic wildflower of the West, Silvery Lupine is one of the most common of the *Lupinus* species found in the region; all readily identifiable as lupine, but identified to the species level only with patience. To confuse matters more, lupines readily hybridize. *Lupinus* (Latin for "wolf") was named because of the mistaken belief that the species degraded land. *Argenteus* from the Latin for "silvery." Wild lupines have been known to cause fatalities in domestic livestock and can be poisonous to humans if taken internally. The young leaves, seeds, and pods are especially toxic.

SILKY LUPINE
(BLUE-BONNET LUPINE)

Lupinus sericeus • Fabaceae (Pea Family)

FIELD DESCRIPTION:

Perennial herb, 8-24" tall, with silky-hairy herbage. Typically, several solid stems arise from plant base. Leaves divided into 5 to 9 narrow leaflets, all originating from one point, like fingers on the palm of a hand (palmate leaf arrangement). Leaflets are covered with long, flat-lying hair on both the upper and lower surfaces. Flowers in whorls along an erect flowering stalk. Petals vary from whitish to bluish tinged and the calyx is silky and without a pronounced spur. Each flower is about 0.5" long with a large upper banner petal, 2 lateral wing petals, and 2 lower keel petals that are fused along the lower edge. The banner petal is distinctly upturned and hairy on its back surface. Fruits are silky pods, about 1" long, produced in late summer, containing 3-6 seeds each.

TIDBITS

Silky Lupine is 1 of 8 or more species of *Lupinus* found in the Yellowstone region, all readily identifiable as lupine, but more difficult to identify to the species level. Silky Lupine is very similar in appearance to Silvery Lupine (*L. argenteus*) but Silvery Lupine is typically larger and its banner petal is hairless and less-strongly upturned. The plant is an important pollen and nectar source for hummingbirds, native bees, and other pollinators. A variety of wildlife, including marmots, eat the plant but it is toxic to cattle and sheep. The young leaves, seeds and pods can be especially toxic.

MONTANE

Flowering: May - August

Habitat: Meadows, grasslands and open forest, montane

Thumbnail photo: Wallowa Co. OR,, July (Gerald D. Carr); Reference & detail photos: Butte Co., ID, June (Matt Lavin)

Medicago sativa • Fabaceae (Pea Family)

ALFALFA
(LUCRENE)

FIELD DESCRIPTION:

Perennial herb, 2-3' tall, with 5-25 mostly erect stems per plant and a very deep taproot. Leaves are alternate, dark green, divided into 3 oblong leaflets (trifoliolate). Leaflets are usually hairy, thin-textured, and arranged pinnately. Stipules are narrow and lance-shaped. Purple-blue (rarely, pink or white) flowers are arranged in tight, rounded, stalked clusters arising from leaf axils. Fruit are many-seeded, net-veined pods coiled in 2-3 spirals.

VALLEYS-FOOTHILLS

Flowering: May - September

Habitat: : Cultivated or disturbed soils, valleys and foothills

TIDBITS

Alfalfa originated in southwestern Asia and is believed to have first been cultivated over 3,000 years ago in Media (present day northwest Iran). The genus *Medicago* reflects that origin. The plant was introduced into the United States in 1736 and is eaten by domestic livestock and a wide range of wildlife. As forage, it is very nutritious, producing more protein per acre than most other crops. It also provides important cover for nesting waterfowl and other birds. Alfalfa is a legume capable of fixing nitrogen, aiding the condition of cultivated soils.

Photos: Bozeman, MT, August (W. Tilt); Illustration: USDA-NRCS Plants Database

YELLOW SWEET CLOVER

Melilotus officinalis • Fabaceae (Pea Family)

FIELD DESCRIPTION:

Highly branched annual or biennial herb that grows up to 9′ tall. Small, yellow, flowers are arranged in tall narrow, terminal clusters. Leaves are alternate, divided into 3 lanceolate, glabrous, finely toothed green leaflets, arranged in pinnate fashion. Fruits are pods with cross-corrugated markings.

TIDBITS

A native of Eurasia, the plant has a sweet smell, giving off the scent of fresh-mown pasture when dried. Sweet clover contains coumarin that converts to dicoumarol (a powerful anticoagulant) when the plant becomes moldy. This can lead to internal hemorrhaging and death in livestock. The leaves can be dried and used as an insect repellent. Yellow and White Sweet Clover (*Meilotus alba*) are commonly considered to be the same species and both provide an important nectar source for bees.

VALLEYS-FOOTHILLS

Flowering: May - October

Habitat: Disturbed soils in pastures and along roads, valleys to foothills

Photos: Butte Co., ID, June (Matt Lavin); Illustration: USDA-NRCS Plants Database

Oxytropis lagopus • Fabaceae (Pea Family)

RABBITFOOT CRAZYWEED

FIELD DESCRIPTION:

Cushioned perennial herb, 3-6" tall. Leaves basal, divided into paired lanceolate leaflets, usually covered with fine silky hairs. Bright, rose-purple, pea-like flowers form dense racemes borne at the ends of leafless stalks. Fruits are oblong pods with long hairs covered by the inflated calyx.

MONTANE
VALLEYS

Flowering: May - June

Habitat: Well-drained soils of sagebrush flats, valleys to lower montane

Thumbnail photo: Bozeman, MT, June (W. Tilt); Reference photo: Bozeman, MT, June (W. Tilt); Seedpods: Bozeman, MT, June (Matt Lavin)

TIDBITS

Crazyweeds are also known as "locoweeds." As these names suggest, this group of plants can cause a number of problems in domestic livestock, resulting in abnormal behaviors, many linked to the toxic effects of the plants. Locoweeds contain swainsonine, an alkaloid that disrupts cellular functions. The generic name, *Oxytropis*, is derived from the Greek meaning "sharp keel," in reference to the sharp beak at the tip of the lowest 2 united petals (keel) of the flower. *Lagopus* is derived from the Greek meaning "hare's foot."

SILKY LOCOWEED
(WHITEPOINT CRAZYWEED)

Oxytropis sericea • Fabaceae (Pea Family)

FIELD DESCRIPTION:

Perennial herb with long, silky hair covering its foliage. Flowering stems are 2-12" high. Its leaves, 4-10" long, are divided into 7 to 17 leaflets that are oblong in outline. Each leaflet is 0.5-1 inch long. Clusters of 6 to 25 white-to-pale yellow flowers are produced at the tops of leafless flowering stems. Each flower is 0.5-1" long and has a typical pea flower structure. Seedpods are erect and crowded together at the tops of flowering stems. Pods are about 0.75" long, thick-walled, and rigid.

ALPINE
SUBALPINE
MONTANE

Flowering: May - July

Habitat: Open sites ranging from grasslands to ridges and slopes, montane to alpine

TIDBITS

As "locoweed" and "crazyweed" suggest, *Oxytropis* and kin can cause a number of problems in domestic livestock. There are reports of sheep and cattle becoming chemically addicted to the plant, eating it even when grass is abundant, resulting in weight loss and abortions. Horses can be even harder hit by the plant's toxic effects. Mountain Crazyweed (*O. campestris*) is similar in appearance to Silky Locoweed and difficult to distinguish from Silky Locoweed unless mature pods are present. Plant is also known as Point Vetch because of the beak at the end of the keel petals.

Photos: Bozeman, MT, July (Matt Lavin); Seedpods: Big Horn, WY, June (Matt Lavin)

GOLDENBANNER
(FALSE LUPINE, GOLDENPEA)

FIELD DESCRIPTION:

Erect perennial herb, to 3′ tall, spreading by rhizomes. Leaves are alternate, compound, divided into 3 narrowly oval leaflets. Two large, leaf-like stipules are present. Yellow pea-like flowers, 0.25-0.5″ long, 5-50 in dense raceme. Flower spikes arise from leaf axils. Spreads by rhizomes. Fruits are long-curving, thin, blue-green, and downy-hairy.

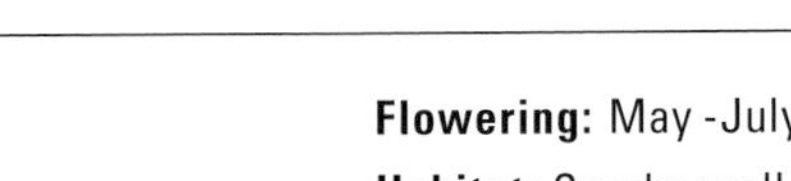

MONTANE
VALLEYS

Flowering: May -July

Habitat: Sandy, well-drained soils, valleys to montane

Thumbnail & reference photos: Willow Creek, MT, June (W. Tilt); Seedpods: Phillips Co., MT, June (Matt Lavin)

TIDBITS

Goldenbanner is an attractive plant considered a weed by some due to its unpalatable foliage and its tendency to crowd out other plants. It grows quickly after snow melt, and by late spring large colonies are in bloom. The plant is sometimes called "False Lupine" because of its superficial resemblance to lupines; its genus even recognizes this similarity. *Thermopsis* translates from the Greek as "lupine-similar." The leaves of Goldenbanner are trifoliate, comprising three leaflets, while lupine's leaves have 5-9 leaflets. *Montana* from the Latin for "relating to mountains."

RED & WHITE CLOVER

Trifolium sp. • Fabaceae (Pea Family)

FIELD DESCRIPTION:

Red Clover ***(Trifolium pretense)*** is a short-lived perennial herb, 6-20" tall. Leaves are trifoliolate, divided into 3 broad, egg-shaped leaflets, which are subtly variegated. Leaves on stalks with lance-like stipules at base. Rose-red flower-heads are made up of 50 to 200 small, narrow flowers. One or more large thrice cut bracts subtend the flower-heads. Fruits are small pods containing 1-2 kidney-shaped seeds.

White Clover ***(Trifolium repens)*** is a perennial, up to 12" tall. Plants glabrous throughout or with scattered hairs. Stems creeping and often rooting at nodes, rarely erect. Leaves are alternate, divided into 3 egg-shaped leaflets with long petioles. Leaflets up to 1" long, margins with slight serrations to nearly entire, with a white blotch near the base. Flower-heads to 1" across, globular with long peduncles. Fruit 4-5 seeded pods.

TIDBITS

Red Clover is one of several clover species introduced from Europe to the United States in the 1800s and now widespread across the region.

White Clover, another introduced clover, is a low growing plant with smaller flower-heads arising from the leaf axils of prostrate stems. Commonly found in lawns.

A wide range of animals from horses and elk to grizzly bears and bees feed on clover. In addition to introduced clovers, there are a number of native clovers, such as the Uinta Clover (*T. dasyphyllum*), that are found in the subalpine and alpine zones.

SUBALPINE
MONTANE
VALLEYS

Flowering: May - July

Habitat: Roadsides, fields, fences, and other disturbed sites, valleys to subalpine

Thumbnail photo (*T. pretence*): Bozeman, MT, June (W. Tilt); Reference photo (*T. repens*): Bozeman, MT, July (Matt Lavin); Inset of leaf (*T. pretense*): Bozeman, MT, June (Matt Lavin)

Vicia americana • Fabaceae (Pea Family)

AMERICAN VETCH

FIELD DESCRIPTION:

Prostrate to ascending or climbing perennial herb, 6-30" tall. Four to 10 reddish-purple to blue-purple flowers are arranged in loose clusters (racemes) on stalks arising from leaf axils. Leaves are alternate, pinnately compound. The 8-18 leaflets are variable in size and shape but typically elliptical to oblong. Fruits borne in flat, hairless pods containing 2 or more brown peas. Tendrils arising from ends allow the plant to grip surrounding vegetation.

MONTANE

Flowering: June - August

Habitat: Fields and prairie and open woods, montane

TIDBITS

Found intermixed with other plants, American Vetch is a legume and provides forage for a range of wildlife and livestock. The plant is commonly used to help restore lands as part of mining reclamation or other habitat remediation efforts. There are a number of varieties of American Vetch as well as similar-looking species. The name "vetch" is applied to members of several genera of the Pea Family. *Vicia* is thought to be derived from the Latin for "to bind," in reference to the climbing habit of these plants.

Thumbnail photo: Bozeman, MT, June (Matt Lavin); Reference photo: Bozeman, MT, June (W. Tilt) ; Illustration: USDA-NRCS Plants Database

GREEN GENTIAN
(MONUMENT-PLANT)

Frasera speciosa • Gentianaceae (Gentian Family)

FIELD DESCRIPTION:

Monocarpic perennial herb with large basal rosette and a flowing stalk to 7′ tall. Leaves hairy-to-glabrous, basal leaves to 2′ long and 4″ wide, spatulate or elliptic-oblong to oblanceolate. Stem leaves much reduced in size upward, lanceolate to oblanceolate. Inflorescence a stout raceme comprising numerous whorls of flowers, each subtended by leaf-like bracts. Flowers pale green-to-white with purple dots; 4 spreading petals with 2 glands at base. Fruit is a oblong capsule, up to 0.8″ long.

ALPINE
SUBALPINE
MONTANE

Flowering: June - August

Habitat: Open slopes and woods, montane to alpine

TIDBITS

Green Gentian grows 20-60 years in a low, vegetative stage, consisting of just a basal rosette. The plant then erupts into the "monument" phase, developing a 4-7′ stalk bearing dozens of flowers that produce 60 seeds each to give rise to the next generation. The dried stalk persists through winter. Plants with life cycles such as Green Gentian are called "monocarpic," growing for many years without flowering, then flowering and dying after the seeds develop. *Frasera* recognizes John Fraser, 18th century nurseryman and botanist. *Speciosa* from the Latin for "showy."

Photos: Driggs ID, June (W. Tilt); Basal rosette, at left

ARCTIC GENTIAN
(WHITE GENTIAN)

FIELD DESCRIPTION:

Tufted perennial, 2-8" tall, with showy flower clusters. Basal leaves up to 5" long and linear. Stem leaves smaller, opposite, lance-shaped with bases joined. Flowers are relatively large (1.5-2" tall), white-to greenish-white petals with 5 pointed lobes with pleats in between fused into a funnel. Flowers are streaked and blotched with purple on the outside and purplish dots on inside.

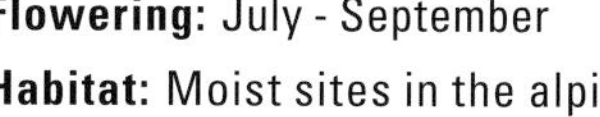

ALPINE

Flowering: July - September

Habitat: Moist sites in the alpine

TIDBITS

This denizen of the region's alpine zone is found across the far northern tundra as well. Arctic Gentian can be abundant over large areas of moist alpine meadows. The flower is almost as tall as the entire plant. Gentians are named after King Gentius of ancient Illyria in Greece, who is said to have discovered the medicinal value of these plants to help cure intestinal maladies. Recognizing this plant's favored climates, *algida* derives from Latin meaning "cold."

Thumbnail photo: SW Colorado, August (Al Schneider); Reference photo: Sierra Nervada Range, NV, August (Jane Richardson, Wikipedia Commons); Illustration: Karl Urban, Umatilla National Forest, OR

NORTHERN GENTIAN
(PLEATED GENTIAN)

Gentianella amarella • Gentianaceae (Gentian Family)
(Synonym: *Gentiana amarella*)

FIELD DESCRIPTION:

Delicate, slender, annual herb with ascending stems growing up to 16" high. Leaves opposite, lanceolate, 0.5-1.5" long, and stalkless. Flowers upright, arising from axils of upper leaves, tubular, 0.5-0.75" long; fine fringe of hair present inside the corolla tube. Flower has 5 pointed lobes and is typically lavender-purple blue in color; color can vary, and often has a greenish hue. Fruits are capsules containing numerous seeds.

SUBALPINE
MONTANE

Flowering: July - September

Habitat: Woodlands and meadows, montane to subalpine

TIDBITS

Barrel-shaped flowers in crowded clusters at tips of stem and branches range in color from pink to blue to purple mark the Northern Gentian. The plant is circumpolar in its distribution, as likely to be found in Iceland as Yellowstone. For hundreds of years, species of gentian were used to treat digestive ailments, fever and skin diseases. King Gentius of Illyria in Greece was reputed to have found the local gentians beneficial for curing malaria among his troops. Northern Gentian is still in use in the treatment of certain gastric disorders as well as use as an anti-inflammatory, an antiseptic, and a worming agent.

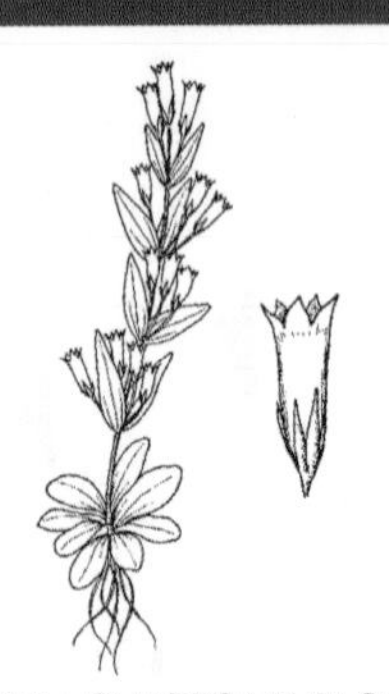

Photos: Slough Creek, MT, July (W. Tilt); Illustration: USDA-NRCS Plants Database

Gentianopsis thermalis • Gentianaceae (Gentian Family)
(Synonyms: *Gentianopsis detonsa, Gentiana detonsa*)

FIELD DESCRIPTION:

Showy annual, 4-12″ tall, with blue vase-like flowers arising from thin stems. Stem leaves opposite, oblong to lanceolate on short petioles. Deep blue-purple flowers are tubular, opening into 4 lobes, and the corolla is fringed along the upper rounded edge. Fruits are 2-valved capsules.

SUBALPINE
MONTANE

Flowering: July - September

Habitat: Moist soils in meadows, montane to subalpine

TIDBITS

Fringed Gentian's flowers untwist and unfold to greet the sun (hence the reference to a windmill). The genus *Gentianopsis* is distinct from *Gentiana* by the absence of pleats between the corolla lobes (see Arctic Gentian for comparison). As the number of synonyms suggests, there is disagreement on the classification of this gentian. The specific epithet *thermalis* (from the Greek for "warmth") references the hot springs of Yellowstone National Park where it can be found in abundance in the geyser basins and meadows. *Gentianopsis* from the Greek for "having the appearance of a Gentian."

Photos: Slough Creek, MT, July (W. Tilt)

RICHARDSON'S GERANIUM (WHITE GERANIUM)

Geranium richardsonii • Geraniaceae (Geranium Family)

FIELD DESCRIPTION:

Perennial herb, 12-40" tall, with large palmately-divided leaves. Flowers in open clusters rise above leaves. Individual flowers consist of 5 white-pinkish petals with distinctive purplish veins and hairs on the inner portion toward the base. Leaves basal and sparse along stem, oppositely or alternately arranged, with 5-7 deeply divided segments and coarsely toothed margins. Fruits are long-beaked, linear capsules.

SUBALPINE
MONTANE
FOOTHILLS

Flowering: June - August

Habitat: Moist woodlands, preferring partial shade, foothills to subalpine

TIDBITS

Sir John Richardson, an English surgeon and naturalist, contributed greatly to the natural history of the boreal and arctic regions of North America in the 1820s. This namesake geranium prefers moister and shadier areas as compared with Sticky Geranium (*Geranium viscosissimum*). The 2 plants may hybridize and produce pink rather than white or purplish flowers. Many species of the genus are referred to as "cranesbill" because of the long-beaked fruit.

Photos: Slough Creek, MT, July (W. Tilt); Illustration: USDA-NRCS Plants Database

STICKY GERANIUM

FIELD DESCRIPTION:

Sticky, glandular perennial herb, 16-36" tall, with bright pinkish-lavender to purple flowers (at times white). Flowers comprised of 5 broad petals with dark reddish purple veins, rounded to slightly notched. Leaves basal and sparse along stem, opposite or alternate, long-stalked, palmately cut more than three-fourths of their length into 5-7 segments with sharp irregular teeth along the edges. Fruits are long-beaked linear capsules.

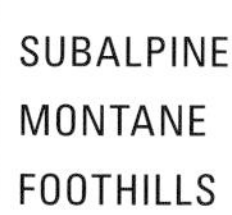

SUBALPINE
MONTANE
FOOTHILLS

Flowering: May - July

Habitat: Dry open areas, foothills to subalpine

TIDBITS

Glandular hairs on the sepals and leaf stems exude a sticky substance with a geranium odor that traps insects. When the petals fall off, the stigma and style elongate into a 1" long structure that resembles a crane's bill. Sticky Geranium prefers sagebrush and open woods as compared with the Richardson's Geranium which prefers moister and shadier habitats. The 2 plants may hybridize, producing pink rather than white or purplish flowers.

Photos: Slough Creek, MT, June (W. Tilt);
Illustration: Karl Urban, Umatilla NF, OR

BALLHEAD WATERLEAF

Hydrophyllum capitatum • Hydrophyllaceae (Waterleaf)

FIELD DESCRIPTION:

Low, hairy perennial herb, 4-14" tall, with blue-purple ball-headed flower cluster below a canopy of leaves. Dense, coiled flower cluster consists of individual cup-shaped flowers with 5 petals, 5 narrow, stiff-haired sepals, and 5 stamens that extend well past petals, giving the flower cluster an overall hairy appearance. Leaves are primarily basal, long-stalked, and pinnately divided in 5-7 leaflets with 2-3 pointed lobes.

TIDBITS

Ballhead Waterleaf is distinctive for its blue-purple bottlebrush flower residing beneath a canopy of green leaves. In bud, sepals and petals appear coarsely fuzzy, prompting the common name of "woollen-breeches." The Waterleaf Family contains several species that have flowers with a bushy bottlebrush appearance. *Hydrophyllum* from the Greek for "waterleaf" in reference to some species that have water-like blotches on their leaves. The leaves of Ballhead Waterleaf can catch and hold rainwater in their cavities and this may be the source of the common name.

SUBALPINE
MONTANE

Flowering: April - July

Habitat: Moist soils in thickets, woods and open areas, montane to subalpine

Thumbnail photos: Big Sky, MT, July (Rip McIntosh); Reference photo: Bozeman, MT, July (W. Tilt); Illustration: Karl Urban, Umatilla NF, OR

Phacelia franklinii • Hydrophyllaceae (Waterleaf)

FRANKLIN'S PHACELIA

FIELD DESCRIPTION:

Erect annual or biennial herb, 6-18" tall, with bluish-purple flower clusters arising from leaf axils. Arranged in dense coils, each flower has 5 petals fused into a tube with a white throat. Filaments extend beyond petals. Basal and alternate stem leaves are pinnately divided. Overall plant is generally hairy, glandular, and somewhat sticky.

MONTANE
FOOTHILLS

Flowering: June - July

Habitat: Dry open sites, often in gravelly soils, foothills to montane

Photos: Slough Creek, MT, June (W. Tilt); Illustration: USDA-NRCS Plants Database

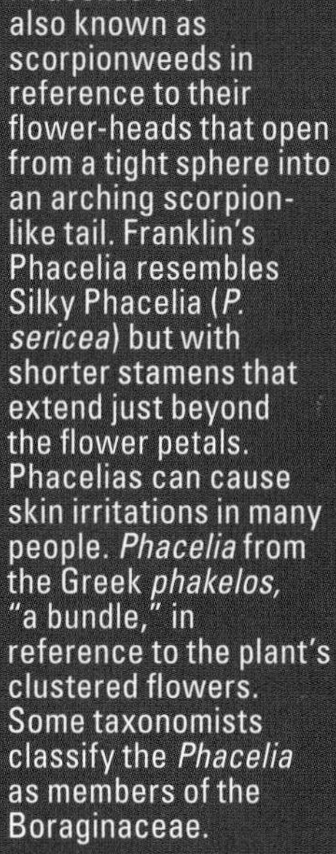

TIDBITS

Phacelias are also known as scorpionweeds in reference to their flower-heads that open from a tight sphere into an arching scorpion-like tail. Franklin's Phacelia resembles Silky Phacelia (*P. sericea*) but with shorter stamens that extend just beyond the flower petals. Phacelias can cause skin irritations in many people. *Phacelia* from the Greek *phakelos,* "a bundle," in reference to the plant's clustered flowers. Some taxonomists classify the *Phacelia* as members of the Boraginaceae.

SILVERLEAF PHACELIA
(PURPLE SCORPIONWEED)

Phacelia hastata • Hydrophyllaceae (Waterleaf Family)

FIELD DESCRIPTION:

Perennial herb, 6-15" tall, with silky-hairy leaves and stems that are trailing or almost erect, and a branched caudex. Basal leaves are lance-shaped, short-petioled, with entire margins and prominent veins, often lobed at base. Stem leaves are smaller. Purple-lavender to dull-white flowers are arranged in tight coil, five-parted with 5 broad petal lobes, 5 hairy sepals, and 5 long stamens expending past petals. Fruits are two-chambered capsules each containing 2 or more seeds.

ALPINE
SUBALPINE
MONTANE
FOOTHILLS

Flowering: May - July

Habitat: Dry open sites, often on disturbed soils, foothills to alpine

TIDBITS

The lance-shaped silver-hairy leaves and prominent veins distinguish Silverleaf Phacelia from other phacelias. Silverleaf Phacelia is known to hybridize with Varyleaf Phacelia (*P. heterophylla*), a similar-looking species that some taxonomists consider to be the same species, but can be distinguished by its branched caudex. All phacelias have bottlebrush-like flowers due to stamens protruding beyond the petals. Some taxonomists classify the *Phacelia* as members of the Boraginaceae. *Hastata* from the Latin for "spear-shaped."

Photos: Bozeman, MT, June (Matt Lavin); Illustration: USDA-NRCS Plants Database

THREADLEAF PHACELIA

FIELD DESCRIPTION:

Erect annual, 5-18" tall, with bluish-purple flower clusters and narrow leaves. Pale blue-pink-purple bowl-shaped flowers, in short-stalked clusters, comprising 5 petals with round lobes and pale throat. Five stamens about same length as petals. Leaves are alternate, linear, hairy, sometimes divided into narrow pointed lobes. Stems and leaves densely pubescent and plant generally single-stemmed or sometimes branched. Fruits are two-chambered capsules.

PLAINS-FOOTHILLS

Flowering: May - July

Habitat: Dry, sandy soils in open areas and parkland, plains to foothills

Photos: Bozeman, MT, June (W. Tilt); Illustration: USDA-NRCS Plants Database

TIDBITS

Threadleaf Phacelia's narrow leaves and relatively large open flower clusters distinguish it from other phacelias. All parts of the plant are hairy. Flower-heads first appear as tight spheres that gradually open outward with the sphere eventually uncoiling into an arching scorpion tail. Threadleaf Phacelia may form dense colonies in sandy soils, shrublands, and open woodlands. *Phacelia* from the Greek for "bundle" in reference to the plant's clustered flowers. *Linearis* references the plant's narrow leaves.

SILKY PHACELIA
(SILKY SCORPIONWEED)

Phacelia sericea • Hydrophyllaceae (Waterleaf Family)

FIELD DESCRIPTION:

Silky, silver-hairy herb, 5-16" tall, with purple, five-petaled flowers clustered in a terminal spike. Long, slender stamens with filaments and yellow-tipped anthers extend beyond edge of the corolla giving the inflorescence a fuzzy bottlebrush appearance. Basal leaves are a distinctive light green, pinnately cleft, forming a mat with stalk leaves smaller, alternate on shorter stems. The previous year's flower stalks may be present.

ALPINE
SUBALPINE
MONTANE
FOOTHILLS

Flowering: May - July

Habitat: Dry open sites, often on disturbed soils, foothills to alpine

TIDBITS

The genus *Phacelia* hosts some 150 species in North America, with Silky Phacelia one of the easiest to recognize. The inflorescence of Silky Phacelia comprises numerous, tightly packed flowers resembling a bottle-brush. The dark blue-to-purple corolla is hairy inside and out, and the filaments are 2-3 times as long as the corolla giving the inflorescence a fuzzy appearance. The anthers are bright yellow or orange, further accenting the flower's appearance. *Sericea* from the Greek for "silky," describes the plant's overall fine hairy appearance.

Photos: Slough Creek, MT, July (W. Tilt); Illustration: Karl Urban, Umatilla NF, OR

Hypericum formosum • Hypericaceae (St. Johnswort)
(Synonym: *Hypericum scouleri* ssp. *scouleri*)

WESTERN ST. JOHNSWORT

FIELD DESCRIPTION:

Low-growing, rhizomatous perennial with stems up to 8" high. Leaves opposite, stalkless (slightly clasping), egg-shaped to elliptic, 0.5-.075" long, dotted with black spots. Yellow, star-shaped, five-petaled flowers are about 0.75" in diameter and are also dotted with black, especially along the petal margins. Stamens conspicuous, 75-100 in number, and joined together at their bases into 3-5 groupings. Fruits are membranous capsules about 0.25" long.

ALPINE
SUBALPINE
MONTANE

Flowering: July - August

Habitat: Stream sides, wet meadows and forests, montane to alpine

Photos: Clackamus Co. OR, July (Gerald D. Carr); Inset: diagnostic perforations present on leaves of *H. perforatum*: Gallatin Co., MT, August (Matt Lavin)

TIDBITS

Western St. Johnswort is a slim and unobtrusive plant, often hidden in the lushness of wet areas. It is most easily found when it is in bloom, for its bright yellow flowers. Petal edges are often dotted in black. The non-native Common St. Johnswort (*H. perforatum*) is a similar-looking non-native plant that is considered a noxious weed in many states. *H. perforatum* may grow to 5' tall with numerous, rust-colored branches that are woody at the base, and the diagnostic characteristic of tiny, transparent perforations on the leaves, thus the species name. *H. perforatum* and other St. Johnsworts have long been used in herbalism to treat a range of maladies, including depression.

ROCKY MOUNTAIN IRIS
(WESTERN BLUEFLAG)

Iris missouriensis • Iridaceae (Iris Family)

FIELD DESCRIPTION:

Erect perennial herb, 8-24" tall, with pale-to-dark lavender-blue flowers resembling domesticated iris. Leaves basal, long narrow, parallel-veined, shorter than flower stem. Flower light-to-dark lavender-blue petals and 3 petal-like sepals that are bent backward with yellow-orange patch and dark blue-purple lines radiating outward. Fruit a three-celled capsule with 2 columns of seeds in each.

MONTANE
FOOTHILLS

Flowering: May - July

Habitat: Wet meadows and stream banks, foothills to montane

TIDBITS

Seeing Rocky Mountain Iris growing wild in a mountain meadow is a delight. The plant can be so abundant in certain meadows that the meadows appear from a distance to be blue water surfaces. The roasted seeds of Rocky Mountain Iris can be used as a coffee substitute. Roots and young shoots are toxic, though roots have been used medicinally to treat toothaches. Iris was the Greek goddess of the rainbow. *Missouriensis* refers to the Missouri River, along which it was first collected.

Photos: SW Colorado, June (Al Schneider); Illustration: USDA-NRCS Plants Database

Sisyrinchium montanum • Iridaceae (Iris Family)

BLUE-EYED GRASS

FIELD DESCRIPTION:

Erect perennial herb, 4-20" tall, with stiff, flattened, and winged stems. Leaves basal, linear grass-like, and folded lengthwise. Flowers are blue-purple with 6 pointed petals surrounding a yellow center. A large, leaf-like bract (spathe) initially encloses the flower bud and then subtends and surrounds the flower on one side once the flower opens. Fruits are round capsules.

SUBALPINE
MONTANE
FOOTHILLS

Flowering: June - August

Habitat: Open grasslands and meadows, foothills to subalpine

TIDBITS

Blue-Eyed Grass is a shy, retiring plant, often hidden amongst the surrounding foliage. Typical of the Iridaceae, the species has long, narrow basal leaves, a showy cluster of flowers at the tip of long stalks, and grows from bulbs. There are a number of other similar species and a good deal of confusion over their collective taxonomic treatment. The plant has been traditionally used to treat a range of ailments from digestive disorders to menstrual problems. *Sisyrinchium* is an ancient Greek name for an Iris-like plant, and *montanum* is "of the mountains."

Photos: SW Colorado, June (Al Schneider); Illustration: USDA-NRCS Plants Database

HORSEMINT
(NETTLELEAF HYSSOP)

Agastache urticifolia • Lamiaceae (Mint Family)

FIELD DESCRIPTION:

Aromatic perennial herb, 1-4' tall, with numerous square, four-sided stems. White-purplish trumpet-shaped flowers have a stigma and 4 stamens projecting from mouth. Numerous flowers are arranged in dense whorls forming a conspicuous spike. Leaves are opposite, arrow-shaped, coarsely toothed, and green on both sides.

TIDBITS

Typical of all mints, Horsemint has square stems and opposite leaves. The spikes, short corolla lobes, and protruding stamens are distinctive of mints. Leaves can be used as flavoring in teas and other foods, and the plant has a number of uses in traditional medicine. The showy flowers are a favorite of bees and other insects. *Agastache* from the Greek *agan*, "very much," and *stachys*, "spike," in reference to the flower clusters. *Urticifolia* from the Latin for "with leaves like nettle" (genus *Urtica*).

Flowering: June - August

Habitat: Moist open sites, foothills to subalpine

Photos: Beehive Basin, MT, July (W. Tilt); Illustration: USDA-NRCS Plants Database

Mentha arvensis • Lamiaceae (Mint Family)

FIELD MINT
(WILD MINT)

FIELD DESCRIPTION:

Aromatic perennial herb, 8-30" tall, with four-sided stems and leaves that are held rigid and horizontal. White-pink, bell-shaped flowers, generally five-lobed fused petals, in dense whorls in leaf axils of upper leaves. Stigma and stamens project from flower mouth. Leaves opposite, lance- to egg-shaped, sharp toothed, glabrous or hairy. Distinctive minty smell. Fruits are 4 small nutlets.

MONTANE
FOOTHILLS

Flowering: July - September

Habitat: Moist to wet soils in open to shaded areas, foothills to montane

Photos: Bozeman, MT, July (Matt Lavin); Illustration: USDA-NRCS Plants Database

TIDBITS

A native mint, Field Mint is often lost in lush greenery of wet areas. Often you will smell it before you see it. The plant has long been used for flavorings, herbal teas, and treating a range of medical conditions, including coughs, flatulence, and digestive problems. Mint extracts are used in food, drinks, and cough medicines. In Greek mythology, Mentha was a nymph pursued by Hades. Hades' wife, Persephone, was not pleased and turned Mentha into a field of mint. *Arvensis* is Latin for "field."

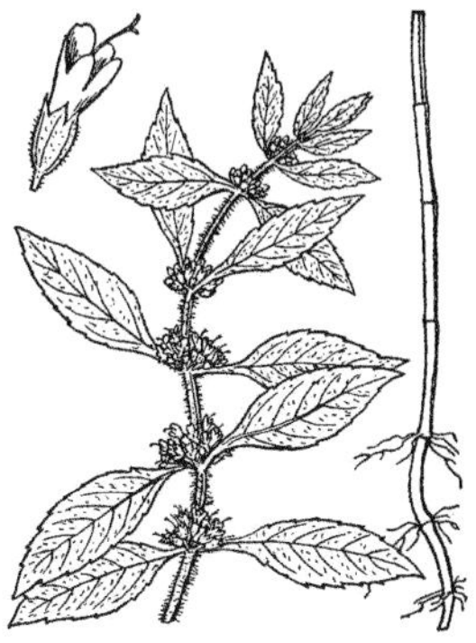

WILD BERGAMOT
(MINTLEAF BEEBALM)

Monarda fistulosa • Lamiaceae (Mint Family)

FIELD DESCRIPTION:

Erect perennial herb, 1-3' tall, with four-sided stems and strong minty odor. Numerous rose-purple tubular flowers form clustered heads atop leafy bracts. Individual flowers open into narrow upper lip and three-lobed lower lip. Two stamens and a single style extend beyond upper lip. Leaves opposite, lance-shaped, sharply-toothed on short stalks. Stems and leaves fine hairy and fruits are smooth nutlets in fours.

TIDBITS

The flower-head of Wild Bergamot looks like a lavender fireworks display. The common name "beebalm" alludes to its attractiveness to native bees and other pollinators. It is a favorite garden plant and its dried leaves and flower-heads are wonderfully aromatic. Wild Bergamot is commonly used as a potherb and brewed as tea. Native Americans utilized the plant for a wide range of medical uses including digestive ailments, as well as perfumes. *Monarda*, after 16th Century Spanish botanist and physician Nicholas Monardes, and *fistulosa* for "tubular."

Flowering: June - August

Habitat: Generally moist soils in open meadows and woods, foothills to montane

Photos: Bridger Range, MT, August (W. Tilt); Illustration: USDA-NRCS Plants Database

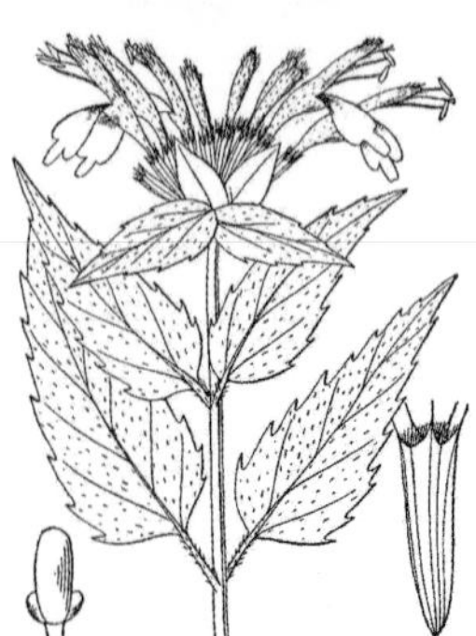

Prunella vulgaris • Lamiaceae (Mint Family)

SELFHEAL
(HEAL-ALL)

FIELD DESCRIPTION:

Small perennial herb, 4-8" tall, with four-sided stems and blue-violet-pink flowers emerging from short, dense spike with green bracts. Individual flowers feature upper hooded lip and three-lobed lower lip. Leaves are few and opposite, lanceolate to broadly ovate in shape, stalked, and lightly hairy on underside.

MONTANE
PLAINS

Flowering: June - August

Habitat: Moist, open to shaded soils, plains to montane

Photos: Gallatin Range, MT, July (W. Tilt); Illustration: USDA-NRCS Plants Database

TIDBITS

Selfheal is a common weed in one's garden or lawn. However, this native plant is worthy of more respect. In addition to being edible, it has been widely used for a range of medicinal purposes, as its common names suggest. Clinical analysis shows the plant to be effective as an antibacterial agent, and it has shown anti-viral properties against the herpes simplex virus. *Prunella* is likely from the Latin prunum, "purple," and *vulgaris* for "common."

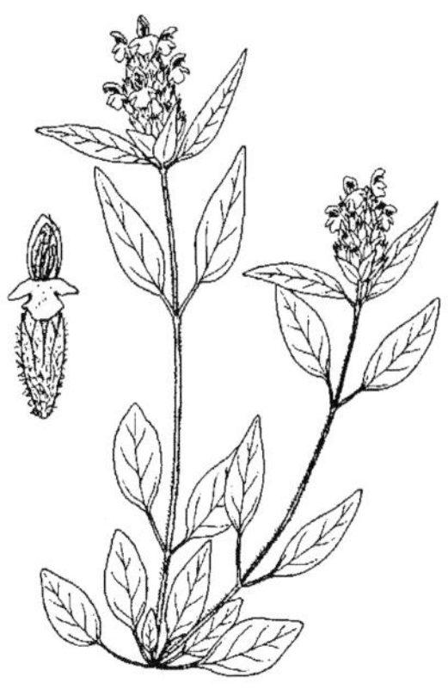

MOUNTAIN DEATHCAMAS

Anticlea elegans • Liliaceae (Lily Family)
(Synonym: *Zigadenus elegans*)

FIELD DESCRIPTION:

Erect perennial herb, 12-24" tall, rather glaucous, glabrous, with slender stem and long, narrow, erect, basal leaves from 2-9" long. Flowers are white-cream, yellow-white, or greenish-white, sometimes tinged with purple in a terminal raceme. Individual flowers have 6 unequal petals that open broadly to expose 6 stamens and 3 styles and an arched, green gland near the base of each petal. Fruits are ovoid capsules.

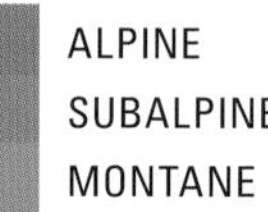

Flowering: June - September

Habitat: Meadows, forests, tundra, montane to alpine

TIDBITS

A conspicuous plant, found primarily at higher elevations, Mountain Deathcamas and the similar looking Meadow Deathcamas (*Toxicoscordion venenosum)*, found at lower elevations, have symmetrically arching leaves and a long stalk with showy raceme of white flowers. The flower of Mountain Deathcamas is about twice as large as that of Meadow Deathcamas with a more open, elongated flower cluster. All parts of the plant are poisonous from alkaloids more toxic than strychnine. Its bulb is similar to the wild onion – a mistaken identity you don't want to make! *Anticlea* was the mother of Odysseus.

Photos: Summit Creek, ID, August (W. Tilt); Illustration: USDA-NRCS Plants Database

Calochortus gunnisonii • Liliaceae (Lily Family)

GUNNISON'S MARIPOSA LILY
(GUNNISON'S SEGO LILY)

FIELD DESCRIPTION:

Perennial herb, 6-18" tall, arising from onion-like bulbs. A single grass-like leaf arises from base. Flowers white to light-lavender with 3 ovate, broadly cupped petals with rounded tips and 3 narrower, white-greenish sepals. A purple gland circles the base of the petals, densely bearded with a yellow fringe. Five erect stamens circle the pistil.

MONTANE
FOOTHILLS

Flowering: July - August

Habitat: Dry soils in fields and open forests, foothills and montane

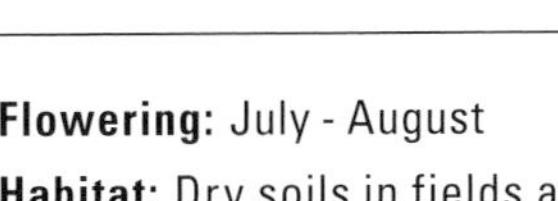

Photos: Boulder River, MT, July (W. Tilt); Illustration: USDA-NRCS Plants Database

TIDBITS

There are a number of mariposa-lily species, primarily distinguished by markings on the inner surface of the petals and the petal colors. The bulbs of mariposa lilies are sweet and nutritious, raw or cooked. They were commonly eaten by settlers and tribes alike, especially when other food was scarce. *Calochortus* from the Greek *kalos*, "beautiful," and *chortos*, "grass." The plant is named for Captain J. W. Gunnison, 1812-1853, surveyor, explorer, and expedition leader who, with 8 companions, was murdered in Utah just after finishing a railroad route survey.

SEGO LILY
(NUTTALL'S MARIPOSA LILY)

Calochortus nuttallii • Liliaceae (Lily Family)

FIELD DESCRIPTION:

Perennial herb from a bulb, to 20" tall. Three very narrow linear leaves, usually withered by flowering time. Stem branches above the middle, producing 1-5 flowers, each stalk subtended by 2 linear, narrow, green bracts to 4" long. The flowers consist of 3 sepals and 3 petals, with the inside of the sepals containing yellow and/or purple markings. The creamy white or lavender petals, to 2.5" long, often terminate in a sharp point. The base of each petal has a circular or U-shaped gland, surrounded by yellow with a V-shaped reddish-purple patch above. The anthers are cream, pink, or purple with an obtuse tip. The capsules are ellipsoid, three-angled, to 2" long.

SUBALPINE
MONTANE
PLAINS

Flowering: May - July

Habitat: Dry soils in grasslands, sagebrush, and open forest, plains to subalpine

TIDBITS

The Sego Lily is most commonly found in the eastern and southern Yellowstone Region where the plant may be abundant and conspicuous, or rarely encountered, depending on the season and from year to year. Sego Lily bulbs are edible and were eaten by Native Americans and settlers alike when other foods were scarce. The Sego Lily is the state flower of Utah in recognition of both its beauty and historical significance. Its bulbous roots were collected and eaten in the mid 1800s during a crop-devouring plague of crickets in Utah. The plant is named in honor of Thomas Nuttall, an English botanist and ornithologist.

Photos: Wasatch Range, UT, July (Steve Hegji); Illustration: USDA-NRCS Plants Database

Camassia quamash • Liliaceae (Lily Family)

BLUE CAMAS

FIELD DESCRIPTION:

Perennial herb, 8-24" tall, that emerges from an edible bulb. Leaves basal, linear-lanceolate. Smooth slender unbranched stem supports bright blue-purple flowers arranged in a terminal raceme. Flower has 3 petals and 3 petal-like sepals arranged in a star with 6 prominent yellow stamens and a single style. Fruit is a three-angled capsule.

MONTANE
FOOTHILLS

Flowering: May - June

Habitat: Moist mountain meadows and forested hillsides, foothills to montane

TIDBITS

The bulb of Blue Camas is a nutritious food which can be eaten raw, cooked, or dried for later use. The bulbs of Blue Camas might be confused with the poisonous white-flowered Death Camas (2 species) as their vegetative forms and habitats are similar when not in flower. With the exception of dried salmon, no other food item was more widely traded in the Pacific Northwest. For the Lewis and Clark Expedition in 1805, the plant represented survival. Facing starvation, the Nez Perce provided food including bread prepared from camas root.

Photos: Upper Mesa Falls, ID, June (W. Tilt); Illustration: Karl Urban, Umatilla NF, OR

GLACIER LILY
(YELLOW AVALANCHE LILY)

Erythronium grandiflorum • Liliaceae (Lily Family)

FIELD DESCRIPTION:

Perennial herb rising 2-15" from bulb-like corms. Single bright yellow, deeply nodding flower atop each stem. Six tepals are curved backward and 6 prominent stamen project downward. A single pair of parallel-veined leaves, 4-8" long, emerge from base of the stem. Fruits are erect three-sided capsules, club-shaped, with dark brown seeds.

SUBALPINE
MONTANE

Flowering: April - May

Habitat: Moist shaded slopes and woodlands, montane to subalpine

TIDBITS

The bright yellow of Glacier Lilies brightens the moist meadows and open woods as the winter snows recede. They are one of the first flowers to bloom, and are often found in large colonies. This is one of several lilies commonly called "Dogtooth Lily" or "Dogtooth Violet." Their deep-seated corms are a favorite of grizzly bears and other wildlife, while mule deer favor the leaves. Meriwether Lewis collected the first specimen of this plant in 1806.

Photos: Gallatin Range, MT, May (W. Tilt); Illustration: USDA-NRCS Plants Database

Fritillaria atropurpurea • Liliaceae (Lily Family)

LEOPARD LILY (CHOCOLATE LILY, SPOTTED FRITILLARY)

FIELD DESCRIPTION:

Erect perennial herb, 4-18" tall, with 1-4 spreading to deeply nodding bell-shaped flowers. Tepals are greenish-purple to chocolate-brown and mottled with yellow or white blotches. Flowers arise from leaf axis. Leaves are narrowly linear, usually alternate in scattered or imperfect whorls. Fruit is an obovoid, angled capsule.

MONTANE
FOOTHILLS

Flowering: May - July

Habitat: Grassy slopes and coniferous forest, foothills to montane

Photos: Gallatin Range, MT, May (W. Tilt); Illustration: USDA-NRCS Plants Database

TIDBITS

The slim profile and nodding flower of the Leopard Lily can make it a challenge to find. Commonly hiding underneath trees and shrubs, it is a delight when discovered. Its blotchy colorful appearance has spawned a wide range of common names including Spotted Missionbells. Native Americans commonly ate the bulbs and some called the bulbs "rice-root." *Fritillaria* from the Latin for "dice box," either a reference to the spotted nature of the flower or the cube-shaped seed capsule and its rattling seeds when dried. *Atropurpurea* means "dark purple."

YELLOWBELLS
(YELLOW FRITILLARY)

Fritillaria pudica • Liliaceae (Lily Family)

FIELD DESCRIPTION:

Delicate perennial herb, 3-10" tall, with solitary, yellow, bell-shaped, 6-petaled flowers nodding at the end of stems (occasionally 2-3 flowers per stem). Purple-to-orange streaks are often apparent at base of flower. Flower fades to orange-brown. Usually 2 linear leaves opposite to whorled on stem. Fruits are egg-shaped capsules erect on stem. Grows from bulb-like corms.

TIDBITS

A sign of spring, Yellowbells are one of the first plants to emerge and flower after the snow melts. The plant is short and the flowers dainty and downturned. Once they emerge, the flowers of Yellowbells are relatively short-lived, fading to an orange-brown and curling outward. The small bulbs can be eaten fresh or cooked. Fritillaries, or mission bells, are a genus of more than 100 species of bulbous plants native to temperate regions of the Northern Hemisphere that flower mostly in the spring in a range of colors. *Fritillaria* from the Latin *fritillus* for "dice-box."

Flowering: April - May

Habitat: Open grassy sagebrush and wooded sites, foothills to montane

Photos: Gallatin Range, MT, May (W. Tilt); Seedhead at left

FAIRYBELLS
(WARTBERRY FAIRYBELLS)

Prosartes trachycarpum • Liliaceae (Lily Family)
(Synonym: *Disporum trachycarpum*)

FIELD DESCRIPTION:

Perennial herb, 1-2′ tall, with narrow bell-shaped flowers, strongly nodding and often in pairs. Delicate creamy-white flowers arise from end of stems and consist of 6 tepals spreading from the base with 6 yellow stamens that typically extend just beyond the tepals. Leaves are alternate ovate-oblong and pointed at tip. Leaves have prominent veins that run parallel to the leaf margin and clasp stem. A terminal pair of leaves often obscures the flowers. Fruits consist of 1-3 red-orange, round berries with a velvety, warty skin.

MONTANE

Flowering: May - July

Habitat: Moist soils in meadows and forests, montane

Thumbnail & reference photos: Gallatin Range, MT, May (W. Tilt); Fruit: Gallatin Range, MT, September (W.Tilt)

TIDBITS

Also known as the Rough-Fruited Fairybells, the plant's flowers are delicate and down-facing with horizontally-held leaves effectively hiding its flowers and fruits. Berries begin as yellow, then orange and red when fully ripe. Their surface has a fuzzy and velvety feel. The Blackfeet Indians placed fairybell berries in their eyes overnight as a treatment for snow blindness. The dampened leaves were also used as a bandage. *Prosartes* from the Greek for "fastened," in reference to the manner in which the fruit parts are attached, and *trachycarpum* from the Greek for "rough fruit."

TWISTED-STALK

Streptopus amplexifolius • Liliaceae (Lily Family)

FIELD DESCRIPTION:

Perennial herb, 24-40" tall. Broad ovate leaves clasp a stem that slightly twists (zigzags) at each leaf attachment. Leaves are alternate, gray-green on underside. A single white-to-yellowish-green flower, hangs under each leaf on a long slender stalk that has almost a perfect right angle to it. Flowers consist of 3 petals and 3 sepals that curl backward. Fruits are bright red, oval-oblong berries.

TIDBITS

Slender stems that are kinked at each node give the species its "twisted-stalk" name. Dainty green-white flowers or orange-red berries dangling singly on long stalks also make for a distinctive plant. By August, bright orange-red, oval berries appear. The berries are reported to be edible, raw or cooked, with a taste like wild cucumber. The plant is known to some as "scootberry" suggesting a possible laxative effect on the person consuming too much of the fruit. *Streptopus* from the Latin for "twisted" and *amplexifolius* for "embracing the leaves," in reference to the plant's clasping leaves.

MONTANE

Flowering: May - June

Habitat: Moist forest and stream banks, montane

Thumbnail & reference photos: Big Sky, MT, July (Rip McIntosh); Fruit: Mt. Blackmore, MT, August (W. Tilt)

BEARGRASS

FIELD DESCRIPTION:

Erect perennial herb, 3-5′ tall, with evergreen leaves. Leaves mostly basal, long and linear, with sharp, finely toothed margins. Stem Leaves are alternate and reduced. Small white, star-like flowers with 6 petals in showy, terminal, "bottle-brush" clusters. Fruits are oval, three-lobed capsules.

SUBALPINE
MONTANE

Flowering: May - August

Habitat: Dry, open soils, montane to subalpine

Photos: Beehive Basin, MT, July (Rip McIntosh); Illustration: Flora of North America (www.efloras.org)

TIDBITS

A dense conical raceme of small white-cream flowers and large tussock of sharp-edged and long grasslike leaves marks Beargrass. Iconic of Glacier National Park, the plant's distribution is much more scattered in the Yellowstone region. Beargrass flowers every 3-10 years and otherwise is found as a basal clump of grass-like leaves. Traditionally Native Americans who wove the tough durable leaves (which turn white as they dry), into tight waterproof weaves. Bears dig for the starchy rhizomes in the spring. *Xerophyllum* translates into "dry class," and *tenax* from the Latin for "tough," in reference to the plant's leaves.

BLUE FLAX
(LEWIS' FLAX)

Linum lewisii • Linaceae (Flax Family)
(Synonym: *Adenolinum lewisii*)

FIELD DESCRIPTION:

Slender, branched perennial herb, 1-2′ tall, often rising above surrounding grasses. Closely spaced leaves are alternate, linear, and one-nerved. Varying shades of blue flowers have 5 broad petals, 5 stamens, and 5 styles that are longer than the stamens.

TIDBITS

When roasted, Blue Flax seeds have a pleasant nutty taste and are very nutritious. Do not eat raw, as seeds contain cyanide which is destroyed in the cooking process. Numerous medicinal uses are reported for Blue Flax and its oil is similar to that of linseed. In season, the blossoms of Blue Flax can fill montane meadows. Meriwether Lewis collected the first specimen of this plant for science in 1806 in the Rockies. Chicory (*Cichorium intybus*) is a similar-looking introduced species with five-toothed edges and similar-color style and anthers.

SUBALPINE
MONTANE
FOOTHILLS

Flowering: May - July

Habitat: Well-drained soils, foothills to subalpine

Photos: Big Sky, MT, July (Rip McIntosh); Illustration: USDA-NRCS Plants Database

TWINFLOWER

FIELD DESCRIPTION:

Evergreen perennial herb or shrublet, 4-6" tall, with trailing stems to 5' long. Pairs of pink, funnel-shaped, nodding flowers. Plant often forms a carpet of trailing stems and flowers on the forest floor. A slender stem rises and splits to support 2 delicate flowers. Corolla is funnel-shaped, pink-to-lavender, five-lobed, with a hairy throat. Evergreen leaves are bright green, opposite, elliptical to roundish, with shallow teeth along the outer margins.

ALPINE
SUBALPINE
MONTANE
FOOTHILLS

Flowering: June - September

Habitat: Moist soils in coniferous forests, foothills to alpine

Photos: Gallatin Range, MT, July (W. Tilt); Illustration: Flora of North America (www.efloras.org)

TIDBITS

Twinflower often forms extensive mats sporting abundant pairs of small nodding flowers, appearing like twin lamp posts pointing at the ground below, as if providing light under the canopy of trees. When not in flower the plant is easily overlooked, but when in flower, its white and pink flowers deserve a closer look, which will likely call for getting on your knees to fully enjoy. Twinflower was a favorite flower of Carl Linnaeus, the Swedish scientist who founded the modern system of biological nomenclature, hence the genus *Linnaea*. *Borealis* means "of the north."

BLAZINGSTAR
(EVENINGSTAR)

Mentzelia sp. • Loasaceae (Blazingstar Family)

FIELD DESCRIPTION:

Tenpetal Blazingstar *(Mentzelia decapetala)* is a stout, coarse perennial, 12-40" tall, with showy star-like flowers. Overall plant coarse with barbed hairs. Leaves are alternate, 2-6" long, lance-shaped, shallowly lobed. Leaf texture fleshy and rough. White-cream flowers are star-shaped comprising 10 long pointed petals (5 petals and 5 petal-like stamens). Flower-heads cyme-like. Fruits are elongate capsules with dark flattened seeds.

Smoothstem Blazingstar *(Mentzelia laevicaulis)* is a biennial or short-lived perennial, 1-3' tall, with showy yellow, star-like flowers and stout, whitish stems. Overall plant coarse with barbed, spiny hairs. Leaves are alternate, oblanceolate, with wavy lobed margins. Leaf texture rough and fleshy. Yellow flowers are star-shaped, comprising 5 long pointed petals and numerous long stamens. Fruits are capsules with numerous winged and flattened seeds.

TIDBITS

Also known as candleflower, the flowers of Tenpetal Blazingstar open in the late afternoon and evening. When flowers are tightly closed during day, the plant is easily overlooked as "just another weed." Leaves will cling to clothing due to short barb-like spiny hairs. Look for this distinctive plant along road cuts and other dry, arid areas where other plants struggle to grow.

Flowering: July - September

Habitat: Dry open soils, foothills to montane

Thumbnail (*M. decapetala*): Big Sky, MT, July (Rip McIntosh); Reference & Inset (*M. laevicaulis*): Yellowstone NP, July (W. Tilt); Illustration: USDA-NRCS Plants Database

Iliamna rivularis • Malvaceae (Mallow Family)

WILD HOLLYHOCK (STREAMBANK GLOBEMALLOW)

FIELD DESCRIPTION:

Perennial herb, 3-6′ tall, with large leaves and showy inflorescence. Pinkish-white to rose-purple cup-shaped flowers are arranged in long, loose raceme. Flowers are 1-2″ wide comprising 5 petals and blunt-tipped sepals above 3 slender bracts. Styles are tipped with head-like stigmas. Leaves are alternate, maple leaf-shaped with 3-7 triangular lobes and coarsely-toothed margins. Fruits are round and hairy with wedge-shaped segments, like a wheel of cheese.

MONTANE
FOOTHILLS

Flowering: June - August

Habitat: Moist soils along wet and open woods, foothills to montane

Thumbnail photo: Beehive Basin, MT, July (Rip McIntosh); Other photos: Gallatin Range, August (W. Tilt); Developing fruits at right

TIDBITS

This tall bushy wildflower looks like it belongs in a garden, where cultivated hollyhocks are commonly found. Wild Hollyhock is an early seral species, becoming abundant following disturbance such as floods, clearcutting, and wildfire. It flowers profusely in full sun and is shade intolerant, quickly disappearing from the post-disturbance communities when overtopped by other vegetation. Wild Hollyhock seeds have a hard coat and can remain viable for 50 years or more, a trait that allows the plant to successfully germinate following disturbance. *Rivularis* from the Latin for "brook-loving."

SCARLET GLOBEMALLOW (COPPER MALLOW)

Sphaeralcea coccinea • Malvaceae (Mallow Family)

FIELD DESCRIPTION:

Low, spreading perennial herb, 4-8" tall, often growing in patches. Flowers are orange-to-brick-red, saucer-shaped with 5-broad petals that are shallowly notched, arranged in small clusters (racemes). Leaves are alternate, gray hairy on undersides, and deeply divided into 3-5 palmate wedge-shaped segments.

TIDBITS

Though commonly known as the Scarlet Globemallow, the plant's petal color is more commonly orange in this region. Scarlet Globemallow establishes well on disturbed sites, aided by survival strategies such as losing its leaves during times of drought. The Blackfeet Indians applied a paste made from this plant to burns, scalds, and external sores as a soothing agent. There are a number of mallows in our area; most grow in large colonies and are very showy. *Sphaer* from the Greek for "a sphere or globe," *alcea* for "mallow," and *coccinea* from the Latin for "scarlet."

MONTANE
FOOTHILLS

Flowering: July - September

Habitat: Dry open soils, foothills to montane

Photos: Bozeman, MT, July (W. Tilt); Illustration: USDA-NRCS Plants Database

Toxicoscordion venenosum • Melanthiaceae (False-Hellebore)
(Synonym: *Zigadenus venenosus*)

MEADOW DEATHCAMAS

FIELD DESCRIPTION:

Erect perennial herb, 12-24" tall, with slender stem and long, narrow, grass-like leaves that are mostly basal. Flowers are white-cream colored in a bell-like terminal raceme. Individual flowers are comprised of 6 unequal tepals that open broadly to expose 6 stamens and 3 styles.

MONTANE
FOOTHILLS

Flowering: April - June

Habitat: Meadows, woods and grassy hillsides, foothills to montane

Photos: Slough Creek, MT, June (W. Tilt); Illustration: USDA-NRCS Plants Database

TIDBITS

Beautiful and deadly, this plant is more potent than strychnine. One bulb, raw or cooked, can be fatal. Petals and sepals of the Meadow Deathcamas are less than 0.25" long and in a fairly crowded, tight raceme. The petals and sepals of the Mountain Deathcamas (*Anticlea elegans*) are more than 0.25 inch long and arranged in an open, airy raceme. Meadow Deathcamas is found at lower elevations than Mountain Deathcamas. *Toxicoscordion* translates as "toxic garlic," while *venenosum* is from the Latin for "venom" or "poison." Recently reclassified from the Liliaceae to the Melanthiaceae.

WESTERN WAKEROBIN (PACIFIC TRILLIUM)

Trillium ovatum • Melanthiaceae (False-Hellebore)

FIELD DESCRIPTION:

Woodland perennial herb, 4-15" tall, with striking three-petaled flower. The plant's single flower comprises 3 broad white petals whorled alternately with 3 green sepals that are framed by 3 broad egg-shaped green leaves. Center of flower contains 6 showy yellow stamens and 3 long styles. Petals turn pink-purplish with age. Fruits are yellow-green, berry-like capsules.

TIDBITS

The common name "wakerobin" alludes to the plant's blooming about the time robins arrive on their spring migration. In the Northern Rockies, robins tend to arrive earlier than the wakerobin blooms, forcing the birds to sit around in the snow awaiting the eventual coming of spring. Wakerobin flowers provide a vibrant splash of color to the early season woods and largely disappear from sight until the next spring. Recently reclassified from Liliaceae to Melanthiaceae.

Flowering: April - June

Habitat: Moist soils in woods recently free of snows, valleys to montane

Photos: Bozeman, MT, May (W. Tilt); Illustration: Karl Urban, Umatilla NF, OR

WILD HYACINTH
(LARGE-FLOWERED TRITELEIA, GOPHERNUTS)

FIELD DESCRIPTION:

Perennial herb, rising 1-3′, on erect leafless stem with 1-2 linear, grass-like, basal leaves. Leaves are flat with keel on underside. Light- to deep-blue flowers are arranged in open umbels atop each stem. Individual flowers are attached by a short stalk and bell-shaped, consisting of 6 fused petals and petal-like sepals that flare at the ends. Fruits are upright, rounded capsules.

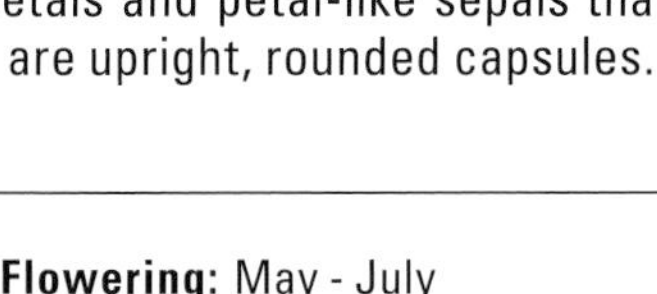

MONTANE
FOOTHILLS

Flowering: May - July

Habitat: Well-drained soils on open or wooded slopes, foothills to montane

Thumbnail photo: Beehive Basin, MT, June (Rip McIntosh); Reference photo: Bozeman, MT, June (Matt Lavin); Seed pods: Bozeman, MT, October (W. Tilt)

TIDBITS

Rodents seek out the corms of Wild Hyacinth that, as suggested by the common name "gopher-nuts." They provided a source of food to both Native American peoples and European settlers, and have had mystical attributes attributed to them – they were included in the medicine bag of some tribes to "make the bag more potent." Wild Hyacinth is distinguished from wild onions or camas by presence of fused petals and sepals. *Triteleia* from the Greek *trios,* "three," and *teleios,* "complete," referring to the flower structure.

CORN LILY
(FALSE HELLEBORE)

Veratrum californicum • Melanthiaceae (False-Hellebore)

FIELD DESCRIPTION:

Robust perennial herb, to 7'' tall, that grows corn-stalk-like in dense patches often covering acres. Conspicuous, large, broad, pleated leaves, up to 14" long, are alternate and have deep parallel veins. Numerous small, yellow-green, star-shaped, 6-petaled flowers with dark green centers are densely clustered in a branched panicle.

SUBALPINE
MONTANE

Flowering: June - September

Habitat: Wet soils along streams and mountain meadows, montane to subalpine

TIDBITS

This large coarse plant of meadow wetlands is conspicuous in the early summer as it grows and flowers, but then withers from sight by late summer. Corn Lily is extremely poisonous and can be lethal in small doses. Alkaloids concentrated in the root and young shoots often poison livestock in the early spring when the plant is just emerging. Humans have used the plant for everything from ridding themselves of head lice to slowing heart rate and reducing blood pressure. *Veratrum* from the Latin for "true black," referring to the black roots. Green False Hellebore (*Veratrum viride*) is a similar species found in much of western Montana.

Photos: Leverich Canyon, MT, July (W. Tilt); Illustration: USDA-NRCS Plants Database

Claytonia lanceolata • Montiaceae (Miner's Lettuce Family)

SPRING BEAUTY

FIELD DESCRIPTION:

Delicate perennial herb, 2-8" tall, with white-pink saucer-shaped flowers. Flowers have 5 spreading petals, shallow notches on their tips and dark-pink-to-purple veins on upper surface. Basal leaves, with long petioles and 2 opposite, stalkless, lance-shaped leaves midstem.

SUBALPINE
MONTANE
FOOTHILLS

Flowering: May - July

Habitat: Cool moist soils, commonly where snow is recently melted, foothills to subalpine

Thumbnail photo: Beehive Basin, MT, June (Rip McIntosh); Reference photo: Bozeman, MT, June (W. Tilt); Illustration: USDA-NRCS Plants Database

TIDBITS

Spring Beauty is a common early spring wildflower. Individually the small herb is easy to overlook, even when a few have flowered. But when large numbers are in bloom, they can turn an entire meadow white with blossoms. Dug after the plant has flowered, the corms are considered a special nutritious treat, raw or cooked. Grizzly bears will dig for the corms, evidenced by soils that look like they have been roto-tilled with plant material scattered helter-skelter. Meriwether Lewis collected the first specimens of this plant for science in 1806. *Lanceolata* from the Latin for "lance-like."

PYGMY BITTERROOT
(ALPINE LEWISIA)

Lewisia pygmaea • Montiaceae (Miner's Lettuce Family)
(Synonym: *Lewisia nevadensis*)

FIELD DESCRIPTION:

Low, succulent perennial, 1-4" tall, from a fleshy, carrot-like root. Leaves are basal, fleshy, linear, and up to 6" long. Flower stems are shorter than leaves with 2 small leaf-like bracts joined midway up stem. Single, small, pink-to-white flowers at the end of stems. Flower comprised of 6-9 petals and 2 distinct oval fleshy sepals, often with tiny teeth on the margin. Fruits are membranous capsules, approximately the size of the sepals.

TIDBITS

A small (1-2" tall) but intense splash of color announces the Pygmy Bitterroot, the smaller, high altitude version of Bitterroot (*Lewisia rediviva*). The flower arises from a woody taproot amid a rosette of fleshy linear leaves. The root of the Pygmy Bitterroot is edible cooked or dried and ground into flour, and a number of medical uses are reported in the literature as well. Recently reclassified from the Portulacaceae to the Montiaceae.

ALPINE
SUBALPINE
MONTANE

Flowering: May - August

Habitat: Open, dry to moist stony soils, upper montane to alpine

Thumbnail photo: Kittitas Co., WA, June (Ben Legler); Reference photo: SW Colorado, July (Al Schneider)

FIELD DESCRIPTION:

Showy, low-growing, perennial herb, 1-4" tall, from fleshy taproot. Large rose, pink or white flowers have yellow centers and 12-18 lance-shaped petals, arising from short stems. Leaves are basal, linear, and fleshy. Leaves are present in fall and spring but dry and wither when plant flowers.

Flowering: May - July

Habitat: Open, dry rocky soils, foothills to montane

Photos: Shields Valley, MT, June (Carol Guzman Aspevig); Illustration: USDA-NRCS Plants Database

TIDBITS

The state flower of Montana, the Bitterroot is unmistakable during its short blooming season. Many Indian tribes timed their spring migrations with the blooming of bitterroots on the gravel river bars and hillsides. Dug, cleaned, and dried, the root provided a lightweight, nutritious supplement to a wild game diet. Frederick Pursh named a new genus *Lewisia* in 1814 in recognition of Meriwether Lewis who collected the first specimens of this genus for science in Montana in 1806. Recently reclassified from the Portulacaceae to the Montiaceae.

YELLOW POND-LILY
(SPATTERDOCK, COW-LILY)

Nuphar polysepala • Nymphaeaceae (Waterlily Family)
(Synonym: *Nuphar lutea*)

FIELD DESCRIPTION:

Aquatic perennial herb, up to 6′ long, with floating leaves. Single, floating, cup-like flowers comprised of 6-9 yellow, waxy, petal-like sepals enclosing 10-20 true petals and red-purple stamens around prominent lobed stigma. Leaves large (up to 16″ long), round to heart-shaped, leathery with wavy edges. Flower and leaf stalks thick and fleshy. Fruit is a leathery, ribbed, egg-shaped capsule. Rhizomes, up to 15′ long, anchor plant to bottom substrate.

SUBALPINE
MONTANE
FOOTHILLS

Flowering: May - August

Habitat: Shallow ponds and backwaters, foothills to subalpine

TIDBITS

Yellow Pond-Lily's network of roots, leaves and seeds provides habitat for a broad range of aquatic animals, from muskrat and ducks to fish and insects. Its conspicuous leaves begin the growing season as round and robustly green, but have a tendency to deteriorate as the season progresses. Pond-lilies can grow and reproduce rapidly, completely covering the surface of small ponds in a few short weeks. Their flowers are said to be "modest" since they appear perpetually reluctant to fully open.

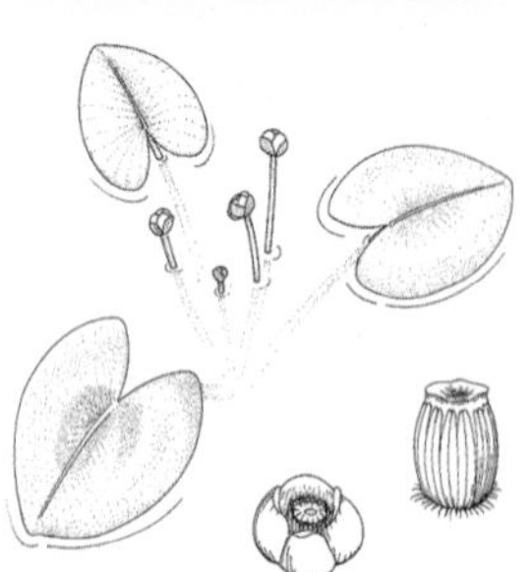

Photos: Shoshone National Forest, WY, June (W. Tilt); Illustration: USDA-NRCS Plants Database

Chamerion angustifolium • Onagraceae (Evening Primrose)
(Synonym: *Epilobium angustifolium, Chamerion danielsii*)

NARROWLEAF FIREWEED

FIELD DESCRIPTION:

Conspicuous perennial herb, 3-5' tall, with unbranched leafy stems. Leaves are alternate and lance-shaped, underside slightly paler with prominent veins. Numerous pink-to-magenta, showy flowers have 4 petals that open first at bottom of the flower spike and move upward. As fireweed goes to seed, its flowers are replaced with linear, purplish fruits that split to release hairy seeds.

MONTANE

Flowering: June - September

Habitat: Favors moist, cool habitats, recently burned or disturbed, montane

Photos: Beehive Basin, MT, August (Rip McIntosh); Illustration: USDA-NRCS Plants Database

TIDBITS

As its common name suggests, fireweed is one of the first plants to colonize burned areas in moist habitats. It appears in great numbers and creates a memorable flower show with its numerous richly colored flowers. Fireweed then develops long seed pods that ripen and burst open with very visible cotton-covered seeds. The plant is rich in vitamin C and a favored food for bears and other wildlife. *Epilobium* species are called "willow herbs" because of their willow-like leaves. *Chamerion* from the Greek *chamae*, "lowly," and *nerium*, "Oleander." *Angustifolium* means "narrow leaves."

DWARF FIREWEED
(DWARF WILLOWHERB, RIVER BEAUTY)

Chamerion latifolium • Onagraceae (Evening Primrose)
(Synonyms: *Epilobium latifolium*)

FIELD DESCRIPTION:

Perennial herb, 2-15" tall. Leaves mostly opposite, lanceolate to ovate, pale green with bluish cast, somewhat fleshy and short-hairy, and stalkless. Flowers pink-magenta, saucer-shaped with 4 broad petals and 8 prominent anthers, 3 or more in terminal clusters. Fruits are hairy elongated capsules.

TIDBITS

As its common name River Beauty attests, this plant commonly adds its bright magenta color to river flats and gravel banks in the Yellowstone region. Dwarf Fireweed is also an alpine plant and its range extends north into the Arctic. The plant is edible, but with a taste described as bitter spinach. Dwarf Fireweed is the national flower of Greenland, where it is known by the Greenlandic name *Niviarsiaq* for "little girl."

ALPINE
SUBALPINE
MONTANE

Flowering: June - August

Habitat: Open, well-drained sites on river bars and open slopes, montane to alpine

Photos: Slough Creek, MT, July (W. Tilt); Illustration: Flora of North America (www.efloras.org)

SCARLET GAURA
(SCARLET BEEBLOSSOM)

FIELD DESCRIPTION:

Perennial herb, 6-12" tall, from spreading rootstock. Stems weak and clustered, hairy (sometimes smooth). Leaves lance-shaped, entire, often with shallow teeth. Flowers, four-parted, few to numerous in spikes, sepals about 1/3" long, petals slightly shorter, light pink to salmon, becoming red-orange to maroon in age. Stamens are long with large reddish anthers. Fruit s are four-angled, hard capsules.

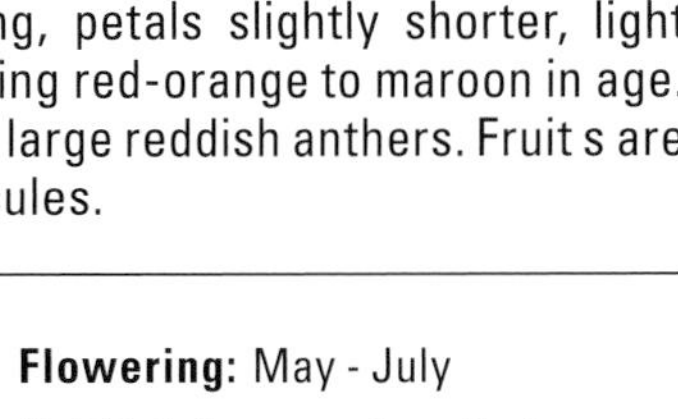

MONTANE
PLAINS

Flowering: May - July

Habitat: Dry, sandy soils in grasslands, sagebrush, and hill-sides, plains to lower montane

Photos: Bozeman, MT, June (W. Tilt); Illustration: USDA-NRCS Plants Database

TIDBITS

A lanky plant with an unkempt appearance and spidery, feathery flowers, Scarlet Gaura is a plant of the Great Plains frequently found in sagebrush-grasslands, dry "badlands" and in disturbed places, such as along roads. Considered weedy in some regions and listed as noxious in California. Common names like Scarlet Butterflyweed and Wild Honeysuckle address the plant's attractiveness to pollinators. Flowers open in evening attracting pollinating moths. Individual flowers last only a brief time. *Gaura* from the Greek for "superb" or "proud."

TUFTED EVENING PRIMROSE

Oenothera caespitosa • Onagraceae (Evening Primrose)

FIELD DESCRIPTION:

Ground-hugging, stemless perennial herb, 4-6" tall, with a basal rosette of oblong leaves with pointed tips. Large, white flowers have 4 heart-shaped petals and 8 yellow stamens. Basal leaves are narrowly spatulate tapered to slender stems. The flowers open in late afternoon, close the next morning, and ultimately wither to pink or red-violet. Lateral roots often give rise to new perennial plants.

TIDBITS

Also known as the Moon-Rose or Fragrant Evening Primrose, Tufted Evening-Primrose specializes in attracting one particular type of pollinator. Its flowers open in the late afternoon and evening to be pollinated by night-flying moths, like hawk moths (family Sphingidae), attracted by a strong, sweet fragrance. The flowers close in bright sunlight. The flowers live only for a day or so with white petals turning pink as they age. *Oenothera* is believed to be derived from the Greek for "wine seeker," possibly in reference to pollinators' attraction to the plant's nectar. *Caespitosa* from the Latin for "tufted."

MONTANE
FOOTHILLS

Flowering: May - July

Habitat: Dry hillsides and open woods, foothills to montane

Photos: Slough Creek, MT, July (W. Tilt); Illustration: Flora of North America (www.efloras.org)

FAIRY SLIPPER ORCHID

FIELD DESCRIPTION:

Small, dainty slipper-like orchid, 2-8" tall, with a spectacularly shaped and colored flower. Flower has cap of 3 pink-purple sepals and 3 petals including one forming a pale lower lip with tuft of yellow hairs, opening into a throat with dark purple stripes or spots. Single, oval, basal leaf emerges before flower appears and remains after flower has gone to seed. Fruits are elliptical capsules.

MONTANE

Flowering: May - June

Habitat: Moist, cool forests with decaying leaf litter, montane

Thumbnail photo: Gallatin Range, MT, May (W. Tilt); Reference photo: SW Colorado, May (Al Schneider); Illustration: USDA-NRCS Plants Database

TIDBITS

The Fairy Slipper Orchid is a small-statured, vibrantly colored orchid that is often difficult to find, but once found, is a real treat for the eyes. Concealment and solitude appear to be the catchwords for the genus *Calypso*, taking its name from the Greek signifying concealment. The plant favors sheltered areas under shrubs and conifers. In Greek mythology Calypso was the daughter of Atlas who lived a solitary life on an island where she made life sweet for the occasional sailor washed up on her shores (including Odysseus). The species was first collected in Siberia and described by Linnaeus in 1753.

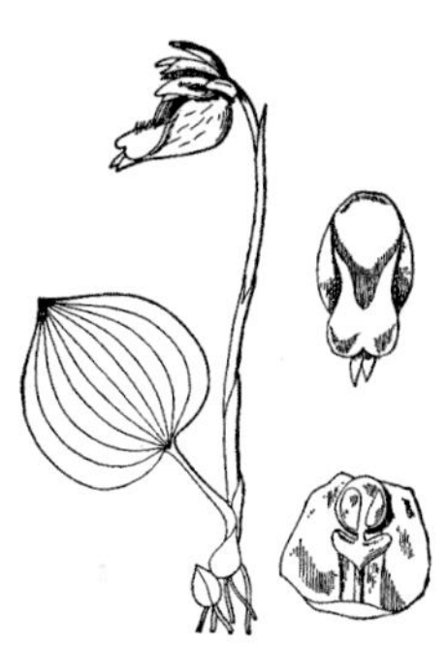

SPOTTED CORALROOT

Corallorhiza maculata • Orchidaceae (Orchid Family)

FIELD DESCRIPTION:

Parasitic perennial herb, 7-24" tall, producing small or large clumps of leafless, erect, reddish stems. Flowers arranged on upper portion of the stem in a loose open raceme. The lip petal and 2 basal lobes on either side are white with purple spots, while the upper 2 petals and 3 sepals are pinkish red. Leaves are reduced to semi-transparent sheaths. Fruits are capsules. As the plant goes to seed, the flowers become thick and stout and droop downward with the whole plant becoming reddish-brown. Plant stalks can persist through winter.

MONTANE

Flowering: May - August

Habitat: Rich moist soils in shaded forests, montane

TIDBITS

Dark red-brown stalks of last year's plant are replaced by yellow-red stalks and new blossoms. Spotted Coralroot can be confused with Pine Drops (*Pterospora andromedea*), but the stalks of the latter are usually much stouter. Coralroots lack green leaves and chlorophyll and cannot photosynthesize. As parasites, they get their nutrients from soil fungi and die when removed from this association. They are, therefore, rarely cultivated or transplanted with success. *Corallorhiza* means "coralroot" in reference to a hard mass of rhizomes that associate with fungi in the soil. *Maculata* from the Latin for "spotted."

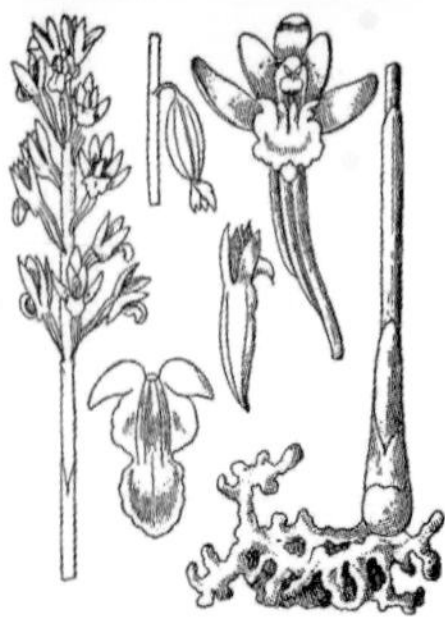

Photos: Bear Canyon, MT, July (W. Tilt); Illustration: USDA-NRCS Plants Database

Corallorhiza mertensiana • Orchidaceae (Orchid Family)

WESTERN CORALROOT

FIELD DESCRIPTION:

Parasitic perennial herb, 6-18" tall, with clumps of erect, reddish stems. Flowers arranged on upper portion of the stem in a loose open raceme of 10-30 funnel-shaped flowers. Individual flowers deep pink, upper petals with yellow to dark red veins, and reproductive column is bright yellow. Leaves are alternate, reduced to semi-transparent sheaths. Fruits are capsules.

MONTANE

Flowering: June - August

Habitat: Moist soils in shaded coniferous forests, montane

Photos: Boulder River, MT, July (W. Tilt); Illustration: Flora of North America (www.efloras.org)

TIDBITS

The flowers of Western Coralroot resemble delicate birds taking flight with yellow upturned beaks, dark pink tongues and brownish-red wings. The seeds of orchids must be infected by a specialized fungus to grow and become self sustaining, as the seeds themselves contain no stored nutrients. Coralroots, in fact, never become self-sufficient, but derive their nutrients from eating mycorrhizal fungi in the soil. "Coralroot" refers to hard, branched rhizomes that resemble coral. *Corallorhiza mertensiana* is named after F.C. Mertens, a German botanist of the late 18th and 19th centuries.

STRIPED CORALROOT

Corallorhiza striata • Orchidaceae (Orchid Family)

FIELD DESCRIPTION:

Parasitic perennial herb, 6-21" tall, growing singly or in small groups. Leafless, erect, purplish stem topped with spike-like raceme consisting of 7-25 flowers. Flowers have conspicuous reddish brown to purple stripes. Leaves are thin, semitransparent sheaths. Fruits are capsules.

TIDBITS

The flowers of Striped Coralroot are about 1.5 times the size of the flowers of Spotted Coralroot (*Corallorhiza maculata*); tend to be more spherical in overall shape; and its flower lip is entire while that of Spotted Coralroot is often wavy edged and has 2 prominent lateral lobes near its base. Overall the flowers of Striped Coralroot have a blue-yellow cast to them and Spotted Coralroot has a pink-yellow cast. Coralroots lack green leaves and chlorophyll and cannot photosynthesize. As parasites, they get their nutrients from soil fungi and die when removed from this association. They are, therefore, rarely cultivated or transplanted successfully.

Flowering: May - August

Habitat: Rich moist soils in shaded forests, montane

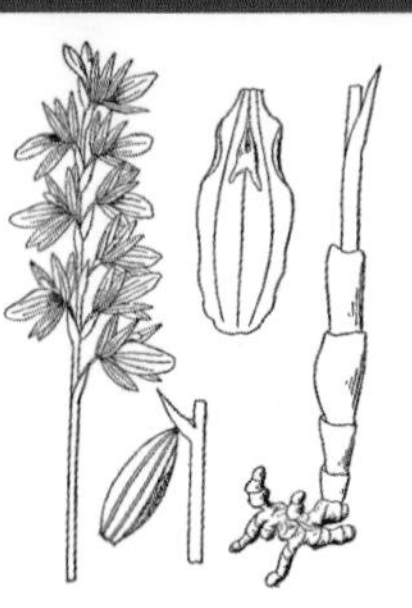

Photos: Gallatin Range, MT, July (W. Tilt); Illustration: USDA-NRCS Plants Database

MOUNTAIN LADY'S-SLIPPER

FIELD DESCRIPTION:

Distinctive perennial, 1-2′ tall with prominent white lip pouch. One to three flowers near tip of stem. Erect green bract arises behind flowers that have 3 brownish-purple, twisted-wavy sepals framing a white pouched lip and yellow throat. Pouch often purple veined. Lance-shaped leaves clasp stems alternately with parallel veins.

MONTANE
FOOTHILLS

Flowering: May - July

Habitat: Dry to moist forests, foothills to montane

TIDBITS

Encountering the Mountain Lady's-Slipper is a treat for the eye. This showy orchid is considered rare through the region with their decline in part the result of thoughtless harvesting; often conducted with hopes of transplanting to home gardens. Alas they seldom transplant successfully and die. As the common name suggests, the flower resembles a delicate slipper. Orchids are known for their highly specific associations with pollinators which result in some of the most magnificent flowers in the plant kingdom. The Lewis and Clark expedition was the first to document Mountain Lady's-Slipper in western North America.

Photos: Smith River, MT, July (W. Tilt); Illustration: Karl Urban, Umatilla NF, OR

YELLOW LADY'S-SLIPPER

Cypripedium parviflorum • Orchidaceae (Orchid Family)

FIELD DESCRIPTION:

Distinctive perennial, 1-2′ tall, with prominent yellow "slipper-like" pouch. One to two flowers near tip of stem. Three green-yellow-brownish sepals with purplish stripes frame a yellow pouched lip and yellow throat. Upper sepal is often erect over the blossom. Leaves are alternate, lance- to egg-shaped, slightly clasping, with strong parallel veins.

TIDBITS

The Yellow Lady's-Slipper orchid remains widespread across the northern Yellowstone region, but is generally found in small, isolated populations. Collection and disturbance of its moist habitats are 2 reasons for its scarcity. While tempting, transplanting orchids from the wild to one's garden seldom succeeds, so it is best to leave in the wild to be enjoyed by all. *Cypripedium* from the Greek for "Venus slipper" in reference to the plant's flower.

FOOTHILLS

Flowering: May - July

Habitat: Moist openings and forests, in the foothills

Photos: Gallatin Co., MT, June (Carolyn Hopper); Illustration: USDA-NRCS Plants Database

Goodyera oblongifolia • Orchidaceae (Orchid Family)

RATTLESNAKE PLANTAIN
(RATTLESNAKE ORCHID)

FIELD DESCRIPTION:

Evergreen perennial herb, 6-14" tall, with prominent white mid-vein on leaves and spike of white-to-greenish-white flowers in raceme arranged one-sided or loose spiral on a tall slender stalk. Petals and one sepal of flower form a hood over lower lip. Leaves are thick, entire, broadly lance-shaped in basal rosette. Fruits are erect, pubescent capsules.

MONTANE

Flowering: July - September

Habitat: Damp, mossy soils in shady conditions under conifers, montane

TIDBITS

The white-striped, mottled leaves in a basal rosette are distinctive of the Rattlesnake Plantain Orchid, and help identify this orchid, especially when not in bloom. A close examination of the flower reveals its orchid features. The plant's common name may arise from the belief that its striped leaves indicated its use to treat snake bite. However no such medicinal qualities are confirmed. An alternative theory is that the eastern species of this plant, *Goodyera pubescens*, has more mottled leaves that resemble a rattlesnake's skin. *Goodyera* for noted British 17th century botanist and botanical writer, John Goodyer.

Thumbnail photo: Smith River, MT, July (W. Tilt);
Reference photo: South Leigh, MT, July (W. Tilt);
Illustration: Karl Urban, Umatilla NF, OR

WHITE BOG ORCHID (SCENTBOTTLE, SPURRED BOG ORCHID)

Platanthera dilatata • Orchidaceae (Orchid Family)
(Synonyms: *Limnorchis dilatata, Habenaria dilatata, Piperia dilatata*)

FIELD DESCRIPTION:

Erect perennial herb with 1-3′ tall spikes of white, fragrant flowers arranged on unbranched stems. Lance-shaped leaves clasp the lower stem portions. Upper sepal and 2 adjacent petals fused to form hood while 2 lower petals spread wide to each side. A prominent white spur extends outward and down from the lower lip.

SUBALPINE

Flowering: May - July

Habitat: Wet meadows, bogs and wet banks, subalpine

TIDBITS

Commonly called bog, rein, or fringed orchids, Platanthera orchids are characterized by having a long, strap-like, or fringed lip petal that terminates at the back into a sac-like spur. The presence of the spur differentiates the White Bog Orchid from the related Ladies-Tresses Orchid (*Spiranthes romanzoffiana*).The bog orchid's spur holds nectar on which moths and other insects with long tongues feed. The process feeds the insects, pollinates the plant (if insect is already carrying pollen) and serves to carry pollen to other orchids.

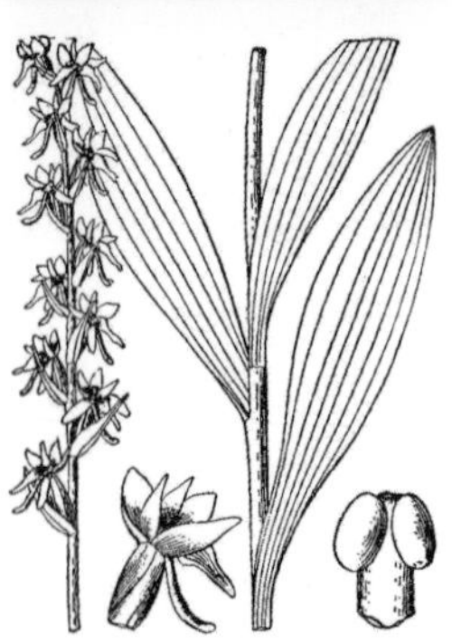

Photos: Slough Creek, MT, June (W. Tilt); Illustration: USDA-NRCS Plants Database

WYOMING PAINTBRUSH

FIELD DESCRIPTION:

Perennial herb, to nearly 3' tall, glabrous to hairy (especially lower on the plant). Leaves to 4" long, linear, glabrous to sparingly hairy, entire or deeply divided. Bracts are red or scarlet, divided into linear lobes. Calyx is scarlet or red, finely hairy. Corolla is from 1-2" long, green yellow. Fruit is a capsule.

MONTANE
PLAINS

Flowering: June - August

Habitat: Dry meadows, forest openings, sandy gravelly soils, plains to montane

Photos: SW Colorado, June (Al Schneider)

TIDBITS

The state flower of Wyoming, the Wyoming Paintbrush is common through much of the West. It is distinguished from other mountain paintbrush by its range of habitats (growing not only in the mountains but also at lower elevations) and by its very narrow leaves (usually entire, but occasionally lobed on upper leaves). Several other characteristics assist, but are not as consistent: the plant is commonly over 2' tall and often branched. Indian Paintbrush and Prairie Fire are 2 other common names for the *Castilleja*. George Bentham named this plant in 1846 from a specimen collected in 1842 by John Fremont in present day eastern Wyoming. Reclassified from the Scrophulariaceae to the Orobanchaceae.

RED PAINTBRUSH (COMMON PAINTBRUSH)

Castilleja miniata • Orobanchaceae (Broomrape Family)

FIELD DESCRIPTION:

Distinctive perennial herb, 8-24" tall, with erect, leafy, glaborous to puberulent foliage. Numerous stems bear leaves that are alternate, three-nerved, and narrowly linear-to-lance-shaped; leaves are typically entire. Bright red-to-scarlet "flowers" are toothed bracts, cut into 1-2 pairs of lateral lobes, with small, inconspicuous, greenish, tubular flowers at the base of the bracts. Fruits are capsules with net-veined seeds.

SUBALPINE
MONTANE

Flowering: June - September

Habitat: Meadows and dry slopes, montane to subalpine

TIDBITS

Conspicuous and iconic plants of the Rocky Mountains, paintbrush come in many different colors; each, usually a distinct species. Red paintbrush mixes up things further with its bracts appearing in red, salmon, and pink attire. To further complicate matters, Red Paintbrush commonly hybridizes with Alpine Paintbrush (*Castilleja rhexiifolia*). Attempts to transplant paintbrush to gardens generally fail as the plant has a semi-parasitic dependence on neighboring plants. *Miniata* from the Latin for "colored red."

Thumbnail photo: South Leigh Creek, ID, June (W. Tilt); Reference photo: Yellowstone NP, July (Jim Peaco); Illustration: USDA-NRCS Plants Database

Castilleja pallescens • Orobanchaceae (Broomrape Family)

PALE PAINTBRUSH

FIELD DESCRIPTION:

Silky-hairy perennial herb, 8-24" tall, with distinctive pale yellow "flowers" in dense clusters. Numerous dense short-hairy stems bear alternate leaves that are linear-lanceolate, entire, or with linear lobes, short-hairy, and stalkless. Inflorescence consists of leafy, green, yellow or purple-tipped bracts that are broader than leaves with 1 or 2 pairs of narrow lobes. Flowers are small, inconspicuous, and yellowish at the base of the bracts. Fruits are capsules.

MONTANE
FOOTHILLS

Flowering: May - August

Habitat: Meadows and dry slopes, foothills to montane

Photos: Slough Creek, MT, June (W. Tilt)

TIDBITS

Paintbrush is easily recognized as a group of wildflowers, but difficult to identify to the species level. Hence, there are numerous red or yellow paintbrushes, and many with colors in between. Some 22 different species of paintbrush, with a rainbow of colors, are found in the region. Attempts to transplant paintbrush to gardens generally fail as the plant has a semi-parasitic dependence on neighboring plants. Indian Paintbrush and Prairie Fire are 2 other common names for the *Castilleja*. Reclassified from the Scrophulariaceae to the Orobanchaceae.

ALPINE PAINTBRUSH (ROSE PAINTBRUSH)

Castilleja rhexiifolia • Orobanchaceae (Broomrape Family)

FIELD DESCRIPTION:

Distinctive perennial herb, 4-16" tall, with bracts that appear as a brush dipped in bright rosy paint. Bracts and sepals are colored purple-rose to pink-red. Bracts often have 2-4 lobes at the tip and hide small purplish-red tubular flowers. Numerous stems bear leaves that are entire (not toothed or lobed), alternate, three-nerved, and narrowly lance-shaped.

TIDBITS

Alpine Paintbrush is similar in appearance to Red Paintbrush (*Castilleja miniata*), and the 2 may be found growing together; Red Paintbrush usually grows at lower elevations. Alpine Paintbrush has vivid rose-pink bracts that are not deeply divided. Many paintbrush hybridize with each other making precise identification more complicated, but also making for marvelous colors. Alpine Paintbrush commonly hybridizes with Red Paintbrush and others. *Rhexifolia* is Greek for "broken foliage" and probably refers to the strongly veined leaves. Reclassified from the Scrophulariaceae to the Orobanchaceae.

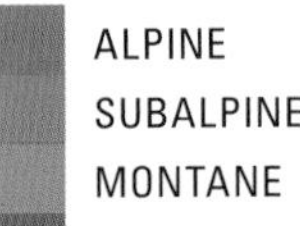

ALPINE
SUBALPINE
MONTANE

Flowering: June - August

Habitat: Meadows and dry slopes, upper montane to alpine

Photos: Beehive Basin, MT, July (Rip McIntosh); Illustration: USDA-NRCS Plants Database

Orobanche fasciculata • Orobanchaceae (Broomrape)
(Synonym: *Aphyllon fasciculata*)

CLUSTERED BROOMRAPE

FIELD DESCRIPTION:

Perennial herb, 2-7" tall. Stems thick fleshy. Stems, leaves, and flowers are yellow (often puplish) with glandular hairs. Tubular flowers formed from fused petals, 5 lobes. Small scale-like leaves on stems with 2-6 flower-heads arising from leaf axils. Fruit is capsule that splits open lengthwise, numerous small seeds.

MONTANE
FOOTHILLS

Flowering: May - July

Habitat: Dry open sites, often near sagebrush, foothills to montane

Photos: Paradise Valley, MT, June (W. Tilt);
Illustration: USDA-NRCS Plants Database

TIDBITS

Broomrapes have no green leaves, lack chlorophyll, and derive their nourishment as parasites, absorbing nutrients from the roots of neighboring host plants, especially various sagebrush species. This may be the origin of another common name for the plant: Yellow Cancerroot. *Orobanche* from the Greek for "vetch choker," and *fasciculata* from the Latin for "bundles," descriptive of the manner in which the leaves are attached to the leaf stem in little bundles.

YELLOW OWLCLOVER

Orthocarpus luteus • Orobanchaceae (Broomrape Family)

FIELD DESCRIPTION:

Annual herb, 4-14" tall, with glandular-hairy, with slender stem, usually simple or branching near the top. Leaves are alternate, linear, 0.3 to 1.5" long, usually entire or rarely three-cleft. Yellow flowers in dense terminal clusters (racemes). Two flower forms: tubular and lobed with 3-5 short bracts. Fruit is a capsule.

TIDBITS

Yellow Owl Clover is the most wide ranging Orthocarpus, and the one most frequently encountered in the Yellowstone region. It may be found growing in sagebrush meadows and open Aspen woodlands. A slender spike of club-shaped flowers and narrow, linear leaves are conspicuous. Thomas Nuttall collected the first specimen of this plant "in humid situations on the plains of the Missouri, near Fort Mandan" in 1812. Nuttall called the genus *Orthocarpus* because of its straight (*ortho*) fruit (*carpus*). *Luteus* from the Latin for "yellow."

MONTANE

FOOTHILLS

Flowering: May - September

Habitat: Meadows, open woods, pastures, foothills to montane

Photos: Bozeman, MT, July (Matt Lavin); Illustration: USDA-NRCS Plants Database

Pedicularis bracteosa • Orobanchaceae (Broomrape Family)

FERNLEAF LOUSEWORT (BRACTED LOUSEWORT)

FIELD DESCRIPTION:

Erect, stout perennial herb, 20-36" tall, with delicate fern-like leaves and a tall flower stalk bearing light yellow flowers in spike-like clusters atop leafy, unbranched stems. Flowers are beak-like in shape. Leaves are alternate, pinnatifid, linear-oblong to lanceolate, and double-toothed with uppermost leaf segments smaller and joined.

MONTANE

Flowering: June - August

Habitat: Woods, meadows, and moist open slopes, montane

Photos: Slough Creek, MT, July (W. Tilt); Illustration: Karl Urban, Umatilla NF, OR

TIDBITS

Fernleaf Lousewort is commonly found in scattered groups of a dozen or more plants. Distinctive, candle-like stalks rise above the surrounding vegetation. Louseworts are parasitic plants whose roots, or haustoria, penetrate the roots of other plants for nourishment. Louseworts got their name from the belief that livestock grazing the plant would get lice and possibly transmit them to humans. While there is no evidence to support this claim, Linnaeus used the Latin word for louse, *pediculus*, to describe the plant.

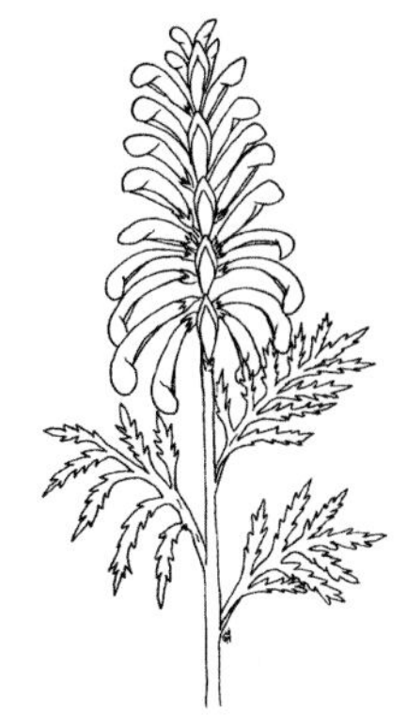

COILED LOUSEWORT

Pedicularis contorta • Orobanchaceae (Broomrape Family)

FIELD DESCRIPTION:

Perennial herb with erect, slender stems growing 6-12" high. Its leaves are mostly basal, 1-6" long and pinnately lobed into narrowly oblong, toothed segments. Its white-to-cream flowers are loosely clustered in a terminal spike, subtended by deeply lobed, leaf-like bracts. Each flower is about 0.5" long and strongly two-lipped, resembling a parrot's beak. The upper lip is elongated into a twisted, hood-like semicircle. The lower lip is short and broad. Fruit are flattened capsules.

ALPINE
SUBALPINE
MONTANE

Flowering: June-August

Habitat: Open forest and high-elevation meadows, montane to alpine

TIDBITS

Plants in the genus *Pedicularis* are parasitic on neighboring plants. They obtain some of their nutrients, water, and carbon by tapping into and drawing food from their neighbors' roots. The particular neighboring species isn't important, and a single plant can form a parasitic relationship with several different plants. Louseworts commonly contain poisonous glycosides, toxic to humans and livestock in large quantities. Reclassified from the Scrophulariaceae to the Orobanchaceae.

Photos: Windy Pass, Gallatin Range, MT, July (W. Tilt)

ELEPHANTHEAD (ELEPHANTHEAD LOUSEWORT)

FIELD DESCRIPTION:

Erect perennial herb, 8-26" tall, with distinctive flowers shaped like an elephant's head. Pink-purple flowers arranged in dense spike-like cluster atop reddish-purple stems. Individual flowers are hooded with short side petals (the ears) and long slender upturned upper lip (galea) resembling an elephant's trunk. Fern-like leaves are pinnately divided into fine, sharp-toothed segments with larger leaves basally arranged while stem leaves are alternate and gradually reduced upwards.

MONTANE

Flowering: June - August

Habitat: Woods, meadows and moist open slopes, montane

TIDBITS

Once you observe this plant, you can honestly say you've seen pink elephants. Red fern-like leaves appear first in early summer, followed by dark stems, and then flowering stalks. Even the dried seed heads continue to show the elephant's trunk. Elephanthead is a parasitic plant whose roots, haustoria, penetrate the roots of other plants for nourishment. Many species of *Pedicularis* are referenced for their potential tranquilizing, sedative, and aphrodisiac effect. While the species name refers to Greenland, the plant does not grow there.

Photos: SW Colorado, June (Al Schneider); Illustration: USDA-NRCS Plants Database

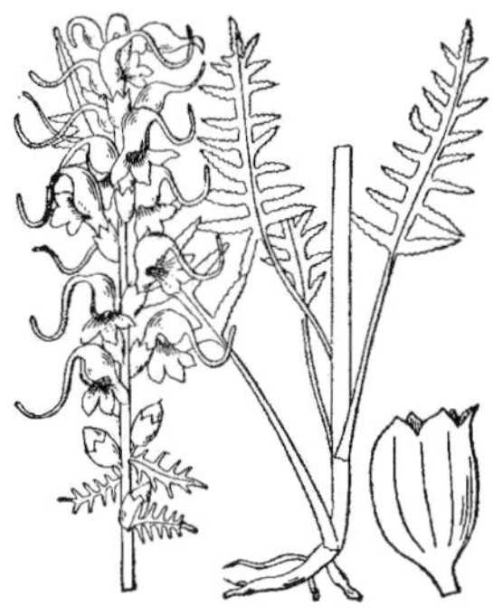

PARRY'S LOUSEWORT

Pedicularis parryi • Orobanchaceae (Broomrape Family)

FIELD DESCRIPTION:

Perennial, 4-10" tall, with erect stems. Leaves pinnately compound, fernlike, mostly basal, becoming reduced and sessile above, with a few smaller leaves on stalks, glabrous. Flowers purple-to-dark-red in dense terminal racemes. Calyx tubular, hooded, tapering to straight lip. Fruit is a flattened capsule.

TIDBITS

The flowers of Parry's Lousewort are commonly white or yellow throughout most of its range. In the Yellowstone region, however, the species is commonly *P. parryi* var. *purpurea*, a purple variation. Parry's Lousewort is a delight to encounter, greeting the eye in high mountain meadows with purple, joined by blues, yellows, and whites of the other wildflowers carpeting the ground. *Parryi* honors Charles Christopher Parry, a highly respected doctor, explorer, and naturalist in the 1800s, who participated in numerous botanical surveys across the Midwest and western United States, particularly Colorado.

ALPINE
SUBALPINE
MONTANE

Flowering: June - July

Habitat: Open slopes and meadows, upper montane to alpine

Thumbnail photo: Gallatin Range, MT, July (W. Tilt); Other photos: Mt. Haggin WMA., MT, July (Hank Jorgensen)

Pedicularis racemosa • Orobanchaceae (Broomrape Family)

PARROT'S BEAK
(SICKLETOP LOUSEWORT)

FIELD DESCRIPTION:

Perennial herb, 6-20" tall, with unbranched stems and showy white flowers arranged in loose racemes. Individual flowers comprised of an upper lip curving downward into a distinct, sickle-shaped beak above a wider three-lobed lip. Leaves are alternate, lance-shaped, and toothed on short petioles. Leaves and stems often reddish.

SUBALPINE
MONTANE

Flowering: June - August

Habitat: Dry, open forests, montane to subalpine

Thumbnail photo: Okanogan-Wenatchee NF, WA, Wikimedia (Walter Siegmund; Reference photo: Linn Co., OR, July (Gerald D. Carr); Illustration: Karl Urban, Umatilla NF, OR

TIDBITS

Parrot's Beak is a showy plant often found at the base of spruce trees. Flowers are beaked, giving rise to its common name. Its bushy herbage gives rise to another common name, Leafy Lousewort. Historically, many plants were given names based on their uses or properties, both real and imagined. The name lousewort from the belief that livestock eating the plant would get lice. While that claim is unfounded, the plant has been recently identified as an alternate host for white pine blister rust (*Cronartium ribicola*), an infectious disease of 5-needled pines.

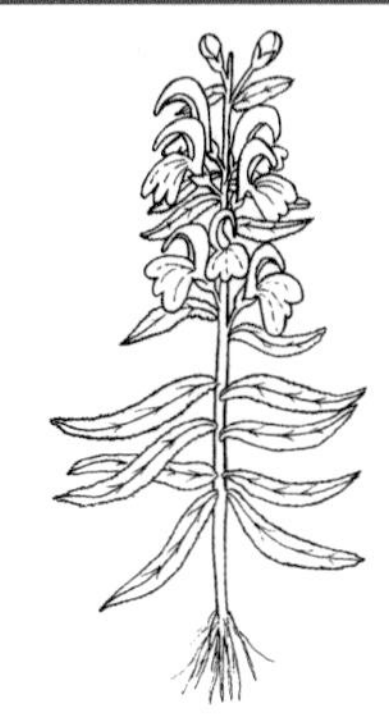

WESTERN PEONY (BROWN'S PEONY)

Paeonia brownii • Paeoniaceae (Peony Family)

FIELD DESCRIPTION:

Bushy perennial, 8-20" tall, with 1 or more erect stems. Leaves deeply lobed, divided 2 or 3 times, fleshy, and coated with whitish-blue waxy powder. Leaflets oval, with rounded tips. One or more nodding, greenish-to-reddish-brown, spherical flowers are clustered at stem ends. Flower is comprised of 5 leathery, greenish-to-purplish sepals and 5 smaller, round, red-to-brownish petals with yellow-to-greenish edges. Numerous stamens surround a thick pistil. Sepals persist until winter and large, leathery, sausage-like fruits develop.

TIDBITS

A large, distinctive flower that cannot be mistaken for any other plant. Found largely along the western portion of the Yellowstone region, the Western Peony is a treat to find lurking under the sagebrush along the Henry's Fork River of eastern Idaho and elsewhere. The large flowers nod and may be missed at first glance while the plant's light green foliage stands out against the surrounding sagebrush. David Douglas collected the plant in 1826 and named it for Robert Brown, a prominent English botanist.

Flowering: May - June

Habitat: Dry flats and slopes, sagebrush steppe, edges and openings in dry forests, valleys to montane

Photos: Harriman State Park, ID, June (W. Tilt); Illustration: Karl Urban, Umatilla NF, OR

Corydalis aurea • Papaveraceae (Poppy Family)

GOLDEN CORYDALIS
(SCRAMBLED EGGS)

FIELD DESCRIPTION:

Biennial herb, 3-11" tall, with bright yellow flowers and fern-like leaves. Flowers are yellow, two-lipped, with an upper spur-like petal, arranged in tight, elongated clusters (racemes). Leaves are alternate, pinnately compound 2-4 times into linear segments. Fruits are curved pod-like capsules, constricted between seeds.

MONTANE
VALLEYS

Flowering: May - August

Habitat: Well-drained soils, valleys to montane

Photos: Stonewall, CO, May (W. Tilt);
Illustration: USDA-NRCS Plants Database

TIDBITS

Golden Corydalis appears at first glance to belong to the Pea Family, but is instead a member of the Poppy Family. Corydalis is not found in large numbers in the region, but its numerous golden-yellow, spurred, tubular flowers make it conspicuous when encountered. Look for it in disturbed areas, on talus slopes, or alluvium along streams. *Corydalis* from the Greek in reference to the spur on the claw of a lark (as in "larkspur"), and *aurea* from the Latin for "golden". Recently reclassified from the Fumariaceae to the Papaveraceae.

STEER'S-HEAD
(LONGHORN STEER'S HEAD)

Dicentra uniflora • Papaveraceae (Poppy Family)

FIELD DESCRIPTION:

Small, delicate perennial with a flower that resembles the skull of a steer. Flower stalks and leaves appear separate above ground, arising from a root cluster. Single pink-white flower at end of stalk with 4 modified petals; 2 outer petals curve out to resemble ears or horns, dependent on the amount of curve, while 2 inner petals are fused and taper to form a rostrum or nose. Leaves are basal, long-stalked and ternate, and again irregularly lobed.

TIDBITS

There may be no more aptly named wildflower. Steer's-Head is a trophy worth the search and a favorite of all who encounter it. While quite common, it is often maddeningly hard to find thanks to a number of characteristics: it is small, early-blooming, and often obscured by other vegetation. The blossoms of Steer's-Head are small (only 0.5-0.6" across), bloom shortly after the snow clears, and as distinctive as the flower is, it blends well into the background vegetation and soil. Flower stem and leaves arise separately from fleshy roots.

SUBALPINE
MONTANE
FOOTHILLS

Flowering: April - June

Habitat: Well-drained slopes, foothills to subalpine

Photos: Beehive Basin, MT, June (Rip McIntosh); Illustration: Karl Urban, Umatilla NF, OR

Mimulus guttatus • Phrymaceae (Lopseed Family)

YELLOW MONKEYFLOWER

FIELD DESCRIPTION:

Annual or perennial herb, 4-20" tall, with yellow flowers comprised of fused petals forming a tube with 2 upper and 3 lower lobes. Lower lip of flower has maroon spots and hairy throat. Fused green calyx is ridged and toothed with upper tooth being the longest. Hollow stems support egg- or lance-shaped, sharply toothed opposite leaves that are often joined at base.

SUBALPINE
MONTANE

Flowering: June - August

Habitat: Wet soils along streams and wetland areas, montane to subalpine

Photos: Bridger Range, MT, July (Matt Lavin); Illustration: Karl Urban, Umatilla NF, OR

TIDBITS

Yellow Monkeyflower is an eye-catching bright yellow with reddish spots. They may appear as scattered plants or may be found in masses. Look for monkeyflowers whenever a small rivulet crosses your trail in the mountains. The plant's sap can be used to heal wounds as it contains agents effective in contracting human tissue. The genus is derived from *mimus,* "buffoon," for the clownish appearance of the flower as you stare into the corolla. *Guttatus* from the Latin for "drops" or "specks" referring to the tiny red dots on the inside of the petals.

LEWIS' MONKEYFLOWER
(PURPLE MONKEYFLOWER)

Mimulus lewisii • Phrymaceae (Lopseed Family)

FIELD DESCRIPTION:

Perennial herb, 1-3' tall, with bright pink-purple snapdragon-like flowers. Flowers consist of fused petals forming a tube with 2 upper and 3 lower lobes. Lower lip of flower has white hairs, yellow patches with maroon dots in throat. Fused green calyx is ridged and toothed with upper tooth being the longest. Leaves are opposite, sticky, hairy, and lanceolate to egg-shaped. Leaves are stalkless and strongly parallel nerved.

TIDBITS

A showy pink-purple flower found along streams and wet areas, similar to the haunts of Yellow Monkeyflower (*Mimulus guttatus*). The complex flower is designed for pollination by bees, and it is a favorite target for hummingbirds as well. The genus *Mimulus* refers to the Latin for "buffoon or actor in a farce," while *lewisii* honors Captain Meriwether Lewis of the Corps of Discovery. The common name alludes to the flowers resembling a grinning ape. Recently reclassified from the Scrophulariaceae to the Phrymaceae.

SUBALPINE
MONTANE
VALLEYS-FOOTHILLS

Flowering: June - August

Habitat: Wet soils along wetland areas, valleys to subalpine

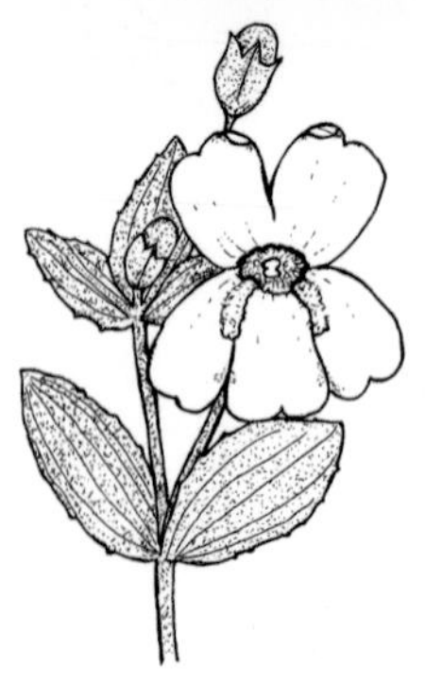

Thumbnail photos: Beehive Basin, MT, July (Rip McIntosh); Reference photo: Beehive Basin, MT, August (W. Tilt); Illustration: Karl Urban, Umatilla NF, OR

Besseya wyomingensis • Plantaginaceae (Plantain Family)

WYOMING KITTENTAILS
(WYOMING BESSEYA)

FIELD DESCRIPTION:

Perennial herb, 3-10" tall, with puberulent stems and leaves. Basal leaves egg-shaped, leathery, margins distinctly round-toothed on long petioles. Stem leaves smaller and stalkless. Numerous flowers arranged in dense terminal spike. Grey-green, woolly flower-heads comprise small flowers with no petals and 2 projecting purple stamens. Fruits are oval, silky capsules containing numerous seeds borne on an elongated stem.

ALPINE
SUBALPINE
MONTANE
VALLEYS

Flowering: April - July

Habitat: Dry open soils, valleys to alpine

Photos: Bozeman, MT, May (W. Tilt)

TIDBITS

After a long winter, spring comes fitfully to the Rocky Mountains. The bright purple appearance of Wyoming Kittentails is one of the first wildflowers to announce the warmer weather to come. The soft, fuzzy hairs of the rounded flower-heads earn the plant its "kitten tail" name while the stamens give the flower-head its purple appearance. After blooming, seedhead is a distinctive green pubescent wand. Recently reclassified from the Scrophulariaceae to the Plantaginaceae.

BLUE-EYED MARY

Collinsia parviflora • Plantaginaceae (Plantain Family)

TIDBITS

One of the smallest wildflowers in the region, Blue-Eyed Mary often grows where other vegetation is sparse. Easily overlooked in shrub-steppe and other areas. It often grows in significantly large numbers, which helps attract attention to it. *Collinsia* honors Zaccheus Collins (1764-1831), an eminent botanist from Philadelphia. *Parviflora* is Latin for "small-flowered." Recently reclassified from the Scrophulariaceae to the Plantaginaceae.

FIELD DESCRIPTION:

Delicate annual herb, 2-4" tall. Leaves opposite, narrow, linear to lance-shaped, with entire margins. Lower leaves broader and stalked, soon withered. Upper leaves narrower, becoming stalkless, often in whorls of 3-5. Small blue flowers with white lips on weak stalks arise in groups of 1-6 from upper leaf axils. Flowers are less than .25" long and are comprised of a brownish calyx, two-lobed upper lip, three-lobed lower lip, and 4 stamens tucked behind middle lobe.

MONTANE
FOOTHILLS

Flowering: April - July

Habitat: Variety of open to shaded sites, foothills to montane

Photos: Butte Co., ID, June (Matt Lavin); Illustration: USDA-NRCS Plants Database

Linaria dalmatica • Plantaginaceae (Plantain Family)

DALMATIAN TOADFLAX

FIELD DESCRIPTION:

Perennial herb, 1-4′ tall, with distinctive snapdragon-like pale-to-bright-yellow flowers arranged in dense cluster atop stem. Lower lip has fuzzy patch of orange-to-white hairs, and flower extends backward in a slender straight spur. Leaves are alternate, ovate or lance-ovate, sharp-pointed, with bases that clasp the stem. Stems and leaves bluish-gray-green, glaucous, with a waxy coating.

MONTANE
FOOTHILLS

Flowering: July - October

Habitat: Disturbed open areas, foothills to montane

Thumbnail photo: Gallatin Range, MT, May (W. Tilt); Reference photo: Utah State University (Bugwood.org); Illustration: Karl Urban, Umatilla NF, OR

TIDBITS

Introduced from Europe as an ornamental but has since escaped, Dalmatian Toadflax is a weedy species that produces large numbers of seeds and spreads by vigorous rhizomatous root systems. Butter-and-Eggs (*Linaria vulgaris*) is a similar plant but with narrow leaves and a distinctive orange patch on the lower lip of the flower. Toadflaxes have a long history of herbal use for liver and other disorders. Toadflax refers to the resemblance of the flowers to toads and the resemblance of its foliage to flax – *Linaria* from the Latin for flax. *Dalmatica* refers to the Dalmatian coast of the Balkan Peninsula.

BUTTER-AND-EGGS (COMMON TOADFLAX)

Linaria vulgaris • Plantaginaceae (Plantain Family)

FIELD DESCRIPTION:

Introduced perennial herb, 8-32" tall, with distinctive snapdragon-like, pale-to-bright yellow flowers arranged in dense cluster atop stem. Lower lip has fuzzy orange patch and flower extends backward in a slender straight spur. Leaves are alternate, linear, and gray-green in color. Plant has an unpleasant smell.

TIDBITS

Introduced from Europe as an ornamental, the plant escaped cultivation and now is a permanent resident. It is known as "Butter-and-Eggs" for its yellow flowers with orange tongues. Like Dalmatian Toadflax (*Linaria dalmatica*), a similar plant with broader egg-shaped leaves with bases that clasp the stem, Butter-and-Eggs can be invasive, aggressively spreading at the expense of native grasses and other perennials, and reducing forage production for livestock and wildlife. The flowers are pollinated by bumblebees, which are strong enough to push past the palate to enter the throat of the corolla.

MONTANE
FOOTHILLS

Flowering: June - September

Habitat: Disturbed open areas, foothills to montane

Thumbnail photos: Beehive Basin MT, July (Rip McIntosh); Reference photo: South Leigh, ID, August (W. Tilt); Illustration: USDA-NRCS Plants Database

Penstemon cyaneus • Plantaginaceae (Plantain Family)

BLUE PENSTEMON
(DARK-BLUE BEARDTONGUE)

FIELD DESCRIPTION:

Perennial herb, 12-28" tall, with erect stems; plant smooth, hairless, glabrous, often waxy-coated (blue-green-colored). Leaves thick with entire margins. Stem leaves stalkless and clasping, linear-lanceolate-to-ovate. Basal leaves lanceolate on short petioles. Inflorescence is a loose spike of showy flowers borne in upper leaf axils. Flowers bilaterally symmetrical with bright blue corolla, often turning pinkish toward back of flower, Snapdragon-like flowers have 2 upper lobes and 3 lower lobes. Flower hairless except for single hairy stamen ("beard-tongue") evident in bottom of flower mouth. Fruits are capsules.

MONTANE

Flowering: June - August

Habitat: Dry open soils, montane

TIDBITS

A showy resident of sagebrush communities with a bright blue-purple spike of flowers, Blue Penstemon is endemic to the Greater Yellowstone Region and southern Idaho. Its large showy flowers attract pollinators, including bumble and mason bees, as well as other insects. Penstemons are one of the largest genera of flowering plants native to North America. *Penstemon from the* Greek for "5 stamens." Recently reclassified from the Scrophulariaceae to the Plantaginaceae.

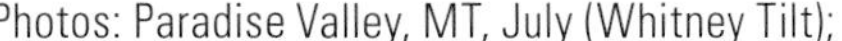

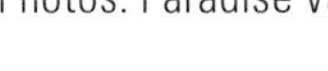

Photos: Paradise Valley, MT, July (Whitney Tilt);

FUZZY-TONGUED PENSTEMON (FUZZY BEARDTONGUE)

Penstemon eriantherus • Plantaginaceae (Plantain Family)

TIDBITS

Several varieties of Fuzzy-Tongued Penstemon are found in the region. The characteristic fuzzy-tongue or "beardtongue" is the single sterile stamen bearing a tuft of hair and protruding from the flower like a tongue. Penstemons are one of the largest genera of flowering plants endemic to North America. *Penstemon* is of Greek origin: *penta* meaning "five," and *stemon* meaning "stamen." Recently reclassified from the Scrophulariaceae to the Plantaginaceae.

FIELD DESCRIPTION:

Showy perennial herb, 5-15" tall with large, pale-lavender-to-purple-red, snapdragon-like flowers presented in whorls from upper leaf axils. Flowers funnel-shaped widening to 2 lobes on upper lip and 3 on lower lip. Lower lip longer than upper lobes, bearded with purplish veins giving the appearance of a tongue. Leaves opposite, oblong-linear. Basal leaves stalked, with stem leaves becoming stalkless and narrower as they rise on stem. Overall plant sticky and glandular-hairy.

MONTANE
VALLEYS

Flowering: May - July

Habitat: Dry open soils, valleys to montane

Photos: Bozeman, MT, June (Whitney Tilt); Illustration: USDA-NRCS Plants Database

WAXLEAF PENSTEMON

FIELD DESCRIPTION:

Perennial herb, 4-12" tall, with waxy leaves and smooth stems. Numerous bright-blue, tubular flowers in tight whorls form elongated clusters. Flower throats prominently yellow-bearded. Leaves are thick, fleshy, entire, broadly lance- to egg-shaped, with whitish-blue bloom.

TIDBITS

The Waxleaf Penstemon is aptly named, for its waxy leaves are distinctive. They are also an adaptation to life in open, dry conditions. The plant is hairless save for yellow, hairy stamens in the flower throats. Penstemons were formerly considered members of the Figwort Family, whose name arises from early European herbalist-physicians who used the plants to cure fig warts. *Nitidus* from the Latin for "shining." Recently reclassified from the Scrophulariaceae to the Plantaginaceae.

Flowering: May - July

Habitat: Open grasslands and hillsides, plains to foothills

PLAINS-FOOTHILLS

Photos: Bozeman, MT, June (W. Tilt & Matt Lavin)

LITTLEFLOWER PENSTEMON

Penstemon procerus • Plantaginaceae (Plantain Family)

FIELD DESCRIPTION:

Slender-stemmed perennial herb, 6-16" tall, with numerous blue-purple flowers crowded into distinct whorls on short stems arising from leaf axils. Flowers more or less nodding. Basal leaves, if present, are stalked and oblanceolate. Stem leaves are opposite, entire, stalkless, and sparse on slender hairless stems. Snapdragon-like flowers consist of 2 lobes on upper lip and 3 on lower lip. Four fertile stamen present along with 1 staminode (non-fertile stamen) giving the appearance of a tongue. Fruits are capsules.

ALPINE
SUBALPINE
MONTANE
VALLEYS

Flowering: June - August

Habitat: Dry meadows and open forests, valleys to alpine zones

TIDBITS

There are dozens of species of penstemon found in the Rocky Mountain region. In general, the blue-purple penstemons are difficult to identify to the species levels but share common characteristics, including leaves in opposite pairs; tubular flowers with 2 lobes on upper lip and 3 on lower lip; and 4 fertile stamen and a staminode (nonfertile stamen), which is often hairy (hence the name "beardtongue"). This species, as its common name suggests, has one of the smallest flowers of the penstemons. Recently reclassified from the Scrophulariaceae to the Plantaginaceae.

Photos: Bozeman, MT, June (Whitney Tilt)

AMERICAN BROOKLINE

FIELD DESCRIPTION:

Slender perennial herb, 4-24" tall, with trailing stems. Foliage is smooth and hairless. Leaves opposite, egg-shaped to broadly lance-shaped with fine-toothed margins on short petioles. Several small (5-10 mm) blue-to-pale-violet, saucer-shaped flowers in open racemes arising from axils of upper leaves. Flowers comprised of 4 broad spreading lobes, 4 glandular-hairy sepals, and 2 anthers. Fruits are smooth, rounded capsules. Grows from system of shallow rhizomes.

MONTANE
FOOTHILLS

Flowering: May - August

Habitat: Moist to wet soils along streams and wet meadows, foothills to montane

Thumbnail photo: Bozeman, MT, June (W. Tilt);
Reference photo: Phillips Co., MT, June (Matt Lavin)

TIDBITS

American Brookline is found in wet areas, often occuring in large numbers, spreading from rhizomes shallowly buried in the soil. The plant can quickly form dense patches in slow-moving or still water. *Veronica* species are edible, often eaten raw like watercress. The genus *Veronica* is derived from the Greek "I bring victory," in reference to the plant's supposed healing powers. It is also believed that *Veronica* recognizes St. Veronica, who is said to have given Jesus her veil to wipe his face as he carried his cross to Golgotha. Recently reclassified from the Scrophulariaceae to the Plantaginaceae.

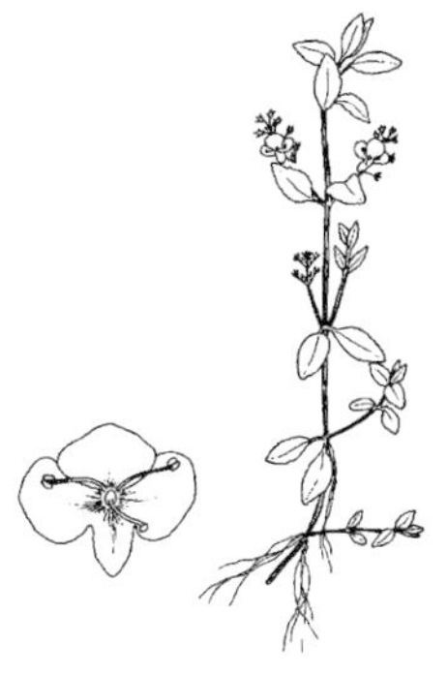

WATER SPEEDWELL (BROOK PIMPERNEL)

Veronica anagallis-aquatica • Plantaginaceae (Plantain Family

FIELD DESCRIPTION:

Biennial or short-lived perennial, 8-40" tall, found near water. Overall form prostrate, hairless, with upraised tips. Stems round and thick. Small, pale-lavender-to-blue flowers, four-petaled, with darker veins, growing in spikes arising from leaf axils. Leaves opposite, elliptic-ovate, stalkless, often clasping. Leaf margins entire to sharply toothed. Fruits are roundish capsules.

VALLEYS-FOOTHILLS

Flowering: July - September

Habitat: Wet soils, along ditches, backwaters, and slow moving water, valleys to foothills

TIDBITS

Introduced from Europe, Water Speedwell is now found throughout much of the United States. Plant is semi-aquatic, often growing in shallow water along steam banks, in ponds, and in other wetland environments. Rich in vitamin C, the leaves are edible, raw or cooked, and have been used in the treatment of scurvy. If eaten, care should be taken to ensure surrounding water is potable. Recently reclassified from the Scrophulariaceae to the Plantaginaceae.

Photos: Bozeman Creek, MT, August (W. Tilt); Illustration: USDA-NRCS Plants Database

ALPINE SPEEDWELL

FIELD DESCRIPTION:

Perennial herb, 2-10" tall, with glandular-hairy stems. Leaves opposite, elliptical to ovate, entire or slightly toothed, stalkless and often silky-hairy. Several minute blue-violet saucer-shaped flowers in short congested terminal clusters. Flowers comprised of 4 broad spreading lobes, 4 glandular-hairy sepals, and 2 anthers. Flowering stalks elongate as plant goes to seed. Fruits are flattened, hairy, heart-shaped capsules. Grows from system of shallow rhizomes.

ALPINE
SUBALPINE
MONTANE

Flowering: June - September

Habitat: Moist and dry open sites and forest understory, montane to alpine

TIDBITS

Alpine Speedwell is a delicate lavender-blue wildflower common along trails in high meadows and alpine areas. But it is easily overlooked while hiking due to its small size. *Veronica* is believed to recognize St. Veronica, who is said to have given Jesus her veil to wipe his face as he carried his cross to Golgotha. The stains on Veronica's cloth were thought to be similar to the markings on some species of *Veronica*. Morton Wormskjoldii was a 19th century Danish botanist.

Photos: Beehive Basin, MT, August (W. Tilt); Illustration: USDA-NRCS Plants Database

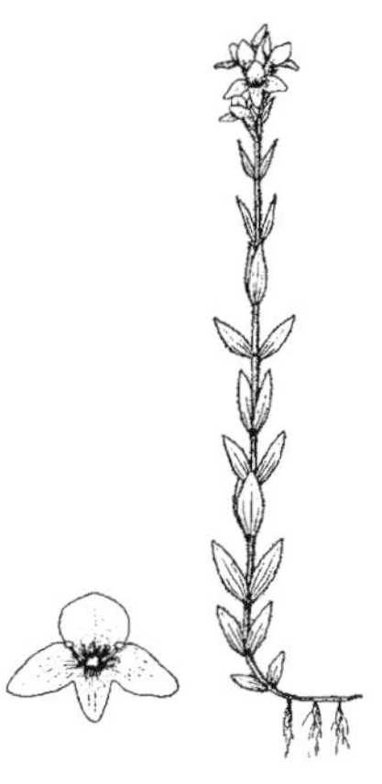

NARROWLEAF COLLOMIA (TINY TRUMPET)

Collomia linearis • Polemoniaceae (Phlox Family)

FIELD DESCRIPTION:

Annual herb, 4-16" tall. Small, pink, trumpet-shaped flowers, with 5 oval flaring lobes, in leafy terminal clusters. Leaves are alternate, linear to lance-shaped, stalkless or nearly so. Leaves increase in size up the stem and smaller leaves arise from leaf axils. Stems erect, fine hairy, becoming glandular on upper parts. Fruits are three-celled capsules enclosed by calyxes.

TIDBITS

The most widespread member of its genus and found in all Western states, the plant's fruit has an interesting twist for dispersing and setting seed. As the calyx dries and shrinks, pressure builds until the capsules split the calyx open sending seeds shooting in all directions. The seeds of Narrowleaf Collomia produce spiraling threads which help anchor them to the soil. *Collomia* from the Greek for "glue," in reference to the plant's mucilaginous seeds, and *linearis* from the Latin for "linear," in reference to the plant's narrow leaves.

MONTANE
FOOTHILLS

Flowering: May - August

Habitat: Open and lightly shaded areas, often on disturbed soil, foothills to montane

Thumbnail photo: Tobacco Root Range, MT, June (W. Tilt); Reference photo: Madison Range, MT, July (Rip McIntosh); Illustration: USDA-NRCS Plants Database

Ipomopsis aggregata • Polemoniaceae (Phlox Family)
(Synonym: *Gilia aggregata*)

SCARLET GILIA
(SCARLET TRUMPET)

FIELD DESCRIPTION:

Biennial or monocarpic, short-lived perennial herb, 1-3' tall, with a distinct unpleasant aroma. Leaves are alternate, pinnately lobed into narrow segments, glandular. Flower-head a simple or branched raceme, bright red trumpet-shaped flowers. Each flower with 5 pointed lobes bent backward. Fruits are a capsule with 1-2 seeds.

MONTANE
FOOTHILLS

Flowering: May - August

Habitat: Dry meadows and other open or lightly wooded sites, foothills to montane

Photos: Teton Range, WY, August (W. Tilt); Illustration: USDA-NRCS Plants Database

TIDBITS

Scarlet Gilia is a favorite of hummingbirds and gardeners alike, providing a delightful splash of red to the open meadows along the western portions of the Yellowstone region. Scarlet Gilia's stem and leaves are sticky and give off an odor when crushed. The shape of its flower and the nectar that forms reminds some observers of honeysuckle. *Ipomopsis* from the Latin for "similar to Ipomoea" (Morning Glories), in reference to similar red, tubular flowers; *aggregata* from the Latin for "brought together" describes its petal growing pattern.

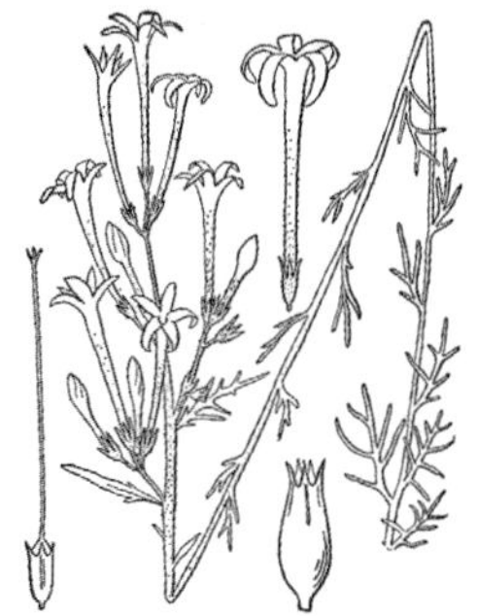

MOSS PHLOX
(CARPET PHLOX)

Phlox hoodii • Polemoniaceae (Phlox Family)

FIELD DESCRIPTION:

Small, compact perennial, 2-6" tall, that forms mats. Flowers are white-pink or bluish with 5 broad, flat-spreading lobes, mostly solitary at end of stems. Leaves are opposite, linear, firm, and sharp-pointed. Overall plant woolly and cobweb-hairy with dense, overlapping leaves. Fruits are elliptic capsules splitting along 3 lines.

TIDBITS

Look for conspicuous clumps of white or pink-flowered phlox along trails. There are several species of similar appearing phlox in the region. The leaves of Moss Phlox are linear and not notched, and the plant has a woolly appearance with cobweb-like hairs and needle-like leaves, forming dense mats on dry open soils. Phlox from the Greek for "flame." *Hoodii* recognizes Robert Hood, a member of the British Royal Navy's ill-fated Coppermine Expedition (1819-1822) into the Arctic to find and map the possibility of a Northwest Passage. Hood named the phlox but was subsequently murdered by a fellow crew member.

Flowering: April - June

Habitat: Dry open soils, foothills

FOOTHILLS

Photos: Bozeman, MT, May (Matt Lavin);
Illustration: USDA-NRCS Plants Database

Phlox longifolia • Polemoniaceae (Phlox Family)

LONGLEAF PHLOX

FIELD DESCRIPTION:

Low perennial herb, 3-14" tall, in loosely tufted groups. Somewhat woody bases and generally erect (as compared to other phlox). White or pink flowers with 5 spreading lobes atop a slender tube. Calyx comprised of 5 green ribs. Leaves are opposite, linear, and up to 3" long. Fruits are elliptical capsules.

MONTANE

FOOTHILLS

Flowering: April - July

Habitat: Dry meadows and other open or lightly wooded sites, foothills to montane

Thumbnail & inset photos: Bozeman, MT, June (Matt Lavin); Reference photo: Bozeman, MT, June (W. Tilt)

TIDBITS

Longleaf Phlox is a conspicuous plant along the trail found across a good portion of the West. The species is large flowered and leaved compared with most phlox. Its flowers vary from white to pink-purple. *Phlox* from the Greek for "flame," as many of the genus are vibrantly colored. *Longifolia* refers to the leaves, which are relatively long (up to 3") and narrow, unlike the leaves of many other types of phlox which have short needle-like leaves like Moss Phlox (*P. hoodii*).

SHOWY JACOBS-LADDER

Polemonium pulcherrimum • Polemoniaceae (Phlox Family)

FIELD DESCRIPTION:

Perennial herb, 3-12" tall, featuring blue flowers arranged in congested clusters. Flowers are broadly bell-shaped with 5 rounded, spreading lobes around small tubes. Five white stamens extend beyond the petals. Leaves are pinnately compound with numerous pairs of leaflets along the main axis. Basal leaves often tufted and stem Leaves are alternate and somewhat reduced. Upper parts of the plant often glandular.

SUBALPINE
MONTANE

Flowering: May - August

Habitat: Moist soils in meadows and along streams, montane to subalpine

TIDBITS

The ladder-like arrangement of leaflets along a main axis gives Showy Jacob's-Ladder its common name. Its sweet-scented flowers attract insects that detect 3 distinctive color zones, guiding them past the stamens and stigma to the nectar. In some years the plant blooms in eye-catching arrays, while in other years few blooms are produced. The plant is often found in colonies around the base of Engelmann Spruce. *Pulcherrimum* from the Greek for "very beautiful." In the Bible, Jacob dreams of a ladder that reached from earth to heaven.

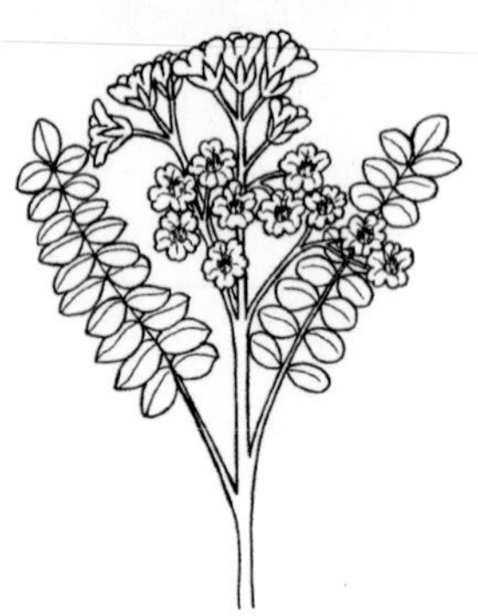

Photos: Slough Creek, MT, June (W. Tilt); Illustration: Karl Urban, Umatilla NF, OR

Polemonium viscosum • Polemoniaceae (Phlox Family)

SKY PILOT
(STICKY POLEMONIUM)

FIELD DESCRIPTION:

Perennial herb, 4-6" tall, spreading from branching caudices. Stems glandular-hairy and stem leaves sparse. Basal leaves to 0.75" long. Leaves are compound, finely cut, and upright. Leaflets very numerous, most or all of them cleft to the base or nearly so. Flowers several to many in dense clusters, funnel-shaped and light blue to dark purple in color. Five-petaled with lobes of calyx shorter than the tube. Fruit is a capsule.

ALPINE

Flowering: June - August

Habitat: Moist alpine tundra near scree, alpine

TIDBITS

Sky Pilot's intense blue-purple flowers makes it a showy denizen of the alpine zone. It prefers rocky, south-facing slopes and scree where the snow melts early and the soil warms up. Its long tubular flowers hang in clusters and the plant may have a sweet skunk-like odor. Sky Pilot was first collected "towards the sources of the Platte" by Thomas Nuttall on his 1834-1837 expedition across the western United States. *Viscosum* references the plant's sticky leaves.

Photos: Beartooth Highway, MT, July (W. Tilt): Leaf detail at right

SULFUR BUCKWHEAT

Eriogonum umbellatum • Polygonaceae (Buckwheat Family)

FIELD DESCRIPTION:

Mat-forming perennial herb, 4-12" tall. Balls of tiny light yellow (sometimes cream) flowers at ends of branches forming an umbel-like cluster on straight, leafless, woolly stems. Each individual ball-like flower cluster is composed of numerous little cups, from which grow several flowers on very slender stalks. Flowers about 0.25" long, often with pinkish tint. The 6 petal-like lobes are hairy on outside margin with a circle of bract-like leaves immediately beneath umbel. Basal leaves lance- or spatula-shaped, green on top and woolly, silver gray on lower side, forming flat mats.

ALPINE
SUBALPINE
MONTANE
FOOTHILLS

Flowering: June - August

Habitat: Generally dry soils, foothills to alpine

TIDBITS

Buckwheats are showy plants with colorful and long-lasting flowers. Sulfur Buckwheat has dense umbels of flowers, subtended by a whorl of leaf-like bracts, arising from a dense mat of small, leathery leaves. The leaves change to red in the fall and persist through the winter. *Eriogonums* are difficult to identify to the species level as they are highly variable; more than 41 varieties of *Eriogonum umbellatum* are described by the *Flora of North America*. *Eriogonium* from the Greek for "wool knee," in reference to the woolly leaves and swollen joints exhibited by species in this genus.

Thumbnail photo: Bridger Range, MT, July (Matt Lavin); Reference & inset photos: Slough Creek, MT, June (W. Tilt)

WATER SMARTWEED

Persicaria amphibia • Polygonaceae (Buckwheat Family)
(Synonym: *Polygonum amphibium*)

FIELD DESCRIPTION:

Amphibious perennial herb, with erect or prostate stem that may grow 6′ or longer. Showy rose-pink flower clusters in a terminal, unbranched cluster. Individual flowers are cup-shaped and five-parted. Leaves are alternate, oval, hairy, and pointed at tip. Seeds are shiny, deep brown, and lens-shaped.

MONTANE
FOOTHILLS

Flowering: July - October

Habitat: Mudflats, shallow still or slow-moving water, foothills to montane

TIDBITS

Also known as Lady's Thumb, Water Smartweed establishes itself in moist soils at the edge of ponds and lakes or in shallow water where its leaves and flowers float at the end of long stems. The species name *amphibium* references this ability to grow on land and in water, and the species is also known as Amphibious Bistort. The plant is found throughout most of the United States and Canada. Waterfowl and other aquatic animals seek out the seeds and other parts of the plant.

Photos: Teton River, ID, August (W. Tilt);
Illustration: USDA-NRCS Plants Database

AMERICAN BISTORT

Polygonum bistortoides • Polygonaceae (Buckwheat Family)
(Synonym: *Bistorta bistortoides*)

FIELD DESCRIPTION:

Long, slender-stemmed perennial herb, 8-22" tall, with small white-pinkish flowers clustered in a short, dense spike at tip of stem. White stamens extend beyond sepals giving flowerhead the appearance of a brush. Basal leaves long and narrow with long petioles. Stem leaves few, small, lance-shaped, and lacking petioles.

TIDBITS

A dainty puff of white like a floral Q-tip announces the bistort. The soft cottony flower-head often has a blush of pink. Partially red stems and leaves are characteristic, with the reds becoming more pronounced in the fall. Explorers Lewis and Clark observed their Native American hosts commonly eating bistort roots and seeds. Fire-roasted, the roots have a chestnut-like taste while the seeds can be roasted or made into flour. This species can be confused with its smaller cousin Alpine Bistort (*Bistorta vivipara*), found in the subalpine and alpine zones.

Flowering: June - August

Habitat: Meadows, shady woods, along stream banks, montane to alpine

Photos: Bozeman, MT, June (Whitney Tilt); Illustration: USDA-NRCS Plants Database

Rumex crispus • Polygonaceae (Buckwheat Family)

CURLYLEAF DOCK
(YELLOW DOCK)

FIELD DESCRIPTION:

Stout perennial herb, 2-5′ tall. Leaves large, smooth, narrowly oblong, blunt-tipped, with curly, wavy margins, alternate on stem. Stems often red. Yellow to green six-parted flowers in dense whorled spikes. Flower stalks conspicuously jointed near base. Fruits are smooth achenes covered in a papery, three-winged membrane. Plant and seedhead persist, turning distinctive rusty brown.

MONTANE
FOOTHILLS

Flowering: June - September

Habitat: Moist soils along roadsides, ditches, prefers disturbed or unmanaged sites, foothills to montane

Photos: Bozeman, MT, July (W. Tilt); Illustration: USDA-NRCS Plants Database

TIDBITS

Introduced from Europe, Curlyleaf Dock is now found across much of North America, and can be locally invasive. Young leaves are rich in vitamins A and C, and are edible raw or cooked in small quantities. However, the plant commonly contains oxalic acid, and may be poisonous to livestock if ingested in quantity. Western Dock (*Rumex occidentalis*) is a similar species that has unbranched stems below the flower cluster and often heart-shaped leaf bases.

FEW-LEAVED DOCK (MOUNTAIN SORREL)

Rumex paucifolius • Polygonaceae (Buckwheat Family)

FIELD DESCRIPTION:

Perennial herb, 8-28" tall, with tall reddish spike of flowers. Small pale-to-dark-red flowers, lacking stamens or pistils, arranged on upward-pointing branches in loose spikes. Flower-heads found on upper half of hairless stems. Male and female flowers on different plants (dioecious). Numerous basal leaves are lance-shaped and tapered at both ends. Stem leaves are alternate and greatly reduced. Fruits are smooth achenes.

ALPINE
SUBALPINE
MONTANE

Flowering: June - August

Habitat: Moist mountain meadows, montane to alpine

TIDBITS

Mountain Sorrel commonly stands higher than surrounding vegetation. Plants are edible and nutritious, but should be consumed in moderation due to the presence of oxalic acid. A number of related *Rumex* species are found in the region, including Sheep Sorrel (*Rumex acetosella*) which is generally smaller in stature and has hastate leaves in the shape of an arrowhead. The 2 species commonly occur together.

Photos: Slough Creek, MT, June (W. Tilt); Illustration: USDA-NRCS Plants Database

ALPINE ROCK JASMINE

FIELD DESCRIPTION:

Low perennial herb, 1-4" tall, with tiny flowers atop silky-hairy, leafless stems. Leaves basal, narrowly lance-shaped and long hairy, in tight rosettes. Flower-heads comprised of 2-8 white flowers in compact umbels with involucral bracts at base. Flowers are white with 5 widely flaring lobes surrounding a yellow eye. Plant spreads by stolons.

ALPINE
SUBALPINE

Flowering: June - August

Habitat: Open rocky slopes, subalpine to alpine

TIDBITS

Alpine Rock Jasmine is a small plant of high elevations with a smell of tropical jasmine. It is easily overlooked due to its diminutive stature but can be found looking up at the attentive hiker with its yellow eyes. Also known as Fairy Candelabras, its flower clusters resemble candelabras sheltering soft rosettes of leaves. The flowers resemble a white forget-me-not whose yellow centers often turn pink as they age.

Photos: Beehive Basin, MT, August (W. Tilt); Illustration: USDA-NRCS Plants Database

SHOOTING STAR
(PRETTY SHOOTING STAR)

Dodecatheon pulchellum • Primulaceae (Primrose Family)
(Synonym: *Dodeceatheon cusickii*)

FIELD DESCRIPTION:

Perennial herb, 6-12" tall, with 1-25 distinctive pink or magenta flowers on long, leafless stem. Five petals sweep backward from a yellow base to reveal yellowish to purple tube and 5 anthers join to form a projecting point. Long, elliptical, and usually hairless leaves form a basal rosette.

TIDBITS

Shooting stars are a distinctive and colorful part of the region's flora. Look for flowers with purple-lavender petals, swept backwards from a yellowish nose, giving the impression of a flower facing a stiff headwind. The plant blooms soon after the snows melt. A great deal of variation occurs within the genera. *Dodecatheon* from the Latin for "12 gods," alluding to the arrangement of flowers suggesting an assembly of deities.

SUBALPINE
MONTANE
FOOTHILLS

Flowering: April - August

Habitat: Moist soils in meadows and along streams, foothills to subalpine

Photos: Gallatin Range, MT, May (W. Tilt); Illustration: USDA-NRCS Plants Database

Douglasia montana • Primulaceae (Primrose Family)

MOUNTAIN DOUGLASIA

FIELD DESCRIPTION:

Low, cushion perennial, 1-3" tall. Leaves basal, narrowly lance-shaped, minutely sharp-toothed, in tight whorled forms, often short-haired. Flowers solitary, bright pink to violet, comprised of a funnel-shaped tube with 5 spreading lobes. Stamens and style do not extend beyond small, central, yellow-rimmed flower opening. Fruits are five-valued capsules.

ALPINE
SUBALPINE
MONTANE
FOOTHILLS

Flowering: June - August

Habitat: Stony soils, exposed ridges, foothills to alpine

Photos: Beartooth Plateau, July (Gordon Wiltsie & Joel Yuodsnukis)

TIDBITS

A low cushion of brilliant pink announces Mountain Douglasia in bloom. Also known as Mountain Dwarf Primrose, the plant begins to bloom in the early summer at lower elevations and continues into July-August as one ascends into the alpine zone. Stamens of Rocky Mountain Douglasia do not extend beyond the yellow-rimmed opening to the floral tube. This helps distinguish douglasia from Moss Campion (*Silene acaulis*) and other members of the Phlox Family (Polemoniaceae) whose stamens and style do extend beyond the confines of the rim.

PARRY'S PRIMROSE

Primula parryi • Primulaceae (Primrose Family)

FIELD DESCRIPTION:

Perennial herb, up to 24" tall, malodorous, from thick rhizomes. Leaves basal, elliptic to lanceolate, glandular and green on both sides. Tubular flowers are magenta to reddish-purple with 5 spreading petals around a yellow center. Fruits are egg-shaped capsules.

TIDBITS

High in the mountains, not long after the snow has receded, the startling magenta of the Parry's Primrose arrests your eye. Its color is intensified by the contrast with its own bright green leaves, as well as the browns and whites of the early summer landscape at elevation. Parry's Primrose prefers moist soils so look for it on wet ledges, snow-melt areas, along streams, and other wetlands. It is often scattered in the extensive patches of white flowering Marsh Marigolds (*Caltha leptosepala*). Touching the plant will bring out an unpleasant fetid odor. *Primula* from the Latin for "early spring."

ALPINE
SUBALPINE
MONTANE

Flowering: June - August

Habitat: Wet meadows, stream sides, montane to alpine

Photos: Beehive Basin, MT, June (W. Tilt); Illustration: Karl Urban, Umatilla NF, OR

FIELD DESCRIPTION:

Perennial herb, 16-60" tall, with distinctive deep blue-purple hood-like flower. Flowers are flattened sideways with petal-like sepals forming a hood with a pointed beak over 2 sepals that are spreading and fan-shaped. Leaves are alternate, palmately divided into 3-5 main lobes, and toothed. Stems are hollow. Fruits are linear pods in erect clusters.

SUBALPINE
MONTANE

Flowering: June - August

Habitat: Moist soils along stream banks and forest borders, montane to subalpine

TIDBITS

The monk-like cowl of the flowers gives the species its common name. Monkshood is poisonous, containing a toxic alkaloid in its seeds and roots. *Aconitum napellus,* a European species of monkshood, is the celebrated "wolfbane" of werewolf lore. Historically, the plant was used to poison bait in wolf traps and its seeds as a parasiticide. *Aconitum* is the classical Latin name and is reported to mean "unconquerable poison," referring to the plant's toxicity.

Thumbnail photo: South Leigh Creek, WY, July (W. Tilt); Reference photo: SW Colorado, July (Al Schneider); Illustration: USDA-NRCS Plants Database

BANEBERRY
(RED BANEBERRY)

Actaea rubra • Ranunculaceae (Buttercup Family)

FIELD DESCRIPTION:

Showy perennial herb, 24-40" tall. Characterized by a white, rounded, cylindrical raceme of densely clustered flowers atop long, naked stalks. Crinkled leaves along stem are compound, coarsely sharp-toothed, lobed, and usually horizontal. Basal leaves clasp stem. Glossy, red berry (sometimes white) retains a dark stigma, which gives the berry the appearance of a doll's eye.

TIDBITS

As the name "Baneberry" suggests, all parts of the plant are poisonous, especially the roots and berries. The Baneberry's toxin suppresses the pneumogastric nerve causing possible cardiac arrest. The plant's red (sometimes white) porcelain-like berries give rise to the plant's common names China Berry and Doll's Eye. The Cheyenne Indians consider Baneberry sacred. *Actaea* from the Latin describing the leaves (elder-like), and *rubra* for "red."

MONTANE

Flowering: May - July

Habitat: Wet forested areas and stream banks, montane

Photos: Middle Cottonwood Canyon, MT, July-August (W. Tilt); Illustration: USDA-NRCS Plants Database

CUTLEAF ANEMONE (GLOBE ANEMONE)

FIELD DESCRIPTION:

Distinctive perennial herb, 8-20" tall, with 1-3 gray-hairy stems topped by single flower comprised of 5-9 sepals, ranging in color from cream to yellow to red, with a combination of colors sometimes appearing on a single plant. Basal cluster of long-petioled leaves divided into 3 or more lance-shaped lobes. Whorl of smaller leaves midway along stems. Fruits are silk tufted achenes in dense round heads.

ALPINE
SUBALPINE
MONTANE

Flowering: June - August

Habitat: Dry open areas, montane to alpine

TIDBITS

Anemone is a large genus of some 120 species worldwide. Like all buttercups, anemones produce protoanemonin, which is toxic and can cause rashes, nausea, and worse if touched or ingested. The Blackfeet Indians used the cotton-like silky hairs from anemone seed heads to burn over hot coals and inhale to soothe headaches. *Anemone* from the Greek for "windflower" in reference to their tufted seed heads. According to Greek mythology, the anemone sprang from Aphrodite's tears as she mourned the death of Adonis.

Photos: Slough Creek, MT, June (W. Tilt); Illustration: USDA-NRCS Plants Database

YELLOW COLUMBINE

Aquilegia flavescens • Ranunculaceae (Buttercup Family)

FIELD DESCRIPTION:

Showy perennial herb, 8-30" tall, with lemon-yellow flowers. Five cream-colored petals open wide in front and taper into spurs that curve inward. Five petal-like sepals surround petals. Compound leaves are mainly basal and divided 2-3 times into sets of 3 leaflets. Leaflets shallow-to-deeply lobed with rounded tips, often with a bluish-white appearance.

TIDBITS

A showy mountain denizen, commonly cultivated in the home garden, columbine flowers are edible, though best consumed in small quantities. Seeds and roots are poisonous and contain cardiogenic toxins. Native Americans used very small amounts of columbine root as an effective treatment for ulcers. *Aquilegia* from the Latin for eagle, in reference to the flower shape, or alternately from *agua* and *ligere*, "water collected," in reference to the nectar collected at spurs tips. *Flavescens* from the Latin for "pale yellow."

SUBALPINE
MONTANE

Flowering: June - August

Habitat: Mountain meadows and glades, montane to subalpine

Thumbnail photo: Slough Creek, MT, June (W. Tilt); Reference photo: Slough Creek, MT, June (Marianne Salas); Illustration: USDA-NRCS Plants Database

Caltha leptosepala • Ranunculaceae (Buttercup Family)
(Synonym: *Caltha biflora*)

MARSH MARIGOLD (ELKSLIP)

FIELD DESCRIPTION:

Low, fleshy perennial herb, 1-8″ tall, with white, saucer-shaped flowers. Flower consists of 5-12 petal-like sepals, oblong to oval, with a central disk with numerous yellow stamens. Flowers usually solitary on stalks. Shiny green, very visibly veined leaves are basal, heart-shaped, and long-stalked. Leaf margins entire to coarse-toothed with wavy margins. Leaf is slightly longer than wide. No leaves on stem.

SUBALPINE
MONTANE

Flowering: May - August

Habitat: Wet open sites, upper montane to alpine

Photos: Beehive Basin, MT, August (W. Tilt); Illustration: USDA-NRCS Plants Database

TIDBITS

Marsh Marigolds commonly form dense colonies in wet, high-mountain meadows. Its bluish buds often push through the melting snow, opening into beautiful white blossoms similar to anemones. *Caltha* is Latin for "marigold" or "yellow-flowered plant" (some *Calthas* are yellow); *leptosepala* from the Latin for "thin sepals." The plant is a buttercup (Ranunculaceae), however, not a marigold. The plant is also called Elkslip, a puzzling description of unknown origin.

SUGARBOWL
(VASE FLOWER, LEATHERFLOWER)

Clematis hirsutissima • Ranunculaceae (Buttercup Family)

FIELD DESCRIPTION:

Perennial herb, 12-24" tall, with a single nodding cup-shaped flower resembling a sugar bowl. Flowers comprised of 4 sepals that are dark blue or purple on inside and paler on the outside. Stems hairy and lacy. Leaves opposite, deeply divided, and covered with silvery hairs. As flower goes to seed, the flower-head becomes erect and produces feathery plumes nearly 2" long.

TIDBITS

Sugarbowls are one of spring's earliest bloomers. Many visitors to region's trails in early summer will miss the dark blue bell or bowl-like flower, with the dark purple interior, and find only the feathery seed plumes. Another common name for the plant is Hairy Clematis and *hirsutissima* is derived from the Latin for very hairy (as in hirsute). Pasqueflower (*Pulsatilla patens*) blooms earlier than Sugarbowl and has basal rather than opposite stem leaves.

MONTANE
FOOTHILLS

Flowering: April - June

Habitat: Forest openings, foothills to montane

Thumbnail & reference photos: Gallatin Range, MT, May (W. Tilt); Fruit: Slough Creek, MT, July (W. Tilt)

FIELD DESCRIPTION:

Climbing, semi-woody perennial vine, growing up to 20′ long. Numerous showy, white-cream flowers arise from leaf axils. Flowers comprised of 4 narrow sepals and several flattened, petal-like stamens. Leaves opposite, pinnately compound with 5-7 egg-to-lance shaped leaflets with toothed margins. Male and female flowers on different plants. Goes to seed as head of hairy achenes.

VALLEYS-FOOTHILLS

Flowering: May - July

Habitat: Wet and well drained soils along streams and field margins, valleys and foothills

Thumbnail photos: SW Colorado, July (Photo ©Al Schneider, www.swcoloradowildflowers.com); Reference photos: Bozeman, MT, July & August (W. Tilt); Illustration: USDA-NRCS Plants Database

TIDBITS

Also known as Old Man's Beard and Virgin's Bower, White Clematis often forms dense mats draped over shrubs, small trees and other structures. The plant has been traditionally used for a wide range of medical treatments, from treating cramps to swollen arms and legs. Seed plumes from this and other clematis species make a good fire starter. Lore has it that crushed roots of the plant, placed in the nostrils of tired horses, revived them. *Clematis* from the Greek for "climbing plant." *Ligusticifolia* from the Latin for "with leaves like lovage."

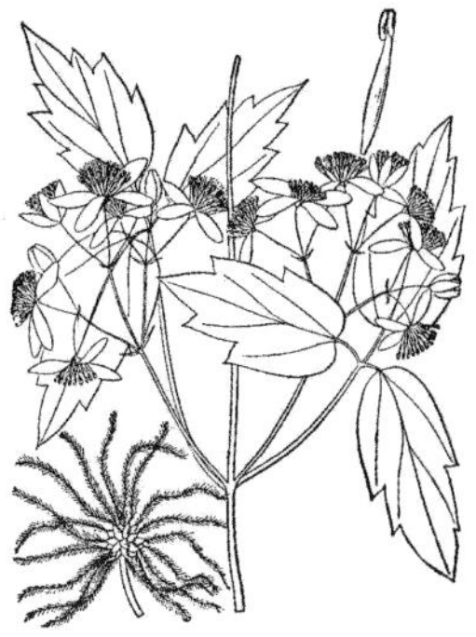

BLUE CLEMATIS (WESTERN BLUE VIRGIN'S BOWER)

Clematis occidentalis • Ranunculaceae (Buttercup Family)
(Synonym: *Clematis columbiana*)

FIELD DESCRIPTION:

Semi-woody trailing vine, up to 7' long, with nodding, blue-to-reddish-purple, paper-like flowers that are solitary on short branches from the axils of three-parted leaves. Leaves are divided into 3 lance-shaped leaflets with faintly toothed margins. Seeds are small achenes with feathery styles that form a fluffy plume.

TIDBITS

A glimpse of blue amid the shady greens of the forest understory often announces the presence of Blue Clematis. The flower resembles lavender-colored paper lanterns strung from one branch to the next. As the summer wears on, the flowers are replaced with "hippy-heads" of flossy white that provide excellent tinder for starting fires. Various species and cultivars of climbing clematis are commonly cultivated in gardens. Clematis is an ancient name given by the Greek physician and botanist Dioscorides to a plant with long, supple branches.

MONTANE
FOOTHILLS

Flowering: May - July

Habitat: Wooded or open areas, foothills to montane

Thumbnail & reference photos: Driggs, ID, June (W. Tilt); Seed head: Gallatin Range, MT, August (W. Tilt)

Delphinium bicolor • Ranunculaceae (Buttercup Family)

LOW LARKSPUR
(LITTLE LARKSPUR)

FIELD DESCRIPTION:

Perennial herb, up to 16" tall. Up to 15 flowers are found in a loose elongated cluster. Bluish-purple flowers are showy and widely flared. Five sepals are widely spread, with the upper one extended backward into a long spur, resembling a witch hat on its side. Leaves are few, generally basal, divided into narrow segments (palmately compound), and rounded in outline.

SUBALPINE
MONTANE
FOOTHILLS

Flowering: May - July

Habitat: Sagebrush flats and meadows, foothills to subalpine

Photos: Gallatin Range, MT, May (W. Tilt)

TIDBITS

Brilliant blue flowers stand out amongst the greens of sagebrush flats and meadows. The plant is widely cultivated as an ornamental. Larkspur is eaten by elk, mule deer, birds, small mammals, and even domestic sheep, but is poisonous to cattle. The plant is most toxic in the early summer and loses its potency as it ages. The flower and leaves have been used to control body lice. A related species, Tall Larkspur (*Delphinium occidentale*) is commonly found in meadows towering over the surrounding vegetation. *Delphinium* from the Greek for "dolphin" in reference to the flower shape; *bicolor* from the Latin for "with two colors," in reference to the plant's purple and white flowers.

TALL MOUNTAIN LARKSPUR

Delphinium occidentale • Ranunculaceae (Buttercup Family)

TIDBITS

This tall plant rises above the other surrounding meadow plants. Larkspurs contain poisonous alkaloids, whose toxicity increases as the plant matures. The seeds are very toxic and can be fatal to humans. *Delphinium,* from the Greek for "dolphin," arises from the story of an ancient fisherman who loses his life while attempting to save a dolphin. The dolphin carries the fisherman's body to Neptune asking for the god to restore the man's life. Neptune transforms the man into a flower the color of the sea and in the shape of a dolphin carrying a load on its back.

FIELD DESCRIPTION:

Tall perennial herb, 3-6′ tall. Pale blue and white flowers in tall, dense, narrow clusters, attached on short stalks. Individual flowers comprise 4 short petals surrounded by 5 sepals; the uppermost sepal extends backwards as a hollow spur. Leaves are alternate, palmate, deeply divided into 5-7 wedge-shaped segments with irregularly toothed margins. Stems hollow, often with a bluish cast, and plant is glandular hairy on upper portion. Fruits are erect, short-hairy, glandular seed pods (follices).

SUBALPINE
MONTANE

Flowering: June - August

Habitat: Moist meadows and glades, montane to subalpine

Photos: Beehive Basin, MT, July (Rip McIntosh); Illustration: USDA-NRCS Plants Database

Pulsatilla patens • Ranunculaceae (Buttercup Family)
(Synonym: *Anemone patens*)

PASQUEFLOWER (PRAIRIE WINDFLOWER)

FIELD DESCRIPTION:

Silky-hairy perennial herb, 12-16" tall, with a cup-shaped purple flower, 1-2" wide. Flower comprised of 5-7 sepals, numerous yellow stamens inside a silky cup and a whorl of 3 bracts below flower. Leaves are basal, stalked, with blades divided into many narrow segments. Fruits are silky achenes forming fluffy heads with long feathery styles.

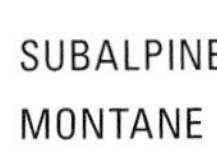

SUBALPINE
MONTANE

Flowering: April - May

Habitat: Well-drained soils in meadows, montane to subalpine

Photos: Triple Tree, MT, May (W. Tilt); Illustration: USDA-NRCS Plants Database

TIDBITS

As the snow melts and the ground becomes moist, Pasqueflower is among the first wildflowers to bloom. Its crocus-like flowers emerge before the finely cut leaves and gives rise to one of its common names, "Prairie Crocus." Late spring and summer visitors will find no flowers, just feathery plumes. All parts of the plant are poisonous and handling can cause skin irritation. Its early blooming time, upright flowers, and deeply cut leaves help distinguish Pasqueflower from Sugarbowl. *Pulsatilla* from the Latin for "pulsing" or "beating," and *patens* for "spreading, open." Pasque is probably from the Hebrew for "relating to Passover."

WATER BUTTTERCUP
(WATER CROWFOOT)

Ranunculus aquatilis • Ranunculaceae (Buttercup Family)

FIELD DESCRIPTION:

Aquatic perennial herb, up to 3' long, with limp stems that root at joints. Solitary, white, saucer-shaped flowers with yellow centers arise from long, stiff stems above the water. Flowers comprised of 5 white petals with yellow bases. Leaves are alternate, highly variable, but commonly of 2 distinct forms: very finely divided, thread-like underwater leaves, and floating palmate with three-toothed or lobed segments.

TIDBITS

Look for small white flowers with yellow centers rising above the surface of a pond. The shape of the narrow leaf segments gives the plant its other common name, Water Crowfoot. Water Buttercup is usually found in slow moving water, less than 3' deep and exposed to full sun. In quiet water, the plants can form dense mats on the water surface. The plant mass provides a refuge for aquatic animals and the seeds are eaten by waterfowl.

SUBALPINE
MONTANE
FOOTHILLS

Flowering: May - August

Habitat: Shallow, still or slow-moving water, foothills to subalpine

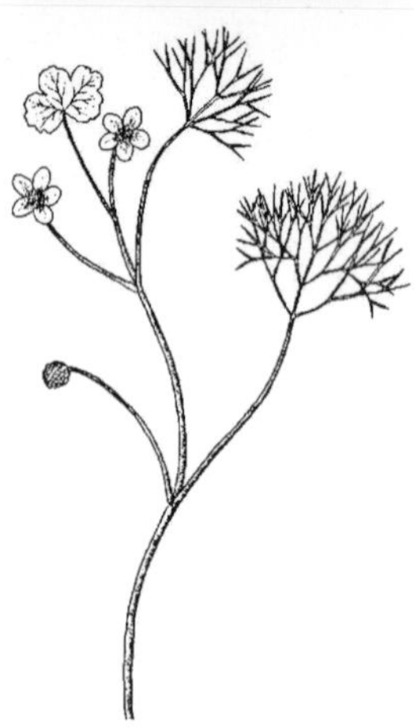

Photos: Afton, WY, August (Rip McIntosh); Illustration: USDA-NRCS Plants Database

FIELD DESCRIPTION:

Perennial herb with erect stems growing 3-10" tall. Most leaves arise from the base of the plant. They are about 1" long, wedge-shaped, and divided into 3- to 5-lobed or toothed segments. There are often no stem leaves, but when present, they are typically divided into 3 linear lobes. Yellow, five-petaled, bowl-shaped flowers are 0.5-0.75" wide. Smooth, tiny, shiny achenes enclose each of the seeds. They have a straight, beak-like projection and are borne in hemispheric clusters.

SUBALPINE
MONTANE
FOOTHILLS

Flowering: June - August

Habitat: Moist meadows where snow collects, subalpine and alpine

Thumbnail photo: Wasatch Range, UT, June (Steve Hegji); Reference photo: North Cascades Range, WA, August (© Walter Siegmund, Wikimedia) Illustration: Flora of North America (www.efloras.org)

TIDBITS

Also known as Snowpatch Buttercup, the Alpine Buttercup is one of the most common high-elevation *Ranunculus* species. There are 34 different species of *Ranunculus* described in Erwin Evert's *Vascular Plants of the Greater Yellowstone Area*, and many are challenging to identify to the species level. The name "buttercup" is from uncertain origins, but many children grew up being told to hold a buttercup to their chins – a yellow reflection bespoke a fondness for butter. Most buttercup species, however, are mildly toxic and commonly contain a juice that can irritate skin.

SAGEBRUSH BUTTERCUP (EARLY BUTTERCUP)

Ranunculus glaberrimus • Ranunculaceae (Buttercup Family)

FIELD DESCRIPTION:

Low perennial herb, 2-8" tall, with long fleshy leaves and clumped stems. Long-stalked, yellow, saucer-shaped flowers comprised of 5 shiny, waxy petals surrounding a mound of green-yellow pistils encircled by numerous stamens. Five sepals have a purplish tint. Basal leaves are elliptic-ovate and fleshy. Margins are entire to deeply lobed. Stems leaves are alternate and short-stalked.

TIDBITS

As the common name, Early Buttercup, suggests, this plant is one of the first to bloom in the Spring, adding their yellow flowers to the dull browns and greens of the winter foliage just beginning to wake up. While the name "buttercup" sounds as if the plant should be edible, they are generally mildly toxic, and their sap can cause skin irritation. *Ranunculus* from the Latin *rana* for "frog," as some buttercups and frogs prefer the same moist habitat. *Glaberrimus* means "completely without hairs," as in glabrous.

Flowering: April - June

Habitat: Dry open sites, sagebrush and woodlands, foothills to lower montane

Photos: Gallatin Range, MT, May (W. Tilt); Illustration: Karl Urban, Umatilla NF, OR

WOODLAND BUTTERCUP (HOOKED BUTTERCUP)

FIELD DESCRIPTION:

Slender perennial herb, 10-30" tall. Basal leaf blades are 1-3" wide and divided into 3 lobed leaflets. Each leaflet is ovate in outline. Stem leaves are smaller with narrower lobes. The inconspicuous flowers are about 0.25 wide with 5 bright yellow petals. Seed heads are globe-shaped and bear a cluster of 1-seeded achenes (fruit). The achenes are less than 0.25" long and sparsely hairy with a curved, beak-like projection.

MONTANE
FOOTHILLS

Flowering: June - July

Habitat: Moist, open forests and shrublands, along streams and in small openings where light filters through the forest canopy, foothills to montane

Thumbnail & reference photos: Benton Co., OR, June (Gerald D. Carr); Inset: SW Colorado, July (Al Schneider)

TIDBITS

Woodland Buttercup is also known as the Little Buttercup and the Small-Flowered Buttercup. It is one of the relatively common, albeit inconspicuous, *Ranunculus* in region. Woodland Buttercup is commonly encountered along trails where its small, hooked fruits readily attach to fur or clothing. All buttercups have a tiny, nectar-bearing pocket at the base of each petal that attracts pollinators. *Uncinatus* means "hooked" and refers to the small hooked beak at the tip of the achene (the fruit).

WESTERN MEADOW-RUE

Thalictrum occidentale • Ranunculaceae (Buttercup Family)

FIELD DESCRIPTION:

Perennial herb, 12-36" tall. Compound leaves, arranged on thin stem, are at least thrice ternate (3x3x3) with a total of 27 or more leaflets. Male and female flowers borne on separate plants (monoecious). Male flower is a conspicuous mass of yellow-tasseled stamens under an umbrella-like sepal, while the female flower is a cluster of naked ovaries resembling snake heads.

TIDBITS

Leaves of Western Meadow-Rue are very similar to columbine at first glance, but meadow-rue is thrice ternate (3x3x3) while columbine leaves are twice ternate (3 x 3) with total of 9 leaflets. Look for both the male and female plants in shady forests. The plant has reportedly been used as a love charm for those seeking attention of a lover, and as a stimulant for horses to increase their endurance. Meadow-rue is also being tested for its potential as a natural biological agent for combating certain kinds of cancer.

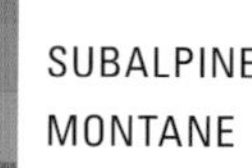

Flowering: May - August

Habitat: Cool, moist woods, montane to subalpine

Photos: Bear Canyon MT, June (W. Tilt); Male flower (upper left); female flower (lower left)

Trollius laxus • Ranunculaceae (Buttercup Family)
(Synonym: *Trollius albiflorus*)

GLOBEFLOWER

FIELD DESCRIPTION:

Perennial herb, 4-16" tall, with clumped stems and saucer-shaped, white-cream-yellow flowers. Flowers are single on stalks, 5-9 petal-like sepals, with numerous yellow stamens arising from the middle. Outer stamens lack anthers and are flattened. Leaves are alternate on long stalks that are palmately divided into 5 deeply toothed or three-lobed segments. Fruits are erect clusters of 10-20 follicles (pods) with spreading tips and conspicuous veins.

SUBALPINE
MONTANE

Flowering: June - August

Habitat: Wet soils in meadows and streambanks, montane to subalpine

Photos: SW Colorado, July (Al Schneider); Illustration: USDA-NRCS Plants Database

TIDBITS

Globeflower blooms early in the season in seeps filled with water from melting snows. The common name refers to the shape of the flower in cultivated species, which is more spherical than the wild species. Marsh Marigold (*Caltha leptosepala*) grows in similar wet habitats but has undivided, heart-shaped leaves, while its flowers have 7 or 8 petals versus 5 for Globeflower. Globeflower's petals are significantly narrower and the flower stalk is shorter. Despite these differences, the 2 plants are easy to mix-up. *Trollius* from the Latin for "globe," and *laxus* for "loose."

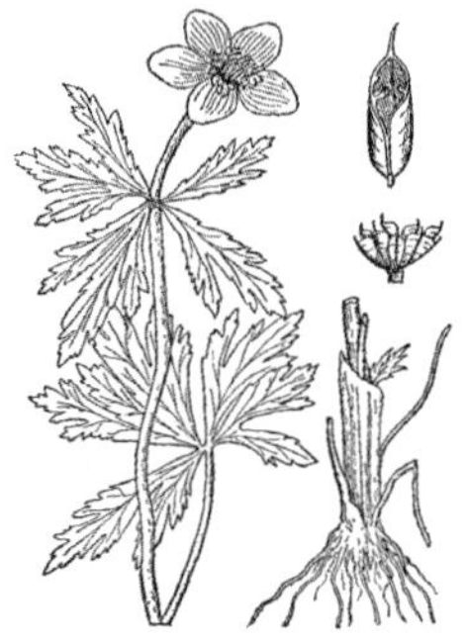

WILD STRAWBERRY

Fragaria sp. • Rosaceae (Rose Family)

FIELD DESCRIPTION:

Woods Strawberry (*Fragaria vesca*), a stolon-producing perennial, 3-6" tall, with white flowers comprised of 5 sepals and roundish petals. Basal leaves are divided into 3 leaflets, which are bright green and have pronounced venation. Leaflet margins are serrate with the terminal tooth the same size as surrounding teeth. Fruit is a fleshy cone with seeds (achenes) on the outside of a fleshy receptacle.

Virginia Strawberry *(Fragaria virginiana)*, a stolon-producing perennial, 3-6" tall, with stems, petioles, and peduncles with appressed to ascending hairs. Petioles from 1-5" long. Leaflets 3, obovate to elliptical, coarsely serrate, silky plumose to glabrate. White, five-petaled flowers in clusters of 2-12. Petals to almost 0.5" long, white. Fruit is a fleshy cone with seeds (achenes) on the outside of a fleshy receptacle.

TIDBITS

Fragaria vesca has bright green leaves, pronounced venation, and the terminal tooth same size as the other teeth along the leaf margin. *Fragaria virginiana* has gray green leaves, less pronounced venation on leaves, and a terminal tooth that is smaller than the other teeth along the leaf margin. *F. vesca* also prefers moister soils than *F. virginiana.*

SUBALPINE
MONTANE
FOOTHILLS

Flowering: May - September

Habitat: Meadows, Moist woods, forest edges, foothills to subalpine

Thumbnail (*F. vesca*): Gallatin Range, MT, June (Matt Lavin); Reference photo (*F. virginiana*): Gallatin Range, MT, June (W. Tilt); Illustrations (Top: *F. vesca*; Bottom: *F. virginiana*): USDA-NRCS Plants Database

LARGELEAF AVENS
(YELLOW AVENS)

FIELD DESCRIPTION:

Perennial herb, 1-2′ tall. Basal leaves ovate to cordate, alternate, pinnately divided into 5-9 leaflets, with smaller leaflets interspersed between larger leaflets. Terminal leaflet significantly larger than others. Stem Leaves are alternate, smaller, often three-parted, stalkless, with leaf-like stipules. Bright yellow flowers, in loose clusters, comprised of 5 broad petals and 5 sepals that are sharp-pointed and bent backward. Fruits are achenes with long hooks (the styles).

MONTANE

Flowering: April - August

Habitat: Moist soils in open or wooded areas, montane

TIDBITS

Largeleaf Avens, as both its common and scientific names suggest, has a distinctive leaf, with 5-9 leaflets, and a tip leaflet much larger than the others. Its fruits, along with that of other *Geums*, are round and bur-like with long-styled (tailed) fruits. The flower has styles that are S-shaped near the tip. This hook shape is retained in the fruits, helping the achenes stick to fur and fabric of passersby. Yellow-flowered *geums* may be confused with Cinquefoils (*Potentilla sp*).

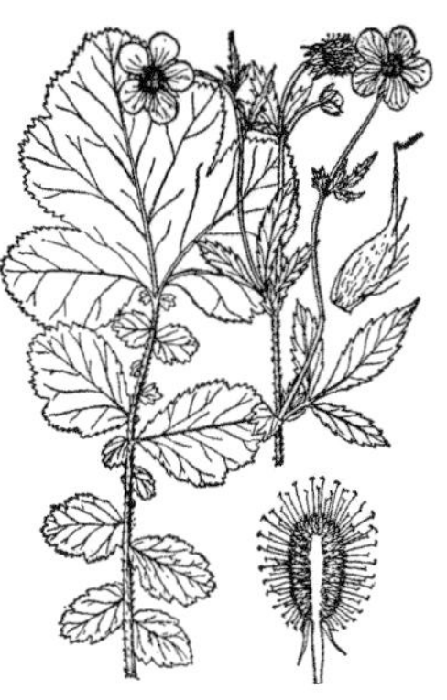

Photos: Gallatin Range, MT, July (W. Tilt); Illustration: USDA-NRCS Plants Database

ALPINE AVENS

Geum rossii • Rosaceae (Rose Family)

FIELD DESCRIPTION:

Perennial herb, 1-7" tall, from rhizomes. Basal leaves 1-8" long, short-petiolate, pinnatifid, glabrous to hairy along the veins on the underside of the leaf, ciliate. Flowers bright yellow, saucer-shaped, 5 petals about 0.3" long, terminal on stalk. Sepals 5, 0.2" long and 1-3 greatly reduced leaves are often present below the inflorescence. Fruits are lance-shaped achenes with long, tapered, persistent styles.

TIDBITS

Alpine Avens is one of the most common alpine species in the region , commonly carpeting the ground. The plant's finely cut shiny leaves, maroon buds, and bright shiny yellow flowers make it distinctive. Alpine Avens may be mistaken for a buttercup (such as *Ranunculus eschscholtzii*) because of its shiny yellow flower petals. Demonstrating the impact of elevation, its leaves are commonly 4-8" when growing below timberline, but barely reach 1-2" long in the alpine zone. Leaves turn red in the fall. *Rossii* recognizes Captain James Ross, an Arctic explorer, who collected the first specimen of this plant in 1820 in the Northwest Territories of Canada.

ALPINE
SUBALPINE
MONTANE

Flowering: June - August

Habitat: Moist meadows, gravels, sands, openings, tundra, montane to alpine

Photos: SW Colorado, July (Al Schneider)

Geum triflorum • Rosaceae (Rose Family)

PRAIRIE SMOKE
(OLD MAN'S WHISKERS)

FIELD DESCRIPTION:

Perennial herb, 6-24" tall, with bell-shaped, nodding flowers with pinkish-green sepals that hide light-yellow or rosy petals within. Bracts curve outward after fertilization, displaying long feathery styles. Commonly 3 flowers per stem. Leaves are hairy, fern-like (irregularly pinnately divided), and mostly basal. Flowing stems are reddish and soft-hairy with pair of small, opposite leaves mid-stem.

SUBALPINE
MONTANE

Flowering: May - August

Habitat: Moist open areas in sagebrush flats, montane to subalpine

Photos: Bozeman, MT, May & June (W. Tilt & Matt Lavin)

TIDBITS

In areas where this wildflower is abundant, the wispy pink plants in seed appear as a low-lying fog or smoke – hence the common name Prairie Smoke. The plant's feathery styles act as sails to disperse its seeds by wind. The plant's leaves persist through the winter and are one of the first to green up in the spring. *Geum* from the Latin *gaeum* for "plant with aromatic roots." *Triflorum* means "three-flowered," in reference to the 3 flowers per stem. Another common name for the plant is Three-Flowered Avens.

TALL CINQUEFOIL
(WHITE CINQUEFOIL)

Potentilla arguta • Rosaceae (Rose Family)
(Synonym: *Drymocallis arguta*)

FIELD DESCRIPTION:

Glandular-hairy perennial herb, 16-32" tall, with densely clustered creamy-white or pale yellow flowers. Flowers, five-petaled, with yellow centers atop stiff, lightly leaved stems. Basal leaves are pinnately compound with 5-9 sharp-toothed leaflets arranged in pairs on the leafstalk. Stem leaves also pinnately compound with 3-5 smaller toothed leaflets. Glandular hairs cover leaves and stems.

SUBALPINE
MONTANE
FOOTHILLS

Flowering: June - August

Habitat: Meadows and open woods, foothills to subalpine

TIDBITS

This white or creamy-yellow flowered plant is found in dry to moderately moist meadows. Stems are tall and usually unbranched, and leaves are serrated and broken into 5-7 leaflets. Leaves are similar to the yellow-flowered Graceful Cinquefoil (*Potentilla gracilis*). Tall Cinquefoil is frequently found in a wide variety of open habitats, though may be hidden amongst taller grasses. *Potentilla* from the Latin for "powerful," in reference to the shrub's medicinal properties; *arguta* from the Greek for "sharp-toothed," describing the leaves.

Photos: Slough Creek, MT, July (W. Tilt); Illustration: USDA-NRCS Plants Database

Drymocallis glandulosa • Rosaceae (Rose Family)
(Synonym: *Potentilla glandulosa*)

STICKY CINQUEFOIL

FIELD DESCRIPTION:

Perennial herb with glandular-sticky foliage and slender stems 4-20" tall. Its basal leaves are oblong in outline and pinnately divided into 5 to 9 ovate, toothed leaflets, each 0.5-1.5" long. Upper stem leaves are smaller. Loose clusters of white-to-yellow flowers are arranged at stem tips. They are saucer-shaped and 0.5-0.75" wide with 5 petals and 5 glandular sepals. Fruit are a cluster of smooth achenes, each with a style attached to its side, below the midline.

ALPINE
SUBALPINE
MONTANE

Flowering: June - July

Habitat: Open, rocky grasslands, slopes, shrublands and woodlands, exposed slopes and ridges, montane to alpine

TIDBITS

More than 30 species and varieties of cinquefoil are described in Erwin Evert's *Vascular Plants of the Greater Yellowstone Area*, and botanists have a fair amount of disagreement over their taxonomy. Another common cinquefoil in the region, Tall Cinquefoil (*Potentilla arguta*), is similar to Sticky Cinquefoil, but its flower clusters are stiff and erect rather than loose and open. Tall Cinquefoil is also typically a more robust plant than Sticky Cinquefoil.

Photos: Bozeman, MT, June (Matt Lavin); Illustration: USDA-NRCS Plants Database

GRACEFUL CINQUEFOIL (SLENDER CINQUEFOIL)

Potentilla gracilis • Rosaceae (Rose Family)
(Synonym: *Potentilla pulcherrima*)

FIELD DESCRIPTION:

Perennial, variably pubescent herbs from a caudex. Stems reclining to erect, from 1-24" long. Basal leaves from 1 to 12" long, palmately or pinnately compound, typically with 5-9 leaflets, serrated or toothed, commonly bi-colored (green on top and hairy silvery gray on bottom). Flowers several to numerous, showy, yellow, and five-petaled. Fruits are numerous achenes.

TIDBITS

Graceful Cinquefoil is often the most common cinquefoil species in high mountain meadows.While *cinque* refers to 5 leaflets, the leaf may range from 5-9 leaflets. The species were first collected for science by David Douglas from plants on the banks of the Columbia River in Oregon, and was then grown from seeds in England. The plant has endured dozens of name changes since first described. *Gracilis* from the Latin for "slender."

SUBALPINE
MONTANE

Flowering: June - September

Habitat: Meadows, woodland openings; montane to subalpine

Photos: Bozeman, MT, July (Matt Lavin); Illustration: USDA-NRCS Plants Database

SULFUR CINQUEFOIL

FIELD DESCRIPTION:

Perennial herb, 8-30" tall with erect, hairy stems, and woody taproot. One to several stems with some branching near the top. Leaves are alternate on stem, no well-developed basal; leaves palmately divided; 5-7 leaflets with distinctly toothed edges and prominent mid-vein. Distinctive stiff hairs on stems and leaves stick straight out from the surface. Flowers pale yellow (sulfur-colored) with 5 heart-shaped petals. Fruits are achenes with thickened margins and net-like pattern.

MONTANE
VALLEYS

Flowering: June - August

Habitat: Open dry to moist soils, including disturbed sites, valleys to montane

TIDBITS

Sulfur Cinquefoil is an introduced species native to Eurasia. The plant is considered invasive in many locations, effectively spreading itself by seed and reproducing vegetatively via new shoots. Some actions such as mowing help spread the plant as the roots send up new shoots after mowing. Sulfur Cinquefoil has stiff-hairy stems and fruits with a net-like pattern, while look-alike native Graceful Cinquefoil (*P. gracilis*) has short hairs that lie flat on the stems and leaves, brighter yellow flowers, and a smooth seed coat.

Photos: Bozeman, MT, June (Matt Lavin); Illustration: USDA-NRCS Plants Database

NORTHERN BEDSTRAW

Galium boreale • Rubiaceae (Madder Family)

FIELD DESCRIPTION:

Fragrant perennial herb, 8-20" tall, with showy white flowers in loose terminal clusters that are repeatedly three-forked. Flowers comprised of 4 petals, 4 stamens, and 2 styles. Stems are hollow and square with 4 narrow, lance-shaped leaves arranged in whorls at nodes that can also have secondary branches.

TIDBITS

A squared stem and narrow leaves in whorls of 4 leaves are distinctive of bedstraw. The plant's sweet smell made it a favorite for use as mattress straw, hence its common name. The plant is also called Catchweed because it clings to clothes as a result of its many small barbed hairs. *Galium* from the Greek for milk (as in galaxy and the Milky Way), and *boreale* from the Latin for "of the north."

ALPINE
SUBALPINE
MONTANE

Flowering: June - August

Habitat: Moist soils in meadows and open forests, montane to subalpine

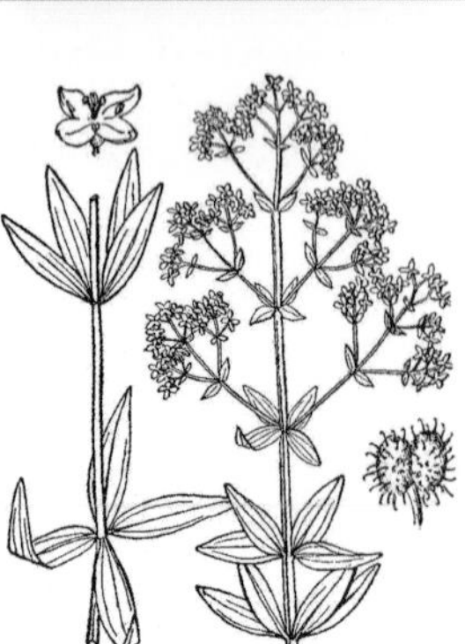

Photos: Gallatin Range, MT, July (W. Tilt); Illustration: USDA-NRCS Plants Database

Heuchera cylindrica • Saxifragaceae (Saxifrage Family)

ROUNDLEAF ALUMROOT

FIELD DESCRIPTION:

Perennial herb, 6-18" tall. White-yellow-green bell-shaped flowers, comprising 5 blunt-tipped sepals, petals minute or absent, stamens shorter than sepals, in a spike-like panicle. Leaves basal, broadly ovate- to heart-shaped on long petioles. Stems glandular-hairy. Fruits are capsules with dark red-brown seeds covered with short spines.

MONTANE
FOOTHILLS

Flowering: June - August

Habitat: Rocky soil, cliffs and talus slopes, foothills to montane

Photos: Slough Creek, MT, July (W. Tilt); Illustration: USDA-NRCS Plants Database

TIDBITS

Roundleaf Alumroot is characterized by leathery, roundish leaves clustered at base of stalks of narrow greenish-white flower clusters. Alumroots commonly hybridize making identification difficult. Roundleaf Alumroot resembles Littleleaf Alumroot (*H. parviflora*) but its flowers are larger (approx. 6-8 mm long). As its common name suggests, alumroots have stypic and astringent properties. The roots are effective in stopping nose bleeds and other hemorrhages. *Heuchera* after Johann Heinrick van Heucher, a German medical professor.

LITTLELEAF ALUMROOT

Heuchera parvifolia • Saxifragaceae (Saxifrage Family)

FIELD DESCRIPTION:

Perennial herbaceous plants with scaly rootstocks and leafless (scapose) stems to over 18" tall. Leaves basal, ovate to reniform, blades 1-2" across, gently lobed 5-9 times, upper surface glabrous, lower usually glandular hairy, margins ciliate. Petioles long and usually glandular hairy. Inflorescence to almost 10" long, very narrow at first and then widening. Flowers cup-shaped, small, five-parted, green to yellow. Fruit is an ovoid or ellipsoid capsule.

ALPINE
SUBALPINE
MONTANE
FOOTHILLS

Flowering: May - September

Habitat: Dry sandy and rocky areas, slopes, shrublands, foothills to alpine

TIDBITS

Littleleaf Alumroot is found in rocky areas, often in small colonies of a dozen or more plants. Their scalloped, thick, bright green leaves and tall swaying stalks make them easy to spot, even from a distance. Littleleaf Alumroot resembles Roundleaf Alumroot (*H. cylindrical*). The roots of alumroot were a common means of relieving diarrhea and stomach cramps. The genus name was given by Linnaeus in 1753 for the German botanist J. H. Heucher. *Parvifolia,* meaning "small leaf," was given by Nuttall who was the first to collect this plant for science.

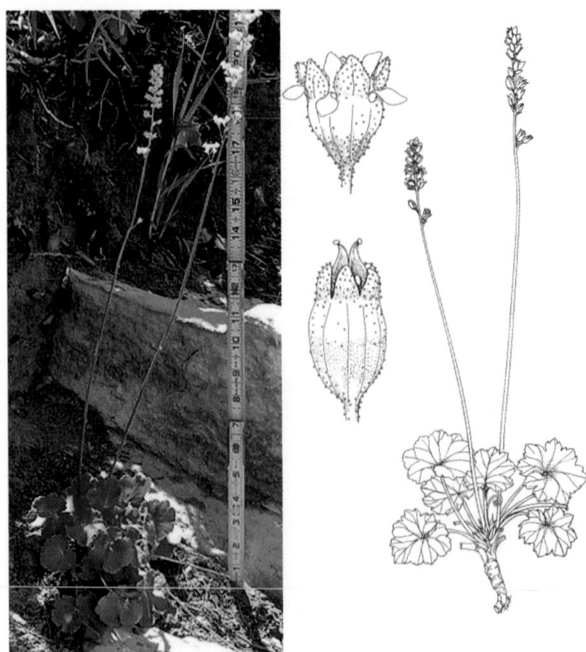

Photos: SW Colorado, June (Al Schneider); Illustration: Flora of North America (www.efloras.org)

Lithophragma parviflorum • Saxifragaceae (Saxifrage Family)

SMALL-FLOWERED WOODLAND STAR

FIELD DESCRIPTION:

Perennial herb, 4-12" tall, with hairy, glandular, often purplish stems. Basal leaves are palmately divided (nearly to their base) into 3-5 divisions, which are divided again into lobed or toothed segments. Stem leaves smaller and deeply divided once or twice. White star-shaped flowers have 5 deeply cleft petals and funnel-like calyx in elongating terminal racemes. Petals appear more numerous due to deep lobes.

MONTANE
FOOTHILLS

Flowering: April - July

Habitat: Dry rocky or sandy soils, open woods, meadows, foothills to montane

TIDBITS

A wildflower of the open forest with a delicate star-shaped flower and deeply cleft petals and leaves. Small-Flowered Woodland Star is quite similar to Bulbous Woodland Star (*L. glabrum*) and Slender Woodland Star (*L. tenellum*), found in the Northern Rockies. Bulbous Woodland Star is distinguished from the other 2 species by the presence of bulblets along its stem. All 3 species are very slender and delicate, quite glandular hairy, and have petals with a number of deep clefts that give them a starburst appearance.

Thumbnail photo: Skagit Co., WA, April (Ben Legler); Other photos: Gallatin Range, MT, June (W. Tilt)

BROOK SAXIFRAGE

Micranthes odontoloma • Saxifragaceae (Saxifrage Family)
(Synonym: *Saxifraga odontoloma*)

FIELD DESCRIPTION:

Perennial herb, 8-24" tall, with round, handsomely scalloped leaves and delicate white flowers. Leaf stalks longer than leaf blades. Single leafless stem bears 10 or more small white flowers in a very open panicle. Flowers comprised of 5 round petals, 5 green-purple sepals, and 10 red stamens that are conspicuous, as long as petals, flattened, and extending outward like spokes on a ship's wheel. Ovary is red and two-celled. Fruit is a purplish capsule.

TIDBITS

Flowers of the Brook Saxifrage are small and easily overlooked – until one looks closely. Crossing a forest stream, one might first observe mats of bright green scalloped leaves. Closer inspection reveals delicate clusters of five-petaled flowers with conspicuous sepals and stamens. Saxifrage means "rock breaker," possibly a reference to where the plants may be found, or possibly to the plant's supposed ability to break kidney stones in humans. *Micranthes* from the Greek for "small flower," *odontoloma* for "tooth-fringe."

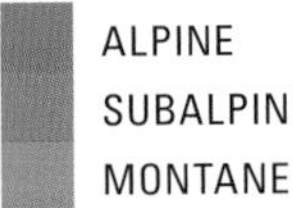

Flowering: July - September

Habitat: Moist soils along streams and wet meadows, montane to subalpine

Photos: Beehive Basin, MT, August (W. Tilt); Illustration: USDA-NRCS Plants Database

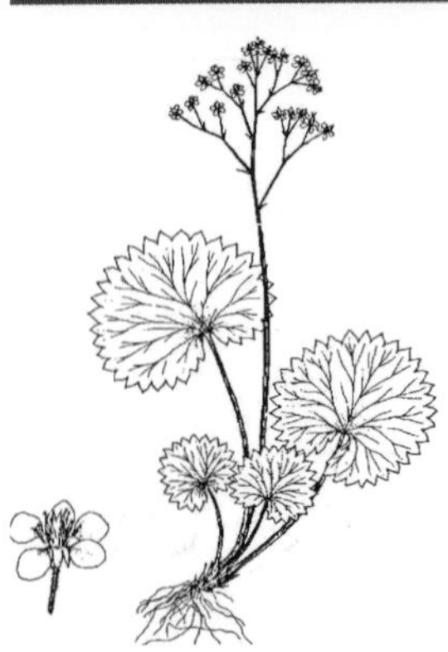

Mitella pentandra • Saxifragaceae (Saxifrage Family)
(Synonym: *Pectiantia pentandra*)

FIVE-STAMEN MITREWORT

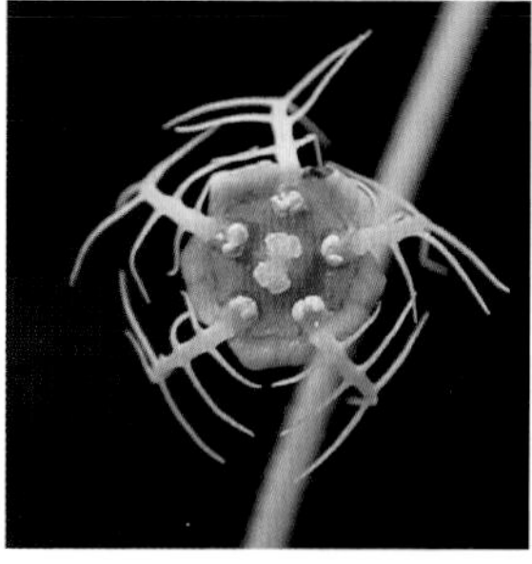

FIELD DESCRIPTION:

Slender perennial herb, 4-12" tall, growing from rhizomes, occasionally with stolons. Stems nearly leafless, occasionally 1-2 membranous bracts present. Leaves mostly basal, heart-shaped, shallowly and indistinctly 5- to 9-lobed, margins with short, rounded teeth, on long petioles. Flower-heads in elongate clusters, 6-25 in number, blossoming upwards. Flowers greenish, purple-tinged with 5 saucer-shaped fringed petals and 5 stamens at petal base. Fruits are two-sided capsules with shiny black seeds.

ALPINE
SUBALPINE
MONTANE

Flowering: June - August

Habitat: Wet meadows and cool moist woods, especially along seeps and streams, montane to alpine

TIDBITS

Five-Stamen Mitrewort has a distinctive flower that is saucer-shaped with 5 green petals divided into narrow, whisker-like lobes. Its flowers have been likened to green snowflakes. Seed dispersal is assisted by a "splash" mechanism where water droplets landing in the fruit cup expel the seeds outward from the plant. The scientific and common names of Five-Stamen Mitrewort arise from "mitra," the cap or mitre worn by a bishop.

Thumbnail photo: Kittitas Co., WA, June (Ben Legler);
Reference photo: Mt. Rainer NP, WA, June (Gerald D. Carr);
Illustration: Flora of North America (www.efloras.org)

COMMON MULLEIN

Verbascum thapsus • Scrophulariaceae (Figwort Family)

FIELD DESCRIPTION:

Erect, very hairy, biennial herb, 15-60" tall, from taproot. Yellow, saucer-shaped, five-petaled flowers in dense terminal spike. Stem leaves are alternate, lance-shaped, pale green, and large. Plant covered with gray-silver felt-like hairs. First year growth consists of basal rosette of leaves to 24" long. Stems persist into winter.

TIDBITS

A native of Eurasia, mullein is widespread across temperate North America. In its first year mullein produces only a basal rosette of broad leaves. The second year, tall, a thick grey-woolly spike arises from the rosette, topped with bright yellow raceme of flowers. Only a few flowers bloom at a time as the flower stalk elongates. This plant has a large number of medicinal uses, including the treatments of chest and lung complaints. A tea made from the roots is said to prevent incontinence. Mullein's large fuzzy leaves have been known to offer a soft alternative for those in need of relief in the field.

MONTANE
FOOTHILLS

Flowering: June - August

Habitat: Dry sandy soils, foothills to montane

Photos: Bozeman, MT, July (W. Tilt); Illustration: USDA-NRCS Plants Database

HENBANE (STINKING NIGHTSHADE)

Hyoscyamus niger • Solanaceae (Nightshade Family)

FIELD DESCRIPTION:

Coarse, leafy, malodorous biennial, 1-3′ tall. Greenish-yellow funnel-shaped, five-parted flowers with purplish net veining and purple throats. Flowers atop stem and from leaf axils. Leaves are alternate, long-hairy, ovate, stalkless, pinnately lobed into triangular pointed segments. Stems are sticky and long hairy. Seeds in thick-lidded capsules enclosed in calyx, visible when blooms fall off.

MONTANE
FOOTHILLS

Flowering: May - August

Habitat: Roadsides and other disturbed areas, foothills to montane

TIDBITS

Introduced from Europe, Henbane is now found throughout much of the western and northern United States. The plant is highly poisonous and should not be handled or eaten. Symptoms are headache, nausea, rapid pulse, convulsions, and possibly death. The plant has an extensive history of medical applications including use as a sedative and pain killer. Henbane is also known as Stinking Nightshade because of its unpleasant odor.

Thumbnail photo: Smith River, MT, July (W. Tilt); Illustration: Flora of North America (www.efloras.org)

BITTERSWEET NIGHTSHADE

Solanum dulcamara • Solanaceae (Nightshade Family)

FIELD DESCRIPTION:

Climbing, semi-woody perennial vine, growing up to 9' long. Blue-purple petals with 5 lobes that flare backwards, in branched clusters. Anthers fused together in a conspicuous yellow column. Leaves are alternate, stalked, ovate to cordate, often with 2 pointed lobes at base. Fruits are hanging clusters of bright red berries.

TIDBITS

Introduced from Europe, Bittersweet Nightshade is found scrambling over fences and surrounding vegetation. Look for vines with small purple star flowers in loose clusters, replaced with red berries in the late summer. The plant's many common names like Poisonberry and Snakeberry speak to the plant's toxic nature and that of other members of the Nightshade Family, which include the Deadly Nightshade or Belladonna (*Atropa belladonna*). The fruits of Bittersweet Nightshade are eaten by a variety of birds and other wildlife but should be avoided by humans (especially children) and pets.

Flowering: May - September

Habitat: Shaded thickets and woodlands, valleys to montane

Thumbnail and reference photos: Bozeman, MT, July (W. Tilt); Fruit photo: Bozeman, MT, September (W. Tilt); Illustration: USDA-NRCS Plants Database

Urtica dioica • Urticaceae (Nettle Family)
(Synonym: *Urtica gracilis*)

FIELD DESCRIPTION:

Erect perennial herb, 18-54" tall, with four-sided stems with stinging hairs. Leaves are opposite, narrowly lanceolate, and coarsely toothed. Stipules prominent and leaf stems nearly one-half length of leaf. Small, inconspicuous, greenish flowers are arranged in hanging clusters (panicles) arising from upper leaf clusters.

Flowering: May - September

Habitat: Moist rich soils, foothills to montane

TIDBITS

The stems of Stinging Nettle are armed with tiny, hollow-pointed hairs containing irritating compounds that cause itching and burning when they come into contact with skin. The discomfort can last from minutes to days, depending on an individual's sensitivity. A common relief is to flood the affected area with water or to apply a paste of baking soda and water. Applying tape to skin can help remove the barbs. Young shoots can be boiled and eaten like spinach and the older stem fibers were commonly used to make rope and cloth. *Urtica* from the Latin for "to burn," and *dioica* for "two homes."

Photos: Gallatin Range, MT, July (W. Tilt); Illustration: USDA-NRCS Plants Database

EDIBLE VALERIAN
(TOBACCO-ROOT)

Valeriana edulis • Valerianaceae (Valerian Family)

FIELD DESCRIPTION:

Tall perennial herb, up to 4′ tall, from a stout taproot. Flowers begin in tight clusters that gradually mature into an elongated, open panicle. Very small, white-to-pale-yellow, tubular flowers have 5 spreading lobes. Basal leaves are thick, linear to obovate, with white-lined entire margin. Conspicuous veins are nearly parallel with midrib. Stems have 2-6 pairs of small pinnatifid leaves divided into 3-7 segments. Fruits are ovate achenes tipped with feathery style. Male and female flowers on separate plants (dioecious).

TIDBITS

Look for Edible Valerian rising above surrounding grasses and wildflowers of montane meadows. As the common and scientific names suggest, the plant is considered edible when cooked, but the taste is very strong with an odor that many find unpleasant. The plant has a number of medicinal uses, and legend has it that the Pied Piper used a valerian to lure the rats out of Hamlin. Valerian from the Latin *valere*, "strength," referring to valerian's alledged potency as a nerve tonic and muscle relaxant.

ALPINE
SUBALPINE
MONTANE

Flowering: June - August

Habitat: Moist to mostly dry soils in open meadows, montane to alpine

Photos: Slough Creek, MT, July (W. Tilt); Illustration: USDA-NRCS Plants Database

Valeriana sitchensis • Valerianaceae (Valerian Family)

SITKA VALERIAN

FIELD DESCRIPTION:

Perennial herb, 1-3′ tall, with small, showy, white (at times pinkish) flowers in rounded, dome-shaped clusters. Flower consists of 5 fused petals forming a tube and encasing 3 stamens and a style. Stamens extend beyond the petals giving the flower-head a pincushion appearance. Leaves mostly opposite, consisting of 2-5 pairs of pinnately compound leaves with 3-5 oval toothed leaflets; terminal leaflet is larger than the others. Flowers also arise from leaf axils below terminal clusters. Stems are squared and often reddish in color.

ALPINE
SUBALPINE
MONTANE

Flowering: June - August

Habitat: Moist, open or wooded habitats, montane to alpine

Photos: Gallatin Range, MT, July (W. Tilt)

TIDBITS

A dome of white, often pink-tinged flowers atop squared stems with compound leaves mark valarians. There are 3 similar-looking valerian species in the region. In addition to the Sitka Valarian, the Woodland or Marsh Valerian (*V. dioica*) is relatively shorter in stature (4-20″ tall) with smaller flower-heads, typically undivided basal leaves, and stem leaves divided into 9-15 leaflets. Western Valerian (*V. occidentalis*) is relatively tall (1-3′), with broader leaflets. Sitka Valarian is commonly found in the Montana portion of the Yellowstone region; Woodland Valerian in the northern and eastern sectors; and Western Valerian throughout the region. Valerian roots were dried and ground by some Native Americans for flour. Herbalists have used the root as a tranquilizer, hunters have used the plants to mask their odor, and cats have a fondness for it akin to catnip.

HOOKEDSPUR VIOLET

Viola adunca • Violaceae (Violet Family)

FIELD DESCRIPTION:

Perennial herb, 6-12" tall, with few leaves on stems. Leaves are alternate, oval to egg-shaped, heart-shaped at base, with shallowly round toothed margins. Leaves and flower stems branch from a main stem above ground on longish stems. Deep-blue-to-purple flowers, five-petaled, with white throats with purple lines pointing to the flower's center. Style tip is hairy. Side petals are white hairy, and a sac-like spur is present at base of lowest petal. Flowers arise from leaf axils. Fruits are capsules with dark brown seeds.

ALPINE
SUBALPINE
MONTANE
FOOTHILLS

Flowering: May - August

Habitat: Moist soils in meadows, forests, riparian and wetland margins, foothills to alpine

TIDBITS

Hookedspur Violets are common in moist soils in a variety of habitats, from the foothills to the alpine. Also known as Early Blue Violet and Western Dog Violet, the flowers, leaves, and stems of plants growing at lower elevations may be 2-4 times the size of those growing at alpine. The species ranges widely across the boreal regions of North America. Leaves and flowers may be eaten and are high in vitamins A and C. The rhizomes, fruits and seeds, however, are poisonous and should not be consumed. *Adunca* from the Latin for "hooked," in likely reference to the spur at the back of the flower.

Photos: Slough Creek, MT, July (W. Tilt); Illustration: USDA-NRCS Plants Database

CANADA VIOLET

FIELD DESCRIPTION:

Perennial herb, 6-12" tall, with white flowers, five-petaled with yellow centers. Flowers may be purple-tinged on the outer petal margin. Lower 3 petals have fine purple lines pointing to the flower's center, and the 2 side petals are hairy at their base. Broad, heart-shaped leaves are sharp-tipped and alternate.

MONTANE
FOOTHILLS

Flowering: May - July

Habitat: Moist soils in shaded woods, especially aspen stands, foothills to montane

TIDBITS

In early spring Canada Violets, also known as Canadian White Violets, can carpet woods from low to high mountains. The plant is easy to spot because of its bright white flowers which are actually often tinged with a faint pink, especially on the back side. Canada Violet is high in vitamins A and C. Violets are edible and often enjoyed raw in salads. Canada Violet is distinguished from other woodland violets by its white (rather than blue or yellow) petals.

Photos: Bozeman, MT, July (W. Tilt); Illustration: USDA-NRCS Plants Database

NUTTALL'S VIOLET (YELLOW PRAIRIE VIOLET)

Viola nuttallii • Violaceae (Violet Family)

FIELD DESCRIPTION:

Low-lying perennial, 4-20" tall. Leaves are basal, long-stalked, narrowly lanceolate-elliptical, commonly 3 times longer than wide, entire to slightly toothed, with conspicuous veins. Yellow flowers with 5 petals; lower 3 petals with purple veins on inner surface, side pairs bearded; upper petals tinged with brownish-red on back side.

Flowering: May - July

Habitat: Dry soils in open sagebrush and forest edges, valley to montane

TIDBITS

Yellow flowers, long-stalked leaves, and a preference for dry, open spaces are distinctive traits of Nuttall's Violet. The plant is named in honor of James Nuttall, a Harvard Professor of Natural History and explorer, botanist, and ornithologist in the western United States in the early 1800s. The leaves and flowers are edible and are high in vitamins A and C. The rhizomes, fruits, and seeds, however, are typically high in saponins and potentially poisonous. Although relatively simple to recognize, identifying violets to species can be more difficult, with some 125 recognized species of *Viola* in North America.

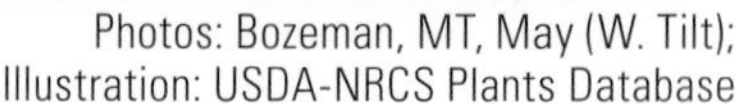

Photos: Bozeman, MT, May (W. Tilt); Illustration: USDA-NRCS Plants Database

ROCKY MOUNTAIN MAPLE

FIELD DESCRIPTION:

Monoecious or deciduous, multi-stemmed shrub or small tree, 6-20′ tall, with opposite leaves that are palmately lobed into 3-5 segments (sometimes cut all the way to the mid-rib) with pointed ends. Leaves are about as long as broad, double-toothed, and paler on underside. Twigs are red-brown and rounded in cross section. Branches are opposite, ascending to erect. Greenish-yellow flowers, with 5 petals and 5 stamens, are loose drooping cymes arising from lateral buds. Fruit is double-winged samara, typical of the Maple Family. Bark is thin and smooth in young trees, developing fissures as it matures.

MONTANE
FOOTHILLS

Flowering: April - June

Habitat: Along streams and other moist, sheltered areas, foothills to montane

Photos: Gallatin Range, MT, July (W. Tilt); Illustration: USDA-NRCS Plants Database

TIDBITS

Known as "rock maple" in reference to the hardness and density of its wood, the Rocky Mountain Maple is one of 2 maples native to the region. Its leaves turn red or yellow in autumn. Its wood makes for good fuel and is used in veneers and laminates, but the trees are too small for broader commercial uses. Bright pink-crimson blotches commonly found on the leaves are typically caused by harmless infestations of eriophyid mites. *Acer* is the ancient Latin name for maples.

BOXELDER
(ASHLEAF MAPLE)

Acer negundo • Aceraceae (Maple Family)

FIELD DESCRIPTION:

Deciduous, multi-stemmed large shrub or small tree, 10-30′ tall (occasionally to 50′), with opposite branching and leaves. Overall irregular form, trunk often with wart-like growths and dividing near ground into a few spreading, rather crooked limbs. Leaves 4-10″ long, comprised of 3-7 leaflets, typically half as wide as long, light green above and grey-green below, coarsely toothed, and hairless. Stems green or purplish, commonly glossy or white-powdered. Male and female flowers on separate plants, small and pale green: male flowers on slender stalks in loose clusters, and female flowers arranged along a separate stem. Fruits are 2 fused, winged samaras hanging in long chains on slender stalks. Seeds 2-3 times as long as wide and markedly wrinkled.

TIDBITS

Boxelder is a fast growing tree with soft wood. Its branches and boles often split from wind and snow. Boxelder is dioecious, with male flowers on one tree and female flowers on another. In late spring, the samaras develop and remain on tree until they are quite dry and uniformly light brown, well into the winter. The plant's sap can be a source of syrup but not as sweet as that drawn from the Sugar Maple (*A. saccharum*). The tree also has its own insect, the Boxelder bug (*Boisea trivittatus*), which feeds on Boxelder and other plants, then often benignly invades certain homes as they search for a site to over-winter.

VALLEYS-FOOTHILLS

Flowering: April - June

Habitat: Along streams and permanent water, also escapes from cultivation, valleys and foothills

Photos: Jefferson River, MT, June (W. Tilt); Illustration: USDA-NRCS Plants Database

Rhus aromatica • Anacardiaceae (Sumac Family)
(Synonym: *Rhus trilobata*)

SKUNKBUSH SUMAC

FIELD DESCRIPTION:

Deciduous shrub, 2-7' tall, strong-smelling, erect to spreading with dense crown. Leaves are alternate, bright green, trifoliate with ovate leaflets with rounded lobes; central leaflet largest of the 3, broadly lobed, tapering to wedge-shaped base. Flower-heads are dense, terminal racemes with pale-yellow flowers, five-petaled, yellow stamens, and reddish sepals. Small cone-like buds and flowers appear before leaves. Fruits are fuzzy red or orange berry-like drupes crowded at stem tips.

MONTANE
FOOTHILLS

Flowering: May - June

Habitat: Dry open, often rocky, soils, grasslands to open forests, foothills to lower montane

TIDBITS

As common name suggests, Skunkbush Sumac is strong-smelling. The small cone-like buds are distinctive of this species as is the three-leaflet leaf where each leaf has lobed margins. Fruits are edible raw or cooked, and the plant has a range of traditional uses. A variety of wildlife browse the shrub, and the fruit is an important winter food source for a range of birds, including grouse and turkey.

Thumbnail photo: Bozeman, MT, May (W. Tilt); Reference photo & fruit: Bozeman, MT, September (Matt Lavin); Illustration: USDA-NRCS Plants Database

POISON IVY

Toxicodendron rydbergii • Anacardiaceae (Sumac Family)

FIELD DESCRIPTION:

Trailing, vine-like, to erect, deciduous shrub, 3-8" tall, with alternate leaves divided into 3 ovate leaflets with pointed tips and entire to round-toothed or lobed margins. Leaves vary from dull light green to shiny deep green. Veins prominent on underside of leaf. Clusters of inconspicuous, yellowish, five-petaled flowers arise from leaf axils before leaves appear. Fruits are white-to-pale-green, berry-like drupes. Leaves turn red and yellow in late summer, early fall.

VALLEYS-FOOTHILLS

Flowering: May - July

Habitat: Well-drained soils in open and shaded areas, along river courses, valleys to foothills

TIDBITS

"Leaves of three, let them be" is the woodsman's adage for avoiding Poison Ivy. The plant contains a yellowish oil called "urushiol," and contact with it causes mild to severe skin irritation when leaves and stems have been broken. The best cure is avoidance, but if you think you have come into contact with the sap, wash immediately in one of several commercially available lotions designed to effectively break down the oils. The plant is toxic even in the winter. *Rydbergii* for Per Axel Rydberg (1860-1931), a respected botanist of his time.

Photos: Smith River, MT, July (W. Tilt); Illustration: USDA-NRCS Plants Database

FIELD DESCRIPTION:

Erect aromatic shrub, 1-4′ tall. Leaves and young twigs typically grayish. Leaves are silver-gray, alternate, entire and linear, terminating in a single tip. Leaves often persist through the winter. Numerous flower-heads in tall narrow clusters consist of small yellow flowers with well-developed bracts. Commonly spreads by rhizomes. Plant has distinctive sage smell when leaves are crushed.

MONTANE
PLAINS

Flowering: August - October

Habitat: Dry open soils, plains to montane

TIDBITS

Silver Sagebrush has a woody base and wispy appearance on top. The sweet smell of sagebrush after a rain is a memory of the West. Crush a few leaves in your hand and rub it on for a little "cowboy perfume." Sagebrush is used as an herb, medicinal remedy, insect repellent, and has been used as mattress stuffing. Young shoots of Silver Sagebrush look similar to White Sagebrush (*A. ludoviciana*), but White Sagebrush does not have woody stems and grows in large patches rather than in shrub form.

Thumbnail photo: Bozeman, MT, June (W. Tilt);
Reference photo: Bozeman, MT, September (W. Tilt);
Illustration: USDA-NRCS Plants Database

PRARIE SAGEWORT (PASTURE SAGE)

Artemisia frigida • Asteraceae (Sunflower Family)

FIELD DESCRIPTION:

Woolly, fragrant perennial herb semi-shrub, 4-16" tall, with erect, leafy stems arising from a branched caudex. Small numerous leaves are alternate, silvery gray-green, silky-hairy, pinnately divided 2-3 times, and packed in attractive, tight clusters. Numerous flower-heads are borne in nodding racemes or open panicles. Each flower-head contains 10-17 small, inconspicuous yellowish disk flowers. The fruits are achenes bearing tiny seeds.

TIDBITS

Members of the *Artemisia* genus are characterized by their distinctive pungent sage aroma and foliage, which is silvery green because of a mat of fine white hairs. Presence of Prairie Sagewort is often considered an indicator of overgrazing or disturbance. Many wildlife species and livestock graze the plant. *Artemisia* for the Greek Goddess Artemis, Apollo's twin sister and daughter of Zeus and Leto (she was the equivalent of the Roman Diana). *Frigida* from the Latin for "cold."

Flowering: June - September

Habitat: Dry, gravelly soils and disturbed sites in grasslands, shrublands and woodlands, foothills to montane

Photos: Bozeman, MT, September (Matt Lavin); Illustration: USDA-NRCS Plants Database

FIELD DESCRIPTION:

Erect aromatic shrub to 9' tall. Leaves and young twigs typically grayish. Leaves are alternate, wedge-shaped with 3 blunt lobes on their tips. Dense gray hairs on both sides lend leaves their silver-blue color. Leaves persist through the winter. Numerous flower-heads in foot-long narrow clusters (panicles) consist of small yellow flowers. Bark on older branches grayish and shredding. Has distinctive sage smell when leaves are crushed.

MONTANE
VALLEYS

Flowering: July - September

Habitat: Dry plains, valleys to montane

Thumbnail photo: SW Colorado, July (Al Schneider); Reference photo: September, Grand Teton NP WY (Matt Lavin); Illustration: USDA-NRCS Plants Database

TIDBITS

Big Sagebrush is the iconic shrub of western rangelands. It provides vital cover and food for a wide range of wildlife and literally defines sagebrush-steppe habitats in the region. The shrub can live more than 50 years. Black Sagebrush (*A. nova*) is shorter (to 16"), with shorter, usually yellowish leaves. The genus is named in honor of the Greek goddess Artemis, while *tridentata* means "three-toothed," like a trident, in reference to the plant's distinctive leaves.

RUBBER RABBITBRUSH

Ericameria nauseosa • Asteraceae (Sunflower Family)
(Synonym: Chrysothamnus nauseosus)

FIELD DESCRIPTION:

Deciduous shrub, to 6′ tall, densely branched with flexible twigs covered with gray felt-like hairs, especially prominent on young twigs. Leaves are alternate, linear, 1-3 veined, velvety and gray. Several flower-heads in rounded, slightly elongate clusters at branch tips. Yellow disk flowers with involucral bracts rounded or abruptly pointed (not-green tipped). Fruits are linear achenes, hairy with pappus of white hairs.

MONTANE
VALLEYS

Flowering: August - October

Habitat: Dry open sites, valleys to montane

TIDBITS

Rubber Rabbitbrush spreads quickly onto barren, sandy soils, and it is a highly variable species. The plant contains latex and has been used like chewing gum. Green Rabbitbrush (*C. viscidiflorus*) is distinguished from Rubber Rabbitbrush by its brittle and hairless (not felt-like) twigs, and is found in more undisturbed habitats throughout the West. The first specimens of Rubber Rabbitbrush were collected by Meriwether Lewis along the Missouri River. *Ericameria* from the Greek for "heath-part," referring to the heath-like leaves. *Nauseosus* means "heavy scented."

Photos: Phillps Co., MT, September (Matt Lavin); Illustration: USDA-NRCS Plants Database

Berberis repens • Berberidaceae (Barberry Family)
(Synonym: *Mahonia repens*)

OREGON GRAPE
(GRAPE HOLLY)

FIELD DESCRIPTION:

Low, trailing, evergreen shrub, 4-10" tall, with stiff branches and stolons (ground level stems). Clusters of yellow flowers are arranged in narrow racemes at end of stem. Flowers mature into grape-like clusters of blue berries with a chalky coating. Holly-like leaves are alternate, glossy, and pinnately compound with 5-7 spine-tipped leaflets per stem.

MONTANE
FOOTHILLS

Flowering: April - July

Habitat: Wide range of dry to moist habitats, foothills to montane

TIDBITS

Oregon Grape is one of the region's earliest flowering plants. The yellow flowers and blue grape-like berries amid holly-like leaves make this a distinctive plant. The tart berries can be used to make a refreshing, lemonade-like drink. Herbalists use this plant for fevers, inflammation, indigestion, and liver disorders. The synonym *Mahonia* honors Bernard McMahon, Thomas Jefferson's favorite nurseryman and friend of Thomas Nuttall, who named this genus for him in 1818. *Repens* from the Latin for "creeping."

Photos: Bozeman, MT, May & September (W. Tilt)

MOUNTAIN ALDER
(GRAY ALDER)

Alnus incana • Betulaceae (Birch Family)

FIELD DESCRIPTION:

Deciduous shrub, 6-30′ tall, with grayish-brown-to-reddish bark. Leaves are alternate, broadly elliptical, rounded to cordate at base and rounding to a pointed tip. Leaf margins strongly wavy-edged and double-toothed. Upper surface is green hairless to soft hairy. Underside paler and soft-hairy, especially along veins. Male and female flowers occur on same branch as catkins, developing before leaves. Female catkins are semi-woody cones, on short pedicels, which develop as the leaves are produced. Cones persist after seeds are shed. Male catkins in slender hanging clusters.

TIDBITS

Like willows, alders are pioneer species, capable of establishing themselves along riverbanks prone to flooding and other disturbance. Their roots also fix nitrogen, allowing them to grow in poor soils. Another species of *Alnus* in the region, Green Alder (*A. viridis*), is typically shorter in stature, grows on dry slopes and hillsides, and has woody seed cones borne from longer pedicels, appearing as leaves develop. Alder has many traditional uses including dyes and medicinal remedies, and its branches are used for divining, or "witching" water.

SUBALPINE
MONTANE

Flowering: May - July

Habitat: Stream banks and wet areas, montane to subalpine

Photos: Slough Creek, MT, August (W. Tilt); Illustration: USDA-NRCS Plants Database

GREEN ALDER

Alnus viridis • Betulaceae (Birch Family)
(Synonyms: *Alnus sinuate, Alnus crispa)*

FIELD DESCRIPTION:

Deciduous shrub, 3-15′ tall, with reddish-brown bark, turning grayish with age. Young branches densely glandular, but becoming hairless. Yellowish-green leaves are alternate, oval to broadly ovate, rounded at base, pointed, finely single- or double-toothed. Male and female flowers occur on same branch as catkins, developing with leaves. Female catkins are semi-woody cones, on long pedicels, which develop as the leaves are produced. Cones persist after seeds are shed. Male catkins in slender hanging clusters.

SUBALPINE
MONTANE
FOOTHILLS

Flowering: May - July

Habitat: Dry to moist soils in open areas, foothills to subalpine

Thumbnail photos: Bridger Range, MT, August (W. Tilt); Reference photo: Bridger Range, MT, May (W. Tilt); Illustration: USDA-NRCS Plants Database

TIDBITS

This typically small, shrubby alder is found on dry slopes and hillsides in the mountains, often lining logging roads in areas protected from the full brunt of weather. Mountain Alder (*A. incana*) is typically taller statured, grows along watercourses, and has woody seed cones borne on short pedicels emerging prior to full leaf expansion. Alder has many traditional uses including dyes and medicinal remedies, and its branches are used for "witching" water in arid locations. Green alder is also an excellent fuel for smoking meats and fish.

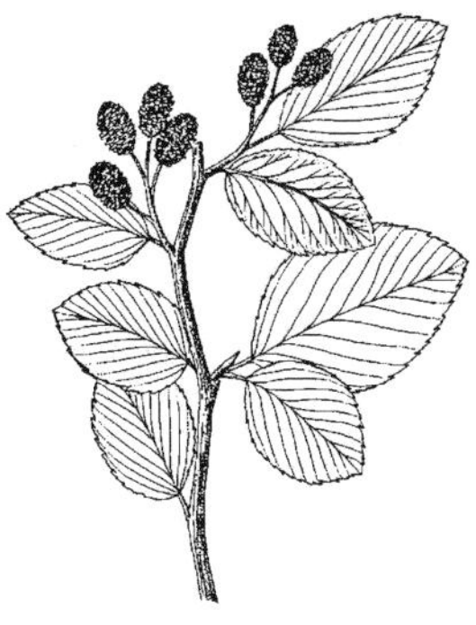

TWINBERRY HONEYSUCKLE

Lonicera involucrata • Caprifoliaceae (Honeysuckle Family)

FIELD DESCRIPTION:

Erect to spreading deciduous shrub, 2-7' tall, with opposite, short-stalked, elliptical, sharp-pointed leaves. Young twigs greenish, 4-sided. Yellow flowers in pairs in leaf axils with conspicuous, broad, green-purple bracts. Flower replaced with black, spherical, three-celled berry.

TIDBITS

The flowers and fruits of Twinberry Honeysuckle are distinctive: yellow flowers in pairs replaced by showy purple black berries framed in dark red bracts. The fruits of twinberry are reported by some to be edible, with a number of medicinal uses. The berry is also used as a dye, as you might learn firsthand when you handle the ripe berries and find your fingers stained purple. *Lonicera* honors German physician and herbalist, Adam Lonicer (1528-1586). *Involucrata* from the Latin for "wrapper," as in the the whorl of bracts, or "involucre," beneath a flower.

SUBALPINE
MONTANE

Flowering: June - August

Habitat: Moist to wet soils in woodlands and thickets, montane to subalpine

Photos: Slough Creek, MT, June & August (W. Tilt); Illustration: USDA-NRCS Plants Database

Lonicera utahensis • Caprifoliaceae (Honeysuckle Family)

UTAH HONEYSUCKLE (RED TWINBERRY)

FIELD DESCRIPTION:

Perennial deciduous shrub, 2-5′ tall. Two white-to-pale-yellow, nodding, trumpet-shaped, five-petaled, fused flowers arise from leaf axils. Funnel-shaped tube is hairy inside. Leaves opposite, oval, smooth, pale green, on short stalks, with paler undersides. Fruit are bright red berries joined at base in pairs.

MONTANE
FOOTHILLS

Flowering: May - July

Habitat: Moist woods and open slopes, foothills to montane

Photos: Gallatin Range, MT, June & August (W. Tilt); Illustration: Karl Urban, Umatilla NF, OR

TIDBITS

Utah Honeysuckle is typically found in the understory of mature forests. It is readily identifiable when its characteristic twinned trumpet flowers or co-jointed red berries are present. Without these signposts, however, the plant is easily overlooked. Each flower has a nectar-filled receptacle, hence the name "honeysuckle." Fruits are edible, and readily consumed by bears, ruffed grouse and other wildlife. Elk and other wildlife also browse the plant. An infusion of the branches and leaves has been used as a wash on sores and infections.

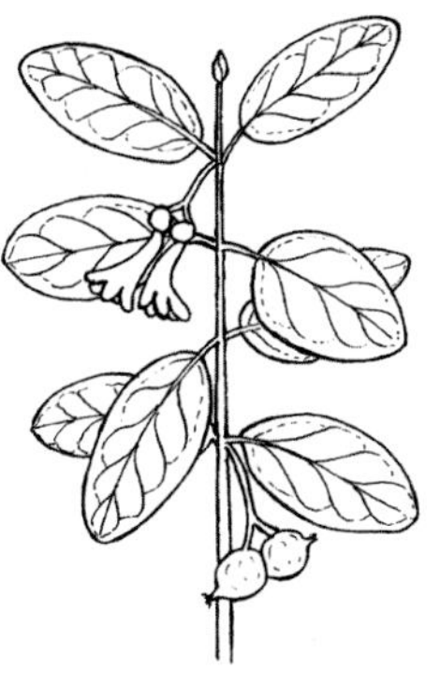

RED ELDERBERRY

Sambucus racemosa • Caprifoliaceae (Honeysuckle Family)

FIELD DESCRIPTION:

Erect deciduous shrub, 3-6′ tall, with highly branched, reddish stems that arch and are brittle and pithy. Leaves are opposite, pinnately compound with 5-17 leaflets, toothed and lance-shaped. Tiny, creamy-white, five-petaled flowers arranged in rounded clusters to 5″ across. Flowers often have a strong, unpleasant smell. Fruits are bright-red or purplish-black drupes in dense clusters.

SUBALPINE
MONTANE

Flowering: June -July

Habitat: Moist, partially shaded soils, montane to subalpine

TIDBITS

The showy clusters of flowers are distinctive as are the red-to-dark-purple berries. While elderberry syrup, pies, and wine are often favorites, in the Northern Rockies the fruits are commonly bitter and possibly toxic because the leaves, stems and roots contain cyanogenic glycosides. They are, however, a favorite of frugivorous birds and many other animals. One account of the common name's origin suggests that humans eating simple foods, including elderberries, stayed in good health, hence becoming "elders." *Sambucus* from the Greek *sanbuke*, a musical instrument, in reference to the plant's stems being made into flutes. *Racemosa* describes the flower cluster.

Photos: Gallatin Range & Slough Creek, MT, June & August (W. Tilt)

Symphoricarpos albus • Caprifoliaceae (Honeysuckle Family)

COMMON SNOWBERRY

FIELD DESCRIPTION:

Deciduous shrub, 2-4′ tall. Branches opposite with slender, hairless stems. Leaves opposite, elliptical to oval, thin, pale green with smooth to wavy-toothed borders. Pink-to-white, funnel-shaped flowers with 5 lobes. Stamens and style do not protrude. White waxy, berry-like fruits appear in clusters and persist into winter. Often forms colonies from rhizomes.

MONTANE
FOOTHILLS

Flowering: May - August

Habitat: Thickets, woodlands and open slopes, foothills to montane

Photos: Gallatin Range, MT, August & September (W. Tilt); Illustration: USDA-NRCS Plants Database

TIDBITS

Find a shrub with twinned white berries in the Yellowstone region and odds are you are looking at snowberry. Its fruits are poisonous, however, and some Native Americans called the plant "snake berry" or "corpse berry." Because of their white color, the berries were believed to be ghosts of Saskatoon berries not to be eaten by the living. Tatarian Honeysuckle (*Lonicera tatarica*) is a similar-looking honeysuckle introduced to the region; it also has opposite leaves, but is taller in stature with deeply-lobed pink flowers and red or orange berries.

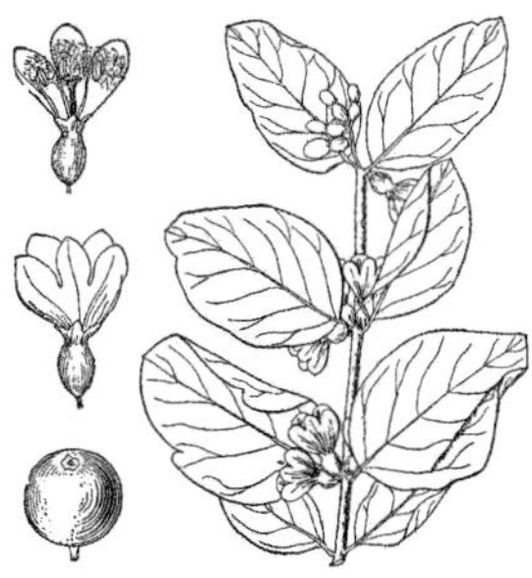

MOUNTAINLOVER (OREGON BOXWOOD)

Paxistima myrsinites • Celastraceae (Bittersweet Family)

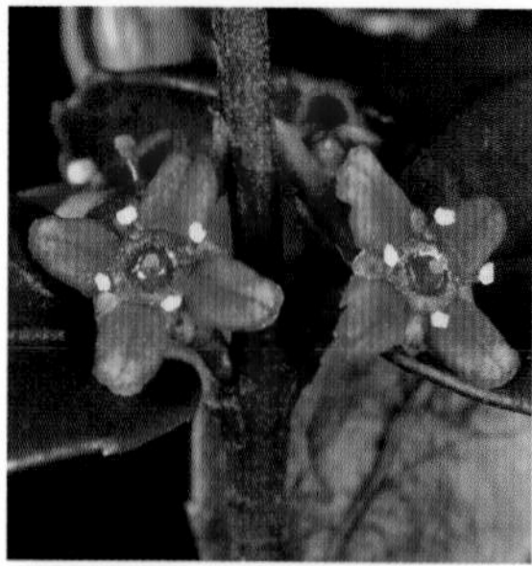

FIELD DESCRIPTION:

Low-growing, evergreen shrub, 8-20" tall, with four-sided, reddish-brown stems. Its leaves are 0.5-1" long, elliptical to oval in outline and produced opposite each other along twigs. The leaves are glossy, leathery, and sharply toothed along the margins. Dark red flowers are very small and produced in leaf axils. Each flower has 4 flared petals. Fruits are 1-2 seeded capsules with a whitish, fleshy coating.

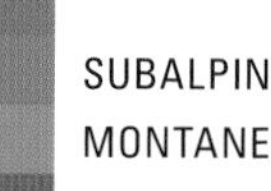

SUBALPINE

MONTANE

Flowering: May - June

Habitat: Open, often moist soils of forests and shrublands, montane to subalpine

TIDBITS

Mountainlover is found sporadically across the Yellowstone region but can be locally abundant, usually in coniferous forests. With an appearance of a miniature boxwood, the plant often goes unnoticed at first glance as it hugs the ground or grows under trees and taller bushes. A close look reveals, tucked into the leaf axils, tiny tubular flowers with red flared petals. Mountainlover is considered important forage for deer, elk, and moose. *Paxistima* from the Greek for "thick stigma," and *myrsinites* for "myrtle," in reference to its resemblance to members of the Myrtle Family (Myrtaceae).

Thumbnail photo: Linn Co., OR, May (Gerald D. Carr); Reference photo: Figalgo Island, WA, Wikimedia (Water Siegmund); Fruit: Ferry Co., WA, June (Gerald D. Carr)

Cornus sericea • Cornaceae (Dogwood Family)
(Synonym: Cornus stolonifera)

RED OSIER DOGWOOD

FIELD DESCRIPTION:

Many-stemmed deciduous shrub, 3-8′ tall, with distinctive maroon stems and opposite branches and leaves. Leaves are egg- to lance-shaped, entire with 5-7 pairs of prominent parallel veins directed toward the leaf tip. Small white flowers comprised of 4 oval petals, 4 small sepals, and 4 stamens are grouped in 2-4′ tight flat-topped clusters (cymes). Fruits are bluish-white, berry-like drupes.

MONTANE
VALLEYS

Flowering: May - August

Habitat: Moist soils along stream banks, valleys to montane

Thumbnail photos: Bridger Range, MT, July (W. Tilt);
Reference photo: Bridger Range, MT, September (W. Tilt);
Illustration: USDA-NRCS Plants Database

TIDBITS

Red Osier Dogwood is a distinctive shrub found in riparian areas. Its leaves turn red in the fall, and the plant's red stems add color to the landscape in the winter, hence the common name "red-twig." These qualities, plus its many clusters of white flowers and white berries, make it a favorite for home gardens as well. The plant's white berries are eaten by wildlife, and the entire plant provides important winter browse. The term "osier" is included in the names of several dogwoods and willows whose flexible twigs are used for furniture and basketry. *Cornus* from the Latin for "hard" or "horn."

COMMON JUNIPER

Juniperus communis • Cupressaceae (Cypress Family)

FIELD DESCRIPTION:

Evergreen coniferous shrub, 1-4' tall, with single or multiple trunks, low, spreading, and often forming mats. Needles mostly in whorls of 3, stiff and very sharp, white above and green below. Male and female cones on different plants (dioecious). Female seed cones mature the second season into blue-black cones (that look like berries), often fleshy and waxy-coated. Male cones small, solitary, round to egg-shaped.

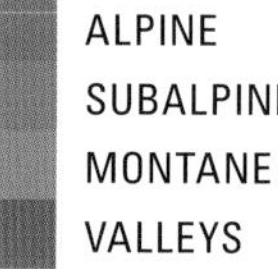

Flowering: June - August

Habitat: Open woods to dry hills and rocky slopes, valleys to alpine

TIDBITS

Considered the most widespread conifer in the world, Common Juniper occupies a wide range of habitats. Creeping Juniper (*Juniperus horizontalis*) is similar in appearance: prostrate shrub with trailing branches with leaves typically less than 5 mm long and often appressed, as compared with Common Juniper with its spreading needle-like leaves. Juniper is used for a range of traditional medicinal uses and its "berries" (actually fleshy cones) are edible, commonly used as seasoning to game and other meats, and provide gin with its distinctive taste.

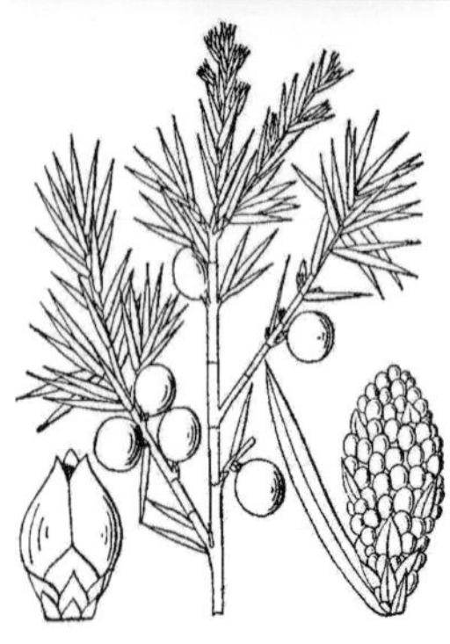

Photos: Bridger Range, MT, September (W. Tilt); Illustration: USDA-NRCS Plants Database

Juniperus scopulorum • Cupressaceae (Cypress Family)

ROCKY MOUNTAIN JUNIPER

FIELD DESCRIPTION:

Evergreen conical-shaped tree, to 30′ tall, with generally regular shape. Trunks red-brown with thin fibrous bark that shreds with age. Leaves typically opposite, scale-like, round-tipped to pointed, light green, in 4 flattened rows. Male and female cones on different plants. Seed (female) cones blue-purple, small, spherical berry-like, often waxy-coated. Male pollen cones solitary at tips of branchlets, small, and egg-shaped.

MONTANE
FOOTHILLS

Flowering: May - June

Habitat: Dry, open, rocky slopes, foothills to montane

TIDBITS

Rocky Mountain Juniper commonly grows to be more than 250 years old. Juniper seeds are mainly dispersed by birds, like Bohemian Waxwings, whose digestive passing of the seeds aids germination by removing the fleshy covering. The plant's durable and aromatic wood is commonly used for furniture and junipers have been used for a range of traditional medicinal uses. The species is commonly dioecious, i.e., it has male flowers on one tree, female flowers (and thus the fruit) on another. *Scopulorum* means "of rocky places," such as the Rocky Mountains.

Photos: Madison Range & Paradise Valley, MT, September (W. Tilt); Illustration: USDA-NRCS Plants Database

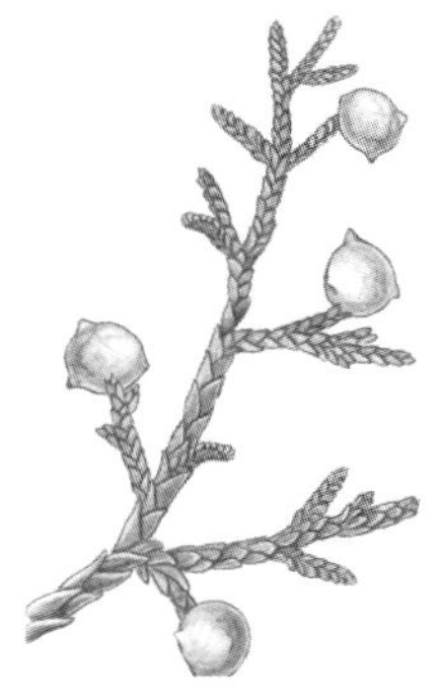

RUSSIAN OLIVE

Elaeagnus angustifolia • Elaeagnaceae (Oleaster Family)

FIELD DESCRIPTION:

Medium-sized tree, to 40′ tall, non-native, with a distinct silvery foliage. Leaves are alternate, narrow, 2-3″ long, and covered with silvery hairs that are star-bursts or scales, more abundant on underside. Trunk and branches often armed with 1-2″ woody thorns. Flowers are very fragrant, yellow, with calyx forming a four-lobed trumpet. Fruits shaped like small olives, silvery when they first appear and turning brown at maturity.

VALLEYS-FOOTHILLS

Flowering: May - June

Habitat: Moist soil sites, road-sides, and planted windbreaks, valleys and foothills

TIDBITS

Russian Olive was intentionally introduced to the United States from southern Europe as an ornamental shade tree and a source of cover for wildlife. It was widely planted across the West in the 1930s as a windbreak to conserve soil. As the tree readily colonizes riparian and wetland areas and is accused of replacing native vegetation, its intentional planting is no longer encouraged and land management agencies encourage eradicating existing trees. At the same time many landowners still argue the tree's benefits for wildlife. *Elaeagnus* from the Greek for "chaste-olive," and *angustifolia* from the Latin for "narrow leaved."

Photos: Bozeman, MT, June & September (W. Tilt)

FIELD DESCRIPTION:

Deciduous shrub, 3-13′ tall, strongly rhizomatous, with an erect, non-spiny form. Leaves are alternate, lance-shaped, approximately 2″ long; leaves silvery as a result of dense star-shaped hairs on both upper and lower surfaces. Flowers yellow, fragrant, funnel-shaped with 4 spreading pointed lobes, arising from leaf axils. Young twigs with dense rusty-brown scales. Fruits are silvery, drupe-like with single nutlet.

MONTANE
PLAINS

Flowering: June - July

Habitat: Open habitats, often gravelly soils along streams, plains to montane

TIDBITS

American Silverberry forms thick, willow-like stands, hence its common name Wolfwillow. Its rhizomatous habit makes it suitable for rehabilitation projects. When in bloom, its flowers are strongly sweet smelling. On the other hand, it is reported that burning the shrub on a campfire will ruin the evening as a result of its foul smell. American Silverberry provides food and shelter to a range of wildlife, including winter browse for moose. The shrub was collected by Captain Meriwether Lewis July, 1806 in the Ovando Valley of Montana.

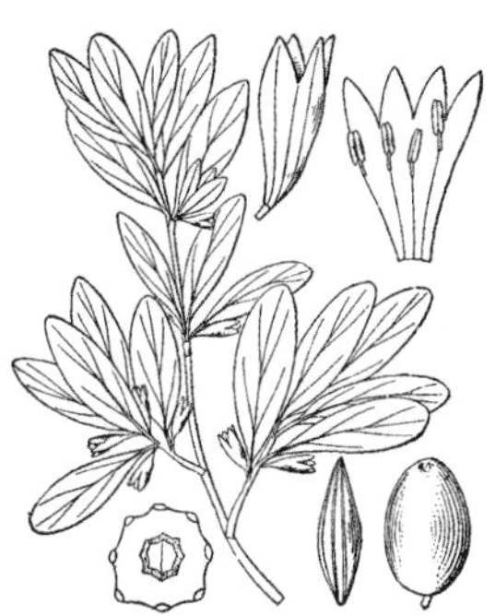

Thumbnail photos: Blackfoot River, MT, July (W. Tilt); Reference photo: Gallatin Gateway, MT, September (Matt Lavin); Illustration: USDA-NRCS Plants Database

SILVER BUFFALOBERRY

Shepherdia argentea • Elaeagnaceae (Oleaster Family)

FIELD DESCRIPTION:

Deciduous shrub, 6-14' tall, many branched with rigid thorns. Species is dioecious with male and female flowers on different plants. Tiny yellow flowers in dense, conspicuous clusters, blossom in very early spring before leaves emerge. Leaves opposite, lanceolate to elliptical, and silvery-gray on both surfaces. Stems on older branches often thorn-tipped. Plant spreads widely from roots. Fruits are bright red berries in small clusters usually covering the plant.

TIDBITS

Silver Buffaloberry is a favored forage for mule deer, pronghorn, and other browsers, while its fruits are eaten by a wide range of birds and other wildlife. Fruits are edible, becoming sweeter and less tart after the first frost, though they contain small amounts of saponin which give the berry a soapy consistency. The plant adapts well to disturbed or degraded wet sites and is also commonly used as a shelterbelt species. *Shepherdia* honors British botanist, John Shepherd. *Argentea* from the Latin for "silvery" in reference to the plant's silver-green leaves.

MONTANE
FOOTHILLS

Flowering: April - May

Habitat: Floodplains and riparian areas, along watercourses, foothills to montane

Photos: Yellowstone River, MT, May & September (W. Tilt); Illustration: USDA-NRCS Plants Database

Shepherdia canadensis • Elaeagnaceae (Oleaster Family)

CANADA BUFFALOBERRY

FIELD DESCRIPTION:

Deciduous shrub, 3-6′ tall, with opposite leaves and without thorns. Species is dioecious with male and female flowers on different plants. Small yellowish flowers, consisting of 4 sepals and no petals, appear on stems with unopened leaves that resemble arrowheads pointing skyward. Once open, leaves are shiny green and veined on top with numerous starburst hairs, lighter underneath, and covered with brownish scales and hairs. Tart, bright red berries appear in late summer to early fall. Fruits are soapy when crushed.

MONTANE

Flowering: June - July

Habitat: Common in open to wooded areas, montane

TIDBITS

Also known as Soapberry and Bearberry (both common names of other plants), the plant's berries are a favorite of bears and many Native American tribes. Picked after the first frosts and whipped with equal parts water and sugar, the berry extract becomes "Buffalo Ice Cream." The fruit contains small amounts of saponin, which give the berry its soapy consistency, and humans should limit their consumption. It is also reported that individuals who consume the fruit are less likely to be bitten by mosquitoes.

Thumbnail photos: Blackfoot River, MT, July (W. Tilt); Reference photo: Gallatin Gateway, MT, September (Matt Lavin); Illustration: USDA-NRCS Plants Database

KINNIKINNICK (BEARBERRY)

Arctostaphylos uva-ursi • Ericaceae (Heath Family)

FIELD DESCRIPTION:

Prostrate evergreen shrub, 4-8" tall, that produces extensive, reddish, trailing stems, extending up to 10' long. Flowers are pink-to-white, urn-shaped with narrow opening, in small hanging clusters at the end of branches (terminal racemes). Branches are flexible. Leaves are alternate, shiny dark green, hairless, paddle-shaped, and rounded at tip. Fruits are bright red berry-like drupes containing 4-5 nutlets.

ALPINE
SUBALPINE
MONTANE
FOOTHILLS

Flowering: May - July

Habitat: Open to wooded areas with well-drained soils, foothills to alpine

TIDBITS

As the common name Bearberry suggests, bears and other wildlife enjoy Kinnikinnick berries. The fruit persist into winter when other fruits are gone. They are not quite as appealing to humans, being somewhat mealy when raw, but tastier when cooked. Also known as uva-ursi by herbalists, the plant is used as an astringent and diuretic, among other uses. Kinnikinnick is an Algonquin word for a smoking mixture. The plant is a host to yellow witch's broom, which infects spruce (see Engelmann Spruce account).

Thumbnail photo: Gallatin Range, MT, July & September (W. Tilt); Illustration: USDA-NRCS Plants Database

Chimaphila umbellata • Ericaceae (Heath Family)

PIPSISSEWA (PRINCE'S PINE)

FIELD DESCRIPTION:

Low evergreen shrub, 4-11" tall, with woody stems near base and overall waxy appearance. Pink-to-rose flowers are nodding with 5 petals and 10 stamens that surround a green ovary. Leaves are leathery, waxy with toothed margins, whorled on stem. Fruits are round, dark-rose capsules.

MONTANE
FOOTHILLS

Flowering: June - August

Habitat: Coniferous forests, foothills to montane

TIDBITS

Pipsissewa is a member of the Wintergreen Family whose members are mostly shrubs. Plant is aromatic, and an extract from its leaves is used to flavor candy and soft drinks. Native Americans used Pipsissewa for a wide range of ailments, including typhus. It was also used during the Civil War to treat rheumatism and kidney disorders. Pipsissewa is said to be Cree for "breaks into pieces," a possible reference to its use in treating gall and kidney stones.

Thumbnail photos: Medford, OR, June (BLM); Reference photo: Gallatin Range, MT, August (W. Tilt); Illustration: USDA-NRCS Plants Database

ALPINE LAUREL
(BOG LAUREL)

Kalmia polifolia • Ericaceae (Heath Family)
(Synonym: *Kalmia microphylla*)

FIELD DESCRIPTION:

Low evergreen shrub, 2-8" tall, with slender, low spreading branches. Leaves opposite, narrowly oblong to elliptical, dark green, glossy, hairless above, and grayish fine-hairy beneath. Leaves often with rolled-under margins. Pink-rose flowers in loose clusters at stem tips, saucer-shaped with 5 lobes. Stamens slightly protruding with densely hairy filaments at base. Flowers often supported by slender, red stem. Fruits are 5-valved, round capsules.

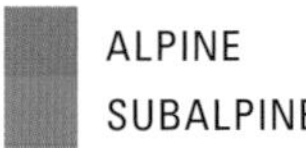

ALPINE
SUBALPINE

Flowering: June - September

Habitat: Moist to wet open sites, subalpine to alpine

TIDBITS

In bloom, Alpine Laurel adds pink accents to the open wet alpine meadows it frequents. A close examination of the flower shows each anther tucked into a pocket in the petal, ready to spring up and dust the passing insect with pollen. When not in bloom, Alpine Laurel could be confused with Trapper's Tea (*Ledum glandulosum*), but that plant is taller and its leaves are alternate and commonly brown-hairy beneath. The plant is poisonous and there are accounts of the leaves being used to commit suicide. *Kalmia* after Swedish botanist Peter Kalm, a student of Carl Linnaeus.

Photos: Beehive Basin, MT, August (W. Tilt); Illustration: USDA-NRCS Plants Database

Phyllodoce empetriformis • Ericaceae (Heath Family)

PINK MOUNTAIN HEATHER

FIELD DESCRIPTION:

Low, evergreen shrub, 3-12" tall. Erect or nodding bell-shaped, five-lobed flowers range in color from pink to deep rose, with petal edges rolled outward. Numerous flowers are arranged in loose umbels. Leaves in a bottlebrush arrangement along stem. Individual leaves are alternate, needle-like, and grooved on underside. Fruits are round capsules with lengthwise slits.

ALPINE
SUBALPINE

Flowering: June - August

Habitat: Moist open sites, subalpine to alpine

Photos: Beehive Basin, MT, August (W. Tilt); Illustration: Karl Urban, Umatilla NF, OR

TIDBITS

A member of the Heath Family, the low-lying Pink Mountain Heather is actually a shrub. The plant's dwarf form and needle-like leaves are adaptations to its high, harsh climate. Leaves are needle-like as a result of their edges being rolled backward along their length. Wood lore has it that the heaths are in full bloom when the mosquitoes are at their hungriest. The genus *Phyllodoce* is named after a sea nymph of the same name, one of the Nereids said by Greek mythology to dwell in the Aegean Sea. *Empetriformus* from the Greek for "on a rock."

TRAPPER'S TEA

Rhododendron columbianum • Ericaceae (Heath Family)
(Synonym: *Ledum glandulosum*)

FIELD DESCRIPTION:

Erect evergreen shrub, 2-5' tall. Leaves are alternate, elliptic to oval in shape, rounded at base, leathery, dark green on top surface and lighter green-grayish with glandular dots and short white hairs beneath. Leaf edges often rounded under. White, five-parted flowers are arranged in dense, round clusters (corymbs) at end of branches. Eight to 12 stamens, with hairy bases, protrude above the flowers. Fruits are nodding, five-chambered capsules that are rounded, short-hairy, and glandular.

ALPINE
SUBALPINE
MONTANE

Flowering: June - August

Habitat: Moist to wet, especially acidic soils in open or wooded areas, montane to alpine

TIDBITS

If you come across a shrub with conspicuous round cluster of rhododendron-looking flowers in a wet mountain area, you are likely looking at Trapper's Tea. While the common name suggests a refreshing brew, Trapper's Tea is considered toxic to livestock and can be poisonous to humans as well. A tea can be made from its leaves to encourage urination and drowsiness. Labrador Tea (*Ledum groenlandicum*), a plant found in the northern Great Lakes and New England, is similar in appearance but has reddish-brown hair rather than white hair on the bottom side of leaves.

Photos: Gallatin Range, MT, July (W. Tilt); Illustration: USDA-NRCS Plants Database

GLOBE HUCKLEBERRY
(BIG HUCKLEBERRY)

FIELD DESCRIPTION:

Deciduous shrub, 1-4' tall, with numerous branches. Bark yellow-green to reddish, slightly ridged on young twigs, and gray on older stems. Leaves are alternate, obovate to elliptical, widest on upper portion and narrowing to point. Leaf prominently veined and somewhat glandular beneath. Flowers inconspicuous, whitish-pink, urn-shaped, translucent, arising singly from leaf axils. Fruits are round, dark-blue-to-purple berries, often with a whitish bloom.

SUBALPINE
MONTANE

Flowering: May - June

Habitat: Moist, cool, open and wooded sites, montane to subalpine

Photos: Madison Range, MT, August (W. Tilt); Illustration: Karl Urban, Umatilla NF, OR

TIDBITS

The huckleberry appears to have gotten its name by being mistaken for the European blueberry, or "hurtleberry," corrupted over time to "huckleberry." They are a favorite of grizzly bears and hikers alike. Typically the most productive huckleberry bushes are found in previously burned clearings. Many botanists group *V. globulare* with the Thinleaf Huckleberry (*V. membranaccum*). The Fool's Huckleberry (*Menziesia ferruginea*) resembles huckleberry, but typically has more than one flower arising from the leaf axis, and its fruit is a woody capsule rather than a berry.

GROUSEBERRY
(GROUSE WHORTLEBERRY)

Vaccinium scoparium • Ericaceae (Heath Family)

FIELD DESCRIPTION:

Dwarf deciduous shrub, 4-10" tall, that often forms a carpet. Twigs are many, green, strongly angled, and broom-like. Leaves are alternate, ovate, thin, serrate, and sharp-pointed. Flowers are solitary, nodding, urn-like pink blossoms in the axils of the lowest leaves. Fruits are round, bright-red berries.

TIDBITS

A common, low-growing shrub, the Grouseberry often appears as green broom-like tufts scattered across the forest understory. In fact it makes a handy broom and is also called Broom Huckleberry. As the common name implies, Grouseberry is an important summer and early fall food for grouse, elk, bear, and other wildlife. Though small and labor-intensive to harvest, the fruits are edible and used in preserves and pies. The plant also has been used as an antiseptic, digestive aid, and to alleviate nausea.

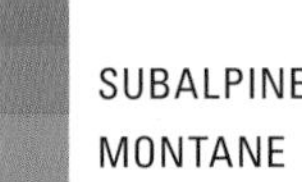

SUBALPINE
MONTANE

Flowering: May - August

Habitat: Moist to dry soils in the understory of conifer trees, montane to subalpine

Photos: Gallatin Range, MT, July & August (W. Tilt)

SIBERIAN PEASHRUB
(CARAGANA, PEATREE)

FIELD DESCRIPTION:

Deciduous shrub, up to 15′ tall, with multiple stems and branches. Leaves are alternate or whorled, pinnately compound with 8-12 leaflets in pairs (end leaflet absent). Leaflets entire, elliptical to ovate, and pointed. Leaves bright to dark green above and paler beneath. Leaves may be covered in fine, soft hairs when young. Bright yellow, pea-like flowers, single or in small clusters, from leaf axis. Fruits are green, linear "peapods" that mature into brownish cylinders that split to eject seeds. Bark is green to gray-brown, smooth with prominent lenticels.

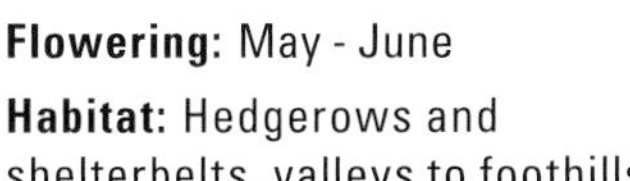

VALLEYS-FOOTHILLS

Flowering: May - June

Habitat: Hedgerows and shelterbelts, valleys to foothills

TIDBITS

Introduced from Siberia for its hardiness and cold tolerance, as well as fast growth, Caragana is commonly planted in the northern Great Plains as windbreaks, hedges and screening. Caragana is also planted for wildlife and erosion purposes, and provides food and cover for a range of birds and other wildlife. Because of its nitrogen-fixing capacity, it is valued as a soil-improving plant. The species has been widely used for medicinal purposes, including treatments of certain breast cancers.

Photos: Bozeman, MT, June & August (W. Tilt)

GOLDEN CURRANT

Ribes aureum • Grossulariaceae (Currant Family)

FIELD DESCRIPTION:

Deciduous shrub, 2-7′ tall, with spreading form. Shrub is spineless and generally glabrous. Leaves up to 2″ across, circular with 3-5 conspicuously rounded lobes. Petioles sometimes as long as leaf blade. Flowers bright yellow, hairless, fragrant, generally five-petaled, yellow or tipped with red, in spreading racemes, 2-15 flowers on short pedicels. Fruits are berries, turning from yellow to orange to dark purple as they mature.

Flowering: April - June

Habitat: Moist areas near lake shores and streams, roadsides, foothills to montane

TIDBITS

Golden Currant's delicate lemon-yellow flowers show brightly in early spring-green foliage. The flowers are followed by golden, then orange, then red, juicy and edible berries. The shrub's scalloped leaves often change to deep maroon in the fall. Golden Currant was first collected by Meriwether Lewis in April, 1806. In determining what general category of *Ribes* you are looking at, if you are looking at a shrub with palmate leaves and spiny, bristly stems, you are likely looking at a gooseberry; if the stems are not spiny and bristly, then it is likely a currant. *Aureum* from the Latin for "gold."

Thumbnail photo: Fort Benton, MT, May (Matt Lavin); Other photos: Bridger Range MT, May & June (Whitney Tilt); Illustration: USDA-NRCS Plants Database

WAX CURRANT

FIELD DESCRIPTION:

Deciduous shrub, to 6′ tall and wide, no thorns, many branched, branchlets hairy and glandular. Leaf blades from 0.2″ to 1″ wide, orbicular or kidney -shaped with 3-7 shallow lobes, each lobe toothed or rounded, hairy and glandular or glabrous except on margins and along veins beneath. Racemes pendulous with 2 or 3 flowers. Flower tube to almost 0.5″ long, pink, hairy, sometimes also glandular. Sepals white or pink. Petals five-parted, white, and minute. Style barely protrudes from flower. Orange-to-red berries with floral tube still attached, sparingly glandular, rarely glabrous.

MONTANE
FOOTHILLS

Flowering: May - August

Habitat: Dry areas, woodlands, rocky areas, foothills to montane

Thumbnail & reference photo: Douglas Co., WA, April (Ben Legler); Fruit: Sawtooth NF, ID, August (W. Tilt)

TIDBITS

The stems of Wax Currant are fuzzy and often very glandular, but lack spines and prickles. The shrub has a pleasant, spicy aroma, and its smooth berries sport a long, dried flower remnant at the tip. Fruits are edible but generally described as rather tasteless. There are a number of *Ribes* species in the Northern Rockies; key distinguishing factors are the presence or lack of thorns, the size and shape of the leaves, and the color and shape of the flowers. *Cereum* means "waxy" and refers to the waxy secretion of the leaves. The species has a variety named "inebrians" and a common name in some regions as Whiskey Currant, suggesting some alternate uses for the fruit.

NORTHERN BLACK CURRANT

Ribes hudsonianum • Grossulariaceae (Currant Family)

FIELD DESCRIPTION:

Erect, deciduous shrub with maple-like leaves, 1-4′ tall, glandular without spines. Bears 6-12 white flowers in showy raceme. Flowers in erect clusters, broadly funnel-shaped, with 5 spreading petals and 5 spreading sepals. Leaves are alternate with 3-5 pointed, toothed lobes and yellow resin glands beneath. Branches are smooth and fruits are black berries with waxy bloom. Plant has strong sweetish "tomcat" odor.

MONTANE
FOOTHILLS

Flowering: May - July

Habitat: Moist, shady woods, foothills to montane

TIDBITS

The fruits of Northern Black Currant are consumed by a wide range of wildlife species. When cooked, the berries make a passable (some reviews say tasty, some say not) currant jam or jelly. Currants and gooseberries have a variety of traditional uses from the treatment of colds to calming restless infants. Three field marks for Northern Black Currant are leaf lobes more or less pointed, leaves with resin dots on underside, and flowers in erect clusters. *Ribes* from Arabic or Persian *ribas*, "acid-tasting," in reference to the tart fruits.

Thumbnail photo: Columbia Co., WA, July (Ben Legler); Other photos: Gallatin Range, MT, July & August (Whitney Tilt); Illustration: USDA-NRCS Plants Database

BRISTLY BLACK GOOSEBERRY

FIELD DESCRIPTION:

Erect-to-sprawling deciduous shrub, 3-5′ tall, with prickles along the branches and thorns at leaf bases. Flowers yellow-green to reddish, five-parted, 7-15, in hanging clusters (racemes). Round and broad sepals, yellow-green-to-reddish flare, bell-like. Petals are wedge-shaped, pink outside with darker red insides. Stamens generally as long as sepals. Leaves are alternate, palmate, with 3-5 deeply cut lobes, coarsely toothed margins, hairless or sparsely hairy, and cordate at base. Branches covered with bristles and armored with 1-3 spines at nodes. Fruits are smooth, sparsely hairy, red-purple-black berries.

ALPINE
SUBALPINE
MONTANE
FOOTHILLS

Flowering: May - July

Habitat: Moist soils in forest or open sites, foothills to alpine

Photos: Snohomish Co., WA, April & July (Ben Legler); Illustration: USDA-NRCS Plants Database

TIDBITS

If you're looking at a shrub with palmate leaves and stems that bite back with prickles and spines, you are likely looking at a gooseberry. Some people experience allergic reactions from contact with the shrub's defenses. Black Gooseberry has edible berries that are tart and juicy, often used in preserves and pies. Its berries are enjoyed by a wide range of wildlife species. *Ribes* species are an alternate host for white pine blister rust. Mountain Gooseberry (*Ribes montigenum*) is very similar to Black Gooseberry but its leaves are hairy-glandular on both sides and berries are bright red.

STICKY CURRANT

Ribes viscosissimum • Grossulariaceae (Currant Family)

FIELD DESCRIPTION:

Deciduous shrub, 3-6′ tall, with stiff spreading branches without spines or bristles. Leaves and stems sticky-glandular and often downy-hairy. Leaves alternate, thick-textured, palmately-shaped, with 3-5 conspicuously rounded lobes, and blunt-toothed margins. Flowers, 6-12 in terminal racemes, somewhat drooping, comprising five-parted, white flowers that are bell-shaped with 5 whitish-greenish sepals which spread at tips, corolla-like, while 5 whitish petals tightly surround the stamens. Fruit is a sticky, purple-black berry.

TIDBITS

As both its common and scientific names suggest, the shrub is covered in sticky, glandular hairs. It is resinous and odorous. The fruits are edible but generally not eaten, at least not by humans. *Ribes* species are alternate hosts for white pine blister rust, which was introduced to North America from Europe in 1910. The disease devastated Western White Pine (*Pinus monticola*) forests, and from the 1930 to 1960s, workers were employed to remove *Ribes* species in an effort to control the disease's impact. The practice was discontinued when the practice was found to be largely ineffective.

SUBALPINE
MONTANE

Flowering: May - June

Habitat: Open dry forests, along stream banks and fire-cuts, montane to subalpine

Photos: Kittitas Co., WA, June (Ben Legler); Fruit: Bozeman, MT, August (W. Tilt); Illustration: USDA-NRCS Plants Database

FIELD DESCRIPTION:

Erect, deciduous shrub, 3-10′ tall. Flowers white, cross-shaped, with 4 broad, rounded, spreading petals around center of numerous bright-yellow stamens. Flowers in showy clusters (racemes) at end of branches. Leaves opposite, lance- to egg-shaped, three-nerved, and edged with hairs. Leaves may feel somewhat rough from short-stiff hairs. Fruits are 4-chambered capsules. Overall shrub is branching with brown, flaky bark.

VALLEYS-FOOTHILLS

Flowering: May - July

Habitat: Well-drained, moist soils, commonly on rocky sites along rivers, valleys and foothills

Photos: Smith River, MT, July (W. Tilt); Illustration: Karl Urban, Umatilla NF, OR

TIDBITS

Lewis' Mock-Orange is a showy shrub with fragrance reminiscent of orange blossoms. When in bloom, it brightens river canyons and other locales with its floral display and fragrance. It is the state flower of Idaho. The genus is named for the Egyptian king Ptolemy Philadelphus, while the species name honors Captain Meriwether Lewis. The hard, straight stems of mock-orange were traditionally used for making tool handles, snowshoes, arrows, and the like. In some areas the shrub is called Syringa, though the name is more properly applied to the lilacs (*Syringa sp.*).

GREEN ASH

Fraxinus pennsylvanica • Oleaceae (Olive Family)

FIELD DESCRIPTION:

Medium-sized, deciduous tree, up to 60′ tall, with oval upright crown, straight trunk (20-30″ in diameter) cm), and gray-brown bark with shallow furrows. Leaves opposite, 8-12′ long, pinnately compound with 5-9 leaflets, lanceolate to elliptic in shape with sharply-toothed-to-entire margins. Flowers are inconspicuous; male flowers in dense, green clusters with reddish anthers; female flowers yellow-green in short clusters. Fruits are single-seeded, paddle-shaped, winged samaras in elongated clusters.

PLAINS-FOOTHILLS

Flowering: May - June

Habitat: Stream banks and moist soils, windbreaks, commonly planted in towns and cities, plains to foothills

TIDBITS

Green Ash is the most widely distributed of the ashes, and one of the most widely planted ornamental trees in the United States. The Yellowstone region is at the western edge of its native range, yet Green Ash is commonly found in windbreaks and frequently planted along streets and boulevards in cities and towns. It is a relatively fast growing and flood tolerant tree whose foliage turns bright yellow in the fall. The tree can produce large seed crops that are eaten by a range of wildlife. The wood of Green Ash is used for paddles and oars, an indication of its strength and durability.

Thumbnail photo: Fort Benton, MT, May (Matt Lavin);
Reference photo: Bozeman, MT, October (Matt Lavin);
Fruit: Livingston, MT, October (W. Tilt)

Abies lasiocarpa • Pinaceae (Pine Family)
(Synonym: *Abies bifolia*)

SUBALPINE FIR

FIELD DESCRIPTION:

Evergreen, up to 110' tall, with slender, spire-like crown that sheds snow and reduces wind resistance. Seed cones are about 3.5" long and dark purple when mature. They grow on upper branches in an erect position on twigs. As cones mature, scales and seeds fall off, leaving an erect, woody, spike-like cone axis. Needles are about 1" long, flexible, and flattened (they won't roll between your fingers). Tips are blunt. Needles arise from all sides of twigs and tend to grow upward.

Flowering: July - September

Habitat: Cool northern exposures and steam bottoms, montane to subalpine

Thumbnail & inset photos: Madison Range, MT, July (W. Tilt); Reference photo: Yoho NP, Alberta, August (W. Tilt)

TIDBITS

Subalpine Fir is the only true fir native to the region, and generally occupies sites characterized by cold winters, cool summers, frequent summer frosts, and heavy snowpack. Stands of Subalpine Fir provide browse and cover for a wide range of wildlife species, and its seeds are eaten by several species of birds and small mammals. The tree's branches often persist right to the ground, forming a protective skirt that animals use to escape heavy snow and wind. Its lumber is used in prefabricated wood products and pulpwood. Small Subalpine Fir trees are extensively used for Christmas trees.

ENGELMANN SPRUCE

Picea engelmannii • Pinaceae (Pine Family)

FIELD DESCRIPTION:

Coniferous tree that may reach 100-150' tall, with a pyramidal shape. Needles somewhat flexible and sharp, square in cross-section (rolls between fingers). Needles arise spirally from twigs and have hairs at base of leaves. Twigs are covered with distinctive, raised pegs, causing twig to feel and appear rough. Branches spreading horizontally or somewhat drooping. Bark usually reddish-to-purplish-brown and thin-scaly. Two-inch seed cones hang down near treetops.

ALPINE
SUBALPINE
MONTANE

Flowering: June - July

Habitat: Cool moist or dry slopes, from montane up to timberline and krummholz

TIDBITS

You know a spruce when you shake hands with it – its needles bite. Engelmann Spruce prefers high, cold environments where its stands provide important cover for big game. Its seeds are eaten by several species of birds and small mammals, and the tree is an important lumber source. Look for "witch's brooms," a broom-like outgrowth of branches caused by a rust (fungus) disease or Dwarf Mistletoe. The species is named after German-born St. Louis botanist, George Engelmann, who was responsible for naming and describing many of the West's plants during the 1800s.

Photos: Gallatin Range, MT, May/July (W. Tilt)
Needle arrangement: Oregon State Univ., *Trees to Know in Oregon*

Pinus albicaulis • Pinaceae (Pine Family)

WHITEBARK PINE

FIELD DESCRIPTION:

A 5-needle pine, 10-60′ tall, with needles growing in clusters at the end of twigs. Bark is white-gray, smooth, and thin in younger trees and broken into scales on older trees. Needles 1.5-2.5″ long in bundles of 5. When in flower, pollen cones are a vibrant red color. Seed cones are 2-3″ long, almost round, dark purple to brown in color. Cones disintegrate after maturing (usually from animal activity), and are rarely found intact on the ground. At timberline, species may occur in shrub or krummholz forms.

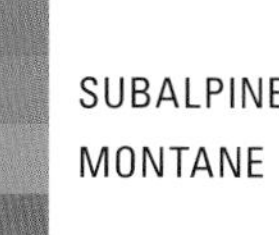

Habitat: High mountain ridges, commonly at elevations of more than 7,500′, upper montane to subalpine

Thumbnail (seed cone): Fresno Co., CA, August (Matt Lavin); Other photos: Gravelly Mountains, MT, September (W. Tilt)

TIDBITS

At lower elevations, Whitebark Pine can be a straight, handsome tree, but at higher elevations it often has a gnarled, windswept appearance. Whitebark Pine produces large seeds, high in fat, which provide an important source of food for many animal species, such as red squirrels and Clark's Nutcrackers. Grizzly bears and black bears raid squirrel caches to consume the hoarded pine seeds. The tree is a keystone species of high elevation habitats. Unfortunately, Whitebark Pine populations are being reduced by a variety of factors, including blister rust from Europe, fire suppression, and mountain pine beetle.

LODGEPOLE PINE

Pinus contorta • Pinaceae (Pine Family)

FIELD DESCRIPTION:

Coniferous tree up to 100′ tall. Needles 2″ long, in bundles of 2, and often twisting. In profile, needles twist apart from one another. Seed cones are yellow-brown, and average about 1.5″ in length. Cones are larger on one side near the base (asymmetrical) and their tips at the cone apex are armed with sharp prickles. Bark is scaly, brown to gray, loosely attached, and thin (rarely exceeding 0.5″ thick), which reduces the tree's resistance to fire.

MONTANE

Flowering: June - July

Habitat: Dry to moist areas in stands, montane

TIDBITS

Lodgepole Pine is one of the most common trees in the Northern Rocky Mountains. The tree often produces serotinous cones that remain on the tree for years, and require temperatures above 113 degrees F to melt the resin and release the seed. In nature, only forest fires generate temperatures of this magnitude. The wood is extensively used for lumber and poles for buildings and fences. Lodgepole stands provide summer range for big game animals. The tree's name arises from Native American use of the poles for lodges. Its needles twist apart from one another, hence the scientific name *contorta*.

Seed cones: Midway Geyser Basin, YNP, September (W. Tilt); Other photos: Island Park, ID, July (W. Tilt); Left: pollen cones

Pinus flexilis • Pinaceae (Pine Family)

LIMBER PINE

FIELD DESCRIPTION:

Coniferous tree, to 50′ tall, often shrubby. Needles in bundles of 5 along twig, 2-3″ long on stout twigs that are very flexible. Trunk is gray, often branched and twisted. Cones 3-7″ long with no prickles, green when immature, thick, woody scales when older. Older cones often intact under tree. The central trunk is usually distorted, many branched, and twisted.

SUBALPINE
MONTANE

Flowering: June - July

Habitat: Open and dry environments such as exposed, rocky mountainsides, montane to timberline

TIDBITS

The twigs of this slow growing, long-lived pine are so flexible that they can be tied in a knot. This characteristic gives rise to both its common name and its species name. Trees may take several hundred years to reach maturity and are capable of living over 1,000 years. Limber Pine grows across a wide range of elevations, inhabiting some of the driest sites capable of supporting trees. The tree has little commercial timber value, but its large seeds have high energy content, providing food for rodents and birds, which cache the seeds for later use. Other animals, such as bears, benefit from raiding these caches.

Thumbnail & reference photos: Bozeman, MT, June (W. Tilt); Right: mature cone: Butte Co., ID, July (Matt Lavin)

PONDEROSA PINE

Pinus ponderosa • Pinaceae (Pine Family)

FIELD DESCRIPTION:

Coniferous tree, up to 140′ tall. Needles in bundles of 3, averaging 7″ in length (5-10″), tufted at the end of branches. Bark is gray to black on young trees. As the tree matures, the bark thickens to as much as 4″ and breaks into large, flat, yellow-brown scaly plates separated by deep furrows. The bark is fragrant and flakes off in small, irregular pieces resembling jigsaw puzzle pieces. The tree has a long clear trunk, its branches are self-pruning, rising to a high open crown.

TIDBITS

Ponderosa Pine is the most widely distributed pine in North America, virtually shading the American West. The name "ponderosa" refers to the ponderous or heavy wood. It reaches maturity in 300 to 400 years. The wood is highly desirable as saw timber. The bark of mature Ponderosa Pines is cinnamon to yellow-orange in a fascinating jigsaw pattern, a characteristic lending the tree another common name, Yellow Pine. The layered bark gives the tree enhanced fire protection. When warmed by the sun. Ponderosa Pine bark exudes a pleasant, soft vanilla/butterscotch fragrance.

MONTANE
FOOTHILLS

Flowering: June - July

Habitat: Dry to moist areas in stands, foothills to montane

Thumbnail & reference photo: Polson, MT, June (Matt Lavin); Bark: Bitterroot River, MT, June (W. Tilt)

FIELD DESCRIPTION:

Large conifer, capable of exceeding 200′ in height (less in the Northern Rockies region), with a short, pyramidal, symmetrical crown at the top of a clear, straight trunk. Distinctive seed cone, 2-4″ long, is brown with protruding three-pronged leaf-like bracts. Cones are almost always present, either on the trees or under them. Buds are also distinctive: sharp-pointed, shiny, with reddish-brown overlapping scales. Needles are flat, flexible, and without sharp tips.

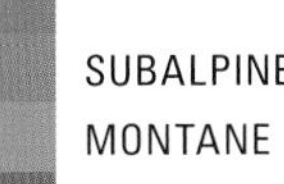

SUBALPINE
MONTANE

Flowering: May - June

Habitat: Cool, moist, north-facing slopes, foothills to montane

Thumbnail & reference photo: Paradise Valley, MT, June (W. Tilt); Cone detail: Oregon State University, *Trees to Know in Oregon*

TIDBITS

The common name, Douglas-Fir, is hyphenated to acknowledge that the species is a not true fir (i.e., not of the genus *Abies*), while *Pseudotsuga* means "false hemlock." The tree's cones are distinctive, with protruding bracts that resemble a mouse's back legs and tail diving into a hole. Douglas-Fir is an important timber tree, accounting for nearly one-quarter of the total lumber produced in North America. The species name recognizes David Douglas, a Scottish botanist who roamed the Northwest in the 1820s, and Archibald Menzies, a fellow Scot who first discovered the tree in 1791.

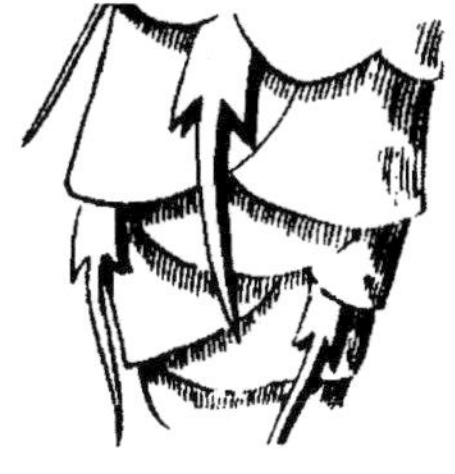

SNOWBUSH
(BUCKBRUSH)

Ceanothus velutinus • Rhamnaceae (Buckthorn Family)

FIELD DESCRIPTION:

Aromatic evergreen shrub, 1-4' tall. Leaves are dark green, shiny, and evergreen, alternately arranged, with 3 prominent ribs arising from leaf base. Twigs brown, becoming dark brown, more or less puberulent. White flowers arranged in dense showy clusters at ends of the branches. Flowers star-shaped, tiny, with 5 white, slender, cupped petals and 5 triangular sepals, which curve sharply between the petals over the flowers. Fruits are three-lobed, sticky, blue-black capsules. Plants produce a cinnamon or balsam-like odor.

MONTANE
FOOTHILLS

Flowering: June - August

Habitat: Moist to dry, fairly open slopes, foothills to montane

TIDBITS

Coming across Snowbush in full bloom on a sunny day is a delight with its bright white floral display, shiny, green leaves, and pleasing aroma. Snowbush provides important fall and winter browse for deer, moose, and elk. Fruits and seeds of the plant are eaten by small mammals. Birds and all types of wildlife use Snowbush for cover and areas to bed down. The leaves contain saponin and have been used to prevent dandruff, diaper rash, and eczema. *Ceanothus* from the Greek for a now-unknown spiny plant, and *velutinus* from the Latin for "like velvet."

Thumbnail photo: Klickitat Co., WA, May (Ben Legler); Reference photo: Boulder River, MT, July (W. Tilt); Illustration: USDA-NRCS Plants Database

Amelanchier alnifolia • Rosaceae (Rose Family)

SERVICEBERRY
(SASKATOON, JUNEBERRY)

FIELD DESCRIPTION:

Bushy, deciduous shrub or small tree, up to 20' tall, with reddish or gray stems. Smooth, dark-gray bark when mature. Leaves are alternate, 1-2", oval to nearly round. Leaf tips rounded and coarsely toothed. White, star-shaped flowers with 5 slender petals arise from rim of a flat cup, in clusters near tips of branches. Fruit matures into purple-black pomes with a waxy covering.

MONTANE
FOOTHILLS

Flowering: April - July

Habitat: Open woods, banks and hillsides, foothills to montane

Photos: Bozeman, MT, May & August (W. Tilt); Illustration: USDA-NRCS Plants Database

TIDBITS

A favorite food of many birds and other animals, the ripe berries of Serviceberry are edible, raw or cooked. The fruit can be dried, and it was a traditional ingredient in pemmican. Native Americans used the plant for a wide range of purposes, including food, medicine, weapons, and tools. The name Serviceberry originated with early settlers who used these early spring blooming flowers for burial services when the ground finally thawed enough to allow them to inter loved ones who had died in the winter. *Alnifolia* means "alder-like foliage."

MOUNTAIN MAHOGANY

Cercocarpus sp. • Rosaceae (Rose Family)

FIELD DESCRIPTION:

Deciduous shrub, 5-16′ tall, with smooth, thornless branches and dense wood. Leaves simple, alternate, leathery, whitish beneath, and short-petiolate. *C. ledifolius* leaves are linear with inrolled margins. *C. montanus* leaves are obovate, finely serrate, and hairy. Flowers greenish-yellow, hairy, bell-shaped, with 5 sepals bent backward and no petals, arising from reddish funnel base. Stamens 25-40, anthers hairy. Fruit is an achene with curling plumose tails (the styles) to 4″ long.

MONTANE
FOOTHILLS

Flowering: May - July

Habitat: Open forests, meadow edges, foothills to montane

TIDBITS

Two species of Mountain Mahogany are found in the region: Curl-Leaf Mountain Mahogany (*C. ledifolius*) and Birch-Leaf Mountain Mahogany (*C. montanus*), with the primary distinction found in the leaves. Favoring dry canyons, the shrub puts on a fragrant display of yellow and red trumpet flowers followed by showy seeds with feathery tails. The shrub provides important forage for mule and whitetail deer and other wildlife. The wood of Mountain Mahogany is hard and brittle. When dried, its smoke adds a rich flavor to barbecued meats.

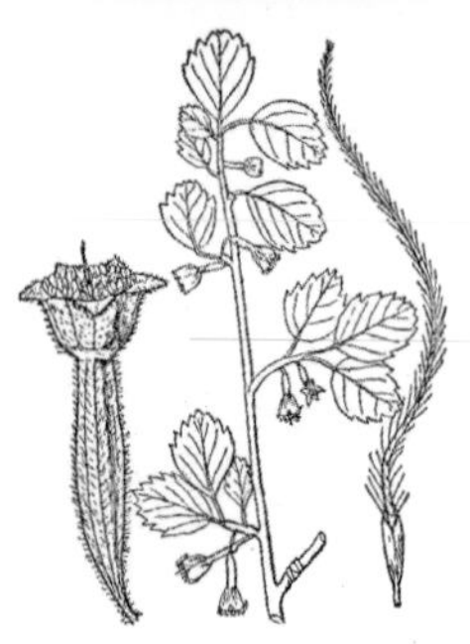

Thumbnail (*C. ledifolius*): Butte, ID, July (Matt Lavin); Reference photo (*C. ledifolius*): Elko, NV, August (Matt Lavin); Inset (*C. montanus*): SW Colorado, May (Al Schneider); Illustration (*C. montanus*): USDA-NRCS Plants Database

FIELD DESCRIPTION:

Deciduous shrub, to 14' tall, with stout, straight 1" thorns on branches. Leaves are alternate, egg-shaped, glossy, leathery, dark green, 1-2 times sharply- toothed, often lobed. Leaf stalks with glands and branches with scaly gray bark. Flowers borne in showy flat-topped clusters (corymbs), saucer-shaped with 5 round petals, 10-20 stamens, and 5 styles. Triangular sepals are bent backward. Fruits are red-purple-black pomes (apple-like), containing 1 large nutlet. Leaves turn red in fall.

MONTANE
FOOTHILLS

Flowering: May - July

Habitat: Open forests, meadow edges, foothills to montane

Photos: Bozeman, MT, May & September (W. Tilt);
Illustration: USDA-NRCS Plants Database

TIDBITS

Hawthorns are most easily identified by long, straight thorns on their branches, well known to hikers and hunters who attempt to push through a hawthorn patch. Hawthorns are native to all 48 lower states. They readily hybridize and are difficult to distinguish to species level. The spiny shrubs provide food and shelter for wildlife since they form protective thickets and produce abundant fruit, called "haws." Hawthorns have a long history of human medicinal uses, especially as a heart tonic. *Crataegus* from the Greek *cratus* for "strength," a reference to the hardness of the wood.

SHRUBBY CINQUEFOIL

Dasiphora fruticosa • Rosaceae (Rose Family)
(Synonym: *Potentilla fruticosa, Pentaphylloides floribunda*)

FIELD DESCRIPTION:

Highly branched, deciduous, rounded shrub, 1-4′ tall, with reddish brown, peeling bark. Bright yellow flowers rise from leaf axils. Saucer-shaped flowers consist of 5 petals enclosed by 5 sepal-like bracts and numerous stamens and pistils. Leaves are alternate, pinnately compound with 5 narrow linear, entire leaflets.

TIDBITS

This hardy shrub has one of the longest blooming periods of any plant in the region, making it a favorite plant for landscaping. Cinquefoil means "five-leaved," and the flower is five-parted. Shrubby Cinquefoil has been used as an astringent and tonic for a range of ailments from weak bowels to flu. The species was formerly classified as *Potentilla*, from the Latin for "powerful," in reference to the shrub's medicinal properties. *Dasiphora* from the Greek for "hair bearing," a likely reference to the plant's hairy bark and seeds.

SUBALPINE
MONTANE
FOOTHILLS

Flowering: June - August

Habitat: Meadows and rocky sites, foothills to subalpine

Photos: Slough Creek, MT, July (W. Tilt); Illustration: USDA-NRCS Plants Database

NINEBARK
(MALLOW NINEBARK)

FIELD DESCRIPTION:

Medium-sized deciduous shrub, 2-6' tall, with brown, shredding bark. Leaves are alternate, palmately divided with 3 shallow lobes and toothed (maple-like in appearance). White saucer-like flowers are borne in dense, terminal clusters. Five rounded petals surround yellow-brown center of flowers with numerous long stamens present. Bark exfoliates in strips. Fruits are reddish, egg-shaped, fuzzy-keeled pods.

SUBALPINE
MONTANE
FOOTHILLS

Flowering: June - July

Habitat: Dry to moist open woods and hillsides, foothills to subalpine

Photos: Gallatin Range, MT, July & October (W. Tilt & Matt Lavin)

TIDBITS

Ninebark is a common shrub of the region, often forming dense thickets. Maple-like leaves and shredding bark are distinctive characteristics of Ninebark. The shrub is a pioneering species, capable of vigorous regeneration from rhizomes and spreading after wildfire and other disturbances. The shrub's vigor is partly due to fact that much of its rhizomes are buried in mineral soil, below the level commonly burned in all, but the hottest, fires. It can outcompete conifer seedlings and is commonly controlled by herbicides following commercial logging. The common name Ninebark describes the erroneous belief that there were nine layers of shredding bark.

CHOKECHERRY

Prunus virginiana • Rosaceae (Rose Family)

TIDBITS

Chokecherry is found across the central and northern United States and southern Canada. Its elongated clusters of white flowers attract a wide range of pollinators, while the tart, edible fruit is commonly canned for use in pies, jellies, jams, and syrups. The berries are also a favorite of birds, bears, and other wildlife. The seeds can contain concentrations of hydrogen cyanide, a poison that gives almonds their characteristic flavor. This toxin is typically present in too small a quantity to do any harm – but best to avoid eating the seeds. *Prunus* from the Latin for "purple."

FIELD DESCRIPTION:

Deciduous shrub or small tree, 3-24′ tall. Leaves are alternate, oval, finely toothed, with 1-2 purplish-red glands near the blade base. Leaves usually abruptly pointed at tips. In flower, numerous whitish or cream-colored saucer-shaped, five-petaled flowers are arranged in terminal, congested, elongated clusters. Bark purplish-gray, with small, raised, horizontal pores. Dark-red-to-black cherries in hanging clusters appear in mid to late summer.

Flowering: May - June

Habitat: Grassland and open forest areas, often along water-courses, foothills and montane

Photos: Bozeman, MT, June & September (W. Tilt); Illustration: USDA-NRCS Plants Database

Purshia tridentata • Rosaceae (Rose Family)

BITTERBRUSH
(ANTELOPEBRUSH)

FIELD DESCRIPTION:

Spreading, deciduous, perennial shrub, 3-6′ tall, and equally wide, with grey or brown shredding bark and tightly branched stems covered with hairs. Leaves are alternate, wedge-shaped, deeply three-toothed, with margins that are usually rolled under. Semi-evergreen leaves are silvery-green and hairy on the upper surface and grey-hairy beneath. Flowers are creamy-yellow, five-petaled, saucer-shaped, and singly borne on short, leafy spurs. Fruits are short-hairy achenes.

MONTANE
FOOTHILLS

Flowering: April - June

Habitat: Dry grasslands and shrub-steppe, foothills to lower montane

Thumbnail photo & fruit: Elko Co., NV, June (Matt Lavin); Reference photo: Big Hole Range, ID, September (W. Tilt); Illustration: Karl Urban, Umatilla NF, OR

TIDBITS

Bitterbrush's trident-shaped leaves are somewhat similar to Big Sagebrush (*Artemisia tridentata*), but the leaves of Bitterbrush are not aromatic. As the common name Antelopebrush suggests, Bitterbrush provides browse for pronghorn and other wildlife, and is often critical winter browse for mule deer. The shrub has excellent drought tolerance and often has nitrogen-fixing root nodules. The species was first collected for science by Meriwether Lewis in July of 1806 near Lewis and Clark Pass, Montana.

WOOD'S ROSE
(WILD ROSE)

Rosa woodsii • Rosaceae (Rose Family)

FIELD DESCRIPTION:

Deciduous shrub, 2-7' tall, armed with prickles along stems and pairs of hooked spines at base of each leaf. Leaves ovate and pinnately divided into 5-9 toothed leaflets, alternate on stems. Large, pink-to-magenta flowers with 5 showy petals. Flowers give rise to round, red rose hips tipped with persistent sepals.

TIDBITS

The Wood's Rose is a bushy shrub with prickly stems and bright, fragrant, pink flowers with yellow centers. Flowers are replaced by dark red fruits (rose hips). The petals of Wood's Rose are edible, and the hips remain on the plant through winter, providing an important food source for variety of wildlife. Rose hips are high in vitamins, especially vitamin C, and are often used in teas to ward off colds. *Rosa* from the Latin for "red rose," and *woodsii* honors Joseph Woods, English architect, botanist, and rose scholar.

MONTANE
FOOTHILLS

Flowering: May - July

Habitat: Dry, sandy, gravelly soils, foothills to montane

Reference photo: Madison Range, MT, July (Rip McIntosh); Other photos: Gallatin Range, MT,July/September (W. Tilt)

Rubus idaeus • Rosaceae (Rose Family)

WILD RED RASPBERRY

FIELD DESCRIPTION:

Erect perennial shrub, 1-5′ tall, with bristles or slender straight prickles on stem. Leaves are alternate, pinnately compound, divided into 3-5 egg-shaped, pointed, double-saw-toothed leaflets; with pale undersides. Flowers greenish-to-white with 5 white petals and 5 glandular-hairy sepals that bend backward. Fruits develop into red woolly-hairy drupelets. Flowers and fruits in nodding clusters.

MONTANE
FOOTHILLS

Flowering: May - August

Habitat: Open to wooded areas, foothills to montane

TIDBITS

Raspberries are a favorite of humans and wildlife alike, eaten on the trail or taken home to be enjoyed as pie fillings and preserves. Stems can grow into long arching canes forming dense tangles. Leaves are rich in vitamin C, and their astringent qualities have a long history of medicinal uses. *Rubus* from the Latin for "red," and *idaeus* is a reference to Mount Ida, south of the ancient city of Troy. The plant was named by Linnaeus in 1753, and it has had numerous taxonomic names since.

Thumbnail & reference photo: Bozeman, MT, June (W. Tilt);
Fruit: Bozeman, MT, July (W. Tilt);
Illustration: USDA-NRCS Plants Database

THIMBLEBERRY

Rubus parviflorus • Rosaceae (Rose Family)

FIELD DESCRIPTION:

Deciduous shrub, 2-6′ tall, with no spines on stem. Alternate, large, maple-like leaves are palmately lobed and toothed, up to 10″ wide. Large, white, saucer-shaped flowers are up to 2″ wide, with 5 paper-like petals on long stem. Fruit resembles a dull-colored raspberry. Plants often form dense thickets.

TIDBITS

The showy, white flower, large undivided leaves, and thorn-less stems of Thimbleberry distinguish it from raspberry (*Rubus idaeus*) and various blackberries. The fruit may be eaten raw, cooked, or dried, and are enjoyed by range of animals including grizzly bears. At times the scientific names of plants do not make much sense. *Rubus* from the Latin for "red," and *parviflorus* for "small flowered" – a seemingly strange scientific name for the large conspicuous white flowers of Thimbleberry, but at least the fruits are red.

SUBALPINE
MONTANE

Flowering: May - July

Habitat: Open to wooded slopes, montane to subalpine

Thumbnail photo: Slough Creek, MT, June (Marianne Salas); Reference photo: Gallatin Range, MT, July (W. Tilt); Fruit: Gallatin Range, MT, September (W. Tilt); Illustration: USDA-NRCS Plants Database

Sorbus scopulina • Rosaceae (Rose Family)

MOUNTAIN ASH

FIELD DESCRIPTION:

Small deciduous tree, to 12′ tall. Leaves are large, alternate and pinnately divided into 11-17 elliptical, finely serrated leaflets. Small, cream-colored flowers with 5 broad petals are borne in terminal, flat-topped clusters. Flowers mature by late summer or early fall into a cluster of glossy, bright orange or scarlet pomes that typically persist into the winter.

MONTANE

Flowering: May - July

Habitat: Moist soils of canyons and mountain hillsides, montane

TIDBITS

Mountain Ash is widespread across western North America. In the fall, its yellow-orange-red foliage and orange-red berries add a splash of color to the surrounding forest. The fruits are eaten by many species of wildlife including Cedar Waxwings. The berries are edible raw, cooked, or dried; best harvested after numerous frosts remove the fruit's bitterness. The European Mountain Ash (*Sorpus aucuparia*) is commonly planted as an ornamental. *Sorbus* from the Latin name for the fruit, and *scopulina* for "of rocky places."

Thumbnail & reference photos: Bridger Range, MT, July (W. Tilt); Fruit: Grand Teton NP, September (W. Tilt); Illustration: USDA-NRCS Plants Database

WHITE SPIREA (BIRCHLEAF SPIREA)

Spiraea betulifolia • Rosaceae (Rose Family)

FIELD DESCRIPTION:

Small, erect, deciduous shrub, 10-24" tall. Leaves are alternate, egg-shaped, irregularly toothed in the upper margins (birch-leaf-like). White flowers are arranged on a fragrant, showy, flat-topped corymb atop stems. Individual flowers are small, with 5 sepals, and 5 petals, and numerous protruding stamens. Flowers give way to small pod-like fruits.

TIDBITS

White Spirea is a small shrub whose rhizomatous habit often forms large colonies. The shrub's relatively deep root system makes it tolerant of disturbance and drought. The shrub is commonly found in forest edges and clearings, where its white flowers brighten the forest floor. Spirea's attractive flowers and foliage make it a favorite for cultivation in gardens as well. Seed heads commonly persist through winter. *Betulifolia* from the Latin for "birch-leaved," an apt description of White Spirea's leaves.

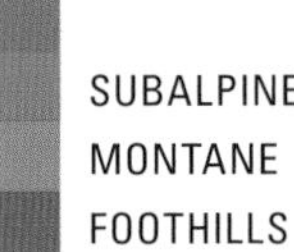

Flowering: June - August

Habitat: Moist to dry soils forest and forest edges, foothills to subalpine

Photos: Bridger Range, MT, August (W. Tilt); Illustration: USDA-NRCS Plants Database

Populus angustifolia • Salicaceae (Willow Family)

NARROWLEAF COTTONWOOD

FIELD DESCRIPTION:

Pyramidal deciduous tree, 20-65′ tall, with interlaced branches on young trees, ascending as tree matures. Bark smooth except near base where it is in furrows and ridges. Twigs glabrous, yellow-green or orange when young. Buds are 0.5″ long, slender, long-pointed, very resinous and somewhat aromatic. Leaves mostly narrowly lanceolate, acute, rounded at base, serrate with margins somewhat revolute, green above, paler green below, glabrous. Petioles short, less than one-third length of the blades. Catkins to 0.25″ long, densely flowered, glabrous. Capsules broadly ovoid.

Flowering: May - June

Habitat: Stream sides, wet areas, foothills to montane

TIDBITS

Narrowleaf Cottonwood forms extensive stands along streams where it commonly grows tightly packed, slender, and to 60′ tall. Green leaves cover most trees from top to bottom because the trunk supports a mass of interlaced branches, evident in winter. The lower bark of Narrowleaf Cottonwood is rough and gray, and leaves are long, narrow, and finely serrated. In contrast, the Plains Cottonwood (*Populus deltoides*) has a tall, branch-less trunk and crown of leaves. *Populus* from the Latin for "people," and *angustifolia* for "narrow leaf."

Thumbnail & inset photos: Jackson, WY, August (W. Tilt); Reference photo: Bozeman, MT, September (Matt Lavin); Illustration: USDA-NRCS Plants Database

BALSAM POPLAR
(BLACK COTTONWOOD)

Populus balsamifera • Salicaceae (Willow Family)

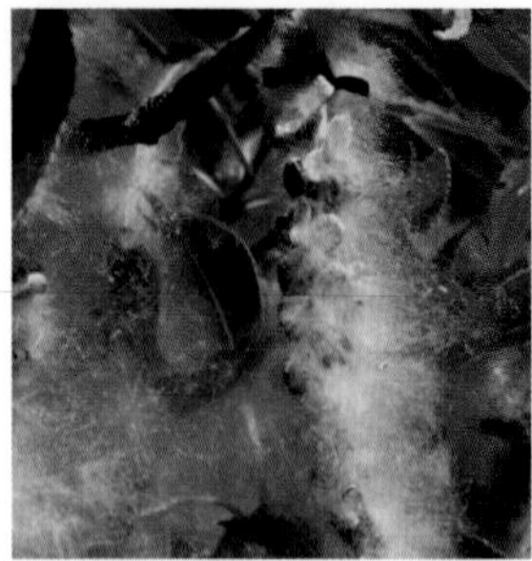

FIELD DESCRIPTION:

Deciduous tree, growing to 60′ tall with an oval-shaped crown and straight, branch-free trunk. Bark is smooth and greenish on young stems, becoming gray and furrowed with age. Leaves are alternate, simple, triangular to spear-shaped, 3-7″ long and 3-4″ wide, thick, leathery, rounded at the base, shiny green on top and whiter below. Terminal bud scales are sticky. Male and female flowers borne in catkins on same tree. Seeds bear enclosed in cotton-like hairs that promote wind and water dispersal.

SUBALPINE
MONTANE
FOOTHILLS

Flowering: June - August

Habitat: Moist to dry soils forest and forest edges, foothills to subalpine

TIDBITS

Cottonwoods get their common name from the cotton-like tufts of hairs that carry the tree's seeds, filling the air with white fluffy snow. Balsam Poplars flash silver when the wind stirs their leaves and leaf buds are coated with a sweet-smelling resin often called balsam. Balsam Poplar commonly hybridizes with other cottonwoods. The Plains Cottonwood (*Populus deltoides*), found at lower elevations, has large deltoid leaves. Narrowleaf Cottonwood (*Populus angustifolia*), has narrowly ovate leaves, and is also commonly found in the region.

Photos: Bozeman, MT, August (Matt Lavin); Illustration: USDA-NRCS Plants Database

PLAINS COTTONWOOD

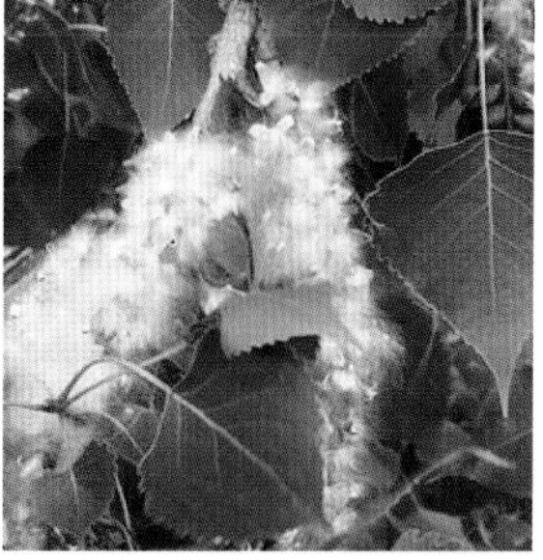

FIELD DESCRIPTION:

Deciduous tree, growing to 90′ tall, with thick, pale gray-brown bark, becoming deeply furrowed on old trunks. Twigs stout, yellow, or orange-brown, and glabrous. Buds hairy, resinous, not aromatic. Leaves broadly deltoid, apex abruptly pointed, base truncate or cordate, coarsely and irregularly serrate, yellow-green, lustrous, and glabrous. Petioles flattened laterally, glabrous. Dioecious; male and female catkins are pendulous, yellow, and appear before the leaves. Fruits are cottony seeds borne in elongated capsules.

MONTANE
PLAINS

Flowering: May - June

Habitat: Stream sides, wet areas, plains to lower montane

Thumbnail photo: Bozeman, MT, July (W. Tilt); Reference photo: Bozeman, MT, August (Matt Lavin); Illustration: USDA-NRCS Plants Database

TIDBITS

When it "snows" in the summer, it's often the result of nearby cottonwoods living up to their name. The Plains Cottonwood is a variant (var. *occidentalis*) of the widely distributed Eastern Cottonwood. It grows primarily on moist alluvial soils found in floodplains and bottomlands. Throughout the West, cottonwoods are the principal overstory tree found along water courses. The Plains Cottonwood is one of the fastest growing native trees in North America. Its wood is coarse, light, and brittle, and is used primarily for pallets, crating, rough construction lumber, and wood pulp.

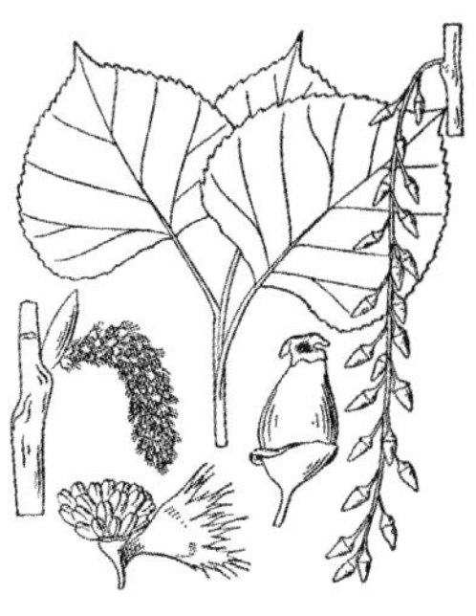

QUAKING ASPEN (TREMBLING ASPEN)

Populus tremuloides • Salicaceae (Willow Family)

FIELD DESCRIPTION:

Distinctive deciduous tree, 20-80′ tall, with smooth white-to-gray-green bark, which becomes gray-black and roughened on older trunks. Leaves are alternate on slender, sideways-flattened leaf stalk. Leaf blades are cordate with sharp-pointed tips. Male and female catkins on separate trees. Primarily spreads through root sprouts that can form extensive clonal colonies.

TIDBITS

The shimmering leaves and white bark of aspen are iconic of the Rocky Mountains. The flat, narrow leaf stalk allows leaves to tremble or quake in the slightest breeze. Leaves turn a vibrant yellow in fall. It is typically a successional species in the West, dependent upon disturbance (primarily fire) for regeneration, yet aspen can form climax communities in some locations. Generally a stand of aspen are all part of the same organism. While individual "ramets" (trunks sprouted vegetatively) are relatively short-lived, the stand may be incredibly long-lived.

Flowering: April - June

Habitat: Moist soils in open forests, hillsides and along watercourses, foothills to montane

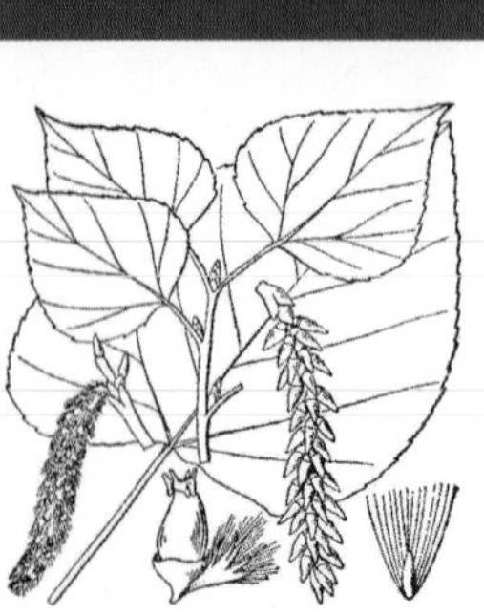

Thumbnail photo: (female catkin) Pine Creek, MT, May (W. Tilt); Reference photo & leaf detail: Gallatin Range, MT, June (W. Tilt); Illustration: USDA-NRCS Plants Database

Salix bebbiana • Salicaceae (Willow Family)

BEBB'S WILLOW
(BEAKED WILLOW)

FIELD DESCRIPTION:

Large, deciduous shrub or small tree, to 20′ tall, with spreading branches. Leaves are alternate, simple, elliptical, sparsely hairy, green on top, and characteristically whitish and reticulate-veined beneath. Twigs purple-brown-hairy and grey-hairy when mature. Male and female catkins appear on separate plants at the same time leaves appear.

SUBALPINE
MONTANE
FOOTHILLS

Flowering: May - June

Habitat: Streams, gravel bars, side channels, and other moist soil areas, foothills to subalpine

Photos: Bozeman, MT, August (Matt Lavin);
Illustration: USDA-NRCS Plants Database

TIDBITS

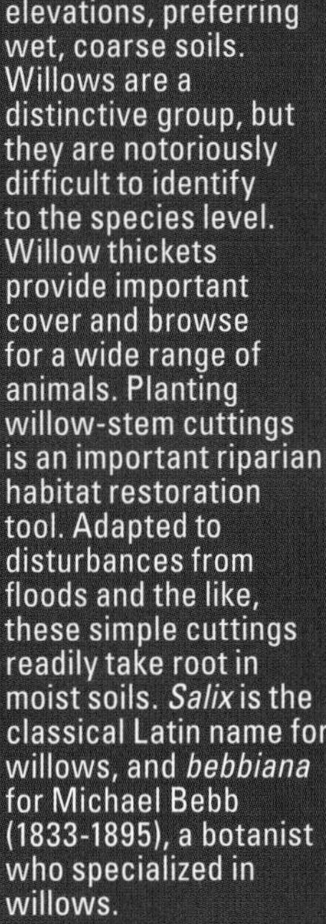

Bebb's Willow is common at mid-elevations, preferring wet, coarse soils. Willows are a distinctive group, but they are notoriously difficult to identify to the species level. Willow thickets provide important cover and browse for a wide range of animals. Planting willow-stem cuttings is an important riparian habitat restoration tool. Adapted to disturbances from floods and the like, these simple cuttings readily take root in moist soils. *Salix* is the classical Latin name for willows, and *bebbiana* for Michael Bebb (1833-1895), a botanist who specialized in willows.

SANDBAR WILLOW (COYOTE WILLOW)

Salix exigua • Salicaceae (Willow Family)

FIELD DESCRIPTION:

Deciduous shrub, to 15′ tall, that grows in thickets on various moist soils. Leaves are alternate, long, and linear with fine grayish hair on upper and lower surfaces. Twigs, brown, sparsely hairy to glabrous. At lower elevations, leaves are shiny green on top and slightly lighter beneath. At higher elevations, leaves are often gray-green with fine, grayish hairs on both surfaces. Female catkins with yellow scales, hairy, emerging with leaves. Generally, male and female catkins are on different plants.

MONTANE
FOOTHILLS

Flowering: April - June

Habitat: Moist or wet soils, foothills to montane

TIDBITS

Sandbar Willow is a common narrow-leaved willow often forming dense, single-species stands along watercourses. Like many willows, it is a pioneer species, establishing itself on newly exposed gravel bars. Exact species identification for most willows is challenging, requiring details for numerous floristic characteristics (timing of flower and leaf development, size and shape of catkin, the size and shape of mature leaves and mature capsules, etc.). Sandbar Willow is, however, one of the easier species to identify. *Exigua* from the Latin for "very little, poor."

Photos: SW Colorado, July (Al Schneider); Illustration: USDA-NRCS Plants Database

CRACK WILLOW
(GOLDEN WILLOW)

FIELD DESCRIPTION:

Medium-sized deciduous tree, 35-60', fast-growing, often multi-trunked, with an irregular crown. Leaves lanceolate, bright green, with tapering bases and finely serrated margins. Stipules small or absent. Leaf undersurfaces distinctly whitish (glaucous) in contrast to glossy green upper leaf surfaces. Twigs very brittle, snapping off cleanly. Dioecious with male and female catkins on separate trees. Bark is dark grey-brown, coarsely fissured in older trees. Fruit are capsules releasing numerous cotton-tufted seeds.

VALLEYS-FOOTHILLS

Flowering: April - June

Habitat: Riparian habitats along rivers and streams, disturbed wet soils, valleys and foothills

Thumbnail photo: Fort Benton, MT, March (Matt Lavin); Reference photo: Madison Co., MT, March (Matt Lavin); Illustration: USDA-NRCS Plants Database

TIDBITS

A native to Eurasia, the tree's profuse golden-yellow stems are very conspicuous during fall, winter, and early spring, when the tree is not in leaf. The common name, Crack Willow, describes how branches easily snap, with an audible crack. The tree's branches are highly susceptible to wind, snow, and ice damage (hence the species name, *fragilis*). This trait, however, is an effective device for propagation since the broken twigs and branches take root readily. Branches falling into waterways are carried downstream to colonize new areas.

GREASEWOOD

Sarcobatus vermiculatus • Sarcobataceae (Greasewood Family)

FIELD DESCRIPTION:

Rigid, thorny, deciduous shrub, 3-7' tall, with gray-white bark. Leaves are alternate, round, linear, and fleshy, generally less than 1" long, and stalkless. Flowers inconspicuous, monoecious with male and female flowers on same plants. Flowers borne in dense spikes arising from leaf axils. Fruits are winged achenes.

TIDBITS

Adapted to harsh, salty habitats, Greasewood is often the dominant species on saline-alkaline flats and clay soils in sagebrush and saltbush steppes. Its green leaves often stand in sharp contrast to the grey-green color of the surrounding shrubs. The leaves contain oxalates of sodium and potassium which can be toxic to livestock if consumed in sufficient quantities. The plant has a number of traditional uses, including use of its crushed leaves to treat insect bites. Formerly classified in the Chenopodiaceae (Goosefoot Family), but recently reclassified as the sole genus in the family Sarcobataceae.

PLAINS-FOOTHILLS

Flowering: May - July

Habitat: Dry, alkaline salt flats, and, less commonly, sagebrush steppe, plains to foothills

Photos: Phillips Co., MT, June (Matt Lavin); Illustration: USDA-NRCS Plants Database

Pteridium aquilinum • Dennstaedtiaceae (Bracken Fern)

WESTERN BRACKEN FERN

FIELD DESCRIPTION:

Large, coarse, deciduous fern, up to 4-6′ tall, with solitary, stiff stems and rhizomes. Fronds are large, dark green, leathery, and triangular in outline, held almost parallel to ground. Fronds pinnately divided 2-3 times into round-toothed pinnae. Pinnae commonly opposite, but may be nearly opposite (almost alternate). Fronds hairy beneath and edges rolled under. Spore clusters present along leaf edges. Stipe smooth, rigid, and grooved on 1 side. The very hairy, tripartite fiddle-heads emerge in early spring. The roots reach deep for moisture, and colonize aggressively.

SUBALPINE
MONTANE

Habitat: Moist to wet meadows, woodlands and forests, montane to subalpine

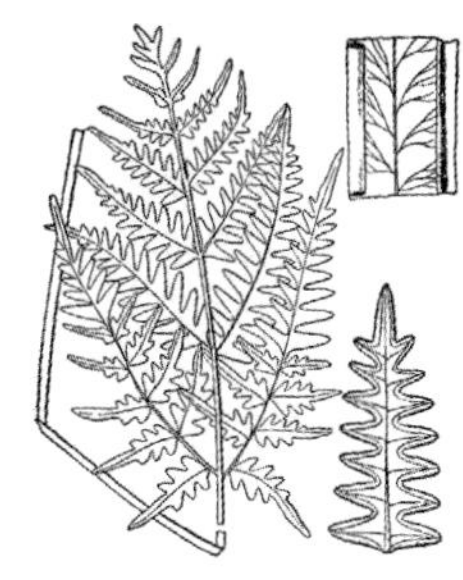

Photo: Yellowstone NP (Bryan Harry); Illustration: USDA-NRCS Plants Database

Cystopteris fragilis • Dryopteridaceae (Wood Fern)

BRITTLEFERN (FRAGILE FERN)

FIELD DESCRIPTION:

Delicate, bright green, hairless fern from short, creeping rhizomes. Stipe erect to arching, lacking scales or hairs. Fronds clustered, varied in overall shape, glabrous, from 10-15" long (including petiole which is about as long as the leaf blade), broadly lanceolate, 2-3 times pinnate. Petioles brown below, yellow above, smooth. Pinnae are ovate to oblong. Sori roundish, sporangia on backs of pinnae.

ALPINE
SUBALPINE
MONTANE
FOOTHILLS

Habitat: Dry to intermittently moist rocky areas, often shady; foothills to alpine

Photo: Pend Oreille Co., WA, July (Ben Legler); Illustration: USDA-NRCS Plants Database

MALEFERN

Dryopteris filix-mas • Dryopteridaceae (Wood Fern)

FIELD DESCRIPTION:

Large clumped fern in a round tuft. Fronds (leaves) clustered on short rhizome, glabrous. Rootstocks stout, erect or declining. Stipe and rachis coarse, distinctly shorter than the blade, densely scaly, conspicuously covered with papery scales. Blade 8-40" long and half as wide at widest point. Twice pinnate leaves; pinnae long, narrow and unlobed. Sori roundish, sporangia on backs of pinnae.

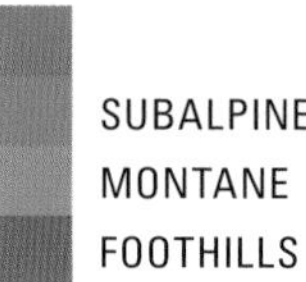

Habitat: Rocky damp woods, rock crevices; foothills to subalpine

Photo: Grant Co., WA, April) (Robert L. Carr); Illustration: USDA-NRCS Plants Database

OREGON CLIFF FERN (OREGON WOODSIA)

Woodsia oregana • Dryopteridaceae (Wood Fern)

FIELD DESCRIPTION:

Fern with leaves to 10" long (including petioles), in tufts, smooth to glandular. Petioles dark red-brown near base, lighter above. Frond (leaf blade) without scales or hairs, glandular, pinnatifid, 2-6" long; pinnae egg-shaped or triangular. Individual segments often lobed or cleft near the base and margins slightly curved. Spori round on the veins on back of pinnea (leaflets).

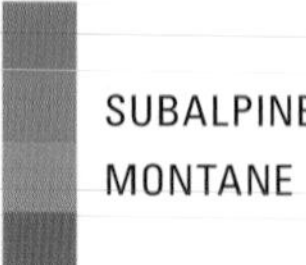

Habitat: Moist cliffs, dry shaded places, talus; montane to subalpine

Photo: Pend Oreille Co. WA, April (Ben Legler); Illustration: USDA-NRCS Plants Database

Woodsia scopulina • Dryopteridaceae (Wood Fern)

ROCKY MOUNTAIN CLIFF FERN

FIELD DESCRIPTION:

Small, delicate, compact fern with basal leaves, to 12" long. Blades 2-3 times pinnate, moderately glandular. Pinnae lanceolate to ovate, longer than wide, and tapering abruptly to rounded or broadly acute tip. Pinnules (secondary leaflets) toothed and often shallowly lobed. Fronds and petioles white hairy with stalked glands. Stems compact, often with persistent petiole bases of unequal lengths. Scales along stem brownish with dark central stripe. Spores in small round groups (sori) on undersides of leaves.

SUBALPINE
MONTANE

Habitat: Rocky ledges and crevices, talus slopes, montane to subalpine

Photo: Grant Co., WA, April (Ben Legler); Illustration: USDA-NRCS Plants Database

Cryptogramma acrostichoides • Pteridaceae (Maidenhair Fern)

ROCKBRAKE (MOUNTAIN PARSLEY-FERN)

FIELD DESCRIPTION:

Hairless, evergreen fern. Rootstocks short and scaly. Fronds egg-shaped with long stalks, numerous, of 2 types on same plant: fertile and infertile. Fertile ones are 2-12" long, surpassing the sterile fronds in size; stipes straw-colored, sterile blades ovate 1-5" long, 2-3 times pinnate, glabrous. Fertile blades simpler with fewer segments, linear, 0.25-0.5" long, margins revolute covering sori. Spores borne on lower side of fertile fronds.

ALPINE
SUBALPINE
MONTANE

Habitat: Amongst rocks, especially scree slopes, montane to alpine

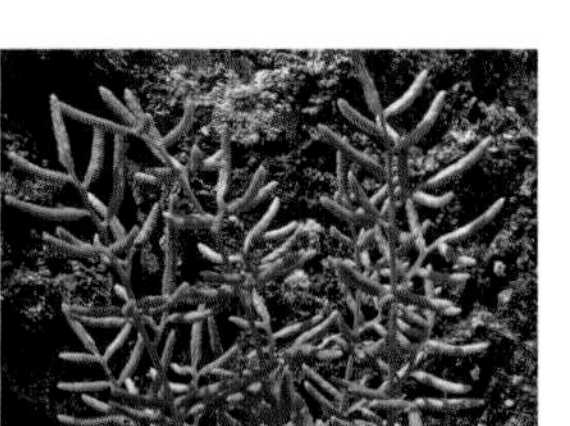

Photo: SW Colorado, September (Al Schneider); Illustration: USDA-NRCS Plants Database

DOUGLAS' SEDGE

Carex douglasii • Cyperaceae (Sedge Family)

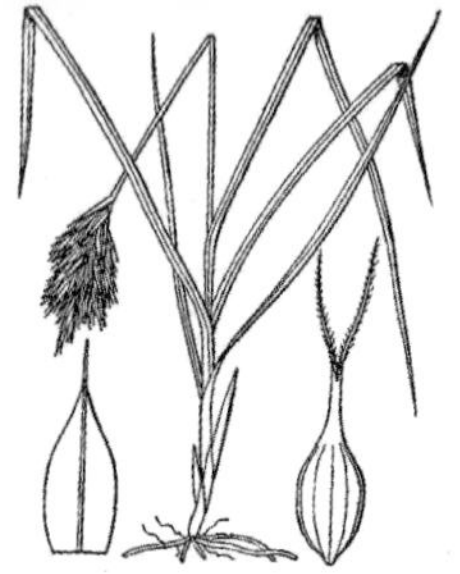

Photo: Pershing, NV, May (Matt Lavin); Illustration: USDA-NRCS Plants Database

FIELD DESCRIPTION:

Native rhizomatous perennial with three-angled stems, generally 6-16" (15-40 cm) tall. Leaves relatively few and basal, hairless; ligules 0-2.8 mm; blades mostly 1-3 mm wide. Inflorescences of dense headlike spikes mostly 1.5-3.5 cm long, typically light brown. Perigynia brown, without evident veins, 3-4 mm long, with a beak 1-2 mm long. Often forming short-statured dense stands along sides of gravel roads or in the middle of 2-track roads on well drained (e.g., sandy or rocky) soils. The seed heads are often thick (e.g., similar in diameter to an average index finger). The three-angled stem is particularly evident just below the seed head.

MONTANE
PLAINS

Habitat: Sandy to clayey soils in open grassland, sagebrush, roadsides and other disturbed sites, plains to montane

NEEDLELEAF SEDGE

Carex eleocharis • Cyperaceae (Sedge Family)
(Synonym: *Carex duriuscula*)

Photo: Butte ID, June (Matt Lavin); Illustration: USDA-NRCS Plants Database

FIELD DESCRIPTION:

Native rhizomatous perennials with three-angled stems generally 6-16" (15-40 cm) tall. Leaves few and basal, the sheaths shredding into fibers; ligules 0-0.8 mm; blades 1-2 mm wide. Inflorescences of small narrow headlike spikes mostly 1-2 cm long, typically dark brown to black. Perigynia dark brown, without evident veins, 2.5-4 mm long, with a beak 0.5-1 mm long. The three-angled stem is particularly evident just below the seed head.

MONTANE
PLAINS

Flowering: May - July

Habitat: Sandy to clayey soils in open grassland and sagebrush, plains to montane

THREADLEAF SEDGE

Carex filifolia • Cyperaceae (Sedge Family)

FIELD DESCRIPTION:

Native bunched or matted perennials with stems generally 3-10" (7-25 cm) tall and sometimes three-angled especially below the seed head. Leaves mostly basal, yellow-green or bright green, very narrow and less than 1 mm wide. Inflorescences of narrow cylindrical spikes 7–30 mm long, usually pale brown. Perigynia pale brown, 2-4.5 mm long, hairy at least towards the tip, with a beak 0–0.8 mm long. The dense bunches or mats of very narrow leaves is distinctive to this sedge that often inhabits open, arid, and disturbed settings such as along 2-track roads and in heavily grazed rangeland.

PLAINS-FOOTHILLS

Flowering: May-July

Habitat: Sandy to clayey soils in open grassland, sagebrush, roadsides and other disturbed sites, plains to foothills

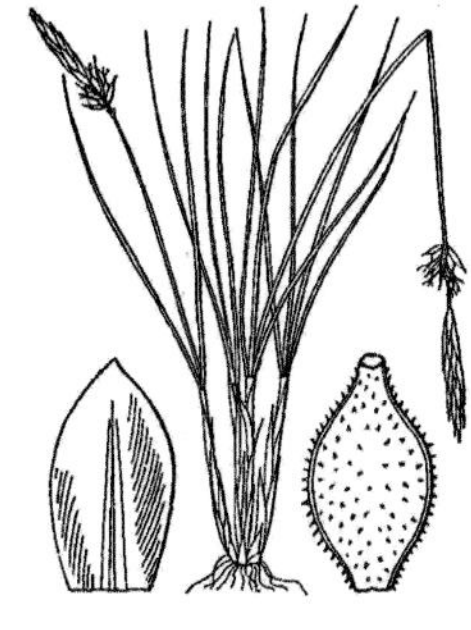

Photo: Golden Valley, MT, July (Matt Lavin); Illustration: USDA-NRCS Plants Database

BEAKED SEDGE

Carex utriculata • Cyperaceae (Sedge Family)

FIELD DESCRIPTION:

Native rhizomatous perennials with stems generally 1-3' (3-10 dm) tall and distinctly three-angled. Leaf blades usually flat or folded along the midrib, yellowish green, and 4-10 mm wide. Inflorescences with cylindrical seed-bearing spikes 3-5 cm long. Florets often straw colored, 5-8 mm long, with an distinct narrowed tip 1-3 mm long. Seeds three-angled (trigonous).

SUBALPINE
MONTANE
PLAINS

Flowering: June - August

Habitat: Wetlands and riparian corridors, including roadside and irrigation ditches, plains to subalpine

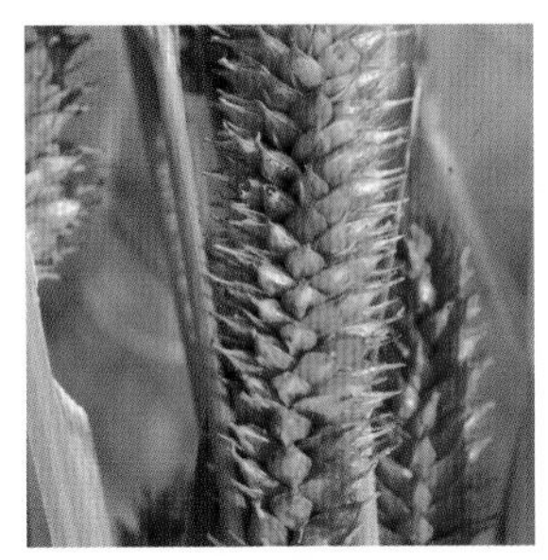

Photos: Bozeman, MT, September (Matt Lavin)

SOFTSTEM BULRUSH

Schoenoplectus tabernaemontani • Cyperaceae (Sedge Family)

FIELD DESCRIPTION:

Slender aquatic perennial, 3-6' (9-18 dm) tall, with stout cylindrical stems. Stems light-to-dark-green, smooth, spongy, up to 1" wide at base and tapering upward. Leaves mostly reduced to sheaths near base. Inflorescence at top of stems in hanging umbels, comprising reddish-brown clusters of branched spikelets arising from base of an erect green bract. Fruits are brown achenes, about as broad as long. As its common name suggests, the stems are easily crushed between one's fingers, as compared with Hardstem Bulrush (*Schoenoplectus acutus*).

MONTANE
VALLEYS

Flowering: June - August

Habitat: Wet soils, in wetlands and along waterways, alkali flats, valleys to montane

Photo: Evergreen MT, August (Matt Lavin); Illustration: USDA-NRCS Plants Database

PANICLED BULRUSH

Scirpus microcarpus • Cyperaceae (Sedge Family)

FIELD DESCRIPTION:

Slender aquatic perennial, 2-4' (6-12 dm) tall, with three-angled stems with distinct edges and concave sides. Stems single or several , growing from stout, well-developed rhizomes. Leaf blades flat, grass-like, and smooth, 10-24" long and 5-15 mm wide. Stem bases and rhizomes have a characteristic rusty or reddish coloration. Inflorescence in terminal umbels comprising clusters of spikelets and conspicuous leaf-like bracts on long, thin branches. Fruits are pale, smooth achenes.

MONTANE
VALLEYS

Flowering: June - August

Habitat: Wet soils, in wetlands and along waterways, valleys to montane

Photo: Gallatin River, MT, July (W. Tilt); Illustration: USDA-NRCS Plants Database

Equisetum arvense • Equisetaceae (Horsetail Family)

HORSETAIL

FIELD DESCRIPTION:

Perennial herb in 2 growth forms: sterile and fertile. The sterile stems to 24" (6 dm) tall are jointed, hollow and erect, supporting numerous whorls of slender branches. Leaves are scale-like and fused into sheaths. The spore clusters (fertile stems) are whitish-brownish (no chlorophyll), 2-12" tall, appearing before sterile form and then withering. Rhizomes are branched and creeping similar to sterile stems but not hollow.

MONTANE
VALLEYS

Habitat: Moist, low-lying areas along streams and creeks, as well as drier and more barren sites, valleys to montane

Photos: Bozeman, MT, June (W. Tilt);
Illustration: USDA-NRCS Plants Database

Equisetum hyemale • Equisetaceae (Horsetail Family)

SCOURING RUSH (ROUGH HORSETAIL)

FIELD DESCRIPTION:

Stiff evergreen perennial herb, 6-36" (2-9 dm) tall, with unbranched stems. Stems are hollow, jointed, ribbed, and rough to the touch. Leaves are reduced to small scales fused into sheaths. Two rows of tubercles on sheaths form black bands up the green stem. Spores produced on short-stalked pointed cones that are persistent.

MONTANE
VALLEYS

Habitat: Moist, low-lying areas along streams and creeks, valleys to montane

Photo: Smith River, MT, July (W. Tilt);
Illustration: USDA-NRCS Plants Database

MOUNTAIN RUSH

Juncus balticus • Juncaceae (Rush Family)

Photos: Bozeman, MT, August - September (Matt Lavin)

FIELD DESCRIPTION:

Native rhizomatous perennials with stems generally 1-3' (3-10 dm) tall. Leaves with no blades, sheaths only. Inflorescences 6 to many flowered, loose to congested, appearing as if arranged on the side of the stem just down from the stem tip. Flowers with usually dark brown to black tepals that are mostly 3.5-5.5 mm long. Anthers are usually 1-2 mm long. The inflorescence is placed at the stem terminus but the subtending green bract of the inflorescence is imperceptible from the stem and thus appears as if arranged along the side of the stem near the tip.

VALLEYS-FOOTHILLS

Flowering: June - August

Habitat: Wet to seasonally dry meadows, sometimes roadsides, valleys to foothills

CRESTED WHEATGRASS

Agropyron cristatum • Poaceae (Grass Family)

Photos: Burke Park, MT, July (Matt Lavin)

FIELD DESCRIPTION:

Introduced perennial bunchgrass, 1-3' (3-9 dm) tall, mostly hairless with erect, leafy stems forming a dense tuft. Leaf blades flat, usually glabrous, 2-9 mm wide, often open and lax. Leaf sheaths are open and collar hairless, ligules are short and auricles pointed and clasping. Inflorescence has a short-broad shape, 4-7 cm long, tapering toward the tip. Spikelets are flattened, 10-29 mm long, and closely overlapping, strongly divergent from the main rachis (40-80 degrees), with 2-8 fertile florets. Glumes approximately half the length of spikelet. Both glumes and lemmas typically taper to a point or to a short awn.

VALLEYS-FOOTHILLS

Flowering: June - August

Habitat: Fields, roadsides and other disturbed sites, valleys to foothills

THICKSPIKE WHEATGRASS

Agropyron dasystachyum • Poaceae (Grass Family)
(Synonym: Elymus lanceolatus)

FIELD DESCRIPTION:

Native rhizomatous perennial, 1-3′ (3-9 dm) tall, with erect stems. Stems mostly hairless and usually smooth with a white bloom. Leaf blades are 2.5-25 cm long, 2-5 mm wide, often stiff and hairless. Leaf sheaths and collar rarely hairy. Inflorescence is slender, compact spike, 2.5-23 cm long, continuous along axis. Spikelets are solitary or occasionally paired, usually greatly overlapping the internodes and flat to the main rachis. Commonly 4-9 fertile florets per spikelet. Glumes are shorter than spikelet, rigid and tapering to a point. Lemmas are lightly to densely hairy and awn-tipped. Thickspike Wheatgrass is an abundant prairie-type grass with a scattered distribution and nondescript appearance.

MONTANE
FOOTHILLS

Flowering: June - August

Habitat: Dry, deep soils, foothills to montane

Photo: Bozeman, MT, June (Matt Lavin); Illustration: USDA-NRCS Plants Database

INTERMEDIATE WHEATGRASS

Agropyron intermedium • Poaceae (Grass Family)
(Synonyms: Thinopyrum intermedium, Elymus hispidus)

FIELD DESCRIPTION:

Introduced rhizomatous to bunched perennial, up to 3-4′ (9-12 dm) tall, with scattered or bunched stems, abundant rhizomes and slender flower spikes. Leaf blades are green to blue-green, firm, flat, 4-12 mm wide, 5-15 cm long, and glabrous or somewhat pubescent. Leaf sheaths often with ciliate margins. Ligule is short and auricles clasping. Inflorescence spike is 10-20 cm long, thick and continuous along axis. Spikelets tight to axis, slightly overlapping, containing 6-12 fertile florets. Glumes shorter than spikelet, thick and bluntly pointed (appear blunt-tipped/cut off). Lemmas blunt to pointed, awnless or sometimes with a very small awn.

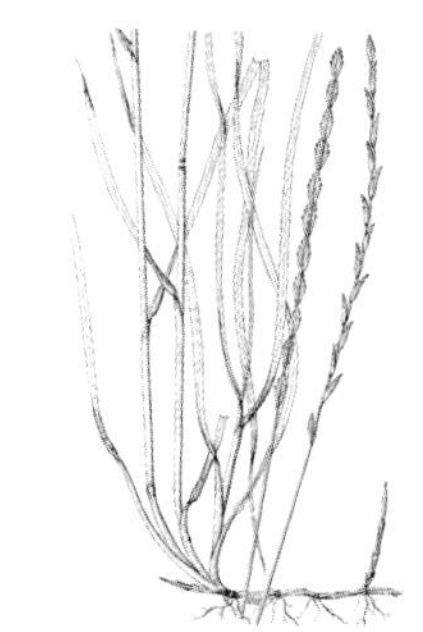

Flowering: June - August

Habitat: Well-drained pastures and fields, valleys to montane

Photo: Bozeman, MT, July (Matt Lavin); Illustration: Texas A&M University Grass Images

QUACKGRASS

Agropyron repens • Poaceae (Grass Family)
(Synonyms: *Elymus repens, Elytrigia repens*)

FIELD DESCRIPTION:

Introduced rhizomatous perennial with slender stems, 25-42" (7-11 dm) tall. Leaf blades are typically broad, 5-10 mm wide, flat and often lax. Sheaths often with down-pointing (retrorse) soft hairs. Inflorescence 5-13 cm long, rachis continuous, slender, the internodes less than 10 mm long. Terminal spikes typically comprise very green spikelets that in turn include mostly short-awned lemmas. Spikelets 9-16 mm long, appressed to the rachis, florets 3-7 per spikelet, glumes shorter than florets, tapering to an awn tip. Lemmas tapering to an awn-tip (rarely unawned) or with an awn usually less than 5 mm long. Ligules short, membranous.

MONTANE
VALLEYS

Flowering: June - August

Habitat: Moist disturbed settings especially around lawns, in gardens, along roadsides, and riparian areas, valleys to lower montane

Photo: Bozeman, MT, September (Matt Lavin); Illustration: USDA-NRCS Plants Database

WESTERN WHEATGRASS

Agropyron smithii • Poaceae (Grass Family)
(Synonym: *Pascopyrum smithii*)

FIELD DESCRIPTION:

Native rhizomatous perennial with mostly hairless and usually glaucous stems, 14-32" (3.5-8 dm) tall. Blades 2-5 mm wide, often stiff and inrolled, sheaths and collar rarely hairy. Inflorescence 3-15 cm long, rachis continuous, the internodes generally less than 10 mm long. Spikelets (sometimes 2 per node) 10-29 mm long, appressed to the main rachis, florets mostly 4-9 per spikelet, glumes shorter than to as long as florets, rigid and gradually long-tapering from the base to a narrow sharp tip (the acuminate tip is often slightly curved). Lemmas awn-tipped or with an awn up to 5 mm.

MONTANE
PLAINS

Flowering: June - August

Habitat: Open dry settings, often where historically disturbed, plains to montane

Photo: Butte Co., ID, August (Matt Lavin); Illustration: USDA-NRCS Plants Database

BLUEBUNCH WHEATGRASS

Agropyron spicatum • Poaceae (Grass Family)
(Synonyms: *Pseudoroegneria spicata, Elymus spicatum*)

FIELD DESCRIPTION:

Top: Buckingham, MT, July (Matt Lavin); Bottom: Bozeman, MT, July (Matt Lavin)

Native perennial bunchgrass, 1-3' (3-9 dm) tall, with erect stems. Leaf blades are flat to rolled, 1-3 mm wide, hairless to slightly hairy, tapering to the tip. The leaf sheath and collar rarely hairy. Inflorescence 4-20 cm long, rachis continuous, internodes generally greater than 10 mm long. Spikelets 10-15 mm long, appressed to the main rachis, florets mostly 3-7 per spikelet, glumes shorter than florets, awnless or short-awned. Lemmas hairless to inconspicuously hairy, with a divergent awn up to 2 cm long, rarely awnless. Historically a dominant grass of the region's grasslands, its abundance has diminished due to competition from introduced grass species and changes in range conditions. Bluebunch Wheatgrass is the state grass of Montana.

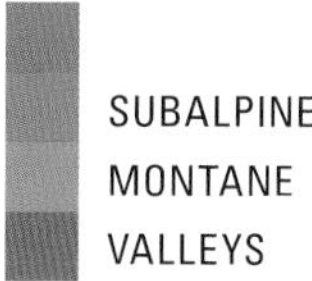

SUBALPINE
MONTANE
VALLEYS

Flowering: June- August

Habitat: Open grasslands and forests on well-drained, dry soils, valleys to subalpine

SLENDER WHEATGRASS

Agropyron trachycaulum • Poaceae (Grass Family)
(Synonym: *Elymus trachycaulus*)

FIELD DESCRIPTION:

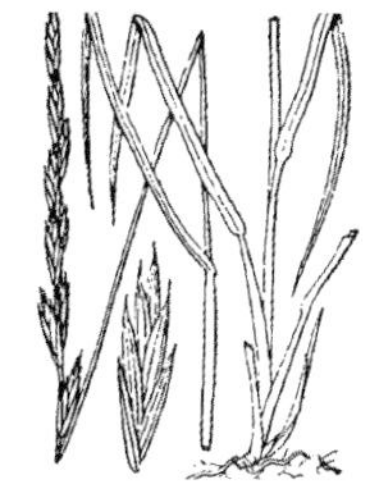

Photo: Butte Co., ID, June (Matt Lavin); Illustration: USDA-NRCS Plants Database

Native perennial bunchgrass, 12-30" (3-10 dm) tall, with erect to decumbent stems. Blades flat or somewhat rolled, 3-8 mm wide, mostly hairless (sometimes hairy), gradually tapering to tip. Sheath hairless or with inconspicuous hairs; ligules short and collar-shaped; auricles small or absent. Inflorescence 5-20 cm long, rachis continuous, the internodes generally less than 10 mm long. Spikelets 12-18 mm long, appressed to the main rachis, florets mostly 3-7 per spikelet, glumes often nearly as long or longer than florets, glumes awn-tipped to long awned. Lemmas awn-tipped or sometimes with a straight awn up to 20 mm long. Slender Wheatgrass is native bunchgrass, widely used for revegetating disturbed rangelands and watersheds.

SUBALPINE
MONTANE
PLAINS

Flowering: June- August

Habitat: Dry to moist sites in wide range of habitats, plains to subalpine

REDTOP BENTGRASS (CREEPING BENTGRASS)

Agrostis stolonifera • Poaceae (Grass Family)
(Synonyms: *Agrostis alba, Agrostis gigantea, Agrostis palustris*)

FIELD DESCRIPTION:

Introduced perennial stoloniferous sodgrass, 8-48" (2-12 dm) tall, often forming dense mats or patches. Stems decumbent at base. Sheath open; auricles absent; and ligule is a well-developed membrane, 2-7 mm long. Leaf blades 2-6 mm wide. Inflorescence is an open panicle at anthesis where the branches have a distinctively whorled arrangement at each node, sometimes contracting after anthesis. Spikelets 2.0-2.5 mm long. Lemmas 2.0-2.2 mm long, awnless or rarely minutely awned from the back; palea up to two-thirds as long as lemma. Redtop Bentgrass, as its name suggests, has a distinctly reddish seed head.

MONTANE
VALLEYS

Flowering: June - September

Habitat: Wet meadows, stream sides, roadsides, pastures and lawns, valleys to lower montane

Photo: Chestnut, MT, August (Matt Lavin); Illustration: USDA-NRCS Plants Database

SWEETGRASS (VANILLA GRASS)

Anthoxanthum hirtum • Poaceae (Grass Family)
(Synonym: *Hierochloe odorata*)

FIELD DESCRIPTION:

Native perennial bunchgrass, 12-40" (3-10 dm) tall, with creeping rhizomes and 1 to few bunched stems. Leaf blades 2-6 mm wide. Sheaths open; ligules membranous, 3-5 mm long; and auricles absent. Inflorescence a pyramidal panicle 4-12 cm long. Spikelets 3-6 mm long. Lemmas the first 2 larger and more hairy that the glabrous uppermost floret (which is concealed by the lower 2), unawned or with an awn up to 0.5 mm long. A sweet-scented grass with purple bases and rhizomes.

SUBALPINE
MONTANE
PLAINS

Flowering: May - July

Habitat: Wet meadows, plains to subalpine

Photo: Manger, MT, September (Matt Lavin); Illustration: USDA-NRCS Plants Database

PURPLE THREEAWN

Aristida purpurea • Poaceae (Grass Family)
(Synonyms: *Aristida fendleriana, Aristida longiseta*)

FIELD DESCRIPTION:

Native perennial bunchgrass, 6-16" (1.5-4 dm) tall. Leaf blades curly to straight, 1-2 mm wide. Sheaths open; auricles absent; and ligules hairy, 0.3-0.5 mm long. Inflorescence a contracted panicle 6-25 mm long. Spikelets 10-18 mm long excluding awns; first glume one-half the length of the second. Lemma 9-15 mm long (including awn column), gradually tapering into a 3-part (tripartite) awn, awn segments 2-5 cm long. Threeawn is a warm-season native perennial that greens up after many other species have started to senesce. The 3-part awn arising from the tip of the lemma is unique to the genus *Aristida*, and tend to irritate the mouths and nostrils of grazing animals.

VALLEYS - FOOTHILLS

Flowering: June- September

Habitat: Open dry areas, often shrub-steppe, on various soils, valleys to foothills

Top: Lavina, MT, July (Matt Lavin); Bottom: Boise, ID, June (Matt Lavin)

WILD OATS
(WEEDY OATS)

Avena fatua • Poaceae (Grass Family)

FIELD DESCRIPTION:

Introduced annual bunchgrass, 20-40" (5-10 dm) tall. Leaf blades 5-10 mm wide. Sheaths of basal leaves often hairy; auricles absent; and ligules 4-6 mm. Ligule is well developed membrane conspicuous from front and side view. Inflorescence an open panicle. Spikelets 20-25 mm long, usually with at least 3 florets. Lemmas hairless to most often long hairy, with a twisted bent blackish awn 3-4 cm long and a conspicuously hairy callus (the sharp base of the floret). Wild Oats thrive along edges of agricultural fields and other frequently disturbed settings.

VALLEYS-FOOTHILLS

Flowering: June- August

Habitat: In and around cultivated fields, roadsides, and pastures, valleys to foothills

Photo: Bozeman, MT, September (Matt Lavin); Illustration: USDA-NRCS Plants Database

SLOUGHGRASS

Beckmannia syzigachne • Poaceae (Grass Family)

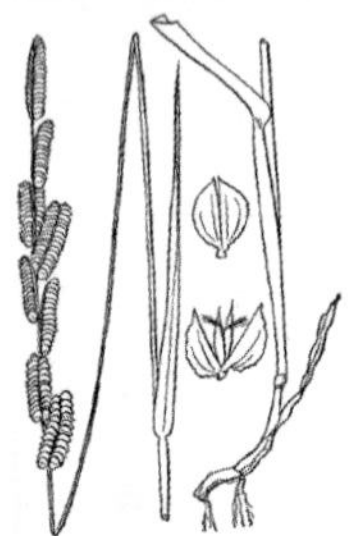

Photo: Bozeman, MT, October (Matt Lavin); Illustration: USDA-NRCS Plants Database

FIELD DESCRIPTION:

Native annual bunchgrass, 4-32" (1-8 dm) tall, with few to many-bunched stems. Leaves mainly along stem, blades scabrous 4-10 mm wide. Sheaths open and ribbed; ligules membranous, 5-11 mm, often folded back; and auricles absent. Inflorescences a contracted secund panicle 5-30 cm long. Spikelets circular, strongly laterally flattened, 2.5-3.0 mm long. Lemmas with an apiculate tip (approaching a very short awn in some spikelets). As its common name suggests, Sloughgrass is found in wet, soggy habitats. It is considered a good forage grass, but grows in fragile habitats easily disturbed by livestock grazing.

MONTANE

VALLEYS

Flowering: June - July

Habitat: Wet meadows, along ditches, streams, and lake edges, often rooted below water level, valleys to montane

BLUE GRAMA

Bouteloua gracilis • Poaceae (Grass Family)

Photo: Golden Valley Co. MT, July (Matt Lavin); Illustration: USDA-NRCS Plants Database

FIELD DESCRIPTION:

Native perennial bunchgrass or sodgrass, 8-20" (2-5 dm) tall. Leaf blades 1-2 mm wide, often curled. Sheath commonly hirsute; auricles absent; ligule and collar regions are distinctively long-hairy. Inflorescence of 1-4 lateral divergent spikes, arranged on 1 side (secund), each 2-4.5 cm long and with 50-80 spikelets; each lateral rachis terminated by a spikelet. Spikelets 4-5.5 mm long, second glume essentially hairless or with clear gland-based hairs. Lemmas essentially hairless, short-awned, these disarticulating from the spikelet. Blue Grama is warm-season grass with distinctive "eyelash" seed heads that provides good quality summer grazing for livestock and wildlife alike.

VALLEYS-FOOTHILLS

Flowering: July - September

Habitat: Open dry shrub-steppe vegetation and open understory, valleys to foothills

MOUNTAIN BROME

Bromus carinatus • Poaceae (Grass Family)
(Synonyms: *Bromus marginatus, Bromus polyanthus*)

FIELD DESCRIPTION:

Native perennial bunchgrass, 20-40" (5-10 dm) tall. Leaf blades 6-12 mm wide. Leaf sheath is fused and lower sheaths often hairy; auricles absent or inconspicuous; and ligule membranous and conspicuous. Inflorescence an open panicle with ascending branches at anthesis, up to 10 cm long. Spikelets 17-22 mm long with 5 to 10 florets. Lemmas with an awn 8-17 mm long. Mountain Brome is a cool-season perennial bunchgrass that commonly inhabits mountain meadows. It is considered one of the best forage grasses on western rangelands. A fused (closed) sheath is characteristic of *Bromus*.

MONTANE

Flowering: June- August

Habitat: Open understory and adjacent meadows, in the montane

Photos: Zion NP, UT, May; Bridger Range, MT, July (Matt Lavin)

SMOOTH BROME (AWNLESS BROME)

Bromus inermis • Poaceae (Grass Family)

FIELD DESCRIPTION:

Native and introduced rhizomatous perennial, 1.5-3' (4.5-9 dm) tall, with a spike-like flower cluster that does not break apart at maturity. Leaf blades are flat, often drooping, 4-12 mm wide (commonly around 5 mm) and 20-38 cm long with raised and keeled midrib below. Blade often has a "W" wrinkle halfway along its length. Sheaths closed, often pubescent; auricles absent; and ligule membranous. Inflorescence a narrow panicle 7-18 cm long. Spikelets 15-30 mm long, with 8 to 15 florets. Lemmas awnless, ≤2 mm long when lemmas glabrous or 3-10 mm long when lemmas hairy. Awns absent or to 3 mm long. Plant is strongly rhizomatous.

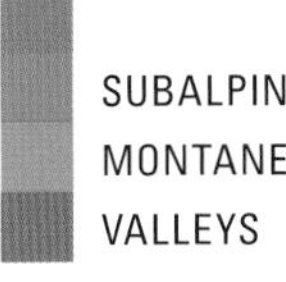

SUBALPINE
MONTANE
VALLEYS

Flowering: June- August

Habitat: Moist to dry sites in meadows as well as along roadsides and in pastures, valleys to subalpine

Photo: Bozeman, MT, June (Matt Lavin); Illustration: USDA-NRCS Plants Database

JAPANESE BROME (FIELD BROME)

Bromus japonicus • Poaceae (Grass Family)
(Synonym: *Bromus arvensis*)

Photo: Bozeman, MT, July (Matt Lavin); Illustration: USDA-NRCS Plants Database

FIELD DESCRIPTION:

Introduced annual bunchgrass, 8-24" (20-60 cm) tall. Leaf blades generally flat, 2-4 mm wide. Inflorescence an open panicle 10-20 cm long, the branches drooping to one side and at least some flexuous, each branch bearing several spikelets. Sheaths closed to near top and soft to densely hairy, auricles usually absent, ligules membranous, to 6 mm. Spikelets 8-13 mm long, with 5 to 11 florets. Lemmas broad; awn 2-6 mm long, straight to curved downward at maturity. Japanese Brome is one of the most common annual bromes found in the region.

VALLEYS-FOOTHILLS

Flowering: June - August

Habitat: Roadsides, pastures, overgrazed sagebrush steppe, sites with strongly fluctuating water levels, and open disturbed dry sites, valleys to foothills

CHEATGRASS (DOWNY BROME)

Bromus tectorum • Poaceae (Grass Family)

Photo: Bozeman, MT, June (Matt Lavin); Illustration: USDA-NRCS Plants Database

FIELD DESCRIPTION:

Introduced annual bunchgrass, 8-20" (2-5 dm) tall. Leaf blades 2-4 mm wide and softly hairy. Inflorescence an open, often nodding panicle 2-15 cm long. Sheaths usually densely pubescent, auricles absent, ligules membranous 2-3mm. Spikelets 10-17 mm long, with 3 to 6 florets. Lemmas 9-12 mm long, gradually tapered into 2 narrow teeth; awn straight, 12-20 mm long, at times twisted. A native grass of Eurasia, Cheatgrass is a prominent invasive in the West where it has filled the void left from the overgrazing of native grasses. Many habitats invaded by Cheatgrass are significantly altered, and no longer support native vegetation.

VALLEYS-FOOTHILLS

Flowering: June - August

Habitat: Roadsides, overgrazed rangeland and sagebrush steppe, and open dry understory, valleys to foothills

Calamagrostis canadensis • Poaceae (Grass Family)

BLUEJOINT REEDGRASS

FIELD DESCRIPTION:

Native rhizomatous perennial often forming dense stands, stems 2-4' (6-12 dm) tall. Numerous slender stems arise from rhizomes topped by large, slightly nodding, branched inflorescence, purplish in flower, turning tan as season progresses. Leaf blades ridged and scabrous, commonly 3-10 mm wide, 7-40 cm long. Sheath open and distinctly veined, ligule membranous to 3-5 mm long. Auricles absent and collar indistinct. Inflorescence an open panicle 7-35 cm long. Spikelets 4-5 mm long. Lemmas with an awn extending at most less than 1 mm beyond lemma tip, callus hairs nearly as long as the lemmas.

SUBALPINE
MONTANE

Flowering: June - August

Habitat: Mountain meadows and open understory, often along streams or lake margins, montane to subalpine

Photos: Park Co., WY, August (Matt Lavin)

Calamagrostis rubescens • Poaceae (Grass Family)

PINE REEDGRASS (PINEGRASS)

FIELD DESCRIPTION:

Native rhizomatous perennial, typically 11-20" (3-5 dm) tall, can reach 40". Stems tall and smooth. Leaves 2-5 mm wide, scabrous below. Inflorescence a dense contracted panicle 4-15 cm long. Spikelets 4.0-4.5 mm long. Sheaths and collars hairy, ligules, 1-5mm long. Lemmas with a bent awn barely surpassing if at all the glume tips, callus hairs less than one-half the lemma length, sometimes less. Pinegrass is often the dominant understory grass species in the region's coniferous and aspen forests where it provides important forage for wildlife and livestock.

MONTANE
FOOTHILLS

Flowering: June- August

Habitat: Dry meadows, open and closed forest understory, foothills to montane

Top: Chestnut, MT, October; Bottom: Montanapolis, MT, July (Matt Lavin)

ORCHARDGRASS (COCK'S-FOOT)

Dactylis glomerata • Poaceae (Grass Family)

Photos: Bozeman, MT, June (Matt Lavin)

FIELD DESCRIPTION:

Introduced perennial bunchgrass, 2.5-6' (8-20 dm) tall, commonly forming tussocks. Leaf blades 4-8 mm wide, lax but conspicuously folded along midrib and whitish scabrous margins. Leaf sheaths generally open and distinctly keeled. Auricles absent; ligules membranous, 3-9 mm long. Inflorescence is a contracted panicle, 4-20 cm long with 2-6 florets per spikelet and spikelets tightly clustered on one side of the branch (secund). Spikelets 5-8 mm long. Glumes shorter than the florets, awn-tipped. Lemmas 4-6 mm long, tapering to short awn. The common name "cock's foot" is an apt reference to the species' inflorescence arranged on ends of short, stiff branches.

VALLEYS-FOOTHILLS

Flowering: June - August

Habitat: Open meadows and open understory where moderately disturbed, including road and trailsides, as well as in lawns, valleys to foothills

TUFTED HAIRGRASS

Deschampsia cespitosa • Poaceae (Grass Family)

Photo: Park Co., WY, August (Matt Lavin); Illustration: USDA-NRCS Plants Database

FIELD DESCRIPTION:

Native perennial bunchgrass, 1-4' (3-10 dm) tall. Leaf blades flat or rolled inward, mostly 1.5-3 mm wide. Ligules membranous, 2-10 mm long; sheaths open; and auricles absent. Inflorescence a loose open panicle, often shiny and purplish in appearance, 8-25 cm long. Spikelets 3.5-6.0 mm long, glumes purplish but distally straw- or silvery-colored. Lemmas 2-5 mm long, usually awned, 1-8 mm long. Its common name describes the hair-like grass blades growing in dense groups. The species is commonly recommended for restoration of disturbed habitats. It is salt tolerant and is found from tidal wetlands to alpine zones in North America.

ALPINE
SUBALPINE
MONTANE
FOOTHILLS

Flowering: June - September

Habitat: Dry open areas and moist meadows, foothills to alpine

Elymus canadensis • Poaceae (Grass Family)

CANADA WILDRYE

FIELD DESCRIPTION:

Introduced perennial bunchgrass 30-60" (8-15 dm) tall. Leaf blades 4-12 mm wide, usually flat, may be smooth or somewhat rough to the touch. Sheaths open to base and mostly smooth, well developed auricles, ligules 0.5-1mm long and finely hairy. Inflorescence 7-19 cm long, the rachis continuous and usually drooping. Spikelets mostly 2 (rarely more) per node, 12-16 mm long (excluding awns), glumes 3-5-veined, tapering to an awn up to 12 mm long. Lemmas mostly 3-4 per spikelet, short hairy, tapering gradually into an awn up to 3.5 cm long, the awns divergent and curved.

VALLEYS - FOOTHILLS

Flowering: June - August

Habitat: Dry to moist, often sandy or gravelly soils in meadows, prairie, steamsides, and along road cuts, valleys to foothills

Photos: Madison Co., MT, July (W. Tilt)

Elymus cinereus • Poaceae (Grass Family)
(Synonym: *Leymus cinereus*)

BASIN WILDRYE (GIANT WILDRYE)

FIELD DESCRIPTION:

Native perennial bunchgrass. Stems 30-65" (1-2 m) tall, forming large bunches or tussocks. Leaf blades 7-12 mm wide, usually flat, and upper surface distinctly ribbed. Stems hairy at nodes. Sheaths open, smooth to soft hairy; auricle well developed, ligules membranous and relative short (less than 2 mm long). Inflorescence is a large spike, 8-22 cm long, the rachis continuous and erect. Spikelets mostly 3 (sometimes more) per node, 11-15 mm long; glumes narrow, gradually tapering from the base to a narrow pointed tip, about as long as 1st lemma, veins not evident or with a single vein. Lemmas mostly 3-5 per spikelet, sparsely short hairy, awnless or with a short awn to 5 mm long.

MONTANE
VALLEYS

Flowering: June- August

Habitat: Dry to moist soils, valleys to montane

Photos: Ennis, MT, August (Matt Lavin)

SQUIRRELTAIL

Elymus elymoides • Poaceae (Grass Family)

FIELD DESCRIPTION:

Native perennial bunchgrass. Stems 4-24" (2-6 dm) tall. Leaf blades 1-5 mm wide, flat to folded. Sheaths open, auricles generally absent, and ligule membranous. Inflorescence 4-14 cm long, the erect rachis readily disarticulating at maturity. Spikelets usually 2 per node (rarely 1 or 3), 11-14 mm long; glumes gradually tapering from the base to a narrow acute tip, often bifid (forked into 2 parts), rarely trifid, distinctly 1-2 veined, imperceptibly tapering into 1 or 2 awns that are 2-11 cm long. Lemmas mostly 2-6 per spikelet, hairless to hairy, tapering into an awn 2-10 cm long. Commonly found in sagebrush communities, its tolerance to disturbance makes it a common species for restoring degraded rangelands.

ALPINE
SUBALPINE
MONTANE
VALLEYS

Flowering: May - July

Habitat: Open dry shrub steppe and moderately disturbed sides such as along gravel backroads, valleys to alpine

Photos: Bozeman, MT, June (Matt Lavin)

BLUE WILDRYE

Elymus glaucus • Poaceae (Grass Family)

Photos: Bozeman, MT, August (Matt Lavin)

FIELD DESCRIPTION:

Native perennial bunchgrass, 24-50" (6-13 dm) tall, that grows in small tufts comprising a few stiff stems. Leaf blades 5-12 mm wide, flat. Sheaths open, auricles long and thin, ligule is membranous arising from a purplish collar. Inflorescence 6-16 cm long, the rachis continuous and erect. Spikelets arranged flat to stem, usually 2 per node, 12-20 mm long; glumes distinctly broadest in the lower half, with 3-5 veins, the base mostly greenish, not indurate, distally tapering to a short awn or awn-tip. Lemmas mostly 2-4 per spikelet, essentially hairless, with a straight awn 10-20 mm long. Blue Wildrye is a common grass in Aspen and mountain brush communities, provides important forage for wildlife and livestock.

MONTANE
FOOTHILLS

Flowering: June - August

Habitat: Meadows and open understory, foothills to montane

Festuca campestris • Poaceae (Grass Family)

ROUGH FESCUE (BUFFALO BUNCHGRASS)

FIELD DESCRIPTION:

Native perennial bunchgrass, 24-40" (6-10 dm) tall, usually without rhizomes. Leaf blades 1-2 mm wide, inrolled to partially flattened, distinctly scabrous. Old leaf sheaths persistent in tuft. Sheath open, scabrous; auricles absent; and ligules membranous, 0.1-0.5 mm. Inflorescence a narrow panicle 5-15 cm long. Spikelets 8-12 mm long, with 4-6 florets. Lemmas awnless or awn-tipped. The reddish- purplish stem bases are characteristic of the species, which has numerous common names including Big Buffalo Bunchgrass and Mountain Rough Fescue. The grass provides good forage for wildlife and livestock alike, but is sensitive to heavy grazing, competition from exotics, and other habitat disturbance.

MONTANE
VALLEYS

Flowering: June - July

Habitat: Dry to moist grasslands and open forests, valleys to montane

Photos: Buckingham, MT, July (Matt Lavin)

Festuca idahoensis • Poaceae (Grass Family)

IDAHO FESCUE

FIELD DESCRIPTION:

Native perennial bunchgrass, 1-3' (3-9 dm) tall, densely tufted, spread by rhizomes. Leaf blades are mostly basal, 1 mm wide, 12-25 cm long, inrolled, and somewhat stiff. Ligules collar-shaped and fringed, while auricles are small or absent. Inflorescence is a narrow, open panicle, 10-18 cm long, with a glabrous peduncle, usually greenish in color. Spikelets 5-10 mm long, with 3-7 florets. Lemmas with an awn tip or awn up to 5 mm long. Idaho Fescue is a bunchgrass that dominates much of the open upland steppe of the region. The species is distinctive for its dense bunches of fine blue-green leaves with narrow panicles of spikelets, and the presence of non-overlapping lemmas with rounded backs.

ALPINE
SUBALPINE
MONTANE
FOOTHILLS

Flowering: May - July

Habitat: Open grasslands, meadows and forests, foothills to alpine

Top: Gallatin Co., MT, August (Matt Lavin); Bottom: Buckingham, MT, July (Matt Lavin)

MANNAGRASS

Glyceria grandis • Poaceae (Grass Family)

FIELD DESCRIPTION:

Native rhizomatous perennial, 3-6′ (1-2 m) tall with thick, stout stems. Leaf blades 2-12 mm wide. Sheaths closed; auricles absent; and ligules 2-6 mm long, often fusing into a membranous cylinder around the stem. Inflorescence is a diffuse, purplish panicle, 20-40 cm long, the branches spreading and often drooping. Spikelets 3-7 mm long, laterally compressed. Lemmas 2-7 (rarely 8) per spikelet. Many species of *Glyceria* are planted in aquatic gardens because of their attractive airy panicles. The species' common name references "manna," the food that sustained the Israelites during their travels in the desert.

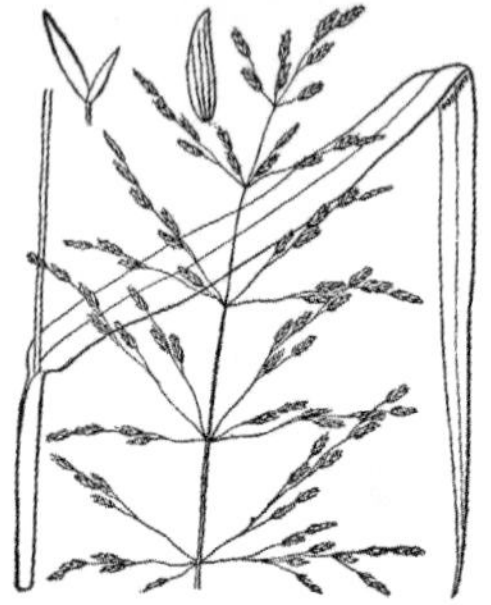

Flowering: July - August

Habitat: Stream sides and along lake margins, foothills to montane

Photo: Bozeman, MT, June (Matt Lavin); Illustration: USDA-NRCS Plants Database

FOXTAIL BARLEY

Hordeum jubatum • Poaceae (Grass Family)

FIELD DESCRIPTION:

Native perennial bunchgrass, 8-28″ (2-7 dm) tall, with erect, bunched stems. Lower blades and sheaths usually hairless, though occasionally hairy but not conspicuously so. Blades flat, lax, 2-5 mm wide, and 12 cm long with raised veins on upper surface. Ligules short, membranous and collar-shaped, auricles absent. Inflorescence a soft, nodding whisk, silvery to reddish like a fox's tail. The inflorescence axis disarticulates at maturity. Spikelets 3 per node. The glumes and lemmas have awns up to 5 cm long. When in flower, the nodding purple to pale-green whisks are distinctive. Foxtail Barley is a prolific seeder. Ripe seed heads break up and disperse by wind or transport in the hair of grazing animals finding their way to roadsides, vacant lots and overused grasslands.

Flowering: June - August

Habitat: : Dry to moist soils, often preferring disturbed areas, valleys to montane

Photos: Bozeman, MT, July & September (Matt Lavin)

PRARIE JUNEGRASS

Koeleria macrantha • Poaceae (Grass Family)

FIELD DESCRIPTION:

Native perennial bunchgrass, 18-24" (46-60 cm) tall, with densely tufted silvery-green flower spikes. Stems and leaf sheaths are distinctly striate (grooved) on both surfaces. Leaf blades smooth or downy, 1-3 mm wide and up to 13 cm long, commonly inrolled or folded, and mostly arranged around base of stem. Sheaths open, auricles absent, and ligules membranous 0.5-2 mm long. Inflorescence is a compact pyramidal panicle, 2.5-13 cm long. Spikelets 4-5 mm long, with 2-4 florets on short branches that point upward. Glumes unequal in size with rough appearance without awns. Lemmas are awnless or awn-pointed. Junegrass is one of the earliest maturing native grasses. Growth and flowering are usually complete by late June or early July, at which time the plants go dormant.

SUBALPINE
MONTANE
PLAINS

Flowering: May - July

Habitat: Sandy, rocky soils in open grassland, sagebrush and forests, plains to subalpine

Photo: Bozeman, MT, June (Matt Lavin); Illustration: USDA-NRCS Plants Database

INDIAN RICEGRASS

Oryzopsis hymenoides • Poaceae (Grass Family)
(Synonym: *Achnatherum hymenoides*)

FIELD DESCRIPTION:

Native perennial bunchgrass, 4-24" (10-60 cm) tall, strongly tufted with a graceful airy appearance. Stems are thick-walled and hollow. Leaf blades elongate, 2-4 mm wide, smooth and lax. Sheaths hairless to short-hairy, auricles absent, and ligules membranous up to 1 cm long. Inflorescence is an open panicle, loosely branched or lacy topped, 8-25 cm long. Spikelets short and plump, 4-5 mm long. Glumes ovate-sharp-pointed, generally 3-veined. Lemmas densely long-hairy, dark, with a deciduous awn 2-3 mm long. Indian Ricegrass has a distinctive delicate lacy, straw-colored inflorescence when in flower. As noted by one botanist, "it looks like a bunch grass that was electrocuted." Its attractive form makes it a favorite for use in dry floral arrangements.

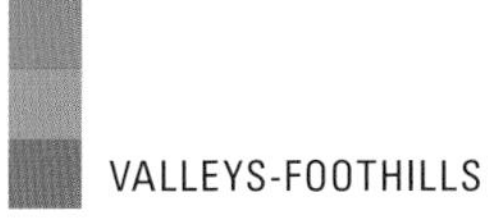

VALLEYS-FOOTHILLS

Flowering: May - June

Habitat: Plains and low hills, especially on sandy or gravelly soils, valleys to foothills

Top: USDA-NRCS Plants Database (unknown); Bottom: Butte Co., ID, August (Matt Lavin)

WITCHGRASS (PANICGRASS)

Panicum capillare • Poaceae (Grass Family)

Photos: Bozeman, MT, August (Matt Lavin)

FIELD DESCRIPTION:

Annual bunchgrass, 4-24" (1-6 dm) tall, with sprawling or spreading stems and fibrous root system. Leaf blades and sheaths lightly to densely glandular hairy, 5-14 mm wide. Ligules a short fringe of hairs, 0.5-1.3 mm long, and auricles absent. Inflorescence an open panicle 15-25 cm long. Spikelets 2-3 mm long, first glume 1.0-1.8 mm long, second glume 2.0-3.0 mm long. Lemmas: sterile lemma not keeled, fertile lemma blunt, yellowish at maturity. Adapted to areas of natural disturbance, the species is densely hairy, has a ligule that is a fringe of hairs, and an open panicle that may account for as much as half of the height of the entire plant. Commonly Witchgrass plants appear bent at base. After maturity, the panicles break off and roll like tumbleweeds.

MONTANE
VALLEYS

Flowering: June - September

Habitat: Disturbed areas along roadsides, railroad tracks, sidewalks, and in lawns, valleys to montane

REED CANARYGRASS

Phalaris arundinacea • Poaceae (Grass Family)

Photos: Bozeman, MT, June (Matt Lavin)

FIELD DESCRIPTION:

Native rhizomatous perennial often more than 6' (18 dm) tall and forming dense stands. Stems are tall and stout. Leaf blades are flat, 6-18 mm wide, with a rough texture. Leaf sheath open, auricles absent, and ligule conspicuous. Inflorescences are a contracted, interrupted panicle. Spikelets 4-5 mm long with 1 well-developed floret and 2 lower sterile florets that are minutely scale-like and covered with long hairs. Glumes are similar in size enclosing 1 fertile and 2 reduced, sterile flowers. Lemmas are rounded and smaller than glumes. Finding yourself in the middle of a dense stand of Reed Canarygrass can make you wish you were atop an elephant rather than on foot.

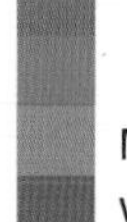

MONTANE
VALLEYS

Flowering: July - August

Habitat: Moist and seasonally wet soils in marshes, wet meadows, prairie and riparian areas, valleys to montane

MOUNTAIN TIMOTHY
(ALPINE TIMOTHY)

Phleum alpinum • Poaceae (Grass Family)

FIELD DESCRIPTION:

Native perennial bunchgrass, 8-20"(2-5 dm) tall, not bulbous at base. Leaf blades 4-7 mm wide. Sheaths open, inflated, subtending the inflorescence. Ligules membranous, 1-4 mm long and auricles generally absent or rudimentary rounded. Inflorescence cylindrical, 1-6 cm long and 5-13 mm wide. Spikelets 3.0-4.5 mm long. Glumes 3-4.5 mm, scabrous, awns to 2.5 mm. Lemmas 2.0-2.5 mm long. Mountain Timothy is a strongly tufted grass that is circumpolar in its distribution. Erect stems are clasped by distinctly inflated leaf sheaths. The tight clusters of spikelets form a rounded cylinder purplish in color.

ALPINE
SUBALPINE
MONTANE

Flowering: June - August

Habitat: Mountain meadows and open understory, montane to alpine

Photo: Stryker, MT, June (Matt Lavin)

TIMOTHY
(FIELD TIMOTHY)

Phleum pratense • Poaceae (Grass Family)

FIELD DESCRIPTION:

Introduced loosely bunched perennial, 20-40" (5-10 dm) tall, with characteristic long cylindrical spikes of purple-silvery flower clusters atop thin stout stems. Stems emerge from a swollen, bulbous base to form large clumps. Stems are light green in color, hairless, round in cross-section, and commonly bent at lower nodes. Leaf blades are flat, 6-9 mm wide, 7-33 cm long, flat, hairless and tapering. Leaf sheath is open, ligules are well developed and auricles generally absent. Inflorescence is a tightly packed cylindrical spike-like panicle, up to 18 cm long. Glume is hairy along its keel and terminates in an awn that is shorter than the glume, 1-2 mm long. Lemma is thin membranous. The grass has widely escaped cultivation and is common across the region.

SUBALPINE
MONTANE
VALLEYS

Flowering: May - June

Habitat: Cultivated pastures, "improved" rangelands, and roadsides, valleys to subalpine

Photos: Gallatin Co., MT, July - August (Matt Lavin)

ALPINE BLUEGRASS

Poa alpina • Poaceae (Grass Family)

Photos: Gallatin Co., MT, September (Matt Lavin)

FIELD DESCRIPTION:

Perennial bunchgrass with stems 4-12" (1-3 dm) tall. Leaves: blades 2.0-4.5 mm wide, ligules 2-4 mm long. Inflorescence a pyramidal panicle 3-7 cm long. Spikelets 4.0-6.5 mm long. Lemmas strongly keeled and uniformly hairy. Alpine Bluegrass grows in scattered dense clumps. Its pyramidal inflorescence and short (usually less than 5 cm long) and broad (up to 5 mm wide) boat-shaped leaves are distinctive. Alpine Bluegrass might be confused with montane forms of Sandberg Bluegrass (*Poa secunda*) with its open panicles, but Alpine Bluegrass has large laterally compressed spikelets with lemmas that are conspicuously hairy and distinctly folded (keeled) along the midrib.

ALPINE
SUBALPINE
MONTANE

Flowering: July - August

Habitat: Open understory, montane to alpine

BULBOUS BLUEGRASS

Poa bulbosa • Poaceae (Grass Family)

Top: Bingham Co., ID, June; Bottom: Pershing Co., NV, May (Matt Lavin)

FIELD DESCRIPTION:

Introduced perennial bunchgrass with stems 8-24" (2-6 dm) tall with a bulbous base. Leaves: blades 1.0-2.5 mm wide, mostly basal, ligules 1-3 mm long. Inflorescence a contracted panicle, 3-10 cm long. Spikelets 4-15 mm long. Lemmas usually transformed into small vegetative bulbs, hairy along veins. Bulbous Bluegrass was introduced to North America accidentally, as a contaminant of alfalfa and clover seed. The species is a short-lived, cool-season grass that is often the first invading species on disturbed moist, shallow soils. The bulblets contain high levels of starch and fat and are sought after by variety of birds and small mammals.

Flowering: May - June

Habitat: Roadsides, trailsides, open dry sites, plains to foothills

PLAINS - FOOTHILLS

Poa compressa • Poaceae (Grass Family)

CANADA BLUEGRASS

FIELD DESCRIPTION:

Introduced rhizomatous perennial, 8-20" (2-5 dm) tall, wiry and flattened. Nodes often distinctly bent and banded with contrasting lighter and darker bands. Leaf blades 1.5-4.0 mm wide, from stem, tip keel-shaped, rarely basal. Sheaths open nearly to base; ligules membranous, 1-3 mm long; and auricles absent. Inflorescence generally a narrow panicle 2-8 cm long, with scabrous branches. Spikelets 3-6 mm long. Lemmas with cobwebby hairs at very base. Canada Bluegrass provides food forage for elk and other wildlife as well as livestock. While some consider it a native species, it is thought to have been introduced from Siberia.

Flowering: June - August

Habitat: Roadsides and other open areas with a combination of moisture and regular moderate disturbance, valleys to montane

Photos: Gallatin Co., MT, August & June (Matt Lavin)

Poa pratensis • Poaceae (Grass Family)

KENTUCKY BLUEGRASS

FIELD DESCRIPTION:

Native and introduced perennial sodgrass, 4-36" (1-9 dm) tall, with vigorous rhizomes. Leaf blades 2-4mm wide, mostly basal with a distinct double midrib and boat-shaped tip. Young shoots are slightly flattened while seed stalks are round. Sheaths open, auricles absent and ligules membranous. Inflorescence is an open panicle, oblong pyramidal, 5-20 cm long, with panicle branches whorled in groups of 3-5. Spikelets are strongly flattened and 3-5 flowered. Glumes have well-developed keels with one slightly larger than the other. Lemmas exhibit a cobwebby base and are generally hairy along the mid and margin veins. Kentucky Bluegrass is a lawn grass gone wild.

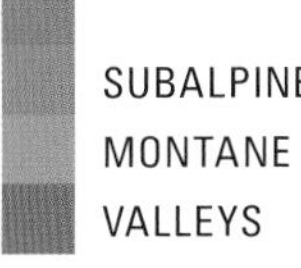

Flowering: May - June

Habitat: Dry to moist soils in open meadows and woodlands, as well as roadsides and lawns, valleys to subalpine

Photo: Bozeman, MT, June (Matt Lavin); Illustration: USDA-NRCS Plants Database

SANDBERG BLUEGRASS

Poa secunda • Poaceae (Grass Family)
(Synonyms: *Poa ampla, Poa canbyi, Poa gracillima, Poa juncifolia, Poa nevadensis, Poa sandbergii, Poa scabrella*)

Photos: Butte Co., ID, June (Matt Lavin)

FIELD DESCRIPTION:

Native perennial bunchgrass, 8-48" (2-12 dm) tall. Leaf blades narrow, 1-3 mm wide, prow-tipped and double mid-rib. Stems arising from basal leaves. Sheaths open, ligules 1-5 mm long, and auricles absent. Inflorescence a narrow panicle mostly 7-24 cm long. Spikelets 6-10 mm long. Lemmas hairless or scabrous to short-hairy, rounded on back. Sandberg Bluegrass is a cool-season, shallow-rooted bunchgrass that is widespread and highly drought-resistant. It is one of the first grasses to green up in the spring and is an important food for ground squirrels and other wildlife, as well as livestock. By mid-summer the grass is cured and dormant.

SUBALPINE
MONTANE
VALLEYS

Flowering: June - August

Habitat: Dry open meadows, ridges, shrub steppe saline settings, valleys to subalpine

NEEDLE AND THREAD GRASS

Stipa comata • Poaceae (Grass Family)
(Synonym: *Hesperostipa comata*)

Photos: Butte Co., ID, June (Matt Lavin)

FIELD DESCRIPTION:

Native perennial bunchgrass, 10-26" (10-66 cm) tall, with a delicate narrowed flower cluster with long awns. Grows in small tufts from profuse roots (no rhizomes). Leaves 2-4 mm wide, 8-30 cm long, glabrous and prominently veined. Sheath open, auricles absent, ligule conspicuous and notched. Seed head is a loose open panicle, 10-20 cm long with lowermost spikelets partly or fully enclosed in the uppermost leaf sheath. One floret present per spikelet. Glumes papery, 15-20 mm long, remaining attached to plant after seeds disperse. Lemmas are evenly whitish hairy with long, flexible, twisted awns up to about 10 cm long.

MONTANE
VALLEYS

Flowering: May - July

Habitat: Sandy and rocky soils on plains and dry hills, valleys to montane

Typha latifolia • Typhaceae (Cattail Family)

COMMON CATTAIL (BROADLEAF CATTAIL)

FIELD DESCRIPTION:

Tall native perennial herb, to 8" tall with erect, smooth, pithy stems. Multitude of tiny flowers (lacking petals or sepals) in a dense cylindrical spike. Male (staminate) yellowish flowers sit above and contiguous to the larger brownish female (pistillate) flower cluster. Staminate flowers disappear by mid-summer. Leaves sheath stem at base and are alternate, long, linear, stiff, and spongy. Goes to seed in a fluff of long, slender hairs. Plant persists through winter. Cattails can form dense stands that provide food, nesting and cover for waterfowl, marsh birds and mammals such as muskrat. Cattail roots are edible raw or cooked, as are the young emergent shoots.

MONTANE
VALLEYS

Flowering: June - July

Habitat: Shallow still or slow-moving water, valleys to montane

Photos: Teton River, ID, July (W. Tilt)

CONIFER KEY

1. Needles in bundles along the twig. PINE (2)
   2. Needles in bundles of 2. (3)
      3. Needles 2" in length or less, and often twisted. Mature cones on tree. LODGEPOLE PINE
      3. Needles 2" in length or more. Upper trunk and branches show orange color. Old cones seldom on tree. SCOTCH PINE
   2. Needles in bundles of 3 (sometimes 2), needles long, about 7" in length. PONDEROSA PINE
   2. Needles in bundles of 5. LIMBER PINE or WHITE BARK PINE

1. Needles, 4 sided or flat, attached singly to the twig. (4)
   4. Needles stiff, sharp and square-sided (rolls between fingers). ENGELMANN SPRUCE
   4. Needles flat, flexible, blunt-tipped (do not roll between fingers). (5)
      5. Needles arise from twigs on all sides (spirally arranged), tending to grow upward. Tree distinctively slender, spire-like, with branches persisting to the ground. Cones, in erect position on upper branches or an erect woody spike-like cone axis may be present. SUBALPINE FIR
      5. Needles attached to the twig by short, twisted petioles, commonly bluish-green in color. Mature cones are 2-4" long with protruding 3-pronged bracts that resemble a "mouse tail." DOUGLAS FIR

TYPICAL FLOWER

PEA FLOWER

COMPOSITE FLOWER

TYPES OF INFLORESCENCE

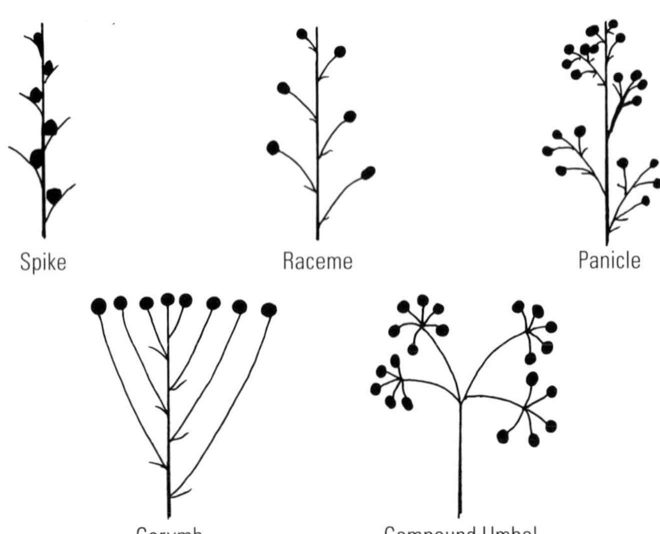

LEAF SHAPES

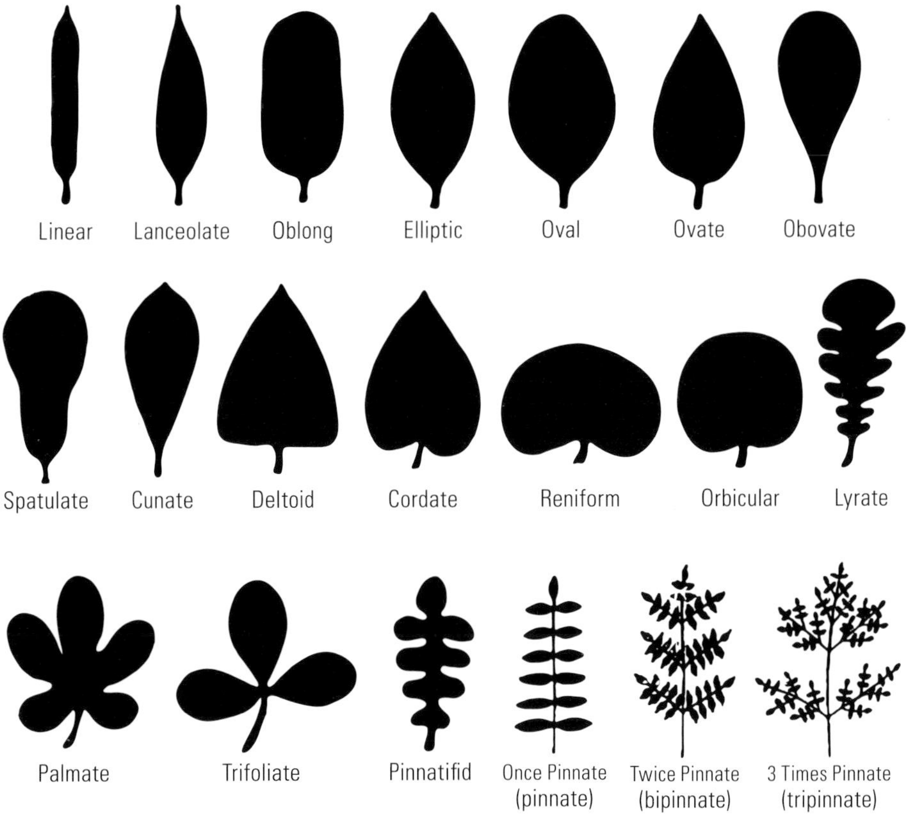

Linear
Lanceolate
Oblong
Elliptic
Oval
Ovate
Obovate
Spatulate
Cunate
Deltoid
Cordate
Reniform
Orbicular
Lyrate
Palmate
Trifoliate
Pinnatifid
Once Pinnate (pinnate)
Twice Pinnate (bipinnate)
3 Times Pinnate (tripinnate)

GRASS ANATOMY

Awn
Lemma
Glume 1
Glume 2
Blade
Ligule
Auricle
Sheath
Midrib
Collar
Stolon
Rhizome

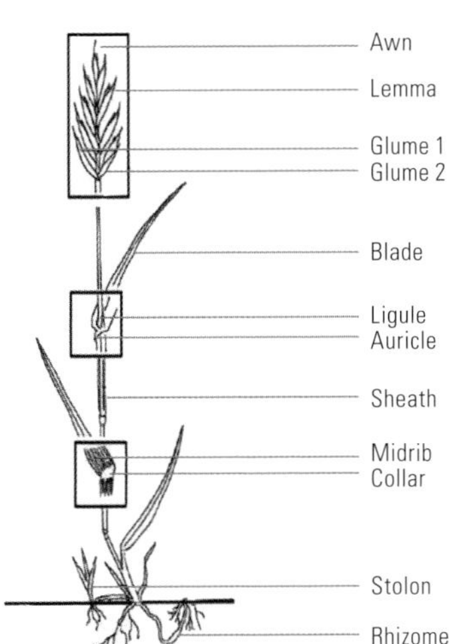

Acaulescent	Without the above ground portion of the stem that has nodes, leaves, and buds. Often defined as "stemless."
Achene	Small, dry, thin-walled fruit that does not split open when ripe. The achene contains a single seed, as in a sunflower seed.
Acute	Tapering gradually to a well-defined point which is less than 90 degrees. See obtuse.
Alkaline	Having alkali properties, i.e., pH greater than 7 (opposite of acidic). Alkaline soils typically have high clay content with high concentrations of salts such as sodium carbonate.
Alpine	Found above timberline at high altitude.
Alternate	Referring to the relative position of leaves on a stem. One alternately positioned leaf grows on one side of the stem, then the next leaf grows higher up on the other side of the stem. See opposite and whorled.
Annual	Used to describe a plant which grows from a seed, flowers, sets on new seeds, and dies in the same year. See biennial, perennial, and monocarpic.
Anther	Expanded, sack-like, pollen-bearing portion of the stamen.
Anthesis	The period during which a flower is fully open and functional.
Antrorsely	Directed forward or upward, as a bristle on a seedhead.
Apiculate	Ending abruptly in a small, short, distinct point.
Appressed	Lying close to or flat against, as in "appressed hairs."
Areole	Area on cactus that gives rise to flowers, spines, and/or glochids.
Ascending	Growing obliquely upward; curving upward during growth.
Auriculate	Small, ear-shaped appendage, as at the base of a leaf. The appendage may be auriculate-clasping or not clasping. See clasping and perfoliate.
Awn	Bristle-like appendage at the tip of a surface. Commonly found on grasses and sometimes on sunflower seeds.
Axil	Upper angle between leaf and stem; the junction of the leaf and the stem.
Axillary	Pertaining to the axil; in the axil.
Axis	Central line around which parts of plant are arranged, i.e., line from which leaflets emanate.
Banner	Upper petal of a Pea Family plant, usually broad, long, and often erect.
Basal	Found at or near the base of a plant or plant part. (Compare with cauline)
Basal rosette	A cluster of leaves radiating from a central point at ground level.
Berry	Fleshy fruit containing 1 to many seeds.
Biennial	Living for 2 years. See annual and perennial.
Blade	The broad part of a leaf.
Branch	Secondary stem, growing from main stem.
Bract	Leaf-like structures, of varying dimensions, which first cover floral parts, and then subtend the floral parts after they emerge.
Bristles	1) Large stiff straight hair. 2) Asteraceae: fine hairs at top of flower arising from inferior ovary.
Bulb	Underground storage organ with thickened fleshy scales, as in the onion.
Caespitose	Growing in clumps, usually close to the ground.
Calyx	Outermost whorl of the flower, collective term for the sepals.
Campanulate	Bell-shaped.
Canescent	Having a gray-white appearance. Hoary.
Capsule	Dry fruit that splits open at maturity. Consists of 2 or more carpels.
Carpel	A leaf modified to produce seed and having a stigma, style, and ovary.
Catkin	Elongate cluster of minute, petal-less flowers; unisexual.
Caudex	Persistent, often woody base of an otherwise annual herbaceous stem.
Cauline	Leaves arising from above ground portion of stem (compare with basal).

Ciliate Bearing a fringe of hairs along the margin, as in some leaves or petals.

Circumboreal Found in the northern (boreal) forests around the globe.

Clasping Leaf base attached to and wrapping part way around the stem.

Compound leaf Leaf divided into 2 or more leaflets (which often appear to be small leaves). The leaflets themselves may be further divided into smaller leaflets. To determine if you are observing a leaf or a leaflet, look for a bud at the point of attachment. If there is a bud, you are looking at a leaf. If there is no bud, you are looking at a leaflet, part of a compound leaf.

Cone A gymnosperm's fruit characterized by overlapping scales.

Coniferous Bearing its pollen and seeds in cones.

Cordate Heart-shaped, with a notch at the center of the base.

Corm Short, vertical, swollen, solid underground stem, distinct from bulbs.

Corolla Collective term for all the petals of a flower.

Corymb Flat-topped flower cluster with varying length pedicels (flower stalks). Outer flowers bloom first (compare with cyme).

Crenate Having rounded teeth on the leaf margin.

Cuneate Wedge-shaped, wider at top and narrowing to base.

Cyanogenic Capable of producing cyanide, toxic.

Cyme Branched inflorescence in which the central flower on the main stem opens before the side flowers (compare with corymb).

Deciduous Falling off at maturity; foliage not persistent, not evergreen.

Decumbent Lying or growing on the ground with erect or rising tips.

Dehiscent Splitting open at maturity, as in seed pods.

Dentate Toothed along the margins with teeth pointing outward; doubly dentate margins have teeth that are in turn toothed. See serrate.

Dicot Group of flowering plants characterized by having 2 cotyledons (seed leaves), netted leaf venation, and flower parts other than in 3s.

Dioecious Having male flowers on 1 plant and female flowers on another.

Disk flower See ray flowers.

Distichous Arranged in 2 vertical rows on opposite sides of an axis.

Drupe Fleshy fruit with a single seed enclosed in a stony covering, e.g., cherry.

Drupelet Small drupe, commonly in a cluster, e.g., a raspberry or thimbleberry.

Elliptic Ellipse, oval-shaped, widest in middle with rounded ends.

Endemic Confined to a region, as in "this plant is endemic is this region."

Entire Leaf margin is smooth, i.e., without teeth, serrations, divisions, lobes, etc.

Evergreen Having green leaves through the winter; not deciduous.

Exserted Projecting beyond, as in "stamens are exserted from the flower tube."

Family In botany, 1 or more genera that share a number of significant characteristics setting them apart from other groupings of genera.

Filament Stalk of a stamen supporting the anther.

Fimbriate Fringed.

Floret Single, small, inconspicuous reproductive unit that includes the lemma, palea, and flower parts; a spikelet usually includes at least 1 floret.

Follicle Dry, single carpel fruit splitting along 1 side only.

Forb Non-woody, broad-leaved plant that dies back to the ground each year.

Frond Leaf of a fern.

Fruit Ripened ovary and any other attached structures that ripen with it.

Gall Amorphous, lumpy, abnormal tissue growth of a plant. Usually caused by the exacerbating effects of insect egg-laying.

Genus	Group of plants sharing a number of characteristics, usually appear similar, and have the same first name of the binomial. *Iris missouriensis* is the name of a species; *Iris* is the genus.
Glabrous	Smooth, without hairs.
Glandular	With glands; producing tiny globules of a sticky or oily substance.
Glaucous	Having a white, waxy powder (bloom) that can be rubbed off.
Glochid	A short, barbed hair on some cacti.
Hastate	Triangular shaped, like that of a spearhead.
Haustorium	Root or appendage of a parasitic fungus that penetrates the host's tissue to draw nutrients from it (plural: haustoria).
Herb	Non-woody plant with herbaceous stems dying at end of growing season.
Imbricate	Shingled, as in bracts that overlap each other.
Imperfect	Having only male parts or only female parts. Unisexual.
Indehiscent	Not opening at maturity.
Inferior	Attached below, often used in reference to an ovary (compare with superior).
Inflorescence	Flower cluster. Raceme, spike, and umbel are types of inflorescences.
Inrolled	Leaves incurved or rolled inwards.
Internode	Portion of stem between 2 nodes.
Introduced	Non-native (exotic), brought in from another region or country.
Invasive	Non-native species capable of economic and/or ecological damage.
Involucre	Whorl of bracts that enclose and then subtend a flower/cluster of flowers.
Irregular	Flowers which are only bi-laterally symmetrical; can only be cut in equal, mirror-image parts in 1 way, in 1 vertical plane (compare with regular).
Keel	A ridge similar to a boat keel; various plant parts can have such ridges. The 2 lower, partly joined petals of pea flowers is called the keel.
Krummholz	Stunted, twisted trees just above "tree-line." Krummholz is formed when severe winds, snow, frost, and cold retard growth and kill buds.
Lanceolate	Lance-shaped, much longer than wide with the widest point toward the bottom, i.e., toward the point of attachment.
Leaflet	Segment of a compound leaf.
Lenticel 100	Raised pores on bark or root.
Ligule	1) Flattened part of ray corolla in Asteraceae; 2) membranous appendage at juncture of blade and sheath in grass and other species.
Lobe	A rounded division, as in "tip of the flower is lobed" (see sinus).
Loment	A legume which is constricted between the seeds.
Lyrate	Pinnatifid with large rounded terminal lobe.
Margin	Border or edge of a leaf.
Monocarpic	Flowering only once and then dying. Typically applied to perennials that live for many years without flowering, finally flower, then die.
Monocot	Group of flowering plants having only 1 cotyledon (seed leaf), parallel venation, and flower parts usually in 3s. Compare with dicots.
Monoecious	Having separate male and female flowers but on the same plant.
Montane	Vegetative zone defined as the treed or forested areas.
Nerve	Prominent vein in leaf or other organ.
Nerved	Veined, as in a leaf (i.e., 10-nerved having 10 observable veins).
Node	The point on a stem where leaves or branches arise.
Nut	Dry, hard fruit, commonly one-seeded, that does not open at maturity.

Oblanceolate Reverse lance-shaped with the broadest part of the leaf above the middle, i.e., away from the point of attachment (compare with lanceolate).
Oblong Rectangular shape with rounded corners.
Obovate Egg-shaped in outline and attached at the narrow end.
Obtuse Blunt, not pointed at the top. With sides coming together at an angle between 90 and 180 degrees (compare with acute).
Opposite Leaves arranged on opposite sides of the stem (compare with alternate).
Orbicular Circular or round in shape.
Ovary Expanded base portion of pistil that contains undeveloped or developing seeds.
Ovate Egg-shaped in outline and attached at the broad end.
Palmate Having divisions, lobes, or veins which radiate from a single point like fingers of a hand.
Panicle Compound raceme with a repeatedly branched inflorescence.
Pappus Bristles, awns, or scales on the apex of seeds of the *Asteraceae*, such as dandelion "fluff."
Parallel-veined Veins parallel to one another, not branching.
Parasitic Living off other organisms.
Pedicle Small stalk bearing a single flower of an inflorescence (see peduncle).
Peduncle Stalk supporting a single flower or group of flowers (see pedicle).
Perennial Plant living for 3 or more years – not an annual, not a biennial.
Perfect A flower with both male and female parts.
Perfoliate Base of a leaf attached to and completely growing around the stem.
Perianth Collective term for both the calyx and corolla.
Persistent Remaining on the plant for an extended time.
Petal An individual segment of the corolla.
Petiolate With a petiole.
Petiole Stalk at base of leaf blade attaching it to the stem.
Phyllary Bract on the cup, or involucre, of many members of the *Asteraceae*.
Phylogenic Related to the evolutionary development and history of a species or taxonomic groupings of organisms.
Pinnate Veins, lobes, or divisions in the form of a feather; arrangement of leaflets on each side of a common axis.
Pinnatifid Pinnately cut into segments, with the cuts in the lobes not reaching to the axis (the midrib).
Pinnatisect Pinnately cut into segments, with the cuts in the lobes reaching to the axis (the midrib).
Pistil Leaf modified to be the female organ of the flower, comprised of ovary, stigma, and style.
Pistillate Bearing a pistil or pistils but lacking stamens.
Plumose Feathery.
Pod Dry fruit that opens to release seeds, especially referring to a legume.
Polymorphic Having 2 or more forms.
Pome Fleshy indehiscent fruit developing from an inferior compound ovary, such as an apple.
Prickle Sharp growth, thorn, or spine, usually restricted to smaller growths.
Puberulent Minutely pubescent; covered in soft, downy hairs.
Pubescent Covered with short, soft hairs.
Raceme Elongated inflorescence with stalked flowers (see spike).

Rachis	Main axis of a structure, such as the main line (axis) from which individual flowers or clusters grow in an inflorescence.
Radially symmetrical	Symmetrical arrangement of parts around a central point. Capable of being divided into equal, similar appearing parts along many vertical planes.
Ray flower	In *Asteraceae*, the flower with the long outer portion, often with 3 lobes.
Receptacle	Top of pedicel to which the sepals, petals, stamens, and pistil are attached.
Reflexed	Bent abruptly backward or downward as in "tip of the petal is reflexed."
Regular	Symmetrical flower, i.e., with parts distributed equally around the flower, allowing it to be divided along many vertical planes into 2 look-alike parts (compare with radially symmetrical, asymmetrical, and irregular).
Reniform	Kidney-shaped.
Revolute	With the margins rolled downward, as in the edges of some leaves.
Rhizome	Horizontal jointed stem, usually underground, arising from nodes, distinguished from a root by presence of nodes, buds, or scale-like leaves.
Rhizomatous	With rhizomes. See stolons.
Root	Underground structure from base of stem that anchors plant absorbs nutrients and water.
Rosette	Cluster of leaves arranged in circle, commonly at base of plant. Usually referred to as a "basal rosette."
Samara	Indehiscent winged fruit, i.e., a fruit that does not split open but does have a thin, flat, protruding margin bordering the seed.
Scabrous	Rough to the touch because of scales, stiff hairs, etc.
Scalloped	Curved projections with sharp depressions between.
Scree	Steep mass of rock debris with scant soil.
Secund	Growing to 1 side, i.e., inflorescence having flowers on 1 side.
Seed	Product of fertilization.
Senesce	To grow old.
Sepal	Fused or free member of the calyx, usually green and leaf-like.
Serrate	Having sharp teeth pointing forward; toothed like a saw.
Sessile	Stalkless and attached directly at the base.
Sheath	Portion of grass leaf that surrounds plant stem.
Shrub	Woody stemmed plant, may be dwarf, mounded, spreading, or erect.
Shrublet	Dwarf shrub.
Silicle	Fruits of *Brassicaceae*; less than 2 times longer than wide (compare with silique).
Silique	Fruits of *Brassicaceae*; at least 2 times longer than wide (compare with silicle).
Simple	Not divided or lobed.
Sinus	The cleft between lobes.
Sorus (sori)	A cluster of sporangia on the surface of a fern leaf.
Sp	Abbreviation for "a single species."
Spp	Abbreviation for "many species."
Spatulate	Narrow base widening toward tip, like a spatula.
Spike	Elongated inflorescence with non-stalked flowers, i.e., the flowers are attached directly to the stem without a pedicel. See raceme.
Spikelet	Unit of inflorescence, consisting of 2 glumes and 1 or more florets.
Spine	Stiff, slender, sharp-pointed structure arising from below the epidermis.
Sporangium	Spore-bearing case (plural sporangia).

Spores For non-flowering plants, such as ferns, the asexual reproductive cell, enclosed in a sporangium.
Stalk Secondary stem, often referring to structure supporting flower.
Stamen Male organ of flower consisting of a filament and pollen-bearing anther.
Stellate hairs Many-branched, star-shaped hairs.
Stem Central support of a plant bearing the other organs, such as leaves.
Stigma Sticky tip of pistil where the pollen lands.
Stipe Stalk supporting a plant structure.
Stipule Appendage, usually leaf-like and growing in pairs at the base of the petiole of most leaves.
Stolon Slender jointed stem or runner growing along the ground, giving rise to roots and shoots. See rhizome.
Stoloniferous Bearing and capable of spreading from stolons.
Striate Having parallel ridges.
Style Stalk connecting stigma and ovary of plant's female organ (pistil).
Subtended Occurring immediately below, as bracts just under a flower.
Superior Attached above, often used in reference to an ovary which is attached above all of the sepals and petals (compare with inferior).
Talus Mass of rock fragments at base of cliff.
Teeth Alternating projections and indentations on the margin.
Tendril Slender twining or coiling structure, supporting a climbing plant.
Tepal One of the segments of a perianth when these are not differentiated into sepals and petals.
Terminal Located at end of, or top of.
Ternate Leaflets in 3s, as in ternately compound.
Throat The expanded portion of a united corolla between the tube and the limb.
Tillers Erect or upwardly ascending shoots growing from the base of a bunchgrass which add to the size of the tuft.
Tree-line Point above which normal tree growth ends; dividing line between sub-alpine and alpine.
Trichome A general term for the hairs on a plant.
Trifoliate 3-leaved.
Tuber Thickened portion of a rhizome bearing nodes and buds; an underground stem modified for food storage.
Tubercle A small tuber; a small bump-like, wart-like outgrowth.
Twig In woody plants, segment produced during the latest growing season.
Umbel Inflorescence where flower stalks radiate from a common point like the spokes of an umbrella.
Unisexual Made up of either all male or all female flowers.
Valve One of the pieces a pod or capsule splits into.
Vein Vessel by which water and nutrients are transported.
Villous Clothed with long, soft hairs.
Vine Trailing or climbing plant with long flexible stem, often supported by tendrils.
Whorl Three or more organs such as leaves, flowers, or petals that are arranged in a circle around a central axis, as in leaves around a stem.
Winged Having a thin, flat border projecting outward, as in the helicopter wing of a samara fruit.

FIELD NOTES

FIELD NOTES

Southwest Montana is a special place; the wide open spaces, meandering streams, golden pastures, majestic mountains; trails that take us somewhere and nowhere at the same time; wildflowers painting color across mountain meadows. Southwest Montana is special because of its outdoors.

For 25 years the Gallatin Valley Land Trust (GVLT) has been protecting this special place through the creation of trail networks and conservation of vital landscapes. GVLT has partnered with many people and organizations to create an 80-mile Main Street to the Mountains trail system in and around Bozeman. GVLT also partners with private landowners to conserve working farms and ranches, wildlife and fish habitat, and scenic views in Gallatin, Park, Madison, and Meagher counties.

By building trails and conserving land GVLT is safeguarding the quality of life we all treasure in Montana. Because of your support we can continue to protect and celebrate the character of this special place for today, for tomorrow, for forever.

For more information about the Gallatin Valley Land Trust, visit www.gvlt.org

The Yellowstone Association is a nonprofit educational organization that, in partnership with the National Park Service, connects people to Yellowstone National Park and the natural world. They operate 12 educational Park Stores, a membership program with 35,000 members world-wide, and the Yellowstone Association Institute which offers more than 600 in-depth courses each year. To learn more visit: www.yellowstoneassociation.org. The Association's Official Park Store is available online at www.yellowstoneassociation.org/shop, offering a large selection of Yellowstone-related books, maps, videos, outdoor gear and educational games.

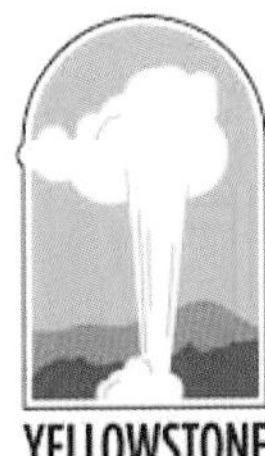

The Yellowstone Park Foundation is a nonprofit organization that is the official fundraising partner of Yellowstone National Park. The Foundation works to fund important projects and programs, many of which are beyond the financial capacity of the National Park Service. The Foundation receives no annual government funding; it relies instead upon the generous support of private citizens, foundations, and corporations to ensure that Yellowstone's great gifts to the world will never diminish. Since its inception, the Yellowstone Park Foundation has raised more than $85 million for Yellowstone National Park, and has successfully funded more than 300 Park projects. To learn more visit: http://www.ypf.org.

About the Author

When not hiking, fishing, bird hunting, or otherwise enjoying the Greater Yellowstone Region, Whitney Tilt serves as Director, Land & Wildlife Conservation for the Arthur M. Blank Family Foundation and the Mountain Sky Guest Ranch in Emigrant, Montana. Throughout his career Whitney has focused on a wide range of conservation issues from Colorado River water allocations and black-footed ferret recovery to Asian tiger conservation and evaluation of federal fisheries programs. Whitney lives in Bozeman, Montana and is also a partner in High Country Apps LLC, developing interactive field guides for smart phones and tablets.